Baseball

on

the Brain

Baseball on the Brain

By Dennis Purdy

Workman Publishing, New York

Library of Congress Cataloging-in-Publication Data is available.

ISBN-13: 978-0-7611-4034-4
ISBN-10: 0-7611-4034-4

Workman books are available at special discounts when purchased
in bulk for premiums and sales promotions as well as for fund-raising
or educational use. Special editions or book excerpts can also be created
to specification. For details, contact the Special Sales Director at the
address below.

Design by Paul Gamarello and Orlando Adiao

Workman Publishing Company, Inc.
225 Varick Street
New York, NY 10014-4381
www.workman.com

Printed in the United States of America

First printing February 2007

10 9 8 7 6 5 4 3 2

CONTENTS

ACKNOWLEDGMENTS

No book like this can be put together without drawing on a lot of raw data from a lot of sources. Among those sources for which I am truly grateful are:

Two fantastic websites, Baseball-Reference.com and BaseballAlmanac.com; the Hall of Fame's website at baseballhalloffame.org; ESPN.com; MLB.com; Baseball.com; and the movie website IMDb.com.

I also utilized a number of fine reference books. Among them: *The Baseball Encyclopedia* (Macmillan); *The Official Major League Baseball Fact Book, 2006 Edition* (Sporting News Books); *The Baseball Maniac's Almanac* by Bert Sugar (McGraw-Hill); *Baseball's Hall of Fame: Cooperstown, Where the Legends Live Forever* by Lowell Reidenbaugh (Crescent Books); *The Baseball Scrapbook* by Peter C. Bjarkman (Dorset); *Professional Baseball Franchises* by Peter Filichia (Facts on File); *The Baseball Chronicle* by Stephen Hanks, et al. (Publications International); *The Ballpark Book* by Ron Smith (Sporting News Books); *Now Batting, Number . . .* by Jack Looney (Black Dog & Leventhal); *The Midsummer Classic: The Complete History of Baseball's All-Star Game* by David Vincent, Lyle Spatz, and David W. Smith (Bison Books); *Ballparks of North America* by Michael Benson (McFarland & Company); *Nineteenth Century Baseball* by Marshall D. Wright (McFarland & Company); *The Baseball Timeline* by Burt Solomon (DK Publishing); *The Ballplayers* by Mike Shatzkin (Arbor House/William Morrow); *Baseball's Greatest Quotes* by Kevin Nelson (Simon & Schuster); *Robert Edward Auctions Catalog* (July 15–16, 2000); *Official Baseball Guide, 1966 Edition* (The Sporting News); and *The Team-By-Team Encyclopedia of Major League Baseball* by Dennis Purdy (Workman Publishing).

And once again I'd like to thank my hard-working editor, Richard Rosen, as devoted a baseball fan as myself, who never failed to keep me on the straight and narrow until the book was finished.

INTRODUCTION

I have two great passions in life. The first is writing about baseball history—an obsession that got a lot of exercise in *The Team-By-Team Encyclopedia of Major League Baseball*. The second is creating baseball trivia games, and the proof of that you are now holding your hands.

I first began writing baseball trivia games in 1987 when I self-syndicated a daily feature called "Baseball Trivia Game" in about two dozen newspapers around the country. In 1995 I added the same game to *The Vintage & Classic Baseball Collector,* a national magazine I published for about six years. After selling the magazine in 2000, I began writing books. But after five books, I yearned to do something again on baseball trivia. Here it is: 1,003 trivia games comprising over 6,000 trivia questions, more than three times as many as any other baseball trivia book ever published.

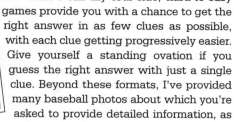

This is not your father's baseball trivia book, with bland questions like "Who hit 61 home runs for the Yankees in 1961?" or "Which team has won the most World Series?" Rather than simply ask a question, I've used different formats to construct trivia "challenges." While my match games of seven clues and seven answers technically gives you a one-in-seven chance of guessing correctly even if you don't know the answer, you'll find that the way the clues are worded and my choices for clues are grouped greatly complicates matters. What I call my four-clue, hard-to-easy games provide you with a chance to get the right answer in as few clues as possible, with each clue getting progressively easier. Give yourself a standing ovation if you guess the right answer with just a single clue. Beyond these formats, I've provided many baseball photos about which you're asked to provide detailed information, as well as some games for the literary-minded that require you to compile "thematic" lineups of ballplayers.

The material in this book might be classified as trivia, but there's nothing trivial about the effect I hope to have on readers. It's my hope that these trivia games will enhance readers' appreciation of the immense role baseball has played in our culture, and also spark a desire to follow some the "trivial" threads in this book back into the remarkable fabric of life stories and history from which they come.

Since baseball was born in the 1800s, its players and devotees have been preoccupied with the game's statistical minutiae with a passion that borders on obsession. Let us not forget that, for every bit of trivia in this game we all so dearly love, we have the players to thank. So I'd like to dedicate this book of baseball trivia to all the players in baseball history, and in particular the hundreds that I have had the pleasure to come to know personally through my baseball card show business. Among them:

Yogi Berra, who once said, "It ain't over 'til it's over." Long ago, Yogi appeared as an autograph guest at one of the large baseball card shows I promoted in the Tacoma Dome. When his session was over, he pulled me aside and asked, "How'd I do for you, Denny? Did I do okay? Are you happy with how everything went?" He knew he was an expensive guest, yet he was concerned about me. No ego here, as with so many of today's players. Just courtesy and concern. For Yogi, it wasn't over when it was over, even with me.

Bobby Thomson, who hit "The Shot Heard 'Round the World." As was often the case with these player signings, we had time to kill after the autograph session before his flight back home to New Jersey. Several hours, in fact. This allowed us time to have a leisurely lunch in a Portland restaurant. To hear firsthand from the man who hit one of baseball's most famous home runs the story of that magical season of 1951 that culminated with his famous clout was—as the credit-card commercial says—priceless.

Buck O'Neil, the ageless Negro League star and first black coach in the major leagues. He was approaching 95 years of age the last time I had him at one of my shows, yet he walked and talked with a zest for life that put me—45 years his junior—to shame. When I took him back to his hotel, there was a young black girl about 14 years old sitting on a bench near the hotel's entrance. Buck marched right up to her, extended his hand, and pronounced, "Hi, I'm Buck O'Neil! How are you doin', young lady?" She didn't have a clue who he was, but shook his hand anyway as she gave me a puzzled look. "How are you doin' in school?" he asked her. "Are you studyin' hard?" Again, puzzled, she just nodded her head. "Well, that's good!" said Buck. "You just keep workin' hard at school, because someday you'll be glad you did." He then breezed into the hotel lobby, where there were a number of people milling about. "Hi, I'm Buck O'Neil!" he said to the first one he met. It took me fifteen minutes to get him through the lobby.

Pete Rose, whose deep yearning to be in the Hall of Fame was quite evident the first time he appeared at one of my shows. For each player who appeared at my shows, I had a professional artist paint a large banner with his name and team logo that was used as a stage backdrop, and which I would have the player sign for me. Over the years, I accumulated hundreds of these colorful banners.

Whenever I promoted my Tacoma Dome show, I would hang these banners of past guests high around the convention hall's walls—an impressive sight to say the least. When we escorted Pete into the convention hall and to the raised stage where he would be signing autographs, with his beautiful Cincinnati Reds banner behind his table (and two thousand people waiting for him, many clapping with approval), he stopped, looked around like a gladiator entering the Coliseum, and announced, "Finally, a show worthy of me."

Johnny Vander Meer, the only pitcher ever to throw back-to-back no-hitters. He appeared at several of my shows; at the first one, we made him laugh with a surprise seventy-seventh birthday party; at the last one, he provided me with one of the best laughs of my life. He was eighty, and had just finished his autograph session. As he slowly left the stage with his six-inch shuffle steps, I asked him if he wanted me to have someone escort him to his room in the hotel adjoining the convention center. (Maybe even get a wheelchair, I thought.) "No," he said, "I'm gonna take this fifteen-hundred bucks you just paid me and head for the bar, and get me some booze and a woman."

Willie Stargell, who hit more home runs completely out of Dodger Stadium than any other player, and who was one of my favorite players growing up, when I was a big Pirate fan. For a big guy, he sure was soft-spoken. We had a bit of time to spare before his autograph session, so he asked if I minded taking him dress shopping. He noticed I was puzzled, so he quickly added, "Oh, not for me, for my fiancé. She's just a little bitty gal, size 1 or 2, I think. I just wanted to bring her home something special." We never did find one that suited him, but, for the record, he tried really hard to find just the right one. I hope his fiancé finds out about this bit of trivia, if she's not aware of it already, because it was his last baseball card show appearance before his death.

There are so many others I could thank as well, all of whom provided me with baseball trivia of a personal nature, but space does not allow it. No matter, gentlemen; I will never forget the memories you gave me—on the field and at my shows. I only hope my words do you justice. Thanks again.

—*Dennis Purdy*

LET THE GAME . . . PROGRESS

1. 1834

A. The first baseball game utilizing the Cartwright rules is played

2. 1846

B. The National Association, baseball's first professional league, begins play

3. 1849

C. The first league, the National Association of Baseball Clubs, is formed

4. 1857

D. The first catcher's mask, invented by Fred Thayer, appears on the scene

5. 1871

E. Albert Spalding and several other players are the first to wear baseball gloves

6. 1875

F. *The Book of Sports,* a baseball instructional manual, first appears on bookstore shelves

7. 1876

G. The Knickerbockers, an amateur team, are the first team to wear an official uniform in a game

2

1. 1871

A. The Providence Grays install the first safety net behind the catcher to protect the fans

2. 1876

B. The first schedules are produced, so fans will know when their favorite team is playing

3. 1877

C. Troy's Roger Connor hits the National League's first grand slam

4. 1879

D. National League and American Association champions square off in baseball's first postseason playoff series

5. 1881

E. Cleveland and Boston become the first teams to start recording players' batting averages

6. 1882

F. Providence's Paul Hines becomes the first player to wear sunglasses in a game

7. 1884

G. The National League begins play

(Note: One date has two answers.)

1. April 22, 1876

A. Candy Cummings of Hartford is the first NL pitcher ever to pitch and win two complete games in the same day

2. May 2, 1876

B. Levi Meyerle collects the first double and triple in National League history

3. July 15, 1876

C. Pete Browning is the first professional player to have his bats custom made

4. Sept. 19, 1876

D. Chicago's Ross Barnes hits the NL's first home run

5. 1878

E. Paul Hines becomes the first player in history to perform an unassisted triple play

6. 1882

F. George Bradley of St. Louis pitches the NL's first no-hitter

G. Hall of Famer Jim O'Rourke collects the first hit (a single) in National League history

4

1. 1884

A. Fleet Walker becomes the first black player to appear in a major league game when he takes the field for the Toledo Blue Stockings

2. 1888

B. For the first time, a rule stipulates that it takes three strikes to make an out

3. 1889

C. The pitcher's mound is moved back to 60.5 feet, the present-day distance

4. April 17, 1892

D. Cincinnati defeats St. Louis, 5–1, in the first-ever Sunday game

5. May 14, 1892

E. Home plate makes its first appearance in the shape of a pentagon

6. 1893

F. Mickey Welch of the New York Giants strikes out in his appearance as the first pinch hitter in major league history

7. 1900

G. Brooklyn's Tom Daly becomes the first pinch hitter in major league history to get a hit—it's a home run

3: 1-B/G, 2-D, 3-F, 4-A, 5-E, 6-C • **4:** 1-A, 2-B, 3-F, 4-D, 5-G, 6-C, 7-E

(Note: One date has two answers.)

1. 1901   A. Major league baseball unveils its first cork-and-rubber-center ball

2. 1903   B. Doc Powers of the Athletics crashes into the wall and is injured so severely that he requires surgery; two weeks later he dies—baseball's first game-related death

3. 1905   C. "Big Ed" Reulbach of the Chicago Cubs becomes the first pitcher to toss two shutouts in the same day

4. 1908   D. The American League begins play

5. 1909   E. The first "moving picture" of a baseball game is made

6. 1911   F. Shibe Park, the first steel and concrete ballpark, opens its doors in Philadelphia as the new home of the Athletics

                         G. Hall of Famer Roger Bresnahan is the first to play wearing a helmet

6

1. 1915   A. Radio station KDKA in Pittsburgh is the first to broadcast a game over the airwaves as the Pittsburgh Pirates beat the Philadelphia Phillies, 8–5

2. 1918   B. The major league season is shortened for the first time in history

3. 1920   C. Resin bags are introduced, appearing on American League mounds

4. 1921   D. Ken Williams of the St. Louis Browns becomes the first 30-30 man in baseball history when he finishes the year with 39 homers and 37 stolen bases

5. 1922   E. The New York Yankees appear in pinstripes for the first time

6. 1923   F. The first nationwide radio broadcast of a World Series game takes place from Yankee Stadium

7. 1925   G. The first Rawlings adjustable-pocket glove is used in play

5: 1-D, 2-E, 3-G, 4-C, 5-B/F, 6-A • 6: 1-E, 2-B, 3-G, 4-A, 5-D, 6-F, 7-C

1. 1933

A. The first night game takes place as the Reds defeat the Phillies, 2–1, in Cincinnati

2. 1935

B. The first annual All-Star Game takes place in Chicago

3. 1936

C. Television station W2XBS telecasts the first baseball games, a doubleheader between the Brooklyn Dodgers and Cincinnati Reds

4. 1939

D. For the first time in history, all major league games scheduled for one date are played at night

5. 1941

E. The Dodgers introduce plastic batting helmets to the game

6. 1944

F. Nels Potter is the first pitcher ejected for violating the new rule that disallows spitballs

7. 1946

G. The first class of Hall of Famers is inducted

8

1. 1947

A. The first franchise shift in 50 years takes place when the Braves move from Boston to Milwaukee

2. 1949

B. The St. Louis Cardinals become the first major league team to be evicted by their own stadium

3. 1951

C. For the first time ever, a major league season takes place without a single player-manager in the game

4. 1953

D. A rule is implemented that requires players in the field to take their gloves back to the dugout with them instead of leaving them on the field, as had been the practice for nearly a century

5. 1954

E. Chuck Connors, who later rose to fame in television as the lead character in *The Rifleman*, is the first player to stand up in opposition to baseball's draft

6. 1956

F. The Little League World Series is played for the first time

7. 1958

G. For the first time, American League players are required to wear batting helmets

7: 1-B, 2-A, 3-G, 4-C, 5-E, 6-F, 7-D • 8: 1-F, 2-B, 3-E, 4-A, 5-D, 6-C, 7-G

1. 1958

A. The Red Sox become the last team to integrate when Pumpsie Green takes the field

2. 1959

B. White Sox owner Bill Veeck has players' names put on the back of their uniforms

3. 1960

C. The National League jumps on the expansion bandwagon by adding teams in Houston (Colt .45s) and New York (Mets)

4. 1961

D. In the first major league game played on the West Coast, the Giants defeat the Los Angeles Dodgers, 8–0, in San Francisco's Seals Stadium

5. 1962

E. Masanori Murakami is the first Japanese player to make it into the major leagues

6. 1963

F. Baseball's two major leagues experience expansion for the first time as the Los Angeles Angels and a replacement Washington Senators team join the American League

7. 1964

G. The Houston Colt .45s defeat the San Francisco Giants, 3–0, in the first-ever Sunday night game

10

1. 1965

A. The Oakland A's use gold-colored bases, but their use is immediately banned after one game

2. 1968

B. The designated-hitter rule is implemented in the American League

3. 1969

C. The era of indoor baseball begins with the opening of Houston's Astrodome

4. 1970

D. The first indoor All-Star Game takes place in the Astrodome. The NL victory is the first 1–0 All-Star Game

5. 1971

E. The first World Series night game, in Pittsburgh; the Pirates defeat the Baltimore Orioles, 4–3

6. 1972

F. The two major leagues are divided into two divisions each, and a best-of-five playoff, the League Championship Series, is introduced

7. 1973

G. Major league baseball's first regular-season players' strike takes place just before the season opens. Teams lose between six and nine games each for the season.

9: 1-D, 2-A, 3-B, 4-F, 5-C, 6-G, 7-E • 10: 1-C, 2-D, 3-F, 4-A, 5-E, 6-G, 7-B

WHO, WHAT, WHEN, WHERE, AND WHY

1. What's the significance of this photograph?

2. What ballpark is this?

3. When was this Series played?

4. Where did the other team play its home games?

11:

1. It shows the first modern World Series, between the Boston Pilgrims (now called the Red Sox) and the Pittsburgh Pirates.

2. Huntington Avenue Base Ball Grounds in Boston.

3. 1903, the first modern World Series.

4. Exposition Park in Pittsburgh.

1. 1974

A. For the first time ever, a father and son take to the field at the same time for the same team when Ken Griffey Sr. and Jr. play for the Mariners

2. 1975

B. The first division playoff game takes place as the Yankees beat the Red Sox, 5–4

3. 1978

C. Dick Woodson becomes the first player to invoke the new free-agency clause; he is followed later by the first high-profile player to do so, Catfish Hunter

4. 1985

D. Frank Robinson hits a home run in his first at bat as a player-manager, a 5–3 win over the Yankees

5. 1987

E. The first night game at Wrigley Field takes place, but it's rained out in the fourth inning, clearly a sign from the displeased gods of baseball

6. 1988

F. The first indoor World Series game is played in the Metrodome in Minneapolis, Minnesota, as the Twins defeat the Cardinals, 10–1

7. 1990

G. The League Championship Series is changed to a best-of-seven format

13

1. 1994

A. Baseball streams its first game between the Rangers and Yankees on 300k broadband Internet video

2. 1996

B. For the first time in major league history, three managers over the age of 70 are active field bosses

3. 1997

C. In a game between Florida and St. Louis, a major league umpire for the first time uses television replay to reverse a call

4. 1999

D. Interleague play begins

5. 2000

E. The major leagues witness their first-ever March regular-season game as the Mariners trip the White Sox, 3–2, on March 31

6. 2002

F. Cincinnati gets the honor of hosting the first season-opening night game in major league history

7. 2005

G. A regular-season game takes place outside North America for the first time ever, as the Mets and Cubs open the season by splitting a two-game series in Japan

12: 1-C, 2-D, 3-B, 4-G, 5-F, 6-E, 7-A • **13:** 1-F, 2-E, 3-D, 4-C, 5-G, 6-A, 7-B

5. doozy marooney   **E. A slow, tantalizing curveball**

6. cunny thumber   **F. An extra-base hit**

7. crocus sack   **G. An impending victory**

17

Aunt Susie and Uncle Charlie are both affectionate nicknames that baseball players have given to curveballs. Can you correctly match the other pitches listed below with their nicknames?

1. Lady Godiva   **A. A spitball**

2. Edison   **B. A curveball**

3. eephus   **C. A fastball**

4. cuspidor curve   **D. An experimental pitch**

5. cream puff   **E. A high-arcing blooper pitch**

6. cheese   **F. An easy pitch to hit**

7. yellow hammer   **G. A pitch with nothing on it**

18

Some of baseball's best slang ends in "er." To "-er" is human; to get every one of these right is divine.

1. cackler   **A. A fastball pitcher**

2. kicker   **B. A complaining, argumentative ballplayer**

3. chinker   **C. An infield hit that is difficult to field**

4. chucker   **D. A bad fielder**

5. clanger   **E. An error**

6. clinker   **F. A weak base hit**

7. squibber   **G. A foul ball**

18: 1-G, 2-B, 3-F, 4-A, 5-D, 6-E, 7-C

16: 1-B, 2-E, 3-D, 4-A, 5-F, 6-C, 7-G • **17:** 1-G, 2-D, 3-E, 4-A, 5-F, 6-C, 7-B

Don't let it "bug" you if you can't match up the following expressions with their correct definitions. Some of them are tough.

1. tumble bug	**A. A sore arm**
2. diamond bug	**B. A rookie sent down to the minors by early summer**
3. bugaboo	**C. An acrobatic player given to crashing and diving in the field**
4. bug bruiser	**D. A hard-hit ground ball**
5. bug on the rug	**E. A fast runner circling the bases on artificial turf**
6. June bug	**F. A game featuring a lot of swinging strikeouts**
7. fanning bee	**G. A 1930s baseball fan**

20

Haven't had your fill of wacky baseball terms yet? You're in luck, because here are seven more tough ones to match up.

1. ugly finder	**A. A hit that falls between two fielders**
2. tweener	**B. A line drive that rattles around the dugout**
3. vulture	**C. A slowly pitched ball**
4. dead mackerel	**D. Opening Day game**
5. daisy cutter	**E. A relief pitcher**
6. cork popper	**F. A hard-hit ground ball that doesn't bounce**
7. wig wagger	**G. First- or third-base coach**

19: 1-C, 2-G, 3-A, 4-D, 5-E, 6-B, 7-F • **20:** 1-B, 2-A, 3-E, 4-C, 5-F, 6-D, 7-G

TEAMWORK

Arizona Diamondbacks hitters.

1. Most consecutive games hit safely—30   A. Tony Womack

2. Most grand slams in a career—7   B. Travis Lee

3. Most runs scored in a season—132   C. Luis Gonzalez

4. Most home runs in a season   D. Tony Clark
   by a switch-hitter—30

5. Most triples in a career—37   E. Jay Bell

6. Most home runs by a rookie—22   F. Andy Fox

7. Most times hit by pitch in a season—18   G. Matt Williams

22

Arizona Diamondbacks pitchers.

1. Most strikeouts in a game—20   A. Bkyung-Hyun Kim

2. Most games pitched in a career—243   B. Randy Johnson

3. Most saves in a career—74   C. Andy Benes

4. Most games lost in a season—16   D. Curt Schilling

5. Most consecutive games won—9   E. Edgar Gonzalez

6. Most consecutive games lost—9   F. Matt Mantei

7. Most runs allowed in a season—117   G. Brandon Webb

23

Atlanta Braves hitters.

1. Most home runs in a career—371   A. Bob Horner

2. Most RBIs in a season—132   B. Rico Carty

3. Highest batting average in a season—.366   C. Ralph Garr

4. Most extra-base hits in a season—87   D. Earl Williams

5. Most home runs in a month—14   E. Chipper Jones

6. Most home runs by a rookie—33   F. Gary Sheffield

7. Highest batting average for a career—.317   G. Dale Murphy

21: 1-C, 2-G, 3-E, 4-D, 5-A, 6-B, 7-F • **22:** 1-B, 2-A, 3-F, 4-G, 5-D, 6-E, 7-C • **23:** 1-G, 2-F, 3-B, 4-E, 5-A, 6-D, 7-C

Atlanta Braves pitchers.

1. Most consecutive games won—14	**A. Tony Cloninger**
2. Most consecutive games lost—11	**B. Phil Niekro**
3. Most wild pitches in a season—27	**C. John Smoltz**
4. Most 20-win seasons—5	**D. Greg Maddux**
5. Most games pitched in a career—689	**E. Tom Glavine**
6. Most games pitched in a season—84	**F. Jim Acker**
7. Lowest ERA in a season—1.56	**G. Chris Reitsma**

25

Baltimore Orioles hitters.

1. Most walks in a season—118	**A. Eric Davis**
2. Highest career batting average—.294	**B. Brooks Robinson**
3. Most consecutive games hit safely—30	**C. Eddie Murray**
4. Most RBIs in a season—150	**D. Brady Anderson**
5. Most hits in a career—3,184	**E. Miguel Tejada**
6. Most triples in a career—68	**F. Ken Singleton**
7. Most stolen bases in a career—307	**G. Cal Ripken Jr.**

26

Baltimore Orioles pitchers.

1. Most games won in a season—25	**A. Dave McNally**
2. Most games started in a career—521	**B. Mike Boddicker**
3. Most games lost in a season—21	**C. Mike Mussina**
4. Most consecutive games won—17	**D. Don Larsen**
5. Most consecutive games lost—13	**E. Milt Pappas**
6. Most wild pitches in a season—14	**F. Jim Palmer**
7. Highest career winning percentage—.645	**G. Steve Stone**

26: 1-G, 2-F, 3-D, 4-A, 5-B, 6-E, 7-C

24: 1-C, 2-F, 3-A, 4-E, 5-B, 6-G, 7-D • **25:** 1-F, 2-C, 3-A, 4-E, 5-G, 6-B, 7-D •

WHO, WHAT, WHEN, WHERE, AND WHY

1. Who is the player at the center of attention?

2. What had he just done?

3. When did he do it?

4. Where was the game played?

Boston Red Sox hitters.

1. Most runs scored in a season—150
2. Most at bats in a season—684
3. Most hits in a season—240
4. Most hits in a career—3,419
5. Most grand slams in a season—4
6. Most home runs by a rookie—34
7. Most RBIs in a season—175

A. Ted Williams
B. Nomar Garciaparra
C. Babe Ruth
D. Walt Dropo
E. Carl Yastrzemski
F. Jimmie Foxx
G. Wade Boggs

29

Boston Red Sox pitchers.

1. Most games pitched in a career—637
2. Most strikeouts in a career—2,590
3. Most strikeouts in a season—313
4. Most games lost in a season—25
5. Most games won in a season—34
6. Lowest ERA in a season—0.96
7. Most consecutive games lost—14

A. Joe Harris
B. Smoky Joe Wood
C. Roger Clemens
D. Dutch Leonard
E. Red Ruffing
F. Bob Stanley
G. Pedro Martinez

30

Chicago Cubs hitters.

1. Most home runs by a rookie—25
2. Grounded into most career double plays—240
3. Most hits in a career—2,995
4. Most runs scored in a season—156
5. Most grand slams in a career—12
6. Most stolen bases in a career—404
7. Most extra-base hits in a season—103

A. Rogers Hornsby
B. Billy Williams
C. Sammy Sosa
D. Ron Santo
E. Frank Chance
F. Cap Anson
G. Ernie Banks

30: 1-B, 2-D, 3-F, 4-A, 5-G, 6-E, 7-C
29: 1-F, 2-C, 3-G, 4-E, 5-B, 6-D, 7-A • **28:** 1-A, 2-B, 3-G, 4-E, 5-C, 6-D, 7-F •

Chicago Cubs pitchers.

1. Most strikeouts in a career—2,038	A. Dutch McCall
2. Most shutouts in a career—48	B. Bill Hutchison
3. Most strikeouts in a season—314	C. John Clarkson
4. Most games pitched in a career—605	D. Mordecai Brown
5. Highest career winning percentage—.706	E. Ferguson Jenkins
6. Highest winning percentage in a season—.941 (16–1)	F. Charlie Root
7. Most consecutive games lost—13	G. Rick Sutcliffe

32

Chicago White Sox hitters.

1. Most stolen bases in a career—368	A. Luke Appling
2. Most RBIs in a career—1,465	B. Harold Baines
3. Most total bases in a season—399	C. Frank Thomas
4. Most grand slams in a career—10	D. Robin Ventura
5. Most career home runs by a lefthander—221	E. Albert Belle
6. Most games played in a career—2,422	F. Eddie Collins
7. Highest career batting average—.340	G. Joe Jackson

33

Chicago White Sox pitchers.

1. Most complete games in a career—356	A. Ed Walsh
2. Most shutouts in a career—58	B. Red Faber
3. Lowest ERA in a season—1.53	C. Patrick Flaherty
4. Most games pitched in a career—669	D. Billy Pierce
5. Most games pitched in a season—88	E. Wilbur Wood
6. Most games lost in a season—25	F. Ed Cicotte
7. Most strikeouts in a career—1,796	G. Ted Lyons

33: 1-G, 2-A, 3-F, 4-B, 5-E, 6-C, 7-D
• **32:** 1-F, 2-C, 3-E, 4-D, 5-B, 6-A, 7-G •
31: 1-E, 2-D, 3-B, 4-F, 5-C, 6-G, 7-A

Cincinnati Reds hitters.

1. Most home runs by a rookie—38
2. Most runs scored in a career—1,741
3. Most triples in a career—188
4. Most grand slams in a career—11
5. Most total bases in a season—388
6. Hit into most double plays in a season—30
7. Most strikeouts in a career—1,306

A. Ernie Lombardi
B. Johnny Bench
C. Pete Rose
D. Frank Robinson
E. George Foster
F. Tony Perez
G. Bid McPhee

35

Cincinnati Reds pitchers.

1. Most games pitched in a season—90
2. Most games started in a career—357
3. Most 1–0 games won in a career—7
4. Most consecutive games won—16
5. Most strikeouts in a season—274
6. Most shutouts in a career—32
7. Most wins in a season
   (tied with Bucky Walters)—27

A. Mario Soto
B. Eppa Rixey
C. Ewell Blackwell
D. Johnny Vander Meer
E. Dolf Luque
F. Bucky Walters
G. Wayne Granger

36

Cleveland Indians hitters.

1. Most consecutive games hit safely—31
2. Most RBIs in a season—165
3. Highest batting average for a career—.375
4. Most home runs by a rookie—37
5. Most total bases in a career—3,200
6. Most home runs in a season—52
7. Most doubles in a season—64

A. Napoleon Lajoie
B. George Burns
C. Manny Ramirez
D. Jim Thome
E. Al Rosen
F. Earl Averill
G. Joe Jackson

36: 1-A, 2-C, 3-G, 4-E, 5-F, 6-D, 7-B
35: 1-G, 2-B, 3-D, 4-C, 5-A, 6-F, 7-E
34: 1-D, 2-C, 3-G, 4-B, 5-E, 6-A, 7-F

Cleveland Indians pitchers.

1. Most games pitched in a career—582   **A. Sam McDowell**

2. Lowest ERA in a season—1.60   **B. Johnny Allen**

3. Most shutouts in a career—45   **C. Bob Lemon**

4. Most 20-win seasons—7   **D. Mel Harder**

5. Most consecutive games won—17   **E. Luis Tiant**

6. Most wild pitches in a season—18   **F. Addie Joss**

7. Most walks allowed in a season—208   **G. Bob Feller**

38

Colorado Rockies hitters.

1. Most home runs on the road in a season—29   **A. Larry Walker**

2. Most home runs at home in a season—32   **B. Dante Bichette**

3. Most consecutive games hit safely—23   **C. Juan Pierre**

4. Most stolen bases in a season—53   **D. Vinny Castilla**

5. Most doubles in a season—59   **E. Andres Galarraga**

6. Hit into most double plays in a career—126   **F. Eric Young**

7. Most singles in a season—163   **G. Todd Helton**

39

Colorado Rockies pitchers.

1. Most games pitched in a career—461   **A. Pedro Astacio**

2. Highest winning percentage in a season—.667 (16–8)   **B. Jason Jennings**

3. Most wins in a season (tied with Kevin Ritz)—17   **C. Julian Tavarez**

4. Most losses in a season—17   **D. Steve Reed**

5. Most saves in a career—102   **E. Jose Jimenez**

6. Most consecutive games won—9   **F. Armando Reynoso**

7. Through 2005 season, the only qualifying Rockies pitcher with a career ERA under 5.00 (4.65)   **G. Darryl Kile**

39: 1-D, 2-B, 3-A, 4-G, 5-E, 6-C, 7-F

37: 1-D, 2-E, 3-F, 4-C, 5-B, 6-A, 7-G • **38:** 1-A, 2-E, 3-B, 4-F, 5-G, 6-D, 7-C

WHO, WHAT, WHEN, WHERE, AND WHY

1. Who are these two players?

2. What is the historical significance of this play?

3. When did it occur?

4. Where did it occur?

5. Bonus 1: A. Who got the hit that precipitated this play; B. Who made the throw to the plate; C. Who was the third-base coach who urged Rose to try and score?

6. Bonus 2: Where did Pete Rose spend his prison time for tax evasion?

40:

1. Pete Rose of Cincinnati and Ray Fosse of Cleveland.

2. It remains as one of the classic plays in All-Star Game history (it also gave the NL a 5–4 win over the AL), and the resulting shoulder injury to Fosse all but ended Fosse's effectiveness as a hitter.

3. July 14, 1970.

4. The brand-new Riverfront Stadium in Cincinnati.

5. A. Jim Hickman; B. Amos Otis; C. Leo Durocher.

6. Marion, Illinois, Ray Fosse's hometown—and the local citizenry loved it.

Detroit Tigers hitters.

1. Most home runs by a rookie—35
2. Most home runs at home in a season—39
3. Most total bases in a career—5,466
4. Most triples in a season—26
5. Most games played in a career—2,834
6. Most at bats in a season—679
7. Most consecutive games with an RBI—10

A. Hank Greenberg
B. Al Kaline
C. Willie Horton
D. Ty Cobb
E. Sam Crawford
F. Harvey Kuenn
G. Rudy York

42

Detroit Tigers pitchers.

1. Most games started in a career—459
2. Lowest ERA in a season—1.81
3. Most games won in a season—31
4. Most consecutive games won—16
5. Most complete games in a career—336
6. Most games pitched in a career—545
7. Most games won in a career—222

A. Denny McLain
B. Hal Newhouser
C. Mickey Lolich
D. John Hiller
E. Schoolboy Rowe
F. George Mullin
G. Hooks Dauss

43

Florida Marlins hitters.

1. Most stolen bases in a season—65
2. Most games played in a career—1,128
3. Most extra-base hits in a career—387
4. Most runs scored in a season—123
5. Most home runs in a season—42
6. Most strikeouts in a career—734
7. Most double plays grounded into in a career—92

A. Jeff Conine
B. Luis Castillo
C. Juan Pierre
D. Gary Sheffield
E. Derrek Lee
F. Mike Lowell
G. Cliff Floyd

43: 1-C, 2-B, 3-F, 4-G, 5-D, 6-E, 7-A

• **41:** 1-G, 2-A, 3-D, 4-E, 5-B, 6-F, 7-C • **42:** 1-C, 2-B, 3-A, 4-E, 5-F, 6-D, 7-G •

Florida Marlins pitchers.

1. Most games pitched in a career—368
2. Most games started in a career—131
3. Only 20-game winner in team's history
4. Most games lost in a season—17
5. Highest winning percentage in a season—.692 (18–8)
6. Most strikeouts in a season—209
7. Most saves in a career—108

A. Carl Pavano

B. Jack Armstrong

C. Braden Looper

D. Dontrelle Willis

E. Ryan Dempster

F. A. J. Burnett

G. Robb Nen

45

Houston Astros hitters.

1. Most home runs by a rookie—21
2. Most consecutive games hitting safely—30
3. Most triples in a career—80
4. Most stolen bases in a career—487
5. Highest batting average in a season—.368
6. Most doubles in a season—56
7. Most stolen bases in a season—65

A. Jose Cruz

B. Lance Berkman

C. Craig Biggio

D. Cesar Cedeno

E. Gerald Young

F. Jeff Bagwell

G. Willy Taveras

46

Houston Astros pitchers.

1. Most games started in a career—320
2. Most games won in a career—144
3. Most strikeouts in a season—313
4. Most strikeouts in a game—18
5. Most strikeouts in a career—1,866
6. Lowest ERA in a season—1.87
7. Most games pitched in a career—563

A. Roger Clemens

B. Don Wilson

C. Joe Niekro

D. Dave Smith

E. J. R. Richard

F. Nolan Ryan

G. Larry Dierker

46: 1-G, 2-C, 3-E, 4-B, 5-F, 6-A, 7-D

• **45:** 1-B, 2-G, 3-A, 4-D, 5-F, 6-C, 7-E •

44: 1-C, 2-F, 3-D, 4-B, 5-E, 6-E, 7-G

WHO, WHAT, WHEN, WHERE, AND WHY

1. Who is this player?

2. What supposedly unbreakable record did he break?

3. When did he break it?

4. Which team did he hit his final home run of this season against?

5. BONUS 1: In what game of the season did he break it?

6. BONUS 2: What was the final score of this game?

47:

1. Roger Maris.

2. Most home runs in a season, 61, breaking Babe Ruth's record of 60.

3. 1961.

4. Boston Red Sox.

5. The season's final game.

6. 1–0.

48

Kansas City Royals hitters.

1. Most strikeouts in a season—172
2. Most at bats in a season—705
3. Most home runs by a rookie—24
4. Most consecutive games hit safely—30
5. Most grand slams in a career—6
6. Most RBIs in a season—144
7. Most home runs in a season—36

A. George Brett

B. Willie Wilson

C. Bo Jackson

D. Mike Sweeney

E. Bob Hamelin

F. Frank White

G. Steve Balboni

49

Kansas City Royals pitchers.

1. Lowest ERA in a season—2.08
2. Most shutouts in a career—23
3. Most wild pitches in a career—107
4. Most games started in a career—392
5. Most games won in a season—23
6. Highest career winning percentage—.587
7. Most consecutive games won in a season—11

A. Roger Nelson

B. Bret Saberhagen

C. Dennis Leonard

D. Larry Gura

E. Mark Gubicza

F. Rich Gale

G. Paul Splittorff

50

Los Angeles Angels hitters.

1. Most triples in a career—70
2. Most hits in a season—240
3. Most strikeouts in a season—181
4. Most career grand slams—7
5. Most consecutive games hit safely—28
6. Most RBIs in a season—139
7. Highest career batting average—.314

A. Garret Anderson

B. Darin Erstad

C. Mo Vaughn

D. Jim Fregosi

E. Rod Carew

F. Don Baylor

G. Joe Rudi

50: 1-D, 2-B, 3-C, 4-G, 5-A, 6-F, 7-E

49: 1-A, 2-C, 3-E, 4-G, 5-B, 6-D, 7-G • **48:** 1-C, 2-B, 3-E, 4-A, 5-F, 6-D, 7-F •

Los Angeles Angels pitchers.

1. Highest winning percentage in a season—.773 (17–5)

2. Most games lost in a career—140

3. Most shutouts in a season—11

4. Besides Ryan, only Angel to win 22 games

5. Highest career winning percentage—.567

6. Most shutouts in a career—40

7. Most consecutive games won—12

A. Bert Blyleven

B. Frank Tanana

C. Chuck Finley

D. Nolan Ryan

E. Clyde Wright

F. Jarrod Washburn

G. Dean Chance

52

Los Angeles Dodgers hitters.

1. Most games played in a career—2,181

2. Highest batting average in a season—.362

3. Most home runs in a career—270

4. Most RBIs in a season—153

5. Most consecutive games hit safely—31

6. Most RBIs in a career—992

7. Highest batting average for a career—.309

A. Willie Davis

B. Pedro Guerrero

C. Bill Russell

D. Steve Garvey

E. Tommy Davis

F. Mike Piazza

G. Eric Karros

53

Los Angeles Dodgers pitchers.

1. Most games won in a season—27

2. Most games pitched in a career—550

3. Most consecutive losses—11

4. Pitched six consecutive shutouts

5. Most consecutive games won—15

6. Most wild pitches in a career—94

7. Highest winning percentage in a season—.864 (19–3)

A. Sandy Koufax

B. Don Sutton

C. Fernando Valenzuela

D. Rick Honeycutt

E. Orel Hershiser

F. Phil Regan

G. Don Drysdale

53: 1-A, 2-B, 3-D, 4-G, 5-F, 6-C, 7-E

52: 1-C, 2-F, 3-G, 4-E, 5-A, 6-D, 7-B • **51:** 1-A, 2-C, 3-G, 4-E, 5-B, 6-D, 7-F •

54

Milwaukee Brewers hitters.

1. Most consecutive games hit safely—39
2. Most walks in a season—99
3. Most strikeouts in a season—188
4. Most career home runs by a lefthander—201
5. Most career home runs by a righthander—251
6. Most doubles in a season—53
7. Most homers hit at home in a season—28

A. Jeromy Burnitz
B. Lyle Overbay
C. Jose Hernandez
D. Richie Sexson
E. Paul Molitor
F. Robin Yount
G. Cecil Cooper

55

Milwaukee Brewers pitchers.

1. Most strikeouts in a season—264
2. Most games pitched in a career—365
3. Most games lost in a season—20
4. Lowest ERA in a season—2.37
5. Most games won in a career—117
6. Most innings pitched in a season—314
7. Most consecutive games lost—10

A. Mike Caldwell
B. Ben Sheets
C. Jim Slaton
D. Danny Darwin
E. Clyde Wright
F. Jim Colburn
G. Dan Plesac

56

Minnesota Twins hitters.

1. Once played all nine positions in a game
2. Most total bases in a season—374
3. Most home runs in a career—475
4. Most triples in a career—90
5. Most home runs by a rookie—33
6. Most consecutive games hit safely—31
7. Most hits in a career—2,304

A. Ken Landreaux
B. Tony Oliva
C. Harmon Killebrew
D. Jimmie Hall
E. Kirby Puckett
F. Rod Carew
G. Cesar Tovar

56: 1-G, 2-B, 3-C, 4-F, 5-D, 6-A, 7-E
54: 1-E, 2-A, 3-C, 4-G, 5-F, 6-B, 7-D • **55:** 1-B, 2-G, 3-E, 4-A, 5-C, 6-F, 7-D •

Minnesota Twins pitchers.

1. Most complete games in a season—25

2. Lowest ERA in a season—2.45

3. Most games won in a season—25

4. Highest winning percentage in a season—.774 (24–7)

5. Most consecutive games won—17

6. Most games lost in a season—20

7. Most games pitched in a season—90

A. Pedro Ramos

B. Johan Santana

C. Allan Anderson

D. Jim Kaat

E. Bert Blyleven

F. Frank Viola

G. Mike Marshall

58

New York Mets hitters.

1. Most RBIs in a career—733

2. Highest batting average in a season—.354

3. Most grand slams in a career—6

4. Most home runs in a month—13

5. Most triples in a career—62

6. Most singles in a career—1,050

7. Most triples in a season—21

A. Mookie Wilson

B. John Olerud

C. Darryl Strawberry

D. Lance Johnson

E. Mike Piazza

F. Dave Kingman

G. Ed Kranepool

59

New York Mets pitchers.

1. Most consecutive games lost—27

2. Most consecutive games lost in one season—18

3. Lowest ERA in a season—1.53

4. Most games won in a season—25

5. Most walks allowed in a season—116

6. Most games lost in a career—137

7. Last Met to strike out 19 in a game

A. Jerry Koosman

B. Tom Seaver

C. Roger Craig

D. Dwight Gooden

E. David Cone

F. Anthony Young

G. Nolan Ryan

59: 1-F, 2-C, 3-D, 4-B, 5-G, 6-A, 7-E

57: 1-E, 2-C, 3-D, 4-F, 5-B, 6-A, 7-G • **58:** 1-C, 2-B, 3-E, 4-F, 5-A, 6-G, 7-D •

WHO, WHAT, WHEN, WHERE, AND WHY

1. Who is at the center of attention?

2. What is he celebrating?

3. When?

4. Which team did he defeat, and who hit two home runs off him in this game?

5. BONUS: What was the final score of the game, and how did it happen?

5. 5–4, when Detroit scored two runs in the bottom of the ninth.

4. The Oakland A's. Reggie Jackson.

3. September 14, 1968.

2. His 30th win of the season, the last time it's been done in the majors.

1. Denny McLain.

60:

61

New York Yankees hitters.

1. Most singles in a career—1,531
2. Most games played in a career—2,401
3. Most times caught stealing in a career—117
4. Most doubles in a season—53
5. Most home runs by a rookie—29
6. Most home runs in a season by a righthander—48
7. Most stolen bases in a career—326

A. Alex Rodriguez
B. Joe DiMaggio
C. Don Mattingly
D. Lou Gehrig
E. Babe Ruth
F. Rickey Henderson
G. Mickey Mantle

62

New York Yankees pitchers.

1. Most games won in a season—41
2. Most complete games in a career—261
3. Most games lost in a career—139
4. Most strikeouts in a game—18
5. Most strikeouts in a career—1,956
6. Lowest ERA for a season—1.64
7. Most consecutive games won—16

A. Roger Clemens
B. Spud Chandler
C. Whitey Ford
D. Ron Guidry
E. Mel Stottlemyre
F. Red Ruffing
G. Jack Chesbro

63

Oakland A's hitters.

1. Most seasons played for Oakland—14
2. Most runs in a season—123
3. Most hits in a season—204
4. Most triples in a season—12
5. Most consecutive games hit safely—25
6. Most strikeouts in a season—175
7. Most home runs by a rookie—49

A. Mark McGwire
B. Miguel Tejada
C. Reggie Jackson
D. Jose Canseco
E. Phil Garner
F. Rickey Henderson
G. Jason Giambi

63: 1-F, 2-C, 3-B, 4-E, 5-G, 6-D, 7-A

61: 1-D, 2-G, 3-E, 4-C, 5-B, 6-A, 7-F • **62:** 1-G, 2-F, 3-E, 4-D, 5-C, 6-B, 7-A

Oakland A's pitchers.

1. Most strikeouts in a season—301
2. Most complete games in a season—28
3. Highest winning percentage in a season—.821 (23–5)
4. Most games won in a season—27
5. Most wins in a career—131
6. Most runs and walks allowed in a career
7. Most games lost in a season—20

A. Dave Stewart

B. Barry Zito

C. Brian Kingman

D. Bob Welch

E. Vida Blue

F. Rick Langford

G. Catfish Hunter

65

Philadelphia Phillies hitters.

1. Most RBIs in a season—170
2. Most RBIs in a career—1,595
3. Most hits in a season—254
4. Most triples in a season—27
5. Most singles in a career—1,811
6. Most home runs by a rookie—30
7. Most doubles in a career—442

A. Chuck Klein

B. Mike Schmidt

C. Lefty O'Doul

D. Ed Delahanty

E. Sam Thompson

F. Willie Montanez

G. Richie Ashburn

66

Philadelphia Phillies pitchers.

1. Most shutouts in a season—16
2. Most games won in a career—241
3. Most strikeouts in a game—232
4. Most games pitched in a career—529
5. Most games lost in a season—24
6. Most strikeouts in a season—319
7. Most hits allowed in a season—348

A. Curt Schilling

B. Grover Alexander

C. Claude Passeau

D. Robin Roberts

E. Steve Carlton

F. Chick Fraser

G. Chris Short

66: 1-B, 2-E, 3-G, 4-D, 5-F, 6-A, 7-C

• **65:** 1-A, 2-B, 3-C, 4-E, 5-G, 6-F, 7-D •

64: 1-E, 2-F, 3-B, 4-D, 5-G, 6-A, 7-C

Pittsburgh Pirates hitters.

1. Most RBIs in a season—131
2. Most games played in a career—2,433
3. Most triples in a career—232
4. Most pinch-hit home runs in a season—7
5. Most extra-base hits in a career—953
6. Most stolen bases in a career—688
7. Most consecutive games hit safely—30

A. Charlie Grimm

B. Paul Waner

C. Roberto Clemente

D. Willie Stargell

E. Craig Wilson

F. Max Carey

G. Honus Wagner

68

Pittsburgh Pirates pitchers.

1. Most wins in a career—202
2. Most games won in a season—41
3. Most innings pitched in a career—3,480
4. Most shutouts in a career—44
5. Most strikeouts in a game—16
6. Most consecutive games won—22
7. Most consecutive games lost—13

A. Wilbur Cooper

B. Bob Veale

C. Ed Morris

D. Roy Face

E. Bob Friend

F. Burleigh Grimes

G. Babe Adams

69

St. Louis Cardinals hitters.

1. Most strikeouts in a career—1,469
2. Most times caught stealing in a season—36
3. Highest career batting average—.359
4. Grounded into most double plays in a season—29
5. Most RBIs in a season—154
6. Most career triples—177
7. Most walks in a season—162

A. Rogers Hornsby

B. Miller Huggins

C. Lou Brock

D. Ted Simmons

E. Mark McGwire

F. Joe Medwick

G. Stan Musial

69: 1-C, 2-B, 3-A, 4-D, 5-F, 6-G, 7-E
• **68:** 1-A, 2-C, 3-E, 4-G, 5-B, 6-D, 7-F •
67: 1-B, 2-C, 3-G, 4-E, 5-D, 6-F, 7-A

St. Louis Cardinals pitchers.

1. Most strikeouts in a game—19

2. Most games won in a season—30

3. Most games pitched in a career—554

4. Lowest ERA in a season—1.12

5. Lowest ERA for a career—2.67

6. Most consecutive losses—12

7. Most complete games in a season—39

A. Bob Gibson

B. Jack Taylor

C. Jesse Haines

D. Bill Hart

E. Dizzy Dean

F. Slim Sallee

G. Steve Carlton

71

San Diego Padres hitters.

1. Most runs scored in a season—126

2. Most home runs in a season by a righthander—50

3. Most doubles in a season—49

4. Highest slugging average for a career—.540

5. Most consecutive games hit safely—34

6. Most strikeouts in a career—773

7. Most stolen bases in a season—70

A. Greg Vaughn

B. Ken Caminiti

C. Nate Colbert

D. Steve Finley

E. Benito Santiago

F. Tony Gwynn

G. Alan Wiggins

72

San Diego Padres pitchers.

1. Most games won in a season—22

2. Highest winning percentage in a season—.778 (21–6)

3. Lowest ERA in a season—2.10

4. Most consecutive losses—11

5. Most games won in a career—100

6. Most strikeouts in a game—16

7. Most strikeouts in a season—257

A. Gaylord Perry

B. Gary Ross

C. Jake Peavy

D. Randy Jones

E. Kevin Brown

F. Eric Show

G. David Roberts

72: 1-D, 2-A, 3-G, 4-B, 5-F, 6-C, 7-E

71: 1-D, 2-A, 3-F, 4-B, 5-E, 6-C, 7-G • **70:** 1-G, 2-E, 3-C, 4-A, 5-F, 6-D, 7-B •

WHO, WHAT, WHEN, WHERE, AND WHY

1. **Who** is sliding into home?

2. **What** had he just accomplished?

3. **When** did he do it?

4. **Where?**

5. **BONUS:** Who was the batter?

73:

1. Hall of Famer Enos Slaughter.

2. Scored all the way from first base on a single with the game-winning run.

3. October 15, 1946, in Game 7 of the World Series.

4. Sportsman's Park in St. Louis.

5. Harry "the Hat" Walker.

San Francisco Giants hitters.

1. Most seasons played in a career—19	**A. Barry Bonds**
2. Highest batting average in a season—.370	**B. Orlando Cepeda**
3. Most home runs in a career by a righthander—459	**C. Jim Hart**
4. Most strikeouts in a season—189	**D. Bobby Bonds**
5. Most RBIs in a season—142	**E. Willie McCovey**
6. Most consecutive games hit safely—26	**F. Jack Clark**
7. Most home runs by a rookie—31	**G. Willie Mays**

75

San Francisco Giants pitchers.

1. Most consecutive games won—16	**A. Mark Davis**
2. Most strikeouts in a game—16	**B. Gaylord Perry**
3. Most losses in a season—18	**C. Jason Schmidt**
4. Most innings pitched in a season—328.2	**D. Bobby Bolin**
5. Most complete games in a season—30	**E. Jack Sanford**
6. One of three Giants to lose nine straight games	**F. Ray Sadecki**
7. Lowest ERA in a season—1.98	**G. Juan Marichal**

76

Seattle Mariners hitters.

1. Most RBIs in a season—147	**A. Edgar Martinez**
2. Most extra-base hits in a career—838	**B. Ichiro Suzuki**
3. Most strikeouts in a career—1,375	**C. Harold Reynolds**
4. Highest batting average in a season—.372	**D. Joey Cora**
5. Most stolen bases in a career—290	**E. Julio Cruz**
6. Most consecutive games hit safely—24	**F. Ken Griffey Jr.**
7. Most stolen bases in a season—60	**G. Jay Buhner**

76: 1-F, 2-A, 3-G, 4-B, 5-E, 6-D, 7-C

74: 1-E, 2-A, 3-G, 4-D, 5-B, 6-F, 7-C • **75:** 1-E, 2-A, 3-C, 4-B, 5-G, 6-A, 7-D

Seattle Mariners pitchers.

1. Most games lost in a career—96
2. Most consecutive wins—16
3. Most innings pitched in a season—272
4. Only pitcher besides Randy Johnson with four shutouts in a season
5. Most wild pitches in a season—16
6. Most consecutive games lost—16
7. Most 20-win seasons—2

A. Mike Parrott
B. Mike Moore
C. Randy Johnson
D. Jamie Moyer
E. Mark Langston
F. Matt Young
G. Dave Fleming

78

Tampa Bay Devil Rays hitters.

1. Most consecutive games hit safely—18
2. Most triples in a season—19
3. Most RBIs in a season—117
4. Most doubles in a season—47
5. Most home runs at home in a season—18
6. Most home runs by a rookie—21
7. Most home runs on the road in a season—22

A. Jorge Cantu
B. Aubrey Huff
C. Jonny Gomes
D. Carl Crawford
E. Quinton McCracken
F. Fred McGriff
G. Jose Canseco

79

Tampa Bay Devil Rays pitchers.

1. Most complete games in a season—5
2. Most games lost in a season—18
3. Most saves in a season—43
4. Most consecutive games lost—10
5. Most games pitched in a career—266
6. Most games started in a career—83
7. Most hit batsmen *and* wild pitches in a season

A. Albie Lopez
B. Esteban Yan
C. Roberto Hernandez
D. Victor Zambrano
E. Ryan Rupe
F. Joe Kennedy
G. Tanyon Sturtze

79: 1-F, 2-G, 3-C, 4-A, 5-B, 6-E, 7-D
78: 1-E, 2-D, 3-A, 4-B, 5-F, 6-C, 7-G • **77:** 1-B, 2-C, 3-E, 4-G, 5-F, 6-A, 7-D •

Texas Rangers hitters.

1. Most at bats in a career—5,830

2. Most home runs in a season—57

3. Most strikeouts in a career—1,076

4. Most consecutive games hit safely—28

5. Most home runs by a rookie—30

6. Most career triples—44

7. Most hits in a career—1,723

A. Gabe Kapler

B. Ruben Sierra

C. Ivan Rodriguez

D. Juan Gonzalez

E. Rafael Palmeiro

F. Alex Rodriguez

G. Pete Incaviglia

81

Texas Rangers pitchers.

1. Most games started in a career—313

2. Most complete games in a season—29

3. Lowest ERA for a season—2.17

4. Most strikeouts in a game—16

5. Most games pitched in a career—528

6. Most consecutive games won—12

7. Most consecutive games lost—9

A. Ferguson Jenkins

B. Nolan Ryan

C. Bobby Witt

D. Mike Paul

E. David Clyde

F. Charlie Hough

G. Kenny Rogers

82

Toronto Blue Jays hitters.

1. Most stolen bases in a career—255

2. Most consecutive games hit safely—28

3. Most homers on the road in a season—28

4. Most walks received in a season—123

5. Most hits in a season—215

6. Highest batting average in a season—.363

7. Most home runs in a career by a righthander—203

A. Carlos Delgado

B. George Bell

C. Joe Carter

D. Shawn Green

E. Vernon Wells

F. John Olerud

G. Lloyd Moseby

82: 1-G, 2-D, 3-B, 4-A, 5-E, 6-F, 7-C

80: 1-E, 2-F, 3-D, 4-A, 5-G, 6-B, 7-C • **81:** 1-F, 2-A, 3-D, 4-B, 5-G, 6-C, 7-E

WHO, WHAT, WHEN, WHERE, AND WHY

1. Who is being congratulated?

2. What had he just done?

3. When?

4. Where did he spend the majority of his time during this game?

83:

1. Hall of Famer Frank Robinson.

2. Hit a first-inning home run in Cleveland's Opening Day game.

3. 1975.

4. The dugout, because he was the team's player-manager-DH—and the first black manager in baseball history.

38

Toronto Blue Jays pitchers.

1. Most games started in a career—408
2. Most games won in a season—22
3. Most games lost in a career—140
4. Highest career winning percentage—.589
5. Tied for most games lost in a season—18
6. Most saves in a season—45
7. Most games pitched in a season—89

A. Jerry Garvin

B. Dave Stieb

C. Duane Ward

D. Jim Clancy

E. Mark Eichhorn

F. Roy Halladay

G. Jimmy Key

85

Washington Nationals hitters.

1. Most runs scored in a season—119
2. Most consecutive games hit safely—17
3. Most triples in a season—7
4. Most walks in a season—110
5. Fewest strikeouts in a season by a regular player—48
6. Most times hit by a pitch in a season—19
7. Most sacrifice hits in a season—14

A. Ryan Zimmerman

B. Nick Johnson

C. Brad Wilkerson

D. Jose Guillen

E. Alfonso Soriano

F. Jose Vidro

G. Livan Hernandez

86

Washington Nationals pitchers.

1. Most games pitched in a season—85
2. Most games lost in a season—16
3. Most consecutive games won—11
4. Most strikeouts in a game—13 (twice)
5. Most saves in a season—47
6. Most consecutive losses—5
   (tied with Michael O'Connor)

A. Livan Hernandez

B. Ramon Ortiz

C. Jon Rauch

D. Ryan Drese

E. John Patterson

F. Chad Cordero

86: 1-C, 2-B, 3-A, 4-E, 5-F, 6-D

84: 1-B, 2-F, 3-D, 4-G, 5-A, 6-C, 7-E • **85:** 1-E, 2-A, 3-C, 4-B, 5-F, 6-D, 7-G •

NAME THAT YEAR

Seven clues. One year. See how few clues it takes you to guess the year.

1 **Cleveland pitcher Ray Caldwell** is struck by lightning during his windup. He stays in the game and earns a 2–1 win over the A's in the August 24 game.

2 **Babe Ruth hits 29 home runs,** a new major league record.

3 **Walter Johnson of the Senators shuts out the A's,** 1–0, on Opening Day, his record fifth Opening Day shutout.

4 **The Giants defeat the Phillies,** 6–1, in a game that takes only 51 minutes.

5 **For the first time since 1903,** the World Series is extended to a best-of-nine format to increase revenue.

6 **Lefty Williams of the White Sox** becomes the first pitcher ever to lose three Series games in three starts.

7 **Ty Cobb wins his last batting title,** hitting .384.

FROM THE HALLOWED HALLS

All of the games in this chapter concern only players who've been enshrined in the Baseball Hall of Fame in Cooperstown, New York.

88

1 **I am the only non-Yankee** American Leaguer to win three MVP Awards.

2 **I won two of my MVP Awards** in back-to-back seasons, and I'm still the only American League first baseman besides Frank Thomas ever to do this.

3 **Lou Gehrig and I share the record** for the most consecutive seasons with 100 or more RBIs, 13.

4 **Nicknamed "The Beast" and "Double X,"** I had what baseball historians believe was one of the most incredible home run years ever, in 1932. I ended up with 58, but eight times I hit outfield screens that had been erected in St. Louis and Cleveland, screens Babe Ruth didn't have to contend with in 1927 when he hit 60 homers. In fact, the screens were built specifically to keep me from breaking the Babe's record.

89

Match up these 19th-century Hall of Famers with each one's particular claim to fame.

1. Only 19th-century player to get seven hits in a game

2. Elected to the Hall of Fame for inventing the curveball

3. Pitched one of just two 19th-century perfect games

4. Bare-handed shortstop whose fielding record stood for 25 years

5. Became city clerk of Chicago after retirement

6. Most games played (2,259) at first base in NL history

7. Hit .409 and .410 in consecutive seasons

A. Cap Anson

B. George Wright

C. Wilbert Robinson

D. Candy Cummings

E. Jesse Burkett

F. Jake Beckley

G. John Ward

1 **My first and last batting titles** were separated by 14 years, the longest span ever between two titles.

2 **Having won three Most Valuable Player Awards** earlier in my career, in 1972 I became the first foreigner ever to win Poland's highest sports award, the Merited Champions Medal.

3 **I hold the record for most career hits**—3,630—by a player who played his entire career with the same team.

4 **Even though I hit nearly 500 home runs** in my long career with the Cardinals, I never once led the league in homers.

91

Match up these famous Hall of Famers with the first teams they played for.

1. Chicago Cubs	**A. Joe Cronin**
2. Boston Red Sox	**B. Babe Ruth**
3. Pittsburgh Pirates	**C. Reggie Jackson**
4. New York Giants	**D. Harmon Killebrew**
5. Kansas City Athletics	**E. Waite Hoyt**
6. Philadelphia Phillies	**F. Ferguson Jenkins**
7. Washington Senators	**G. Lou Brock**

92

1 **I am the only player to hit four home runs** in a World Series *twice.*

2 **In 1949, one of the greatest hitters of all time, George Sisler,** was hired specifically to help me "establish an acquaintance with the strike zone."

3 **Nicknamed the "Silver Fox,"** I christened Los Angeles' Dodger Stadium by getting the first-ever hit in its confines.

4 **Also known as the "Duke of Flatbush"** and one of the "Boys of Summer," I participated in six World Series from 1949 to 1959 and hit 326 home runs in the 1950s, more than New York's other two center fielders, Mickey Mantle and Willie Mays.

90: Stan Musial • **91:** 1-G, 2-B, 3-A, 4-E, 5-C, 6-F, 7-D • **92:** Duke Snider

Match up these Hall of Fame pitchers with each one's particular achievement.

1. Most career complete games—749   **A. Grover Alexander**

2. Most consecutive Opening Day starts—16   **B. Tom Seaver**

3. Most seasons as the league leader in starts—6   **C. Kid Nichols**

4. Most 20-win seasons by a lefthander—13   **D. Warren Spahn**

5. Most wins in a season since 1900—41   **E. Robin Roberts**

6. Last to win 30 or more games three years in a row   **F. Cy Young**

7. Most seasons with 30 or more wins—7   **G. Jack Chesbro**

94

1 **I retired from baseball at the age of 33,** largely because of the effects of diabetes.

2 **In 1968, at the age of 22,** I became the youngest player ever to pitch a perfect game. This was the first regular-season perfect game in the American League in 46 years.

3 **Toiling for the Yankees in 1975,** I became the last major league pitcher to hurl at least 30 complete games in a season.

4 **After leading the Oakland A's to three straight World Series titles** from 1972 to 1974, with 67 wins, I became a free agent in 1975 and signed with the Yankees for $3.5 million, an astronomical sum at the time, thereby inspiring many others, especially Oakland stars, to seek free agency.

95

Each of these famous Hall of Famers achieved one of the following distinctions. See if you can match them up.

1. Last player-manager to win a pennant   **A. Brooks Robinson**

2. Once hit eight home runs in three days   **B. Phil Rizzuto**

3. Most career strikeouts in World Series and All-Star games   **C. Ralph Kiner**

4. Considered the best bunter in major league history   **D. Mickey Mantle**

5. Hit into the most career triple plays—4

6. Recorded the most hits in a rookie season—223

7. Refused to play in a World Series because he was superstitious

E. **Lou Boudreau**

F. **Kiki Cuyler**

G. **Lloyd Waner**

96

1 **Playing first base and catching at the age of 45,** I hit .285 in 114 games. No other nonpitcher has ever played as much at such an advanced age.

2 **When I hit .344 to win my fourth and final batting title,** I became the last player-manager to win both a pennant and a batting title in the same year.

3 **I was the first player in the history of professional baseball** to collect 3,000 hits in a career.

4 **Although I was the National League's biggest star** for its first 25 years, I was extremely prejudiced. In fact, I am the man who is most credited with establishing baseball's infamous color line, which kept blacks out of major league baseball until Jackie Robinson's debut in 1947.

97

Each American League Hall of Famer in the right column was the first to accomplish one of the feats in the left column. Go for it.

1. First player to homer in the All-Star Game

2. First player to bat three times in one inning

3. First player to get five extra-base hits in a nine-inning game

4. First player to hit four home runs in a nine-inning game

5. First player to receive six walks in a nine-inning game

6. First player to strike out five times in a nine-inning game

7. First to receive an intentional walk with the bases loaded

A. **Jimmie Foxx**

B. **Lou Boudreau**

C. **Babe Ruth**

D. **Lefty Grove**

E. **Ted Williams**

F. **Napoleon Lajoie**

G. **Lou Gehrig**

95: 1-E, 2-C, 3-D, 4-B, 5-A, 6-G, 7-F • **96:** Cap Anson • **97:** 1-C, 2-E, 3-B, 4-G, 5-A, 6-D, 7-F

45

WHO, WHAT, WHEN, WHERE, AND WHY

1. Who is this?

2. Why is this baseball card so significant?

3. When was the card released?

4. Where was the card originally made available, and where is it today?

98:

1. Hall of Famer Honus Wagner of the Pittsburgh Pirates.

2. It is the most valuable baseball card in existence and the only one that has ever sold for more than $1 million. This particular card has a notable provenance, once having being owned by hockey great Wayne Gretzky and Los Angeles Kings owner Bruce McNall.

3. 1909.

4. It was inserted in packs of cigarettes as a premium to increase sales and as a stiffener to protect the fragile cigarettes. In its recent past, this card was purchased by Wal-Mart for $1 million plus and given away in a promotion to one lucky winner. Unfortunately for that winner, she couldn't afford to pay the more than $300,000 in taxes that were owed, so she had to put the card up for auction in order to pay the tax bill.

1 **Cy Young and I are the only two pitchers** in major league history to twice win 20 or more games in a season after the age of 40.

2 **A battling lefthander,** I pitched my only two major league no-hitters at the ages of 39 and 40.

3 **Even though I didn't win my first game until I was 25,** I became the winningest pitcher in baseball since World War II, with 363 wins, leading the National League in complete games nine times, a major league record.

4 **As a member of the Braves,** I was a 14-time All-Star, won 20 or more games 13 times in 17 seasons, and became the oldest 20-game winner in history when I went 23–7 in 1963 at the age of 42.

100

Each of these Hall of Fame pitchers made famous one of the pitches listed in the right column. See what your batting average is.

1. Christy Mathewson	**A. Bat Dodger**
2. Hoyt Wilhelm	**B. Express**
3. Dizzy Dean	**C. Fogball**
4. Ferguson Jenkins	**D. Puffball**
5. Gaylord Perry	**E. Flutterball**
6. Satchel Paige	**F. Dirtball**
7. Nolan Ryan	**G. Fadeaway**

101

1 **I was the first player in major league history** to have his uniform number retired.

2 **Not only did I break more of Babe Ruth's records** than any other player did in history, but I also was the first American League player ever to hit four home runs in one game.

3 **During my career I had seven seasons** with 150 or more RBIs and five seasons with 400 or more total bases—both major league records.

4 **A disease called amyotrophic lateral sclerosis**—later to bear my name— ended my consecutive-game streak at 2,130, my career with the Yankees at 35, and my life at 37.

99: Warren Spahn • 100: 1-G, 2-E, 3-C, 4-F, 5-D, 6-A, 7-B • 101: Lou Gehrig

102

Some Hall of Fame nicknames.

1. Enos Slaughter	**A. Buck**
2. George Kelly	**B. Cocky**
3. Bob Gibson	**C. Hoot**
4. William Ewing	**D. Country**
5. Adrian Anson	**E. Pop**
6. Amos Rusie	**F. Hoosier Thunderbolt**
7. Eddie Collins	**G. Highpockets**

103

1 **Once I broke into the starting lineup,** they just couldn't get me out of it. As a matter of fact, I held the record for playing the most consecutive games from the start of a career—424—until Hideki Matsui of the Yankees broke it in 2005.

2 **As a rule, it's pretty tough** for a shortstop to win his league's MVP Award, but I won it in back-to-back seasons. To this day, Cal Ripken Jr. and I are the only shortstops to win more than one MVP Award.

3 **Oh, sure, the MVP Awards were nice,** but playing in a World Series would have been nicer. During my career I hit 512 home runs, but never played in the Fall Classic.

4 **A lot of folks aren't aware of this:** Not only was I the first black player to suit up for the Chicago Cubs, but I'm a cousin of O. J. Simpson's.

104

More nicknames. No sweat.

1. Lou Gehrig	**A. Sultan of Swat**
2. Hank Aaron	**B. Georgia Peach**
3. Willie Mays	**C. Hammerin' Henry**
4. Honus Wagner	**D. Big Six**

102: 1-D, 2-G, 3-C, 4-A, 5-E, 6-F, 7-B • **103:** Ernie Banks

5. Ty Cobb   **E. Iron Horse**

6. Babe Ruth   **F. Say Hey Kid**

7. Christy Mathewson **G. Flying Dutchman**

105

1 **I was speedy and I was daring;** that's why I am the only National League player in history to steal my way from first to home five times in a career.

2 **And I could hit, too.** I won a batting title at the age of 37, the oldest player to do so in the first 126 years of the NL's existence until Barry Bonds won in 2002 at the age of 38.

3 **Not only could I run and hit,** I could field. I won 11 fielding titles as a slick-fielding shortstop, and I didn't even wear a glove. In fact, I was the last of the bare-handed fielders.

4 **I hit over .300 in 16 of my first 17 seasons,** won eight batting titles with the Pittsburgh Pirates, and was one of baseball's first inductees into the Baseball Hall of Fame, in 1936. Today, however, most people associate me with being pictured on the only baseball card ever to sell for more than $1 million.

106

More Hall of Famer nicknames, even tougher.

1. Richie Ashburn   **A. Arky**

2. Jim Palmer   **B. Cakes**

3. Willie Wells   **C. Rock**

4. Joseph Vaughan   **D. Goofy**

5. Andrew Foster   **E. Put Put**

6. Earl Averill   **F. Rube**

7. Lefty Gomez   **G. The Devil**

104: 1-E, 2-C, 3-F, 4-G, 5-B, 6-A, 7-D • **105:** Honus Wagner • **106:** 1-E, 2-B, 3-G, 4-A, 5-F, 6-C, 7-D

Baseball Trivia

107

1. **As a rookie catcher,** I participated in 15 double plays, a record that no other National League rookie has ever broken.

2. **Cal Ripken Sr. of the Baltimore Orioles** was the second manager in major league history to have his son play for him. I was the first when my son Earle played for me.

3. **Nicknamed the "Tall Tactician,"** as a manager I never left the dugout during a game, nor did I ever wear a uniform, always preferring a suit and tie. I even had a stadium named after me.

4. **I was born Cornelius Alexander McGillicuddy,** but was better known by another name during my 53-year managerial career, 50 of which were spent with the Philadelphia Athletics.

108

Several Hall of Famers sport unusual middle names. See how you do with the seven immortals below.

1. Victor Willis	**A. Gazaway**
2. Charles Radbourn	**B. True**
3. Cy Young	**C. Trowbridge**
4. Al Spalding	**D. Mountain**
5. Eddie Collins	**E. Goodwill**
6. Lou Gehrig	**F. Heinrich**
7. Judge Landis	**G. Gardner**

109

1. **At my induction into the Hall of Fame** I told the audience, "I'm just a human being gifted with the ability to play baseball. I'm nothing special. I'm just another person. I'm not very good at making speeches, but I sure can ride a motorcycle."

2. **Stan Musial and I are the only two members of the 3,000-hit club** who have ever been named league MVPs twice while playing a different position each award-winning year.

107: Connie Mack • 108: 1-A, 2-G, 3-B, 4-E, 5-C, 6-F, 7-D

50

3 **The youngest regular starting player** in American League history at the age of 18, I also held the AL record for highest slugging average in a season by a shortstop until Alex Rodriguez beat it in 1996.

4 **The only player ever to have two four-hit games** in World Series play, I had them both in the same Series, 1982, as I led my Brewers against the Cardinals.

110

Still more Hall of Famers with unusual middle names.

1. Ed Walsh	**A. Emory**
2. Lefty Grove	**B. Moses**
3. Herb Pennock	**C. Augustine**
4. Kid Nichols	**D. Centennial**
5. Mordecai Brown	**E. Jefferis**
6. Jimmie Foxx	**F. Glee**
7. Paul Waner	**G. Augustus**

111

1 **I hold the record for the quickest induction** into the Hall of Fame after the end of a playing career.

2 **Even though the press was quick to write** that I faked injuries in order to get out of playing, I'll stand by my numbers: the 2,370 games I played in right field was the most by any player in history. I also won four batting titles and hit .362 in 14 World Series games.

3 **Willie Mays and I are the only two outfielders** to win 12 Gold Glove Awards, but he played four more seasons than I did.

4 **My 3,000th career hit for the Pittsburgh Pirates in 1972** was also my last. On December 31, 1972, I died in a plane crash just after takeoff at San Juan, Puerto Rico, while taking relief supplies to earthquake victims in Central America.

WHO, WHAT, WHEN, WHERE, AND WHY

1. **Who** is this player?

2. **What** product is he endorsing?

3. **When** was it released?

4. **When** was it discontinued and why?

5. **When** was it reintroduced and why?

112:
1. Hall of Famer Reggie Jackson.
2. A candy bar.
3. 1978.
4. 1987, when he retired.
5. 1993, after he was inducted into the Baseball Hall of Fame.

Back to Hall of Famer nicknames.

1. Lloyd Waner	**A. Deacon**
2. Harry Heilmann	**B. Scoops**
3. Al Simmons	**C. Slug**
4. Ray Schalk	**D. Buck**
5. Zachary Wheat	**E. Cracker**
6. Max Carey	**F. Little Poison**
7. Bill McKechnie	**G. Bucketfoot**

114

1 **Only five players have ever homered** in 1–0 World Series games, and I was the first to do it, while playing outfield for the Giants.

2 **When my number, 37,** was retired by both the Yankees and Mets, I became one of only a handful of men to have his uniform number retired by two teams.

3 **As a player with the Dodgers,** I was acclaimed to be the world's greatest player—from the neck down. Yet in 12 seasons of managing in the American League, I was smart enough never to have a losing season.

4 **Dubbed "The Old Professor,"** I was both a comedian and a genius when it came to baseball. In 12 years of managing the New York Yankees, we went to the World Series ten times.

115

Another round of Hall of Famer nicknames.

1. Eppa Rixey	**A. Big Poison**
2. John Ward	**B. Jephtha**
3. Miller Huggins	**C. Ol' Stubblebeard**
4. Paul Waner	**D. Monte**
5. Burleigh Grimes	**E. The Little Steam Engine**
6. Luke Appling	**F. Mighty Mite**
7. Pud Galvin	**G. Old Aches and Pains**

4-A, 5-C, 6-G, 7-E

113: 1-F, 2-C, 3-G, 4-E, 5-D, 6-B, 7-A • **114:** Casey Stengel • **115:** 1-B, 2-D, 3-F,

1 **I am the last player in either league** to win a batting championship without hitting a home run. Strangely enough, that was the only year in my 19-year career that I didn't hit a homer.

2 **On August 4, 1985** (the same day Tom Seaver won his 300th career game), I collected my 3,000th career hit off Frank Viola of the Minnesota Twins, becoming the first infielder since Eddie Collins, in 1925, to join the 3,000-hit club.

3 **I was always a daring base runner.** In 1969, for example, I stole home seven times, one short of Ty Cobb's record of eight, set in 1912.

4 **In 1967 I won the American League Rookie of the Year Award** playing second base for the Minnesota Twins.

117

Still more Hall of Famer nicknames.

1. Ted Williams	**A. The Thumper**
2. Branch Rickey	**B. The Mahatma**
3. Joe Medwick	**C. Muscles**
4. Waite Hoyt	**D. Schoolboy**
5. Earle Combs	**E. The Kentucky Colonel**
6. Charles Hafey	**F. Beauty**
7. Dave Bancroft	**G. Chick**

118

1 **Of all the starting pitchers** to play since 1920 when the lively ball was introduced, I have the lowest career earned run average—2.75.

2 **No other rookie starting pitcher** has ever had a better qualifying winning percentage than my .900, in 1950.

3 **Even though I hold the record** for the most consecutive scoreless innings pitched in World Series history, with 33.2, I also hold the record for most career losses in World Series play, with 8.

4 **I was the only pitcher** ever to start four consecutive opening World Series games, and I did it twice, once in the 1950s and again in the 1960s as a member of the New York Yankees. I also hold the Yankee records for most career strikeouts, 1,956, and most games won in a career, 236.

116: Rod Carew • **117:** 1-A, 2-B, 3-C, 4-D, 5-E, 6-G, 7-F • **118:** Whitey Ford

Match each of the Hall of Famers listed below with the team he retired from. Careful now. . . .

1. Babe Ruth	**A. Pirates**
2. Paul Waner	**B. Red Sox**
3. Eddie Mathews	**C. Tigers**
4. Hank Greenberg	**D. Orioles**
5. Frank Robinson	**E. Yankees**
6. George Kell	**F. Braves**
7. Luis Aparicio	**G. Indians**

120

NAME THAT YEAR

Seven clues. One year. See how few clues it takes you to guess the year.

1 **For the first time in history,** four different pitchers earn a win for the World Series champion.

2 **Johnny Cooney of the Braves** hits his first career home run after 18 seasons in the majors. The next day he hits another.

3 **The Baseball Hall of Fame,** in Cooperstown, New York, is officially dedicated and opens on June 12.

4 **The average major league salary** this year is $7,300.

5 **National League president Ford Frick** requires all NL ballparks to install nets on all foul poles to help eliminate fair-foul disputes.

6 **The Yankees sweep Cincinnati** in the World Series, giving them 28 wins in their last 31 Series games.

7 **Lou Gehrig bids a tearful farewell** to Yankee fans.

1 **Some days I think I chose the wrong career.** I mean, how would *you* feel if you lost 313 games, as I did, and knew that no other pitcher in the history of the game had lost as many?

2 **I got my break in the major leagues** when Cleveland purchased my contract from the Canton, Ohio, minor league team for a suit of clothes for the team's manager.

3 **And I never was paid very well,** even though I pitched 7,357 innings during my career, over 1,400 more innings than my closest competitor.

4 **It wasn't all bad, though.** You should have seen the party the team threw for me on July 19, 1910, right after I won my 500th career game. And now they even name the award given to each league's best pitcher after me.

122

Match the Hall of Famer below with his career major league record.

1. Highest on-base percentage in a career—.482   **A. Tris Speaker**

2. Most career five-hit games—14   **B. Reggie Jackson**

3. Highest career slugging average—.690   **C. Ty Cobb**

4. Most doubles in a career—792   **D. Hank Aaron**

5. Most grand slams in a career—23   **E. Ted Williams**

6. Most total bases in a career—6,856   **F. Babe Ruth**

7. Most career strikeouts—2,597   **G. Lou Gehrig**

123

1 **In my major league debut,** at the tender age of 17, I struck out the first eight batters to face me, then seven more in the game, for a total of 15.

2 **In my third major league season,** while still a teenager, I threw 20 complete games, by far the all-time record for teenagers. That same season I became the first pitcher in the 20th century to strike out 18 batters in a nine-inning game.

121: Cy Young • 122: 1-E, 2-C, 3-F, 4-A, 5-G, 6-D, 7-B

3 **I threw baseball's only Opening Day no-hitter** in 1940, a 1–0 victory against the White Sox. I also pitched the first no-hitter against New York in Yankee Stadium, in 1946.

4 **Nicknamed "Rapid Robert,"** during my 18-year career with Cleveland I pitched 12 one-hitters, which ties me with Nolan Ryan for the most ever.

124

Each Hall of Fame second baseman listed holds one of these all-time records for the keystone position. Can you correctly get 'em all?

1. Highest batting average in a season—.426

2. Most doubles in a season—60

3. Most hits in a season—250

4. Most stolen bases in a season—81

5. Most National League games played at second base—2,427

6. Most consecutive games played at second base—798

7. Most consecutive errorless games—123

A. Eddie Collins

B. Nellie Fox

C. Napoleon Lajoie

D. Rogers Hornsby

E. Ryne Sandberg

F. Charlie Gehringer

G. Joe Morgan

125

1 **Ron Guidry and I are the only two lefthanders** in the history of the American League to hurl nine shutouts in one season.

2 **No Red Sox pitcher has won four career World Series games,** although a number have won three—but at 3–0, I am the only Boston pitcher to be undefeated in World Series play.

3 **I was also a pretty fair hitter in my day,** retiring with a career batting average of .342, including 136 triples and 123 stolen bases.

4 **Oh, I forgot to mention that I also hit 714 career home runs,** most of them after being traded to the Yankees and becoming an outfielder.

1 **Talk about respect . . .** During my Triple Crown season, I became the first player ever to receive an intentional walk with the bases loaded!

2 **Because of my immense status in baseball,** when the first baseball movie was made, I was the star of the show.

3 **A very popular player in my day,** I was fought over in the courts by two teams, the Philadelphia Phillies and the Philadelphia Athletics. The Athletics had me, but lost the court battle, so they quickly traded me to Cleveland to spite the Phillies and the judge. The next season I had to sit out all the road games at Philadelphia to avoid the court's jurisdiction.

4 **My .426 batting average** in 1901 is still the best ever in the American League. When I was traded to Cleveland in 1902, they were so happy to get me that they renamed the team the Cleveland Naps in my honor.

127

1 **When I retired from the Dodgers** in 1975, I had the best control of all pitchers who had at least 3,000 innings pitched since 1961: I issued only 1.82 walks per nine innings pitched.

2 **In 18 innings of All-Star Game pitching,** I gave up only one earned run.

3 **Even though I won 25 or more games** three times in my career, retired with a 243–142 record, had a career ERA of 2.89, and was elected to the Hall of Fame, I never won a Cy Young Award.

4 **On August 22, 1965,** one of the most violent brawls in baseball history took place in San Francisco's Candlestick Park after I rapped the Dodger catcher, John Roseboro, over the head with my bat.

128

1 **Despite playing in only 52 games** in my rookie season, having hit .354, I was unanimously voted the National League Rookie of the Year.

2 **I'm the only player in history** to hit two home runs in the same inning *twice,* accomplishing the feat in 1973 and 1977.

3 **A six-time All-Star,** I became the last player to homer twice in an All-Star Game when I led the National League to a 9–3 romp in the 1969 Summer Classic.

4 **Nicknamed "Stretch,"** when I retired as a four-decade player—mostly with the San Francisco Giants—after the 1980 season, I was the NL's career leader in home runs by a lefthander, with 521.

126: Napoleon Lajoie • **127:** Juan Marichal • **128:** Willie McCovey

1 **My .391 batting average** for a season is still the highest ever for a National League third baseman.

2 **One little-known fact** is that I have the highest on-base average in NL history (.466) and third best overall, trailing only Ted Williams and Babe Ruth.

3 **My main claim to fame,** however, is as a manager. In fact, I was one of the first managers ever elected to the Hall of Fame.

4 **I was small, but tough.** I guess that's why they called me "Little Napoleon." I was also successful. In 33 years—31 with the Giants—I won ten pennants.

130

1 **Faithfully keeping my word** to my mother, I always refused to play on Sundays.

2 **That Ty Cobb fella sure was a tough guy.** In 1918, during World War I, he was accidentally gassed in a military training exercise and it never even bothered him. Gassed in that same room with Cobb, I, on the other hand, contracted tuberculosis and died seven years later.

3 **Between 1903 and 1914,** I never won fewer than 22 games in a season and am the only pitcher in history to toss three shutouts in one World Series.

4 **Nicknamed "Big Six,"** I won 373 games, mostly for John McGraw's Giants, and was one of the original inductees into the Baseball Hall of Fame in 1936.

131

1 **During the first 80 years of the 20th century,** only Orlando Cepeda and I were unanimously selected to be named National League MVP.

2 **In 1989, even though I was retired,** the fans voted me in as one of the starters in the All-Star Game. I appreciated their votes, but did not play.

3 **No other player** has ever led the National League in home runs more than my eight times.

4 **A 12-time All-Star,** ten-time Gold Glove winner, and three-time MVP, as a lifetime member of the Philadelphia Phillies I'm considered to be the best all-around third baseman ever to play the game.

129: John J. McGraw • **130:** Christy Mathewson • **131:** Mike Schmidt

1 **My right arm was so strong** I actually equaled George Washington's alleged feat of throwing a silver dollar across the Rappahannock River.

2 **As for feats on the diamond,** in my first three games in the American League, I shut out New York all three times!

3 **In 1983, Nolan Ryan** broke my career strikeout record, a mark that had stood for 56 years.

4 **I never intentionally brushed a batter back.** Heck, I rarely even pitched inside because I always feared that with my velocity I would accidentally kill an opponent. And, in spite of allowing opposing batters to dig in against me, I still threw 110 shutouts for the lowly Washington Senators, far more than any other pitcher in major league history.

133

1 **In 1973, as the main designated hitter of the California Angels,** I homered in the 32nd different ballpark in use during my long career, the most ever up to that time.

2 **The Cleveland Indians** had more than their share of player-managers. I was their last.

3 **I was the unanimous selection** for National League Rookie of the Year in 1956 when I hit .290 with 38 homers and a league-leading 122 RBIs while playing with the Cincinnati Reds.

4 **I was not only the only player ever to win MVP Awards** in both the National and American Leagues (1961 with Cincinnati and 1966 with Baltimore), but also the first black manager in both leagues as well.

134

1 **During the decade of the 1960s,** I was the only player besides Bobby Bonds to hit at least 30 homers and steal at least 30 bases in the same season.

2 **Joe Adcock got the first hit** off Pittsburgh's Harvey Haddix in the longest perfect game in history, a 13th-inning home run, but was called out for passing me on the base paths.

3 **One of only a few players** to have his uniform number retired by two teams, my number, 44, was retired by both the Atlanta Braves and Milwaukee Brewers.

4 **On April 8, 1974,** and despite death threats, I made a "Ruthian" hit off Al Downing, breaking a record that most baseball experts had been saying for years would never be surpassed.

135

1 **I hold the major league pitching record** for most consecutive Opening Day assignments—16.

2 **On the same day that Rod Carew** collected his 3,000th career hit, I collected my 300th career victory, a 4–1 win over the Yankees.

3 **In a 1970 game against the San Diego Padres,** I struck out ten consecutive batters (the last ten of the game, too!), and that is still the major league record.

4 **In 1973 I became the first pitcher in history** to win a Cy Young Award without being a 20-game winner as I led my New York Mets teammates to another World Series berth.

136

1 **I was pretty good,** even as a kid. In fact, I still hold the major league record for highest batting average in a season by a teenager—.322.

2 **I hit over .300 11 times in my career,** but I never won a batting title. I almost won the home run crown in 1929, but in the last game of the season, Philadelphia's pitchers walked me intentionally five times so that I wouldn't have a chance to catch their teammate, Chuck Klein. He ended up winning the title, 43 homers to 42.

3 **As a National League outfielder,** I did, however, win six home run titles. Many baseball experts couldn't understand how I could hit so well with my trademark high front-leg kick just as the pitch was coming in.

4 **I also hold the major league record** for most home runs hit in the same park, 323. I accomplished this while playing for the old New York Giants in the Polo Grounds.

WHO, WHAT, WHEN, WHERE, AND WHY

1. Who is the batter in this artist's rendering?

2. What is he alleged to have been doing?

3. When did he do it?

4. Where did the game take place?

5. BONUS: Who was the pitcher?

137:

1. Hall of Famer Babe Ruth.

2. Pointing to the center-field stands where he intends to hit the next pitch.

3. Game 3 of the 1932 World Series.

4. Wrigley Field in Chicago.

5. Charlie Root.

1 **It was quite a celebration,** that first game in the brand-new Houston
Astrodome. I feel honored to have hit the first home run in the new
stadium.

2 **I was the first outfielder** in major league history to win back-to-back
MVP Awards.

3 **In 1956 I hit .353** and became the first switch-hitter ever to win a
batting title. I also hold the American League record for most career
home runs by a player who played his entire career with the same team.

4 **I hit 54 home runs in 1961,** but finished as the runner-up to the league
leader, who just happened to be one of my teammates.

139

1 **I am the only pitcher** in major league history with two career Opening
Day home runs.

2 **Talk about trivia.** I threw the first pitch in all of the following: the first
indoor All-Star Game, the first West Coast All-Star Game, and the first
West Coast World Series.

3 **The only pitcher ever to start two All-Star Games** in one season (1959),
I also hold the career record for most strikeouts in All-Star Game play
(19).

4 **Besides being the only pitcher** in history to pitch six consecutive
shutouts, I hold the Dodger record for most Opening Day victories, with
five.

140

1 **I hold the distinction of being the first player** in history to hit a pinch-
hit home run in the World Series.

2 **When Bill Mazeroski** hit his dramatic home run to win the 1960 World
Series, I was the Yankee left fielder who watched helplessly as the ball
sailed over my head and the wall.

3 **New York fans are very demanding.** So it was with great pleasure that
I, as manager, was able to take both the Yankees and the Mets to the
World Series.

4 **I'm most remembered,** however, as a catcher for the Yankees who was
given to saying such things as, "It ain't over 'til it's over!" and "Ninety
percent of this game is half mental."

138: Mickey Mantle • **139:** Don Drysdale • **140:** Yogi Berra

1 **Since 1917,** I have been the only National League pitcher to win 30 games in a season.

2 **Judge Landis, then baseball's commissioner,** had me removed as broadcaster for the all–St. Louis World Series of 1944 because he felt my clowning and syntax were too undignified for a national audience.

3 **Prior to Game 7 of the 1934 World Series,** I told the Detroit batters that I would throw 'em only fastballs. I did, and still shut them out, 11–0.

4 **Born Jay Hanna in 1911,** I was better known by another name when I was a star pitcher, along with my brother Daffy, for St. Louis's Gas House Gang.

142

1 **A suspected member of the Ku Klux Klan,** I once had to stay out of Ohio for 18 months to avoid arrest for knifing a black waiter in Cleveland.

2 **I was once suspended indefinitely** for attacking a heckling fan in the stands. When my teammates refused to play until I was reinstated, management had to bring in a replacement team until the matter was settled.

3 **When Maury Wills stole 104 bases** in 1962, he broke my single-season record of 96, set back in 1915.

4 **I toiled in the American League for 24 years,** 22 of them with the Tigers. I hit better than .300 for 23 consecutive seasons, three times hitting over .400, and retired as baseball's all-time batting champion, with a .367 average.

143

1 **As a player I was as loyal as I was good.** I still hold the record for the highest career batting average by a player who played his entire career with the same team.

2 **In 1969 I was named** the American League Manager of the Year.

3 **I was once fined $5,000** for "contemptuous actions toward the press and paying customers of Boston." That was a fancy way of saying I made obscene finger gestures and spit at 'em.

4 **In my last career at bat** for the Red Sox in 1960, I hit my 521st career home run. Not bad, considering I lost nearly five years in my prime to military service and injury.

141: Dizzy Dean • **142:** Ty Cobb • **143:** Ted Williams

1 **At times I was a bit wild.** I am the only pitcher since 1900 to issue over 200 walks in a season more than once.

2 **Other times, however,** I found the groove, and that's what helped me to become the last pitcher to win at least 100 games in both leagues.

3 **In 1974 I had one particularly hot streak.** In a three-game span I struck out 47 batters.

4 **And it was just the year before** that I set the modern-era record for most strikeouts in a season—383—while pitching for the Angels. Yet in spite of numerous strikeout and ERA records, I never won a Cy Young Award.

145

1 **I still hold the record for best home-run-to-strikeout ratio** in baseball history. Though no player has ever had as many home runs as strikeouts, I came the closest, with 361 homers and 369 strikeouts.

2 **Although my career was shortened** by military service, I still managed to set a few records—26 to be exact. I still hold the American League record for most runs scored in a season by a rookie, 132.

3 **In 1933, while just 19 years old** and playing in the Pacific Coast League, I shattered the all-time minor league record for most consecutive games with at least one hit. My 61-game hitting streak bested the existing record of 49 straight games set by Jack Ness in 1914.

4 **Mostly, though, I'll be remembered** for setting a record that most baseball experts feel will never be broken: my 56-game hitting streak in 1941 while playing for the Yankees.

146

1 **My National League fielding record** for double plays by a rookie first baseman stood for many years after I set it in 1947.

2 **An aggressive base runner,** I stole home 19 times during my ten-year career.

3 **Who says baseball rivalries aren't intense.** After ten brilliant years with the Dodgers, I was traded to the hated Giants. Rather than report, I retired.

4 **I was responsible for a lot of "firsts"** during my career. I was the first black Rookie of the Year, first black MVP, first black batting champion, and the first black to enter the Hall of Fame. In fact, I was the first black player of the 20th century.

144: Nolan Ryan • **145:** Joe DiMaggio • **146:** Jackie Robinson

147

1 **I am the only pitcher** ever to allow three home runs in one All-Star Game.

2 **The first pitcher ever to post World Series wins** in three different decades, I was also the first American League pitcher ever to win the Cy Young Award three times.

3 **In 1966, at the age of 20,** I became the youngest player ever to pitch a complete game shutout in the World Series, when I defeated Sandy Koufax and the Dodgers, 6–0.

4 **In 1984 I retired as the Baltimore Orioles' all-time leader** in wins, strikeouts, games pitched, innings, and shutouts. This gave me more time to model for Jockey brand underwear.

148

1 **In 1966 I became the first player** in All-Star Game history to win the game's MVP Award while playing for the losing team.

2 **In 1977 I became the first player** ever to play 23 seasons for the same team. Carl Yastrzemski later tied my record.

3 **In 1958, in one of the weirdest trade stories of all time,** Kansas City and Baltimore very nearly traded complete rosters. The only thing that prevented it was the Oriole management's desire to keep me in their organization.

4 **I played more games at third base** (2,870) than anyone else in history, and along the way won 16 Gold Gloves, all with the Baltimore Orioles.

149

1 **Of all the pitchers enshrined in the Hall of Fame,** my career winning percentage of .475 is the lowest.

2 **Although a considerable part of my career is legend,** it is enhanced by the fact that on more than one occasion, just to prove my ability, I called all my outfielders into the infield at the start of an inning and then struck out the side.

3 **Not only was I the oldest player** ever to appear in an All-Star Game when I appeared in the 1953 Summer Classic at the age of 47, I was the oldest rookie ever when I debuted in 1948 at the age of 42.

4 **My charismatic reputation** made me the preeminent gate attraction in the Negro leagues. My classic maxim was, "Don't look back. Something might be gaining on you."

147: Jim Palmer • **148:** Brooks Robinson • **149:** Satchel Paige

WHO, WHAT, WHEN, WHERE, AND WHY

1. **Who** is this?

2. **Why** is the photograph important?

3. **When** was this picture taken?

4. **Where** did this take place?

150:

1. Hall of Famer Satchel Paige.

2. At age 59, he was the oldest player in major league history to appear in a game.

3. 1965.

4. Kansas City.

1 **I hold the distinction** of being the only player in either league ever to win at least three batting titles, yet retire with a career batting average below .300.

2 **I guess you could say I was a durable player;** after all, I played in 3,308 games during my career, and that's more than any other player in American League history.

3 **Was 1968 really the year of the pitcher?** Well, I was the only player in the American League to hit .300. In fact, my .301 batting average that season still ranks as the all-time lowest average ever by a batting champ.

4 **Normally I'm modest** about most of my accomplishments, but I'm very proud of the fact that in 1967 I led the Boston Red Sox to the pennant, and in the process became the last player to win baseball's coveted Triple Crown.

152

1 **In 1976 I won a disputed batting title** on the last day of the season by one point when I hit a routine fly ball to left field that some say Steve Brye deliberately misplayed into a hit so my closest rival wouldn't win the crown.

2 **In 1979 I became only the second American League player** ever to hit at least 20 doubles, 20 triples, and 20 home runs in the same season.

3 **Besides Wade Boggs,** I am the only American League third baseman ever to win more than one batting title.

4 **For me, the best year in my long career** with the Kansas City Royals was 1980, when I hit .390, the highest seasonal average ever for an AL third sacker. For others, the most memorable moment in my career was the famous "Pine Tar Incident," in which I had a home run taken away from me because the umpires ruled I had pine tar too far up the bat.

153

1 **Signed to a contract right off the sandlots,** I never played a game of minor league ball. I was so good, in fact, that when I was only 20 years old, I hit .340 and in the process became the youngest player ever to win a batting title.

2 **Of all the 3,000-hit club members** whose lifetime average was below .300, mine was the highest, at .297.

3 **On September 24, 1974,** I collected my 3,000th base hit and became the first American League player in nearly 50 years to reach that milestone.

4 **After retiring with more career games played** and home runs than any other Tiger in Detroit history, I joined the Tiger broadcast team, where I spent the next three decades. I guess that's why they call me "Mr. Tiger."

154

1 **When I was a power-hitting outfielder** for the Baltimore Orioles in 1976, my hands were quick but not too nimble. My league-leading .502 slugging average was offset by my league-leading 11 errors.

2 **In 1982 I won the American League home run crown** with 39 and led the Angels to the division title and their best record in team history.

3 **I was the first player ever to have a candy bar** named after him. They should have called it the Whiff Bar, though, considering I struck out more times in my career (2,597) than anyone else in history.

4 **Being the only player ever** to hit five home runs in a single World Series helped me attain my nickname, "Mr. October."

155

1 **Talk about long seasons!** I had one year in which I allowed 412 hits, an American League pitching record that has never been broken.

2 **Although my pitching career was short,** at only ten years, I still managed to win 246 games, leading the league in wins five times.

3 **I must admit that even though it wasn't easy,** I did keep myself in great shape. That's what allowed me to continue pitching effectively in the minor leagues until my mid-50s.

4 **They used to call me "Iron Man,"** not because of the times I pitched both games of a doubleheader but because I usually finished what I started. During my career I started 381 games and completed an amazing 314 of them, most during my career with the New York Giants.

1 **Determined to save my eyes** for baseball, I didn't smoke, drink, go to the movies, or even read newspapers during my career! I was strictly business. In fact, I didn't even attend my mother's funeral because it would have interfered with the World Series.

2 **Winning the Triple Crown** is a next-to-impossible feat, but I did it twice.

3 **Considered the greatest righthanded hitter** in the history of the game, I retired with a career batting average of .358, including one five-year stretch in which I hit .401. Only Ty Cobb's .367 lifetime average is higher.

4 **Not only did I win six consecutive batting titles,** I also won nine fielding titles while playing second base for the St. Louis Cardinals.

157

1 **As a member of "dem bums,"** the Brooklyn Dodgers of 1955, I once struck out in 12 consecutive plate appearances, and that is still the major league record.

2 **In 1972 I became the youngest person** ever to be elected to the Hall of Fame in Cooperstown.

3 **I was the first Cy Young winner** to be a unanimous selection. In fact, all three of my Cy Young Awards were unanimous.

4 **In 1966 I won 27 games,** a 20th-century record for a pitcher playing in his last season. My career was cut short by a terrible case of arthritis in my pitching elbow.

158

1 **In 1973, as a member of the Red Sox,** I became the first designated hitter ever to hit a home run, when I connected off Sparky Lyle of the Yankees.

2 **I accomplished a lot of "firsts"** in my career. Not only was I the first National Leaguer to be a unanimous selection for MVP, I was the first player in either league to be a unanimous selection for Rookie of the Year.

3 **Although most people agree** that my lifetime stats warranted election to the Hall of Fame earlier in my career, the fact that I spent time in prison for drug smuggling probably kept me out for many years.

4 **Nicknamed the "Baby Bull,"** I became more popular in San Francisco in the 1960s than my teammate Willie Mays.

156: Rogers Hornsby • **157:** Sandy Koufax • **158:** Orlando Cepeda

1 **The debut issue of the popular magazine** *Sports Illustrated* (August 16, 1954) featured me on the cover.

2 **Ty Cobb once said of me,** "I've only known three or four perfect swings in my time. This lad has one of them."

3 **I am the only player in history** to play in three different cities for the same franchise.

4 **In my long career with the Braves** (Boston, Milwaukee, and Atlanta), home runs were my specialty and only Mike Schmidt of the Phillies has more career home runs as a third baseman. Also, of all the members of the prestigious 500-home run club, only Mark McGwire played fewer seasons than my 17.

160

1 **I held the record** for most consecutive starting appearances without a relief appearance *in the same league* at 534, until Roger Clemens broke it in 2001.

2 **In 1969 I became the only pitcher** in baseball history to strike out 19 batters in a game, yet lose. In the All-Star Game that year I got a double, and that marks the last time that a pitcher got an extra-base hit in the Summer Classic.

3 **The first pitcher ever to win four Cy Young Awards,** I was also the first lefthander in major league history to reach 4,000 strikeouts.

4 **1972 was a bittersweet year for me.** My personal record was 27–10. My Phillies team, however, finished a dismal 59–97, and that's the only time in history a Cy Young Award winner played for a last-place team.

161

1 **In 1972 I became the first player** in the history of the American League to be a unanimous selection for Rookie of the Year.

2 **In 1985 I hit 33 home runs,** an American League record for catchers until Ivan Rodriguez broke it with 35 in 1999.

3 **When I retired in 1993,** I had played more games at catcher than anyone else in baseball history.

4 **The 1975 World Series featured me in the spotlight** when I drilled a Pat Darcy pitch off the left-field foul pole in the 12th inning of Game 6, a home run that ended what many consider the most dramatic game in World Series history.

159: Eddie Mathews • 160: Steve Carlton • 161: Carlton Fisk

1 **I was a very consistent player** during my career. To this day I am the only player ever to hit at least three home runs in All-Star Game play, the League Championship Series, and the World Series.

2 **I was exceptionally good** when I was young. So good, in fact, that my minor league uniform number was retired when I was promoted to the majors. And when I won the MVP Award in 1970, at the age of 22, I was the youngest player in history up to that time to capture the award.

3 **My ten Gold Glove Awards** are still the most ever by a National League catcher.

4 **Until Javy Lopez of Atlanta** surpassed me in 2003, I held the record for most home runs in a season by a catcher (38—but I hit seven more when playing other positions!), which I accomplished in 1970 while playing with Cincinnati.

163

1 **Like so many other great players,** I rose to the occasion. Of all players who played at least 20 career World Series games, my .391 batting average is the highest.

2 **I am the only player** to collect at least 3,000 hits in National League play and not win a batting title.

3 **In 1964 I split my time** between the St. Louis Cardinals and Chicago Cubs, yet I still broke the 200-hit barrier, becoming the last player to reach that mark while playing for two teams until Randy Velarde matched the feat in 1999.

4 **Among my many stolen-base accomplishments** in my 16 seasons with the Cardinals: 12 seasons with 50 or more steals, more than anyone except Rickey Henderson; most stolen bases in a World Series (7), and I did it twice; and the National League record for steals in a season with 118.

164

1 **From 1964 to 2001,** seven pitchers won the American League MVP Award. I was the only *National League* pitcher during that same period to win the award.

2 **During the decade of the 1960s,** I pitched eight straight complete games in the World Series.

3 **Speaking of the World Series,** no other pitcher has even come close to my records of 17 strikeouts in one World Series game and 35 in a single World Series.

4 **Along with the MVP Award,** in 1968, I also won the National League's Cy Young Award after pitching 13 shutouts, compiling an incredible 1.12 ERA, and leading the Cardinals to the pennant.

165

1 **Although I am currently in the all-time top 10** in RBIs, I never once led either league in runs batted in.

2 **My first career hit,** after a long hitless drought that begin my career, was a home run off Warren Spahn, later a fellow Hall of Famer. Thank goodness my manager, Leo Durocher, had faith in me.

3 **In 1966 I broke Mel Ott's National League record** for career homers when I hit the 512th of my career on May 4. When I was eventually elected to the Hall of Fame, in 1979, the 409 votes for me were the most ever up to that time.

4 **The last Giant to win a batting title** (1954) until Barry Bonds in 2002, I also have the most career hits in All-Star Game play, 23, and was the first black player ever to collect 3,000 career hits.

166

1 **I am the only National League player** ever to hit safely in seven consecutive All-Star Games.

2 **One of my strongest abilities** was to work the pitcher for a walk. In 1965, my first full season with the Astros, I led the league in walks. In 1980, my last season with the Astros, I also led the league in walks. In 1984 I retired with 1,865 walks—good for third on the career list at the time—and was the only black player in the top 14 in career walks.

3 **I still hold the National League record** for most career games played at second base—2,427.

4 **As a member of Cincinnati's "Big Red Machine"** in 1975 and 1976, I won back-to-back MVP Awards, the only second baseman ever to do so.

WHO, WHAT, WHEN, WHERE, AND WHY

1. Who is the player?

2. What just happened?

3. When?

4. What position did the player play that day?

4. Left field.

3. In Game 7 of the 1960 World Series, bottom of the ninth inning.

2. Bill Mazeroski hit the first Series-ending walk-off home run in major league history.

1. Hall of Famer Yogi Berra.

167:

The next series of games concerns the accomplishments of Hall of Famers grouped by the position for which they were inducted. (Note: For statistical purposes, each Hall of Fame player's lifetime totals are used, even though some of their career stats may have been earned while playing other positions.)

Hall of Fame catchers.

1. First catcher to be elected to the Hall of Fame
2. Catcher most recently elected to the Hall of Fame
3. HOF catcher with the most career hits—2,356
4. HOF catcher with lowest career batting average—.253
5. HOF catcher with highest career batting average—.320
6. HOF catcher with fewest career games played—1,215
7. HOF catcher with most career RBIs—1,430

A. Mickey Cochrane
B. Carlton Fisk
C. Yogi Berra
D. Gary Carter
E. Buck Ewing
F. Roy Campanella
G. Ray Schalk

169

More Hall of Fame catchers.

1. HOF catcher with most career strikeouts—1,386
2. HOF catcher with most career home runs—389
3. HOF catcher who was thrown out the most times attempting to steal—69
4. HOF catcher with the fewest career strikeouts—99
5. Only HOF catcher with a career on-base percentage over .400
6. HOF catcher with the most career walks—931
7. HOF catcher with the most career triples—178

A. Ray Schalk
B. Buck Ewing
C. Carlton Fisk
D. Mickey Cochrane
E. Rick Ferrell
F. Johnny Bench
G. Roger Bresnahan

168: 1-E, 2-D, 3-B, 4-G, 5-A, 6-F, 7-C • **169:** 1-C, 2-F, 3-A, 4-G, 5-D, 6-E, 7-B

Hall of Fame first basemen.

1. The first baseman most recently elected to the Hall of Fame

2. Of the two four-decade HOF first basemen, the one who played the most years—22

3. The only HOF first baseman with more than 2,000 career RBIs

4. HOF first baseman with the most career homers—573

5. The HOF first baseman with the highest career batting average—.340

6. HOF first baseman with the fewest career hits—1,273

7. The HOF first baseman with the highest career on-base percentage—.447

A. Cap Anson

B. Eddie Murray

C. Frank Chance

D. Willie McCovey

E. Lou Gehrig

F. Harmon Killebrew

G. Dan Brouthers

171

More Hall of Fame first basemen.

1. Only HOF first baseman to be inducted in the 1990s

2. HOF first baseman with most career runs scored—1,996

3. Hit the most career triples among HOF first sackers—243

4. HOF first baseman with most career at bats—11,336

5. HOF first baseman with fewest career walks—386

6. HOF first baseman with the lowest career batting average—.256

7. HOF first baseman with the most career stolen bases—401

A. Eddie Murray

B. Harmon Killebrew

C. Cap Anson

D. Frank Chance

E. Orlando Cepeda

F. Jake Beckley

G. George Kelly

Hall of Fame second basemen.

1. The first second baseman ever inducted into the Hall of Fame

2. The HOF second baseman with the most career walks—1,865

3. The HOF second baseman with the fewest career hits—1,518

4. HOF second baseman with the lowest career batting average—.260

5. Most stolen bases among HOF second basemen—744

6. Fewest career homers among HOF second basemen—12

7. HOF second baseman with most career homers—301

A. Johnny Evers

B. Rogers Hornsby

C. Bill Mazeroski

D. Jackie Robinson

E. Joe Morgan

F. Napoleon Lajoie

G. Eddie Collins

173

More Hall of Fame second basemen.

1. Second baseman most recently inducted into the Hall of Fame

2. HOF second baseman with fewest runs scored (769) and stolen bases (27) for his career

3. Most career triples of all HOF second basemen—188

4. HOF second baseman who was thrown out the most times attempting to steal in his career—187

5. HOF second baseman with the highest career batting average (.358), slugging average (.577), and on-base percentage (.434)

6. HOF second baseman with the most career hits—3,315

7. HOF second baseman with the most career RBIs—1,599

A. Rogers Hornsby

B. Eddie Collins

C. Ryne Sandberg

D. Bill Mazeroski

E. Bid McPhee

F. Napoleon Lajoie

G. Rod Carew

174

Hall of Fame third basemen.

1. The first third baseman inducted into the Hall of Fame

2. HOF third baseman with the most career triples—164

3. HOF third baseman with the most career stolen bases—235

4. HOF third baseman who's played the most games—2,896

5. HOF third baseman with the fewest career hits—1,747

6. HOF third baseman with the most career hits—3,154

7. HOF third baseman with the highest career batting average—.328

A. Freddie Lindstrom

B. Wade Boggs

C. Pie Traynor

D. Brooks Robinson

E. Jimmy Collins

F. Home Run Baker

G. George Brett

175

More Hall of Fame third basemen.

1. HOF third baseman with fewest career home runs—58

2. HOF third baseman who struck out the fewest times—182

3. Major league third baseman most recently to be inducted into the Hall of Fame

4. HOF third baseman with most career runs scored—1,583

5. HOF third baseman with the fewest career runs scored—881

6. HOF third baseman with most career home runs—548

7. HOF third baseman with lowest career batting average—.267

A. George Brett

B. Home Run Baker

C. Mike Schmidt

D. George Kell

E. Wade Boggs

F. Pie Traynor

G. Brooks Robinson

174: 1-E, 2-C, 3-F, 4-D, 5-A, 6-G, 7-B • **175:** 1-F, 2-B, 3-E, 4-A, 5-D, 6-C, 7-G

WHO, WHAT, WHEN, WHERE, AND WHY

1. **Who** are these three men?

2. **What** are they discussing?

3. **When?**

4. **Where?**

5. **BONUS:** What was the score of the game when Commissioner Landis had one of the men removed for his own safety and what was the final score?

176:

1. Cardinals manager Frank Frisch, Cardinals outfielder Joe Medwick, and baseball commissioner Kenesaw Mountain Landis, Hall of Famers all.

2. They were trying to decide what to do about the Tiger fans' violent reaction (they were throwing bottles, food, and garbage) to Medwick after his rough slide into third baseman Marv Owen in the top of the sixth inning. Commissioner Landis had Medwick removed for his own safety.

3. Game 7, bottom of the sixth inning, of the 1934 World Series.

4. Detroit's Navin Field.

5. 9–0 in favor of St. Louis when Medwick was removed, and 11–0 final.

Hall of Fame shortstops.

1. HOF shortstop with the highest career batting average—.327

2. HOF shortstop with the lowest career batting average—.258

3. HOF shortstop with the most career walks—1,302

4. HOF shortstop with the fewest career RBIs—563

5. After the original class of 1936 inductees, he was the first shortstop to be enshrined in the Hall of Fame

6. HOF shortstop with the fewest career runs scored—774

7. HOF shortstop with the most career strikeouts—1,350

A. Hughie Jennings

B. Luke Appling

C. Honus Wagner

D. Joe Tinker

E. Robin Yount

F. Phil Rizzuto

G. Rabbit Maranville

178

More Hall of Fame shortstops.

1. HOF shortstop with the fewest career doubles—231

2. HOF shortstop who played the most games—2,856

3. Shortstop most recently to be enshrined in the Hall of Fame

4. HOF shortstop with most career home runs—512

5. Highest career on-base percentage by an HOF shortstop—.406

6. HOF shortstop with the fewest career home runs (18) and hits (1,527)

7. HOF shortstop with the most career runs scored (1,736), hits (3,415), doubles (640), triples (252), RBIs (1,732), and stolen bases (722)

A. John Ward

B. Robin Yount

C. Ozzie Smith

D. Hughie Jennings

E. Honus Wagner

F. Arky Vaughan

G. Ernie Banks

177: 1-C, 2-G, 3-B, 4-F, 5-A, 6-D, 7-E • **178:** 1-A, 2-B, 3-C, 4-G, 5-F, 6-D, 7-E

Baseball Trivia

Hall of Fame left fielders.

(Reminder: Although some of these players played other positions during their careers, left field was their primary position and the one for which they were inducted into the Hall of Fame.)

1. The left fielder most recently to be inducted into the Hall of Fame

A. Lou Brock

2. HOF left fielder with the most career triples—220

B. Ed Delahanty

3. HOF left fielder with the highest career batting average—.346

C. Stan Musial

4. Only HOF left fielder to be walked more than 2,000 times during his career—2,021

D. Carl Yastrzemski

5. HOF left fielder with the most career hits—3,630

E. Ralph Kiner

6. HOF left fielder with the lowest career batting average—.279

F. Fred Clarke

7. HOF left fielder with the most career stolen bases—938

G. Ted Williams

More Hall of Fame left fielders.

1. HOF left fielder who hit the most career home runs—521

A. Chick Hafey

2. HOF left fielder who hit the fewest career home runs—62

B. Ted Williams

3. HOF left fielder with the fewest career runs scored (777) and RBIs (833)

C. Lou Brock

4. HOF left fielder who struck out the fewest times—345

D. Willie Stargell

5. HOF left fielder with the lowest career on-base percentage—amazingly, just .343

E. Heinie Manush

6. HOF left fielder who struck out the most times (1,936) and stole the fewest bases (17)

F. Stan Musial

7. HOF left fielder with the most career runs (1,949) and RBIs (1,951)

G. Jim O'Rourke

179: 1-D, 2-F, 3-B, 4-G, 5-C, 6-E, 7-A • **180:** 1-B, 2-G, 3-A, 4-E, 5-C, 6-D, 7-F

Hall of Fame right fielders.

1. The first right fielder inducted into the Hall of Fame

   A. Dave Winfield

2. HOF right fielder with the fewest career homers—33

   B. Frank Robinson

3. HOF right fielder with the most career hits—3,771

   C. Ross Youngs

4. HOF right fielder who played the fewest games—1,211

   D. Hank Aaron

5. Right fielder most recently elected to the Hall of Fame

   E. Babe Ruth

6. HOF right fielder with the lowest career batting average—.262

   F. Willie Keeler

7. After Aaron and Ruth, the HOF right fielder with the most career home runs—586

   G. Reggie Jackson

182

More Hall of Fame right fielders.

1. HOF right fielder who played the most games—3,298

   A. Hank Aaron

2. HOF right fielder who struck out the most times—2,597

   B. Reggie Jackson

3. HOF right fielder who had the fewest career stolen bases—71

   C. King Kelly

4. HOF right fielder with the highest career batting average—.342

   D. Enos Slaughter

5. HOF right fielder with most career stolen bases—495

   E. Babe Ruth

6. HOF right fielder with most career triples—309

   F. Sam Crawford

7. HOF right fielder whose playing career ended first

   G. Willie Keeler

Hall of Fame center fielders.

1. First center fielder elected to the Hall of Fame	**A. Billy Hamilton**
2. HOF center fielder with the most career doubles—792	**B. Mickey Mantle**
3. HOF center fielder with the fewest career stolen bases—30	**C. Ty Cobb**
4. HOF center fielder with the most career stolen bases—912	**D. Lloyd Waner**
5. HOF center fielder with the fewest career home runs—27	**E. Tris Speaker**
6. HOF center fielder with the most career home runs—660	**F. Willie Mays**
7. HOF center fielder with the most career strikeouts—1,710	**G. Joe DiMaggio**

184

More Hall of Fame center fielders.

1. HOF center fielder with the lowest career batting average—.283	**A. Hack Wilson**
2. HOF center fielder with the most career triples—295	**B. Larry Doby**
3. Center fielder most recently elected to the Hall of Fame	**C. Mickey Mantle**
4. HOF center fielder with the fewest career hits—1,461	**D. Joe DiMaggio**
5. HOF center fielder who received the most walks—1,733	**E. Duke Snider**
6. Only center fielder elected to the Hall of Fame in the 1980s	**F. Kirby Puckett**
7. HOF center fielder with the highest career slugging percentage—.579	**G. Ty Cobb**

The *batting* accomplishments of Hall of Fame pitchers.

1. HOF pitcher with the most career at bats (2,960), runs scored (325), hits (623), and RBIs (290)
   A. John Clarkson

2. HOF pitcher with the most career triples—41
   B. Sandy Koufax

3. HOF pitcher with the most career stolen bases—31
   C. Red Ruffing

4. HOF pitcher with the most career doubles (98) and highest career batting average (.269)
   D. Pud Galvin

5. HOF pitcher with the lowest career batting average—.088
   E. Cy Young

6. HOF pitcher with the most career home runs—37
   F. Walter Johnson

7. HOF pitcher who struck out the most times as a batter—631
   G. Bob Lemon

186

Now for the *pitching* accomplishments of Hall of Fame pitchers.

1. HOF pitcher with the most career wins—511
   A. Dennis Eckersley

2. HOF pitcher with the lowest career ERA—1.82
   B. Robin Roberts

3. HOF pitcher who appeared in the most games—1,071
   C. Walter Johnson

4. HOF pitcher who allowed the most home runs—505
   D. Ed Walsh

5. HOF pitcher with the most career strikeouts—5,714
   E. Whitey Ford

6. HOF pitcher with the most career shutouts—110
   F. Nolan Ryan

7. HOF pitcher with the highest career winning percentage—.690
   G. Cy Young

WHO, WHAT, WHEN, WHERE, AND WHY

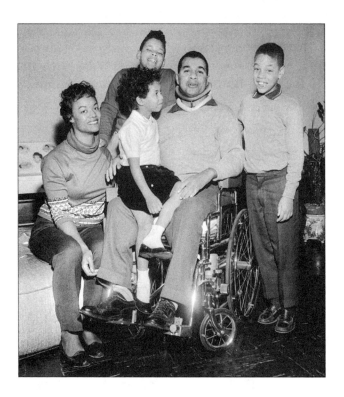

1. **Who** is in the wheelchair?

2. **What** caused his paralysis?

3. **When** and where did it occur?

4. **How?**

187:

1. Hall of Fame catcher Roy Campanella of the Dodgers.

2. He was injured in a car accident.

3. January 29, 1958, in Long Island, New York.

4. While driving home after closing his liquor store for the evening, Campanella hit an icy patch on a city street and crashed into a telephone pole. His spinal cord was nearly severed.

More Hall of Fame pitchers. (Note: Only regular, full-time pitchers who had a full career in major league baseball are considered for this game—no Negro league transfers, such as Satchel Paige; pitchers converted to hitters, such as Babe Ruth; pitchers who played predominantly another position, such as Bobby Wallace; or pitchers who were enshrined primarily for something else, such as Candy Cummings.)

1. Only HOFer with a losing record (114–118, .491)   **A. Jesse Haines**

2. HOFer with the fewest career wins—150   **B. Ted Lyons**

3. HOF *starting* pitcher with the fewest complete games—151   **C. Rollie Fingers**

4. HOF *starting* pitcher with the fewest career shutouts—24   **D. Red Ruffing**

5. HOF pitcher with the highest career ERA—3.80   **E. Jim Bunning**

6. HOF pitcher who appeared in the fewest games—286   **F. Addie Joss**

7. HOF pitcher with the second highest career ERA—3.67   **G. Dizzy Dean**

189

Because Cy Young dominated so many career pitching categories, many Hall of Fame pitchers who finished second to him (and others) are often overlooked.

1. HOFer with the second most games started—773   **A. Walter Johnson**

2. HOFer with the second most career wins—417   **B. Lefty Grove**

3. HOFer with the second most career complete games—646   **C. Ferguson Jenkins**

4. HOFer with the second best career winning percentage—.680   **D. Pud Galvin**

5. HOFer who allowed the second most home runs—484   **E. Grover Alexander**

6. HOFer with the second most career shutouts—90   **F. Nolan Ryan**

7. HOFer who appeared in the second most games—1,070   **G. Hoyt Wilhelm**

188: 1-C, 2-G, 3-E, 4-A, 5-D, 6-F, 7-B • **189:** 1-F, 2-A, 3-D, 4-B, 5-C, 6-E, 7-G

Hall of Fame managers and their achievements. (Note: This game takes into account only those who were inducted as managers, not those who were inducted as players who also happened to manage during their careers.)

1. HOF manager who managed the most career games (7,755), for the most years (53), and had the most wins (3,731) and losses (3,948)

    A. Casey Stengel

2. The first of only two HOF managers to win seven World Series

    B. John McGraw

3. Of the two HOF managers to win ten pennants, he did so in the fewest years (25)

    C. Ned Hanlon

4. HOF manager with the second most career victories—2,763

    D. Sparky Anderson

5. HOF manager with the second most career losses—2,218

    E. Connie Mack

6. Won five pennants, but never a World Series

    F. Bucky Harris

7. Most recent HOF manager inductee

    G. Joe McCarthy

191

This game takes into account only those Hall of Fame managers who were inducted first and primarily for their playing careers and secondarily for their managing careers.

1. Won the most pennants—6

    A. Charles Comiskey

2. Of those in this game, the most recent HOF inductee

    B. Clark Griffith

3. Won the most World Series—2

    C. Harry Wright

4. Had the highest career winning percentage—.608

    D. Frank Chance

5. Had the most career wins—1,602

    E. Dave Bancroft

6. Managed the most career games—2,918

    F. Red Schoendienst

7. Lowest career winning percentage—.407

    G. Fred Clarke

190: 1-E, 2-G, 3-A, 4-B, 5-F, 6-C, 7-D • **191:** 1-C, 2-F, 3-D, 4-A, 5-G, 6-B, 7-E

Now for the eight Hall of Fame umpires.

1. Tom Connolly

A. Became baseball's youngest umpire at the age of 22, was a contributing writer to several magazines, and authored the book *Umpiring from the Inside*.

2. Bill McGowan

B. A calm and dignified ump in baseball's roughest era, he once went ten years without ejecting a player. He worked eight World Series in his 34-year career.

3. Jocko Conlon

C. Was the first person elected to three different sports halls of fame, having earlier been elected to both the college and pro football shrines.

4. Bill Klem

D. Once a White Sox outfielder, he took over the umpiring in a game between the Sox and Browns when the regular umpire was overcome by heat. The next year, with his trademark polka-dot tie, he became a full-time ump.

5. Nestor Chylak

E. A longtime AL crew chief, he won the Silver Star and Purple Heart for his part in World War II's Battle of the Bulge, in which he nearly lost his eyesight to shrapnel.

6. Cal Hubbard

F. He was credited with bringing dignity to the umpiring profession. Proficient at calling balls and strikes, he worked almost exclusively behind the plate his first 16 years, and umpired 18 World Series.

7. Al Barlick

G. In 30 American League seasons, he was the umpire's equivalent of Cal Ripken Jr., umpiring every inning for 16 years at one stretch—2,541 consecutive games.

8. Billy Evans

H. Extremely intelligent, he was a strict, yet fair, interpreter of the rules during his 30-plus years as an NL ump. He was very active in the umpires' union, leading the drive for better pay and respect.

192: 1-B, 2-G, 3-D, 4-F, 5-E, 6-C, 7-H, 8-A

Do you know the paths to fame for these Hall of Fame executives and pioneers?

1. Ed Barrow
2. Morgan Bulkeley
3. Alexander Cartwright
4. Henry Chadwick
5. Happy Chandler
6. Charlie Comiskey
7. Candy Cummings

A. Helped create the National League in 1876 and was its first president

B. Served in almost every capacity except player; built the Yankees dynasty

C. A star pitcher in baseball's early years, he is often credited with inventing the curveball

D. Baseball's second commissioner, he presided over the racial integration of the game

E. Called "The Father of Baseball," he helped formalize and publish the first set of baseball rules

F. A renowned baseball writer, he invented the modern box score and introduced statistics such as batting average and ERA to the game

G. A successful player, manager, and owner

194

More Hall of Fame executives and pioneers.

1. Rube Foster
2. Ford Frick
3. Warren Giles
4. Clark Griffith
5. William Harridge
6. William Hulbert
7. Ban Johnson

A. Eighteen-year NL president who presided over the league's expansion, several franchise shifts, and the construction of numerous new ballparks

B. A successful pitcher, manager, and owner

C. Successful promoter of the American League as its president for 28 years

D. Babe Ruth's former ghostwriter, he became baseball's third commissioner and later would require that an asterisk be placed next to Roger Maris's 61 home runs in the official record books (signifying Maris hit his in a 162-game season, whereas Ruth hit his in a 154-game season)

E. Founder of the Negro National League in 1920

F. Founded the American League in 1901

G. Cofounded the National League in 1876 and later became the circuit's second president

193: 1-B, 2-A, 3-E, 4-F, 5-D, 6-G, 7-C • **194:** 1-E, 2-D, 3-A, 4-B, 5-C, 6-G, 7-F

More Hall of Fame executives and pioneers.

1. Kenesaw Mountain Landis

A. A great innovator, he initiated night baseball, travel by airplane, player pensions, and the regular broadcasting of games

2. Larry MacPhail

B. A successful player, manager, and Negro league owner whose teams often outdrew their white counterparts

3. Lee MacPhail

C. She used her position as a Negro league team co-owner to push for civil rights and sought (and earned) the respect by major league baseball of Negro league contracts

4. Effa Manley

D. Former owner of several Negro league teams, he was also a longtime scout who helped open the doors to the major leagues for many Caribbean players

5. Alex Pompez

E. A 50-year front-office executive with vision, he invented the modern farm system, pioneered the utilization of statistics, and broke the color barrier by signing Jackie Robinson as baseball's first black player

6. Cum Posey

F. A 45-year front-office executive, AL president, and president of the player relations committee

7. Branch Rickey

G. As baseball's first commissioner, he dealt with the Black Sox scandal with an iron fist, banning eight White Sox players for life

196

One final game of Hall of Fame executives and pioneers.

1. Al Spalding

A. A highly successful GM who won the Executive of the Year Award four times when his Yankees won ten pennants in 14 years

2. Bill Veeck

B. The best pitcher in the game in the 1870s, he later became a manager and team president, then left the game to tend his highly successful sporting goods business

3. George Weiss   **C. A star outfielder in baseball's early days, he introduced the practice of hitting pregame fungoes to the outfielders, defensive shifts, and backing up fielders as a defensive strategy**

4. George Wright   **D. A maverick owner who used ingenious promotions and sometimes outrageous prizes for fans, he introduced Bat Day, fireworks, exploding scoreboards, players' names on uniform backs, and signed the AL's first black player**

5. Harry Wright   **E. The highly respected owner of the Red Sox for 44 years and the AL vice president for 18**

6. Tom Yawkey   **F. A star player in baseball's early days, he helped revolutionize the playing of the shortstop position**

197

NAME THAT YEAR

Seven clues. One year. See how few clues it takes you to guess the year.

1 **Lou Gehrig establishes a major league record** by hitting 14 home runs against the Cleveland Indians, the most by any player against one team in one season.

2 **Fenway Park erects a 23-foot-high screen** on top of the left-field wall because of all the broken windows on Lansdowne Street.

3 **In a fan poll,** Boston Braves fans choose the Bees as their new team nickname, a moniker that will last for five seasons.

4 **The Yankees have five players** with at least 100 RBIs.

5 **Carl Hubbell of the Giants** wins 16 straight decisions.

6 **Tony Lazzeri of the Yankees** has 11 RBIs in one game.

7 **The Hall of Fame is created** and Ty Cobb is the leading vote getter in the first class.

See if you can match up these Hall of Fame members, who played in or were associated with the Negro leagues, with their primary teams.

1. Cool Papa Bell   **A. Detroit Stars, Kansas City Monarchs**

2. Ray Brown   **B. Homestead Grays**

3. Willard Brown   **C. Newark Eagles**

4. Oscar Charleston   **D. Newark Dodgers, Newark Eagles, New York Cubans**

5. Andy Cooper   **E. St. Louis Stars, Homestead Grays, Pittsburgh Crawfords, Kansas City Stars**

6. Ray Dandridge   **F. Indianapolis ABCs, Harrisburg Giants, Pittsburgh Crawfords, Philadelphia Stars**

7. Leon Day   **G. Kansas City Monarchs, several Puerto Rican teams**

199

More Negro leaguers.

1. Martin Dihigo   **A. Homestead Grays, Pittsburgh Crawfords**

2. Bill Foster   **B. Cuban Stars East, Hilldale Daisies, New York Cubans**

3. Rube Foster   **C. Newark Eagles**

4. Josh Gibson   **D. Chicago American Giants, Leland Giants, Philadelphia Giants**

5. Frank Grant   **E. Cuban Giants, Philadelphia Giants, Buffalo Bisons**

6. Pete Hill   **F. Chicago American Giants, Cole's American Giants**

7. Monte Irvin   **G. Leland Giants, Cuban X-Giants, Philadelphia Giants, Chicago American Giants**

More Negro leaguers.

1. Judy Johnson
2. Buck Leonard
3. Pop Lloyd
4. Biz Mackey
5. Effa Manley
6. Jose Mendez
7. Satchel Paige

A. Hilldale Daisies, Pittsburgh Crawfords, Madison Stars

B. Newark Eagles

C. Homestead Grays, Brooklyn Royal Giants

D. Cuban Stars, All Nations, Kansas City Monarchs

E. New York Lincoln Giants, Chicago American Giants, Brooklyn Royal Giants, Atlantic City Bacharach Giants

F. Birmingham Black Barons, Pittsburgh Crawfords, Kansas City Monarchs

G. Hilldale Giants, Philadelphia Stars, Newark Eagles, Baltimore Black Sox

201

Still more Negro leaguers.

1. Ben Taylor
2. Cristobal Torriente
3. Willie Wells
4. Sol White
5. J. L. Wilkinson
6. Joe Williams
7. Judd Wilson

A. Baltimore Black Sox, Homestead Grays, Philadelphia Stars

B. Cuban Stars (West), All Nations, Chicago American Giants, Detroit Stars, Kansas City Monarchs, Cleveland Cubs

C. White owner of the Kansas City Monarchs

D. Indianapolis ABCs, Birmingham Giants, West Baden Sprudels, St. Louis Giants, New York Lincoln Giants, Chicago American Giants, Harrisburg Giants

E. New York Lincoln Giants, Homestead Grays

F. Philadelphia Giants

G. St. Louis Stars, Newark Eagles

One last game of Negro leaguers.

1. Alex Pompez   **A. Kansas City Monarchs**

2. Cum Posey   **B. Detroit Stars, Kansas City Monarchs, Cole's American Giants**

3. Joe Rogan   **C. Birmingham Black Barons, St. Louis Stars, Chicago American Giants, Newark Eagles**

4. Louis Santop   **D. Kansas City Monarchs, Monroe Monarchs**

5. Hilton Smith   **E. New York Lincoln Giants, Brooklyn Royal Giants, Hilldale Daisies, Philadelphia Giants**

6. Turkey Stearnes   **F. Cuban Stars, New York Cubans**

7. Mule Suttles   **G. Homestead Grays**

203

NAME THAT YEAR

Seven clues. One year. See how few clues it takes you to guess the year.

1   **Yankee pitchers Mike Kekich and Fritz Peterson** swap wives, children, houses, and even pets.

2   **George Steinbrenner** buys the Yankees.

3   **Wilbur Wood (24–20)** becomes the first pitcher in 57 years to both win and lose at least 20 games in a season.

4   **Pete Rose** wins the NL MVP Award.

5   **Nolan Ryan becomes the fifth pitcher** in major league history to toss two no-hitters in one season.

6   **The American League** implements the designated-hitter rule.

7   **The brash Oakland A's** win their second of three straight World Championships.

202: 1-F, 2-G, 3-A, 4-E, 5-D, 6-B, 7-C • **203:** 1973

BASEBALL BIRTHPLACES

(Year indicates first year in majors.)

204

1. Afghanistan	A. Joe Quinn, 1884
2. Aruba	B. Brian Lesher, 1996
3. Australia	C. Jeff Bronkey, 1993
4. Austria	D. Kurt Krieger, 1949
5. Austria-Hungary	E. Andre Rodgers, 1957
6. Bahamas	F. Tommy Bond and Andy Leonard, 1876 (same day)
7. Belgium	G. Amos Cross, 1885
8. Ireland	H. Gene Kingsale, 1996

205

1. Belize	A. Rafael Almeida and Armando Marsans, 1911 (same day)
2. Canada	B. Bill Phillips, 1879
3. Canal Zone	C. Ed Porray, 1914
4. China	D. Chito Martinez, 1991
5. Colombia	E. Hensley Meulens, 1989
6. Cuba	F. Luis Castro, 1902
7. Curaçao	G. Pat Scantlebury, 1956
8. Atlantic Ocean	H. Harry Kingman, 1914

206

1. Honduras	A. Julio Bonetti, 1937
2. Italy	B. John Houseman, 1894
3. Jamaica	C. Chili Davis, 1981
4. Japan	D. Masanori Murakami, 1964
5. Korea	E. Mel Almada, 1933
6. Mexico	F. Gerald Young, 1987
7. The Netherlands	G. Chan Ho Park, 1994

204: 1-C, 2-H, 3-A, 4-D, 5-G, 6-E, 7-B, 8-F • **205:** 1-D, 2-B, 3-G, 4-H, 5-F, 6-A, 7-E, 8-C • **206:** 1-F, 2-A, 3-C, 4-D, 5-G, 6-E, 7-B

207

1. Nicaragua	A. Dennis Martinez, 1976
2. Norway	B. Henry Peploski, 1929
3. Panama	C. Hi Bithorn, 1942
4. Philippines	D. John Anderson, 1894
5. Poland	E. Bobby Chouinard, 1996
6. Puerto Rico	F. Jake Gettman, 1897
7. Russia	G. Humberto Robinson, 1955

208

1. Samoa	A. Charlie Hallstrom, 1885
2. Scotland	B. Tony Solaita, 1968
3. Singapore	C. Jim McCormick, 1878
4. Spain	D. Otto Hess, 1902
5. Sweden	E. Robin Jennings, 1996
6. Switzerland	F. Al Cabrera, 1913
7. Okinawa	G. Bobby Fenwick, 1972

209

1. Taiwan	A. Ted Lewis, 1896
2. Venezuela	B. Danny Graves, 1996
3. Vietnam	C. Joe Christopher, 1959
4. Virgin Islands	D. John Otten, 1895
5. Wales	E. Rob Belloir, 1975
6. West Germany	F. Alex Carrasquel, 1939
7. Holland	G. Chin-Feng Chen, 2002

209: 1-G, 2-F, 3-B, 4-C, 5-A, 6-E, 7-D

• **208:** 1-B, 2-C, 3-E, 4-F, 5-A, 6-D, 7-G •

207: 1-A, 2-D, 3-G, 4-E, 5-B, 6-C, 7-F

1. Czechoslovakia	**A. Joe Woerlin, 1895**
2. Denmark	**B. Harry Wright and George Hall, 1876 (same day)**
3. Dominican Republic	**C. John Michaelson, 1921**
4. Finland	**D. Charlie Getzien, 1884**
5. France	**E. Elmer Valo, 1940**
6. Germany	**F. Al Campanis, 1943**
7. Greece	**G. Olaf Henriksen, 1911**
8. England	**H. Ozzie Virgil, 1956**

211

Now let's try all the foreign-born Hall of Famers. (Note: Some countries claim more than one Hall of Famer.)

1. Luis Aparicio	**A. Puerto Rico**
2. Rod Carew	**B. Canada**
3. Orlando Cepeda	**C. Venezuela**
4. Henry Chadwick	**D. Dominican Republic**
5. Roberto Clemente	**E. Panama**
6. Tom Connolly	**F. Cuba**
7. Martin Dihigo	**G. England**
8. Ferguson Jenkins	
9. Juan Marichal	
10. Tony Perez	
11. Harry Wright	

210: 1-E, 2-G, 3-H, 4-C, 5-A, 6-D, 7-F, 8-B • **211:** 1-C, 2-E, 3-A, 4-G, 5-A, 6-G, 7-F, 8-B, 9-D, 10-F, 11-G

WHO, WHAT, WHEN, WHERE, AND WHY

1. Who was Harry Wright?

2. What is the significance of this card?

3. When was this photograph taken?

4. Why was the photograph taken?

212:

1. Wright was one of professional baseball's early players and pioneers and was considered the "father of professional baseball."

2. It is considered to be the first baseball card ever produced with the actual picture of a player instead of an artist's rendering or generic caricature.

3. 1863.

4. As a memento for a famous benefit baseball game that took place in Hoboken, New Jersey, in 1863.

Each of the following states can claim just one Hall of Famer born within its borders (as of 2006).

1. Delaware
2. Idaho
3. New Hampshire
4. New Mexico
5. South Carolina
6. South Dakota
7. Vermont

A. Ralph Kiner
B. Bill McGowan
C. Carlton Fisk
D. Harmon Killebrew
E. Frank Selee
F. Sparky Anderson
G. Larry Doby

214

Match the state to the appropriate distinction.

1. State that has produced the most major leaguers—1,797

2. State that has produced the fewest major leaguers—9

3. State that has produced the second most major leaguers—1,310

4. State that has produced the most major league third basemen who have made it to the Hall of Fame—2

5. State whose players have won the most Triple Crowns—3

6. State which produced the only Triple Crown winner *not* to make it into the Hall of Fame

7. State that produced only three Hall of Famers, yet two of them won the Triple Crown

A. Arkansas
B. Alaska
C. Virginia
D. Rhode Island
E. California
F. Pennsylvania
G. Texas

213: 1-B, 2-D, 3-E, 4-A, 5-G, 6-F, 7-C • **214:** 1-E, 2-B, 3-F, 4-A, 5-G, 6-C, 7-D

This time, let's do Hall of Fame distinctions.

1. Only state to have a player inducted as a designated hitter

2. Only state east of the Mississippi River without a Hall of Famer

3. State whose three HOF members are all outfielders

4. The state in this game with the most Hall of Famers—11

5. Only state in this game whose entire HOF contingent is made up of Negro leaguers (two out of two)

6. State in this game with seven Hall of Famers, none of which were first, second, or third basemen

7. State with the highest number of HOF inductees (3) without any of them being a position player (1B, 2B, 3B, SS, OF, or C)

A. Mississippi

B. New Jersey

C. Minnesota

D. Virginia

E. Alabama

F. Maine

G. North Carolina

216

Try another round.

1. Of this state's six Hall of Famers, four are outfielders

2. Only state with at least one HOFer from each of the following positions: C, 1B, 2B, 3B, SS, OF, P

3. State with the most second basemen elected to the Hall of Fame—4

4. One of two states to have seven pitchers elected to the Hall of Fame (New York is the other)

5. State which has had the most former Negro league players enshrined in the Hall of Fame—4

6. Only state besides Pennsylvania to have three managers sent to Cooperstown

7. Five of this state's ten HOF members are outfielders

A. Massachusetts

B. New York

C. Illinois

D. Indiana

E. Pennsylvania

F. Oklahoma

G. Texas

215: 1-C, 2-F, 3-B, 4-E, 5-A, 6-G, 7-D • **216:** 1-F, 2-C, 3-B, 4-E, 5-G, 6-A, 7-D

NAME THAT YEAR

Seven clues. One year. See how few clues it takes you to guess the year.

1 **John Rocker of the Braves** is suspended by Major League Baseball for making negative comments about New Yorkers and various minorities.

2 **Ken Griffey Jr. is traded** from the Mariners to the Reds and becomes the youngest player ever to hit 400 home runs.

3 **After an ugly incident** with fans in a May 16 game at Wrigley Field, 16 Dodgers are fined or suspended.

4 **Pedro Martinez wins his second** straight Cy Young Award.

5 **Pac Bell Park opens** in San Francisco; Comerica Park opens in Detroit.

6 **The Mets and Cubs open the season**—in Japan.

7 **In the World Series,** the Yankees defeat the Mets in five games, all of which come down to the last at bat.

217: 2000

THE WORLD SERIES

See if you can match each of these distinctions with a World Series pitcher.

1. Most career World Series shutouts—4   **A. Whitey Ford**

2. Most consecutive scoreless innings pitched—33.2   **B. Moe Drabowsky**

3. Oldest ever to hurl a complete game shutout—38   **C. Bill Bevens**

4. Most hits allowed in one World Series—38   **D. Randy Johnson**

5. Most consecutive hitless innings, career—11   **E. Don Larsen**

6. Most walks given up in one Series game—10   **F. Christy Mathewson**

7. Most strikeouts in one game by a reliever—11   **G. Deacon Phillippe**

219

This time, match the World Series hitting achievements with their owners.

1. Highest batting average in one World Series—.750   **A. Babe Ruth**

2. Most at bats in one World Series—36   **B. Billy Hatcher**

3. Most career World Series extra-base hits (26)   **C. Jimmy Collins**

4. Most career games appeared as a pinch hitter—12   **D. Thurman Munson**

5. Most consecutive games where player scored at least one run—9   **E. Luis Polonia**

6. Most singles in a four-game Series—9   **F. Mickey Mantle**

7. Only NL player to homer in first two World Series at bats   **G. Andruw Jones**

218: 1-F, 2-A, 3-D, 4-G, 5-E, 6-C, 7-B • **219:** 1-B, 2-C, 3-F, 4-E, 5-A, 6-D, 7-G

More World Series distinctions—National League only.

1. Only NL player to play for six losing World Series teams

A. Mike Morgan

2. NL second baseman who played in the most World Series—7

B. Frank Frisch

3. Youngest player ever (18) to play in the World Series

C. Pee Wee Reese

4. Most years between World Series appearances—22

D. Pepper Martin

5. Player who played the most seasons in his career (21) before seeing action in the World Series on the National League side

E. Tommy Leach

6. Only NL player with four career triples

F. Fred Lindstrom

7. NL player with the highest career batting average (.418) with a minimum of 50 at bats

G. Willie Mays

221

Here are a few more World Series pitching feats.

1. Longest game pitched without allowing a walk—12 innings

A. Ed Walsh

2. Most innings pitched in one World Series without giving up a walk—26

B. Bob Gibson

3. Only pitcher ever to strike out four batters in one inning

C. Carl Mays

4. Only NL pitcher ever to strike out at least one batter in every inning of a nine-inning game

D. Dave Stewart

5. Only AL pitcher ever to strike out at least one batter in every inning of a nine-inning game

E. Jack Morris

6. Only pitcher in World Series history with more than one career balk (he had two)

F. Orval Overall

7. One of only two pitchers (Hal Schumacher was the other) to have five career wild pitches in World Series play

G. Schoolboy Rowe

220: 1-C, 2-B, 3-F, 4-G, 5-A, 6-E, 7-D • **221:** 1-G, 2-C, 3-F, 4-B, 5-A, 6-D, 7-E

WHO, WHAT, WHEN, WHERE, AND WHY

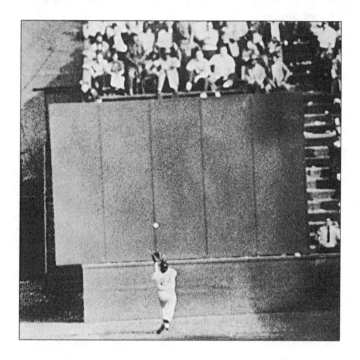

1. **Who's** this?

2. **What** had he just done?

3. **When?** Against what team?

4. **Where?**

5. **BONUS:** Who hit the ball?

5. Vic Wertz.

4. The Polo Grounds in New York.

3. In Game 1 of the 1954 World Series against Cleveland.

won it in the tenth on a three-run homer from Dusty Rhodes.
runner to advance only to third. Giant pitchers preserved the tie game and
and fired to second, keeping the trailing runner on first and allowing the lead
amazing catch about 450 feet away from home plate on a 2–2 game. Mays made his
second and no outs in the top of the eighth in a 2–2 game. Mays made his
greatest defensive plays in World Series history. With runners on first and
2. He had made an over-the-shoulder catch that is considered to be one of the

1. Hall of Famer Willie Mays.

222:

See if you can hit these.

1. One of only two pitchers (Mort Cooper was the other) ever to start a World Series game by striking out the first five batters

2. One of only two pitchers (Walter Johnson was the other) to lose when striking out 12 batters in one game

3. Most strikeouts in a seven-game Series—35

4. Most strikeouts in a five-game Series—18

5. Most triples allowed in one game—5

6. Most doubles allowed in one game—8

7. Most home runs allowed in one inning—3

A. Orlando Hernandez

B. Dick Hughes

C. Sandy Koufax

D. Christy Mathewson

E. Walter Johnson

F. Bob Gibson

G. Deacon Phillippe

224

Now a little more heat.

1. Most hits allowed in one inning—8

2. Only NL pitcher in history to hit three batters in one game

3. Only pitcher with two career complete game 1–0 wins

4. Most shutout losses in a career—3

5. Most runs allowed in one game—10

6. Only four times in Series history has the side been retired on just three pitches. He did it *twice!*

7. Lowest career ERA (minimum 30 innings)— 0.83

A. Eddie Plank

B. Jay Witasick

C. Bruce Kison

D. Harry Breechen

E. Art Nehf

F. Bill Kennedy

G. Christy Mathewson

225

Don't bail out. Here are some more.

1. Most complete games pitched in a career—10
2. Most consecutive complete games pitched in a career—8
3. Most games won in a career—10
4. Most innings pitched in one game—14
5. Most games started in one World Series—5
6. Most Game 1 victories in a career—5
7. Only pitcher to lose five consecutive World Series games

A. Christy Mathewson

B. Whitey Ford

C. Babe Ruth

D. Joe Bush

E. Red Ruffing

F. Deacon Phillippe

G. Bob Gibson

226

Here's one final game of World Series pitching feats.

1. Most hits allowed in one World Series game—15
2. Only pitcher to appear in all seven games of a seven-game Series
3. Most consecutive games won in a career—7
4. Only AL pitcher to have an ERA of 0.00 with 27 innings pitched in one Series
5. Youngest (20) pitcher ever to pitch a complete-game shutout
6. Oldest pitcher (39) to pitch a complete game in the Series
7. Fewest hits allowed in two consecutive games—4

A. Walter Johnson

B. Jim Palmer

C. Darold Knowles

D. Pete Alexander

E. Bob Gibson

F. Waite Hoyt

G. Jim Lonborg

227

Now for some World Series hitting feats.

1. Most World Series games played in a career—75   **A. Home Run Baker**

2. Only player in history with two four-hit games in one Series   **B. Robin Yount**

3. Highest batting average for a seven-game Series—.583   **C. Reggie Jackson**

4. Only American League hitter to lead his team in batting average for three different World Series   **D. Yogi Berra**

5. Highest career on-base percentage (minimum 50 at bats)—.475   **E. Paul Molitor**

6. Highest on-base percentage for a seven-game Series—.700   **F. Barry Bonds**

7. Highest career slugging percentage (minimum 50 plate appearances)—.755   **G. Danny Bautista**

228

The hitting feats just keep on happenin'.

1. Only player in history to hit two doubles in one inning   **A. Scott Podsednik**

2. Only player in history with eight plate appearances in one game   **B. Matt Williams**

3. Only player in history to have five plate appearances in one game and have no official at bats (four walks and a sacrifice hit)   **C. George Earnshaw**

4. Only player in World Series history to have two plate appearances in an inning *three* times in his career   **D. Fred Clarke**

5. Most career consecutive at bats without a hit—31   **E. Dal Maxvill**

6. Most at bats in one Series without a hit—22   **F. Joe DiMaggio**

7. Most career World Series at bats without a hit—22   **G. Marv Owen**

227: 1-D, 2-B, 3-G, 4-A, 5-E, 6-F, 7-C • **228:** 1-B, 2-A, 3-D, 4-F, 5-G, 6-E, 7-C

All together now: "I love New Yooork . . ."

1. Most runs scored in a World Series career—42   **A. Lou Gehrig**

2. Most hits in a World Series career—71   **B. Yogi Berra**

3. Only American Leaguer with seven   **C. Thurman Munson**
   consecutive hits

4. Most consecutive games played in   **D. Babe Ruth**
   consecutive years—30

5. Highest slugging average for one   **E. Mickey Mantle**
   World Series—1.727 (yikes!)

6. Only player ever to hit two or more home runs   **F. Bobby Richardson**
   in four World Series

7. Most home runs in two consecutive World Series—7   **G. Reggie Jackson**

230

More New Yorkers.

1. Most RBIs by a pinch hitter in one World Series—6   **A. Casey Stengel**

2. Most times grounded into a double play in one   **B. Frank Frisch**
   World Series game—3

3. Only National Leaguer with five total bases   **C. Benny Kauff**
   in one inning (he hit a double and a triple)

4. Only National Leaguer with ten career doubles   **D. Dusty Rhodes**
   in World Series play

5. Only player to hit .400 or higher in an   **E. Travis Jackson**
   eight-game World Series

6. First player ever to go 0 for 6 in a   **F. Willie Mays**
   World Series game

7. First National Leaguer to hit two home runs   **G. Buck Herzog**
   in one World Series game

8. Only player in the first 45 World Series (1903–1948)   **H. Bill Dahlen**
   to hit a home run in a 1–0 game

9. First player in World Series history to steal home   **I. Ross Youngs**

10. First black player in World Series history to   **J. Monte Irvin**
    steal home

229: 1-E, 2-B, 3-C, 4-F, 5-A, 6-D, 7-G • 230: 1-D, 2-F, 3-I, 4-B, 5-G, 6-E, 7-C, 8-A, 9-H, 10-J

WHO, WHAT, WHEN, WHERE, AND WHY

1. **Who** are these two players?

2. **What** brought them together?

3. **When?**

4. **Which** two ballparks hosted this affair?

231:
1. Hall of Famers Honus Wagner and Ty Cobb.
2. Their teams met in the World Series. The Pirates beat the Tigers in seven.
3. 1909.
4. Forbes Field, Pittsburgh, and Bennett Park, Detroit.

How about hitting records from Yankee-free World Series?

1. Most extra-base hits in one World Series—7   **A. Buck Weaver**

2. Only American League player in history with two   **B. Bernie Carbo**
   pinch-hit home runs in one World Series

3. One of only two players (Fred Clarke was the other) **C. Tommy Herr**
   ever to have 34 at bats in one World Series and
   not have an RBI

4. Only player in history to collect four extra-base hits **D. Joe Carter**
   in one game (he had four doubles)

5. Most times hit by a pitch in one World Series—3   **E. Frank Isbell**

6. Only player ever to collect *two* RBIs on one   **F. Max Carey**
   sacrifice fly

7. Most sacrifice flies hit in one World Series—3   **G. Willie Stargell**

233

"New York, New York"—just hum it if you don't know the
lyrics. (Note: Two questions have the same answer.)

1. Most putouts in World Series history by any   **A. George Shuba**
   noncatcher—326

2. The last National Leaguer to receive four   **B. Cookie Lavagetto**
   walks in one World Series game

3. First National Leaguer to hit a pinch-hit home run   **C. Gil Hodges**
   in World Series play

4. Only player in history to hit four or more home   **D. Duke Snider**
   runs in two World Series

5. One of only two NL players (Frank Secory is   **E. Jackie Robinson**
   the other) in history with five pinch-hit at bats
   in one World Series

6. First NL player to lead his team in batting average **F. Pee Wee Reese**
   in three different World Series

7. First National Leaguer to play four different
   positions in World Series

232: 1-G, 2-B, 3-A, 4-E, 5-F, 6-C, 7-D • **233:** 1-C, 2-E, 3-A, 4-D, 5-B, 6-F, 7-E

Try some more general World Series records/feats.

1. Oldest pitcher (46) to work in a World Series game   **A. Jim Kaat**

2. Most Series qualified to play in, but did not play—6   **B. Charlie Silvera**

3. Player with the most years of major league   **C. Sam Rice**
service (21) before playing in the World Series
n the American League side

4. Oldest nonpitcher (43) to play in the World Series   **D. Johnny Kucks**

5. Most years between player's first and second   **E. Joe Niekro**
World Series—17

6. Only National League pitcher to appear in relief in   **F. Jack Quinn**
six different World Series

7. Only 20th-century pitcher to appear in four   **G. Mike Stanton**
World Series his first four years in the big leagues

235

Relax, we're not at the tough ones yet. Here are more general World Series records and feats.

1. Only player ever to appear in the World Series   **A. Lonnie Smith**
with four different teams

2. Youngest pitcher ever (19) to appear in   **B. Bob Lemon**
a World Series game

3. Last player to play four different positions   **C. Pete Rose**
in World Series play

4. Only player to play four different positions   **D. Ken Brett**
in the World Series, *including* pitcher

5. Only player to play four different positions   **E. Elston Howard**
in the World Series, *including* catcher

6. Most runs allowed in a four-game Series   **F. Moe Drabowsky**
by an AL pitcher—11

7. Only American League pitcher in history to strike   **G. Babe Ruth**
out six consecutive batters in a World Series game

234: 1-F, 2-B, 3-E, 4-C, 5-A, 6-G, 7-D • **235:** 1-A, 2-D, 3-C, 4-G, 5-E, 6-B, 7-F

You should be warmed up by now. Time for some tough ones.

1. Only pitcher ever to lose a World Series no-hitter with two outs in the ninth

2. Only pitcher ever to hit two consecutive batters in one inning

3. Only pitcher ever to hit at least one batter in four different World Series

4. Only pitcher ever to throw two wild pitches in the ninth inning of one World Series game

5. Only pitcher ever to pitch in all five games of a five-game Series

6. Most innings pitched in a seven-game Series—32

7. Only four pitchers in World Series history have ever pitched 18 innings in a four-game Series, and he was the last

A. Ed Willett

B. Mike Marshall

C. Bill Bevens

D. Sandy Koufax

E. George Mullin

F. Eddie Plank

G. Johnny Miljus

237

If you can make it there, you can make it anywhere, blah blah.

1. Most career consecutive games with at least one hit—17

2. Only player in history with ten hits in a four-game Series

3. Most consecutive walks received in World Series play—5

4. Only American League player in history to ground into seven career double plays

5. Only American League player in history to be hit by a pitch twice in one game

6. Only player in history to strike out in eight consecutive at bats

7. Only player in history to strike out five times in one game

A. George Pipgras

B. Lou Gehrig

C. Babe Ruth

D. Yogi Berra

E. Joe DiMaggio

F. David Justice

G. Hank Bauer

236: 1-C, 2-A, 3-F, 4-G, 5-B, 6-E, 7-D • **237:** 1-G, 2-C, 3-B, 4-E, 5-D, 6-F, 7-A

Try these tough miscellaneous World Series hitting distinctions.

1. Most at bats in a World Series without a strikeout—30
2. Most at bats in a World Series without a walk—34
3. Only player in history to strike out twice in one inning
4. Only player in history to record five sacrifice hits in one World Series
5. Only player in history to reach base three times in one game on errors
6. Only player in history to ground into five double plays in one World Series
7. Only player in the 20th century to collect three sacrifice hits in one World Series game

A. Tim Foli

B. Joe Tinker

C. Edgar Renteria

D. Irv Noren

E. Buck Weaver

F. Jake Daubert

F. Fred Clarke

239

Here's some tough miscellaneous World Series American League pitching trivia.

1. Only pitcher in history to lose two 1–0 shutouts in World Series play
2. Only American League pitcher in history with two career home runs
3. One of only two players, and the only pitcher, to receive two walks in one inning
4. Most career consecutive batting strikeouts by a pitcher—8
5. Only pitcher in history to receive two bases-loaded walks in the same game
6. One of only two American League pitchers (Stan Coveleski was the other) to win three games in a Series without a defeat
7. Only American League pitcher in history to win three games in a five-game Series

A. Lefty Gomez

B. Jack Coombs

C. Dave McNally

D. Jim Palmer

E. Mickey Lolich

F. Eddie Plank

G. Vida Blue

238: 1-A, 2-E, 3-C, 4-F, 5-G, 6-D, 7-B • **239:** 1-F, 2-C, 3-A, 4-G, 5-D, 6-E, 7-B

Now, tough miscellaneous World Series pitching trivia, National League style.

1. Only pitcher in history to collect two hits in one inning

2. Only National League pitcher in history with two career home runs

3. First National League pitcher to hit a home run in World Series play

4. Only National League pitcher in history to allow eight earned runs in one game

5. One of only two pitchers in history (Hooks Wiltse is the other) to allow seven runs in one inning

6. Only National League pitcher in history to have a 0.00 ERA in a World Series with at least 27 innings pitched

7. One of only five National League pitchers (and the last) to win three games in a World Series without a defeat

A. Rosy Ryan

B. Pete Alexander

C. Carl Hubbell

D. Christy Mathewson

E. Randy Johnson

F. Dizzy Dean

G. Bob Gibson

241

Want some relief?

1. Most career World Series saves—9

2. Most saves in one World Series—4

3. Only relief pitcher in history to win two games in either a four- or five-game Series

4. The only other American League relief pitcher in history besides the answer to question 3 to win two games in a World Series

A. Mike Stanton

B. John Wetteland

C. Joe Hoerner

D. Rawly Eastwick

240: 1-F, 2-G, 3-A, 4-B, 5-C, 6-D, 7-E

5. The last of five National League relief pitchers to win two games in one World Series   **E. Mariano Rivera**

6. Only relief pitcher in history (or starter, for that matter) to allow six consecutive hits in six consecutive plate appearances, and it happened in the ninth inning, to blow a one-run lead   **F. Ed Summers**

7. One of only two National League relief pitchers (Art Reinhart is the other) to walk three consecutive batters in one inning   **G. Duane Ward**

242

Now, let's switch gears and try some World Series team trivia.

1. The only National League team ever to employ 26 players in a single World Series   **A. 1903 Pirates**

2. Only team ever to use just 13 players in a four-game Series   **B. 2005 Astros**

3. Only team in World Series history to use just nine players in a game six times during one Series   **C. 1997 Marlins**

4. Only National League team ever to use 21 players in one nine-inning game   **D. 1961 Reds**

5. The last National League team not to use a single pinch hitter for an entire Series   **E. 1976 Reds**

6. The only team in history to use six pinch hitters in one nine-inning game   **F. 1963 Dodgers**

7. The only team ever to utilize four different second basemen during one World Series   **G. 1959 Dodgers**

WHO, WHAT, WHEN, WHERE, AND WHY

1. Who are these two players?

2. What unique feat did they accomplish together?

3. When did they do it?

4. What famous challenge did one of them issue to his opponents before Game 7?

243:

1. Paul Dean and Hall of Fame brother Dizzy Dean.

2. Between them they won all four of the Cardinals' victories in the World Series.

3. 1934.

4. Dizzy Dean told the Tigers players he would throw nothing but fastballs in the final game, kept his word, and still shut them out, 11–0.

244

More World Series team trivia.

1. The last of only three teams in history to use six different starting pitchers in one World Series

2. Only team ever to use nine different pitchers in one World Series game

3. Only team in World Series history to use four different catchers during one Series

4. Highest team batting average for one World Series—.338

5. Lowest team batting average for one World Series—.142

6. Most at bats in a nine-inning game—46

7. Most at bats in an extra-inning game during one World Series—54

A. 1973 Mets

B. 1960 Yankees

C. 1971 Pirates

D. 2005 White Sox

E. 2001 Diamondbacks

F. 1978 Dodgers

G. 1966 Dodgers

245

See how you score in the runs-scored category of World Series team trivia.

1. Most runs scored in a four-game Series—37

2. Most runs scored in a seven-game Series—55

3. Fewest runs scored in a four-game Series—2

4. Fewest runs scored in a seven-game Series—8

5. Most runs scored in one World Series game—18

6. Most runs scored in the first inning—7

7. One of only two teams in history (the 1929 A's were the other) to score ten runs in one inning in World Series play

A. 1920 Dodgers

B. 1966 Dodgers

C. 1936 Yankees

D. 1968 Tigers

E. 1960 Yankees

F. 1958 Braves

G. 1932 Yankees

244: 1-C, 2-D, 3-F, 4-B, 5-G, 6-E, 7-A • **245:** 1-G, 2-E, 3-B, 4-A, 5-C, 6-F, 7-D

Do you know these World Series team hitting records?

1. Fewest hits in a four-game Series—17

A. 1960 Yankees

2. Most hits in a seven-game Series—91

B. 1979 Pirates

3. Fewest hits in a seven-game Series—40

C. 2001 Diamondbacks

4. Most hits in a four-game Series (two-team tie; 1932 Yankees were the other team)—45

D. 1985 Cardinals

5. Most hits in one World Series game—22

E. 1929 A's

6. Most hits in one World Series game *by a losing team*—17

F. 1966 Dodgers

7. Most hits in one inning—10

G. 1990 Reds

247

Match up these distinctions and World Series teams.

1. Most singles in one World Series—64

A. 2002 Giants

2. Most doubles in one World Series—19 (accomplished in five games; the 1946 Cardinals also had 19 in a seven-game Series)

B. 1910 A's

3. Most triples in one World Series—16

C. 1960 Yankees

4. Most home runs in one World Series—14

D. 1924 Giants

5. One of only two teams (1952 Yankees were the other) to homer in all seven games of a seven-game Series

E. 1925 Senators

6. The only team in history not to hit a homer in a seven-game Series

F. 1903 Red Sox

7. The only team in history to have two pitchers hit a home run in the same Series

G. 1920 Dodgers

And these as well.

1. Only team in history to hit three homers in one inning   **A. 1989 A's**

2. One of only two teams ever to hit five home runs in one World Series game (the 1928 Yankees were the other)   **B. 1967 Red Sox**

3. One of only two teams ever to hit two grand slams in one World Series (the 1956 Yankees were the other)   **C. 1907 Tigers**

4. The only team in history to hit two home runs in an inning three times in one World Series   **D. 1991 Braves**

5. Team with the fewest extra-base hits in any World Series—3   **E. 1987 Twins**

6. Team with the most extra-base hits in one Series game—9   **F. 1925 Pirates**

7. Most total bases in one World Series game—34   **G. 2002 Giants**

249

More World Series team trivia.

1. Only team in history to receive five walks in one inning   **A. 2001 Diamondbacks**

2. This team suffered far and away the most strikeouts ever in one World Series—70   **B. 1919 White Sox**

3. This team holds the record for being the victim of the fewest strikeouts ever in one World Series—7   **C. 1927 Pirates**

4. The only team in history whose hitters struck out 17 times in one World Series game   **D. 2002 Angels**

5. The only team in the first 63 years of World Series play to suffer six consecutive strikeouts in one World Series game (which aroused even more suspicion)   **E. 1926 Yankees**

6. The only team in the last 45 years of World Series play not to have struck out even once in a World Series game   **F. 1944 Cardinals**

7. The only team in history to have three pinch hitters strike out in one inning   **G. 1968 Tigers**

Even more.

1. The most sacrifice hits in one World Series—13
2. One of only two teams (2001 Diamondbacks are the other) to suffer six hit batsmen in one World Series
3. One of only two teams with 18 stolen bases in one World Series, this club accomplished it in a five-game Series (the 1909 Pirates did it in a seven-game Series)
4. Most times caught stealing in one World Series—13
5. By a very wide margin, this team left the most runners on base in one World Series—72
6. The only team in history to leave 15 runners on base in a nine-inning World Series game
7. The only team in history to play a full nine-inning World Series game and leave no runners on base

A. 1906 Cubs

B. 1911 Giants

C. 1973 Mets

D. 1956 Dodgers

E. 1907 Cubs

F. 2002 Angels

G. 1909 Pirates

251

Time for some World Series team pitching trivia.

1. This team had more pitching appearances in one World Series by its staff than any other team during the 20th century—33
2. The only team in history to have five complete games in a seven-game World Series
3. One of only two teams ever to record four saves in one World Series, and they did it in six games (the 1973 Oakland A's did it in a seven-game Series)
4. The only team in history to record four shutouts in one World Series
5. The only American League team to win with three consecutive shutouts in one World Series
6. The only team staff with five wild pitches in one World Series
7. The only team since 1956 to win a 1–0 extra-inning game

A. 1905 Giants

B. 1996 Yankees

C. 1991 Twins

D. 1997 Indians

E. 1956 Yankees

F. 1960 Pirates

G. 1966 Orioles

WHO, WHAT, WHEN, WHERE, AND WHY

1. Who is the player crossing home plate?

2. What famous first in baseball history had he just achieved?

3. When did he do it?

4. Where?

252:
1. Hall of Famer Babe Ruth.
2. Hit three home runs in one World Series game.
3. Game 4 of the 1928 World Series.
4. Sportsman's Park in St. Louis.

Let's play catch with some World Series team fielding trivia.

1. One of only two teams in history to have a team fielding average of 1.000 for a World Series. This team had it for a five-game Series while the 1966 Orioles played errorless ball in just a four-game Series.

    A. 1920 Indians

2. The team with the worst fielding average ever for one World Series—.934

    B. 1969 Mets

3. Most double plays made in one World Series—12

    C. 2001 Diamondbacks

4. The only team in history to record a triple play in World Series play

    D. 1909 Tigers

5. The only team in history to play an entire Series and not record even one double play

    E. 1966 Dodgers

6. The only team in history to play six errorless games in a seven-game Series

    F. 1937 Yankees

7. The only team since 1917 to commit six errors in one game

    G. 1955 Dodgers

254

Feats by World Series first basemen.

1. Most games played at first base in World Series history—38

    A. Fred McGriff

2. One of only two first basemen in history (George Kelly is the other) to record 19 putouts in one World Series game

    B. Fred Merkle

3. Most assists by a first baseman in a World Series career—29

    C. Gil Hodges

4. Most assists in one World Series—10

    D. Hank Greenberg

5. Most errors by a first baseman in a World Series career—8

    E. Cecil Cooper

6. The only first baseman in World Series history to start two double plays in the same game

    F. Bill Skowron

7. The only American League first baseman ever to make two errors in one inning of a World Series game

    G. Eddie Murray

253: 1-F, 2-D, 3-G, 4-A, 5-B, 6-C, 7-E • **254:** 1-C, 2-A, 3-F, 4-E, 5-B, 6-G, 7-D

World Series second basemen.

1. Most games played at second base in World Series history—42

A. Bill Wambsganss

2. Most putouts by a second baseman in a seven-game Series—26

B. Bucky Harris

3. Most assists by a second baseman in a seven-game World Series—29

C. Jim Gantner

4. Most consecutive errorless games by a second baseman in a World Series career—23

D. Dick Green

5. Most errors by a second baseman in one World Series—6

E. Davey Lopes

6. The only second baseman in World Series history to start three double plays in one game

F. Billy Martin

7. The only second baseman ever to make an unassisted triple play in a World Series game

G. Frank Frisch

256

World Series third basemen.

1. Most games played at third base in World Series history—31

A. Home Run Baker

2. Most putouts by a third baseman in a World Series career—37

B. Gil McDougald

3. Most assists by a third baseman in a World Series career—68

C. Graig Nettles

4. Only third baseman in World Series history to make an unassisted double play

D. Ron Cey

5. Most errors by a third baseman in a World Series career—8

E. Bill Mueller

6. The only third baseman since the 1910 Series to make two errors in one inning

F. Larry Gardner

7. Most consecutive errorless games at third base in a World Series career—22

G. Doug DeCinces

255: 1-G, 2-B, 3-C, 4-F, 5-E, 6-D, 7-A • **256:** 1-B, 2-A, 3-C, 4-E, 5-F, 6-G, 7-D

Feats by World Series shortstops.

1. Most games played at shortstop in World Series history—52

A. Tim Foli

2. Most putouts by a shortstop in a seven-game World Series—22

B. Roger Peckinpaugh

3. Most chances accepted at shortstop in one World Series game—13

C. Derek Jeter

4. Only shortstop in World Series history to make three putouts in one inning

D. Mickey Stanley

5. Most assists by a shortstop in a seven-game Series—32

E. Buck Weaver

6. Only shortstop in World Series history to record nine assists in a nine-inning game

F. Ozzie Smith

7. Most consecutive errorless games at shortstop in a World Series career—26

G. Phil Rizzuto

258

World Series outfielders.

1. Most games played in the outfield in World Series history—63

A. Tris Speaker

2. Most putouts by an outfielder in a World Series career—150

B. Dan Gladden

3. Most putouts by an outfielder in a seven-game Series—25

C. Willie Davis

4. Only outfielder in World Series history to record nine putouts in one game

D. Amos Otis

5. Only outfielder in history to make two double plays in one World Series game

E. Mickey Mantle

6. Only outfielder in history to record an unassisted double play in the World Series

F. Edd Roush

7. Only outfielder ever to make three errors in one inning of a World Series game

G. Joe DiMaggio

257: 1-G, 2-F, 3-E, 4-D, 5-A, 6-B, 7-C • **258:** 1-E, 2-G, 3-B, 4-D, 5-F, 6-A, 7-C

World Series catchers.

1. Most games played at catcher in World Series history—63

2. Most putouts by a catcher in a seven-game World Series—69

3. Most putouts by a catcher in one World Series game—18

4. Most runners thrown out attempting to steal in one World Series—10

5. Only catcher in World Series history to have four chances accepted (chances accepted = putouts + assists) in one inning

6. Most runners thrown out attempting to steal in a World Series career—20

7. Most runners thrown out attempting to steal in one World Series game—5

A. Jorge Posada

B. Yogi Berra

C. Wally Schang

D. Jack Lapp

E. Tim McCarver

F. Ray Schalk

G. John Roseboro

260

Accomplishments by World Series pitchers.

1. Most games played at pitcher in World Series history—22

2. Most putouts by a pitcher in a seven-game World Series (and he got them all in just one game!)—5

3. Most assists by a pitcher in a World Series career—34

4. Only American League pitcher in history to have three career World Series errors

5. Only pitcher in World Series history to have 11 chances accepted (chances accepted = putouts + assists) in one game

6. Only three pitchers in World Series history have ever recorded 12 assists in one Series; he did it in the fewest games—6

7. Only pitcher since the 1906 World Series to record eight assists in one Series game

A. Nick Altrock

B. Christy Mathewson

C. Whitey Ford

D. Lon Warneke

E. Ed Cicotte

F. Jim Kaat

G. Mordecai Brown

259: 1-B, 2-A, 3-G, 4-F, 5-E, 6-C, 7-D • **260:** 1-C, 2-F, 3-B, 4-E, 5-A, 6-G, 7-D

How about some World Series miscellany?

1. The only team in history to lose seven consecutive one-run games in World Series play (they lost the last four of one Series and the first three of the next one they played in)   **A. Cubs**

2. The only team in history to win six consecutive one-run games in World Series play (they won the last four of one Series and the first two of the next one they played in)   **B. Yankees**

3. They won the first night game in World Series history   **C. Phillies**

4. The team that has lost the most World Series—13   **D. Pirates**

5. The first of only two teams (the Dodgers are the other) to lose seven consecutive World Series   **E. Tigers**

6. The only American League team to lose the World Series in three consecutive seasons   **F. Red Sox**

7. The only National League team to lose the World Series in three consecutive seasons   **G. Giants**

262

Now, try to match the particular World Series distinction with the year it occurred (since 1903 only).

1. One of only two years to feature a 14-inning game—tied for the longest in Series history (the other was 1916)   **A. 1944**

2. The year that featured the highest single-game attendance—92,706   **B. 2005**

3. The year that featured the lowest single-game attendance—6,210   **C. 2002**

4. The highest scoring Series ever—85 runs by both teams   **D. 1908**

5. The lowest scoring Series ever—15 runs by both teams   **E. 1993**

6. The Series featuring the highest-scoring game ever (15–14 final score)—29 runs   **F. 1959**

7. The only Series in history not to feature a stolen base by either club   **G. 1966**

261: 1-C, 2-F, 3-D, 4-B, 5-A, 6-E, 7-G • **262:** 1-B, 2-F, 3-D, 4-C, 5-G, 6-E, 7-A

WHO, WHAT, WHEN, WHERE, AND WHY

1. Who are these guys?

2. What is their nickname?

3. When were they given it?

4. Why?

263:

1. The Chicago White Sox.

2. The Black Sox.

3. 1917.

4. At first (1917) for refusing to wash their uniforms as a form of protest against Sox owner Charles Comiskey, who docked their pay for washing their uniforms. Later (1920) they were called the Black Sox because of the game-fixing scandal that took place during the 1919 World Series. Today's references to Black Sox, however, refer almost exclusively to the 1919 team.

Here are more World Series distinctions and the years they occurred (since 1903 only).

1. The first World Series to feature night games   **A. 1994**

2. The first World Series to be played entirely at night   **B. 2001**

3. The only year the World Series was canceled because one league champion refused to play the other   **C. 1985**

4. The only year the World Series was canceled by a vote of the owners   **D. 1971**

5. The only year the World Series was played entirely in the month of September   **E. 1918**

6. The only year the World Series ended in November   **F. 1965**

7. The year helicopters and blowtorches were used to dry off the wet field in order to get a game under way   **G. 1904**

265

How well do you know your World Series managers? Let's start with just the Hall of Famers.

1. Most career World Series games won by a manager—37   **A. John McGraw**

2. Most career World Series games lost by a manager—28   **B. Joe Cronin**

3. He managed three different teams in the World Series: the Pirates, the Cardinals, and the Reds   **C. Hughie Jennings**

4. Youngest manager ever in World Series history—26   **D. Bill McKechnie**

5. Youngest manager ever to win a World Series—27   **E. Bucky Harris**

6. Only manager in history to win six consecutive World Series in which his team participated   **F. Casey Stengel**

7. One of only two managers in history (John McGraw was the other) to lose the World Series in three consecutive seasons   **G. Joe McCarthy**

No Yankees allowed.

1. Played more World Series games than any other non-Yankee—50

A. **Jackie Robinson**

2. Scored more World Series runs than any other non-Yankee—22

B. **Eddie Collins**

3. The non-Yankee Hall of Famer with the highest career World Series batting average—.418

C. **Frank Frisch**

4. Has more career World Series home runs than any other non-Yankee—11

D. **Paul Molitor**

5. Received more career World Series walks than any other non-Yankee—25

E. **Duke Snider**

6. The non-Yankee with the highest career World Series batting average—.471

F. **Barry Bonds**

7. One of two non-Yankees (Lou Brock is the other) who sits atop the World Series career stolen base list, with 14

G. **Mickey Cochrane**

267

Still no Yankees allowed.

1. Lowest career World Series ERA—0.36 (minimum of 25 innings pitched)

A. **Jack Billingham**

2. More career pitching wins than any non-Yankee—7

B. **Bob Gibson**

3. Pitched in more career World Series games than any other non-Yankee—16

C. **Rollie Fingers**

4. Pitched more career World Series innings than any other non-Yankee—101.7

D. **Sandy Koufax**

5. Lowest career World Series ERA (minimum of 50 innings pitched)—0.95

E. **Christy Mathewson**

6. The non-Yankee with the best undefeated career record in World Series play—5–0

F. **Schoolboy Rowe**

7. The non-Yankee with by far the best walks/ 9 IP ratio (minimum of 45 innings pitched) in a World Series career—0.39

G. **Jack Coombs**

266: 1-C, 2-A, 3-D, 4-E, 5-G, 6-F, 7-B • **267:** 1-A, 2-B, 3-C, 4-E, 5-D, 6-G, 7-F

Baseball Trivia

268

More World Series team potpourri.

1. Of all the *current* teams, the one with the worst career Series record (they've lost all three World Series they've played)

   A. Athletics

2. Of all the current National League teams that have played in more than one World Series, they are the only team to be undefeated in World Series play (2–0)

   B. Padres

3. Of all the current American League teams that have played in more than one World Series, they are the only team to be undefeated in World Series play (2–0)

   C. Marlins

4. The American League team with the most World Series titles after the Yankees—9

   D. Astros

5. Of all current teams that have played in the World Series, the only one that has never won a single World Series game

   E. Cardinals

6. Besides the winless team in question 5, this is the next worst current team in Series history, with a 1–8 record in nine World Series games played

   F. Giants

7. Of all the current teams, the only one besides the Yankees to play at least 100 World Series games in its history

   G. Blue Jays

269

Some World Series are remembered as classics because of a famous play, the overall action of the Series, or the way it ended. See if you can match these classic World Series and their classic moments.

1. 1909: Tigers-Pirates   **A. Cinderella team shocks the heavy favorite**

2. 1975: Reds-Red Sox   **B. One of the most famous errors in history**

3. 1954: Indians-Giants   **C. A snag of a vicious line drive saves Game 7**

4. 1969: Mets-Orioles   **D. Matchup of two of baseball's greatest players**

5. 1960: Yankees-Pirates   **E. Dramatic Game 7 home run**

6. 1986: Red Sox-Mets   **F. The most famous catch in Series history**

7. 1962: Giants-Yankees   **G. Dramatic Game 6 home run**

268: 1-F, 2-C, 3-G, 4-A, 5-D, 6-B, 7-E • **269:** 1-D, 2-G, 3-F, 4-A, 5-E, 6-B, 7-C

How about these?

1. 1985: Royals-Cardinals

A. The home team wins all seven games

2. 1965: Dodgers-Twins

B. Game 7 ends when that year's best home run hitter is thrown out trying to steal second

3. 1987: Twins-Cardinals

C. Players are accused of throwing games

4. 1926: Yankees-Cardinals

D. Team wins the Series after dropping Games 1 and 2 with two of the best pitchers in baseball

5. 1919: White Sox-Reds

E. Long Game 6 delay while players and owners argue over how to split the gate receipts

6. 1905: Athletics-Giants

F. First-base umpire blows call in Game 6

7. 1918: Red Sox-Cubs

G. One pitcher tosses three shutouts

271

Try one more round of World Series distinctions.

1. 1920: Indians-Dodgers

A. The huge crowds at one of the stadiums (more than 92,000 fans at each of three games)

2. 1948: Indians-Braves

B. The only perfect game in Series history

3. 1956: Yankees-Dodgers

C. Series ends in dramatic fashion with an unusual 4–3–5 double play on final play of 1–0 game

4. 1970: Reds-Orioles

D. A second baseman is "fired" by his owner for making costly errors in the Series

5. 1973: Athletics-Mets

E. Game 5 relief appearance by legendary Negro league pitcher Satchel Paige, the first black pitcher ever to play in the World Series

6. 1959: Dodgers-White Sox

F. The many fantastic defensive plays at third base

7. 1921: Yankees-Giants

G. First Series grand slam and only unassisted triple play ever

270: 1-F, 2-D, 3-A, 4-B, 5-C, 6-G, 7-E • **271:** 1-G, 2-E, 3-B, 4-F, 5-D, 6-A, 7-C

WHO, WHAT, WHEN, WHERE, AND WHY

1. Who is this player?

2. What is he celebrating?

3. Why was it so personally significant?

4. When did he do it?

5. Where?

272:

1. Kirk Gibson.

2. His two-out, two-run, pinch-hit game-winning World Series home run off Hall of Famer Dennis Eckersley.

3. It was his only at bat in the Series.

4. 1988.

5. Dodger Stadium in Los Angeles.

MOUND
MAGNIFICENCE

1. Pitched the first-ever perfect game   **A. Don Larsen**

2. Pitched the only postseason perfect game   **B. Cy Young**

3. The youngest ever (20) to pitch a perfect game   **C. Lee Richmond**

4. The oldest ever (40) to pitch a perfect game   **D. Randy Johnson**

5. Pitched the fastest perfect game
   (1 hour, 23 minutes)   **E. Mike Witt**

6. Pitched the slowest perfect game
   (2 hours, 40 minutes)   **F. John Ward**

7. Pitched his perfect game on the last
   day of the season   **G. David Wells**

274

Did you get a perfect score? Here's more.

1. Had the only regular-season interleague
   perfect game   **A. Len Barker**

2. Pitched his in front of the smallest crowd—6,298   **B. Don Larsen**

3. Pitched his in front of the largest crowd—64,519   **C. Sandy Koufax**

4. Pitched the only October regular-season
   perfect game   **D. Catfish Hunter**

5. Pitched his perfect game on Father's Day   **E. David Cone**

6. Pitched first perfect game against a
   Canadian team   **F. Addie Joss**

7. His perfect game was his fourth no-hitter in
   four years   **G. Jim Bunning**

273: 1-C, 2-A, 3-F, 4-D, 5-B, 6-G, 7-E • **274:** 1-E, 2-D, 3-B, 4-F, 5-G, 6-A, 7-C

Almost perfect: There have been six "unofficial" perfect games that Major League Baseball currently does not recognize as perfect games for a variety of reasons. However, most of these games were once recognized in the past as official perfect games, before Major League Baseball amended its own rules of what constitutes a perfect game. Four of these weren't counted as perfect games because they didn't go nine innings. Two went nine perfect innings (or more), but went into extra innings as scoreless ties, before being ruined in extra innings. In addition, there have been nine games in MLB history in which a pitcher lost a perfect game after getting the first two outs in the ninth inning. The following trivia game deals with these six unofficial perfect games and nine near-perfect games.

1. Pitched 12 perfect innings, lost it in the 13th on an error

2. Pitched nine perfect innings, lost it in the tenth on a hit

3. Retired 27 straight batters after coming into game as a reliever with one on and no outs in the first inning, after the starting pitcher, Babe Ruth, was ejected for arguing balls and strikes with the home-plate ump

4. Had 8.2 perfect innings, lost it when he hit the batter

5. Had 8.2 perfect innings, lost it by giving up a walk

6. Had 8.2 perfect innings, lost it when he gave up a home run

7. Had 8.2 perfect innings, lost it when he gave up a double. This was his third no-hitter lost with two outs in the ninth in less than a year, and his fifth one-hitter in two seasons, including three one-hitters in a four-game stretch.

A. Dave Stieb

B. Ernie Shore

C. Milt Pappas

D. Pedro Martinez

E. Harvey Haddix

F. Brian Holman

G. Hooks Wiltse

275: 1-E, 2-D, 3-B, 4-G, 5-C, 6-F, 7-A

Try your hand at some American League no-hitter trivia.

1. Detroit Tigers

2. California Angels

3. Chicago White Sox

4. Boston Red Sox

5. Tampa Bay Devil Rays

6. Oakland A's

7. Kansas City Royals

A. First AL team to pitch a no-hitter

B. AL team with the best ratio of no-hitters for and against (four no-hitters for, one against)— .800

C. Team that holds the AL record for most consecutive years without pitching a no-hitter—39

D. Along with the White Sox, they've had the most no-hitters thrown against them—14

E. Last AL team to have two no-hitters in the same season

F. AL team with the most no-hitters—17

G. Only AL team without a no-hitter to its credit

Now some National League no-hitter trivia.

1. Philadelphia Phillies

2. Los Angeles Dodgers

3. New York Mets

4. Chicago Cubs

5. Cincinnati Reds

6. San Diego Padres

7. Arizona Diamondbacks

A. Last NL team to pitch two no-hitters in the same season

B. First NL team to pitch two no-hitters in the same season

C. NL team that has pitched the most no-hitters—20

D. Besides the Mets, the other NL team whose ratio of no-hitters is 0 for and 7 against

E. Team that holds the NL record for most consecutive years without pitching a no-hitter—45

F. NL team with the most no-hitters pitched against it—17

G. Last NL team to pitch a no-hitter

276: 1-C, 2-E, 3-A, 4-F, 5-G, 6-D, 7-B • **277:** 1-F, 2-C, 3-E, 4-A, 5-B, 6-D, 7-G

THE ALL-STAR GAME

Can you match these All-Star Game pitching records and feats with their authors?

1. Most consecutive strikeouts to start a game—4

    A. Fernando Valenzuela

2. Most innings pitched in a career—19.1

    B. Lefty Gomez

3. Most innings pitched in one game—6

    C. Don Drysdale

4. Only pitcher to allow three home runs in one game

    D. Pedro Martinez

5. Most hits allowed in one game—9

    E. Tom Glavine

6. Most games finished in a career—6

    F. Jim Palmer

7. Struck out five consecutive batters in one game

    G. Goose Gossage

279

Now match these hitters with their All-Star Game feats.

1. Most career All-Star Game at bats—75

    A. Stan Musial

2. Most doubles in a career—7

    B. Mickey Mantle

3. Most games used as a pinch hitter—10

    C. Willie Mays

4. Only player with four consecutive strikeouts in All-Star play

    D. Fred Lynn

5. Most career RBIs—12

    E. Roberto Clemente

6. Hit the only grand slam in All-Star Game history

    F. Ted Williams

7. Most times struck out in All-Star Game career—17

    G. Dave Winfield

278: 1-D, 2-C, 3-B, 4-F, 5-E, 6-G, 7-A • **279:** 1-C, 2-G, 3-A, 4-E, 5-F, 6-D, 7-B

280

Here are some more All-Star Game pitching feats.

1. Most All-Star Games pitched—10

A. Robin Roberts

2. Only NL hurler to pitch in six consecutive games

B. Lefty Gomez

3. Only AL hurler to pitch in six consecutive games

C. Ewell Blackwell

4. Only AL pitcher to start five All-Star Games

D. Tom Seaver

5. First of two NL pitchers to start five All-Star Games

E. Roger Clemens

6. Last pitcher in either league to start five All-Star Games

F. Don Drysdale

7. Only NL pitcher to appear in relief in seven All-Star Games

G. Early Wynn

281

And back to some All-Star Game hitting accomplishments.

1. First player to play in 24 consecutive All-Star Games

A. Stan Musial

2. Most runs scored in a career—20

B. Willie Mays

3. Only player ever to score four runs in one All-Star Game

C. Charlie Gehringer

4. Only NL player with seven consecutive hits in All-Star play

D. Mickey Mantle

5. First of two AL players with seven consecutive hits

E. Joe Medwick

6. First player to reach base safely five times in one game

F. Joe Morgan

7. Only NL player with four hits in one All-Star Game

G. Ted Williams

280: 1-E, 2-C, 3-G, 4-B, 5-A, 6-F, 7-D • **281:** 1-A, 2-B, 3-G, 4-F, 5-D, 6-C, 7-E

Batter up! Some more All-Star Game hitting feats.

1. Most All-Star Game at bats without a hit—10

A. Joe DiMaggio

2. The only player ever with two *official* at bats in an inning

B. Al Rosen

3. Most at bats in one All-Star Game—7

C. Terry Moore

4. The only player besides Ted Williams with five RBIs in one All-Star Game

D. Willie Jones

5. The only AL player to ground into three career double plays

E. Pete Rose

6. The only NL player to ground into three career double plays

F. Jim Rice

7. Most career singles in All-Star Game play—15

G. Willie Mays

283

And now for another round of All-Star Game pitching feats.

1. Only pitcher with more than one career balk—2

A. Bill Hallahan

2. Of the four pitchers in All-Star Game history to strike out six batters in a game, he did it in the fewest innings—2.2

B. Tom Glavine

3. The last pitcher to strike out six batters in one game

C. Johnny Vander Meer

4. Most hits allowed in one inning—7

D. Ferguson Jenkins

5. Most runs allowed in one game—7

E. Mel Harder

6. Most career innings pitched with a 0.00 ERA—13

F. Dwight Gooden

7. Most walks allowed in one game—5

G. Atlee Hammaker

282: 1-C, 2-F, 3-D, 4-B, 5-A, 6-E, 7-G • **283:** 1-F, 2-C, 3-D, 4-B, 5-G, 6-E, 7-A

The votes are in—one more round of All-Star Game hitting highlights.

1. Only player ever to steal home in an All-Star Game   **A. Willie Mays**

2. Most stolen bases in his All-Star Game career—6   **B. Rod Carew**

3. The most career extra-base hits—8   **C. Mickey Owen**

4. First player to hit two home runs in one All-Star Game   **D. Gary Carter**

5. Last player to hit two home runs in one All-Star Game   **E. Pie Traynor**

6. Only player to hit two triples in one All-Star Game   **F. Stan Musial**

7. Hit the first pinch-hit home run in All-Star Game history   **G. Arky Vaughan**

285

Time for some catchers' All-Star Game glove work.

1. Most chances accepted in one game—15   **A. Ivan Rodriguez**

2. Most games played at catcher—14   **B. Yogi Berra**

3. Most innings caught in one game—15   **C. Lance Parrish**

4. Most career errors by a catcher—2   **D. Smoky Burgess**

5. Most career double plays by a catcher—2   **E. Bill Freehan**

6. Most assists in one All-Star Game—3   **F. Johnny Bench**

7. Only NL catcher with 11 chances accepted in one game   **G. Roy Campanella**

284: 1-E, 2-A, 3-F, 4-G, 5-D, 6-B, 7-C • **285:** 1-G, 2-B, 3-E, 4-D, 5-A, 6-C, 7-F

WHO, WHAT, WHEN, WHERE, AND WHY

1. Who are these guys?

2. Why is this photograph significant?

3. When did it occur?

4. Where?

286:
1. The National League All-Star team.

2. It's the first All-Star Game ever played.

3. July 6, 1933.

4. Comiskey Park in Chicago.

Now some outfielders' achievements.

1. Most games played as an outfielder—22   **A. Dave Parker**

2. Most putouts in one All-Star Game—9   **B. Darryl Strawberry**

3. Most career outfield assists—3   **C. Stan Musial**

4. First of only two players to record two assists in one game   **D. Joe DiMaggio**

5. Only outfielder to make two errors in one game   **E. Pete Reiser**

6. Besides the answer to question 5, the only other outfielder with two career errors   **F. Willie Mays**

7. The most recent outfielder of only three in history to make a double play in an All-Star Game   **G. Larry Doby**

288

Now some All-Star shortstops.

1. Most All-Star Games played at shortstop—15   **A. Ozzie Smith**

2. Most chances accepted in a career—39   **B. Cal Ripken Jr.**

3. Most assists in a career—24   **C. Marty Marion**

4. Most putouts in one All-Star Game—5   **D. Joe Cronin**

5. Only shortstop with two errors in one All-Star Game   **E. Chico Carrasquel**

6. Most double plays in a career—6   **F. Nomar Garciaparra**

7. Only NL shortstop with ten chances in one game   **G. Ernie Banks**

On to the hot corner.

1. Most career errors by an All-Star third baseman—6

    A. Red Rolfe

2. Most putouts in a nine-inning game—4

    B. George Kell

3. One of only two third basemen ever to collect six assists in one game (Frank Malzone is the other)

    C. Ken Keltner

4. Only AL third sacker with two errors in one game

    D. Brooks Robinson

5. Most chances accepted in a career—43

    E. Eddie Mathews

290

How about some second base fielding marks?

1. Most games played as a second baseman—13

    A. Nellie Fox

2. Most double plays made in a career—5

    B. Roberto Alomar

3. Most chances accepted in a nine-inning game—9

    C. Bill Mazeroski

4. Most putouts made in one game—7

    D. Juan Samuel

5. Most assists in a career—23

    E. Willie Randolph

6. Most assists in one All-Star Game—6

    F. Billy Herman

7. Of the four second basemen to have two career errors in All-Star Game play, the only one not to appear as an answer elsewhere in this game

    G. Steve Sax

291

And, finally, the first basemen.

1. Most putouts in a career—53

    A. Bill White

2. Most games played at first base—10

    B. Harmon Killebrew

3. Most putouts in a nine-inning game—14

    C. George McQuinn

4. Most chances accepted in a game—15

    D. Steve Garvey

5. Most double plays in one All-Star Game—3

E. Lou Gehrig

6. Only NL player with six career double plays

F. Pete Runnels

7. Only AL player ever to make an unassisted double play

G. Stan Musial

292

Match each record-setting All-Star Game performance with the year in which it occurred.

1. All-Star Game with fewest at bats by one team (27), NL

A. 1998

2. Longest-ever All-Star Game (15 innings)

B. 1992

3. All-Star Game with the highest batting average by one team (.442), AL

C. 1968

4. All-Star Game with the fewest hits by one team (2), NL

D. 1971

5. All-Star Game with the most hits by one team (19), AL

E. 1990

6. One of three All-Star Games (and the last) to feature six total home runs by both teams

F. 1967

7. First All-Star Game to feature 13 runs scored by one team, a record that has been tied twice since

G. 1983

293

Try these record-setting All-Star Game performances and their years.

1. Highest scoring All-Star Game ever, 21 runs (won by the AL, 13–8)

A. 1999

2. All-Star Game featuring the most runs in an inning by one team—7

B. 1983

3. First All-Star Game played at night

C. 1981

4. Only All-Star Game in which one team (NL) had no batters strike out

D. 1943

5. All-Star Game which featured 22 strikeouts, the most ever

E. 1978

6. Only All-Star Game to feature three triples

F. 1937

7. Year of the All-Star Game's highest attendance—72,086

G. 1998

293: 1-G, 2-B, 3-D, 4-F, 5-A, 6-E, 7-C

• **292:** 1-C, 2-F, 3-A, 4-E, 5-B, 6-D, 7-G • **291:** 1-E, 2-D, 3-C, 4-B, 5-G, 6-A, 7-F

WHO, WHAT, WHEN, WHERE, AND WHY

1. Who are these two players?

2. What incredible feat did each perform this year?

3. When was this photograph taken?

4. Where?

5. BONUS: Who had the better game in the 1941 All-Star Game?

294:

1. Hall of Famers Ted Williams of the Red Sox and Joe DiMaggio of the Yankees.

2. Williams hit .406 for the season (the last player ever to reach the .400 plateau), and DiMaggio had his 56-game batting streak (unsurpassed to this day).

3. July 8, 1941.

4. Briggs Stadium in Detroit, in the locker room after the 1941 All-Star Game.

5. Ted Williams, although DiMaggio was no slouch. DiMaggio was 1–4 with three runs scored and one RBI while Williams was 2–4 with one run scored and four RBIs, including the game-winning three-run homer with two out in the bottom of the ninth.

DEFUNCT, BUT NOT FORGOTTEN

Brooklyn Dodgers (1890–1957) hitters.

1. Most hits in a season—241
2. Most hits in a career—2,318
3. Highest career batting average—.352
4. Most home runs in a season—43
5. Most career grand slams—13
6. Most career stolen bases—298
7. Highest career on-base percentage—.409

A. Gil Hodges
B. Jackie Robinson
C. Willie Keeler
D. Babe Herman
E. Zack Wheat
F. Tom Daly
G. Duke Snider

296

Brooklyn Dodgers (1890–1957) pitchers.

1. Most games pitched in a career—382
2. Most wins in a career—190
3. Most career shutouts—38
4. Most 20-win seasons—4
5. Most games pitched in a season—62
6. Lowest career ERA—2.31
7. Most home runs allowed in a career—180

A. Brickyard Kennedy
B. Dazzy Vance
C. Nap Rucker
D. Burleigh Grimes
E. Clem Labine
F. Jeff Pfeffer
G. Carl Erskine

297

Washington Senators (original team, 1901–1960) hitters.

1. Most games played in a career—2,307
2. Most runs in a season—127
3. Most home runs by a rookie—30
4. Most home runs in a career—127
5. Most total bases in a season—331
6. Washington's first-ever Rookie of the Year
7. Most consecutive games hit safely—33

A. Goose Goslin
B. Sam Rice
C. Heinie Manush
D. Bob Allison
E. Albie Pearson
F. Joe Cronin
G. Roy Sievers

297: 1-B, 2-F, 3-D, 4-A, 5-G, 6-E, 7-C
296: 1-A, 2-B, 3-C, 4-D, 5-E, 6-F, 7-G • **295:** 1-D, 2-E, 3-C, 4-G, 5-A, 6-F, 7-B •

298

Washington Senators (original team, 1901–1960) pitchers.

1. Most games lost in a career—279   **A. Alvin Crowder**

2. Most consecutive games lost—15   **B. Bob Groom**

3. Most strikeouts in a game—15   **C. Al Orth**

4. Most home runs allowed in a season—43   **D. Camilo Pascual**

5. Most games pitched in a season—64   **E. Pedro Ramos**

6. Most runs allowed in a season—172   **F. Firpo Marberry**

7. Most consecutive wins   **G. Walter Johnson**
   (tied with Walter Johnson)—16

299

St. Louis Browns (1902–1953) hitters.

1. Most consecutive games hit safely—41   **A. Beau Bell**

2. Most home runs in a career—185   **B. Ken Williams**

3. Most runs scored in a season—145   **C. George Sisler**

4. Most singles in a season—179   **D. Wally Judnich**

5. Most doubles in a season—51   **E. Jack Tobin**

6. Most triples in a season (tie)—20   **F. Heinie Manush**

7. Most home runs by a rookie—24   **G. Harlond Clift**

300

St. Louis Browns (1902–1953) pitchers.

1. Most games won in a season—27   **A. Urban Shocker**

2. Most complete games in a career—210   **B. Elam Vangilder**

3. Most strikeouts in a game—17   **C. Bobo Newsom**

4. Most games started in a season—40   **D. Fred Glade**

5. Most consecutive wins in one season—10   **E. Jack Powell**

6. Most games pitched in a career—323   **F. Alvin Crowder**

7. Most games lost in a season—25   **G. Rube Waddell**

300: 1-A, 2-E, 3-G, 4-C, 5-F, 6-B, 7-D • **299:** 1-C, 2-B, 3-G, 4-E, 5-A, 6-F, 7-D •
298: 1-G, 2-B, 3-D, 4-E, 5-F, 6-C, 7-A

301

New York Giants (1883–1957) hitters.

1. Most games played in a career—2,730   A. Bill Terry

2. Most consecutive games hit safely—33   B. Bobby Thomson

3. Most career home runs by a righthander—189   C. John Montgomery Ward

4. Most extra-base hits in a season—87   D. Mel Ott

5. Highest batting average in a season—.401   E. Mike Tiernan

6. Most triples in a career—162   F. Willie Mays

7. Most stolen bases in a season—111   G. George Davis

302

New York Giants (1883–1957) pitchers.

1. Most consecutive games won—24   A. Christy Mathewson

2. Most consecutive games won *in one season*—19   B. Tim Keefe

3. Most strikeouts in a game—16   C. Rube Marquard

4. Highest career winning percentage—.682   D. Joe McGinnity

5. Highest winning percentage in a season— .833 (15–3)   E. Hoyt Wilhelm

6. Most innings pitched in a season—434   F. Carl Hubbell

7. Most runs allowed in a career—1,860   G. Amos Rusie

303

Milwaukee Braves (1953–1965) hitters.

1. Most home runs in a season—47   A. Hank Aaron

2. Most triples in a career—80   B. Eddie Mathews

3. Most strikeouts in a season—122   C. Rico Carty

4. Most home runs in season by a switch-hitter—6   D. Red Schoendienst

5. Most home runs in a month—15   E. Joe Torre

6. Most singles in a season—132   F. Mack Jones

7. Most home runs by a rookie—22   G. Joe Adcock

303: 1-B, 2-A, 3-F, 4-D, 5-G, 6-E, 7-C
301: 1-D, 2-G, 3-B, 4-F, 5-A, 6-E, 7-C • **302:** 1-F, 2-C, 3-A, 4-B, 5-E, 6-D, 7-G •

304

Milwaukee Braves (1953–1965) pitchers.

1. Most games won in a season—24
2. Most games started in a season—39
3. Most consecutive games won—11
4. Most games pitched in a season—62
5. Most batters hit in a season—12
6. Most walks allowed in a season—121
7. Led National League with four shutouts in 1958

A. Bob Buhl
B. Billy O'Dell
C. Warren Spahn
D. Carl Willey
E. Bob Shaw
F. Lew Burdette
G. Tony Cloninger

305

Boston Braves (1876–1952) hitters.

1. Most stolen bases in a career—431
2. Most home runs in a career—199
3. Most games played in a career—1,795
4. Most runs scored in a season—160
5. Most strikeouts in a season—134
6. Most stolen bases in a season—93
7. Most hits in a career—2,002

A. Hugh Duffy
B. Fred Tenney
C. Herman Long
D. Wally Berger
E. Rabbit Maranville
F. Billy Hamilton
G. Vince DiMaggio

306

Boston Braves (1876–1952) pitchers.

1. Most strikeouts in a game—18
2. Most games pitched in a career—557
3. Most wins in a season—49
4. Most shutouts in a season—11
5. Twice won a team-record 13 consecutive games
6. Most 20-win seasons (tied with Warren Spahn)—4
7. Most consecutive games lost—18

A. Warren Spahn
B. Charlie Buffinton
C. Kid Nichols
D. Johnny Sain
E. John Clarkson
F. Cliff Curtis
G. Tommy Bond

306: 1-A, 2-C, 3-E, 4-G, 5-B, 6-D, 7-F
305: 1-C, 2-D, 3-E, 4-A, 5-G, 6-F, 7-B • **304:** 1-G, 2-F, 3-C, 4-B, 5-E, 6-A, 7-D •

WHO, WHAT, WHEN, WHERE, AND WHY

1. **Who** is in the center of the photograph?

2. **How** did he break so many hearts?

3. **When** did he do it?

4. **Where** did he move his team to?

4. Los Angeles.

3. Following the 1957 season.

2. Moved his team out of Brooklyn after nearly 80 years.

1. Brooklyn Dodgers owner Walter O'Malley.

307:

Seattle Pilots (1969) hitters.

1. Most runs scored in a season—88
2. Most home runs in a season—25
3. Most stolen bases in a season—73
4. Most consecutive games hit safely—18
5. Most triples in a season—6
6. Lowest batting average by team regular—.165
7. Had only one HR, 19 RBIs, and 22 runs all season as the team's regular second baseman

A. Tommy Davis
B. John Donaldson
C. Tommy Harper
D. Ray Oyler
E. Don Mincher
F. Mike Hegan
G. Wayne Comer

309

Seattle Pilots (1969) pitchers.

1. Most wild pitches in a season—8
2. Most strikeouts in a game—11
3. Most consecutive games won—5
4. Most games won in a season—13
5. Most consecutive games lost—9
6. Oldest pitcher on the team—34
7. Lowest ERA for a season—2.18

A. Bob Locker
B. Diego Segui
C. George Brunet
D. Marty Pattin
E. John Gelnar
F. Jim Bouton
G. Gene Brabender

310

Philadelphia A's (1901–1954) hitters.

1. Most games played in a career—1,702
2. Most hits in a season—253
3. Most consecutive games hit safely—29
4. Most triples in a season—87
5. Most RBIs in a season—169
6. Most home runs in a month—15
7. Most stolen bases in a career—376

A. Home Run Baker
B. Jimmie Dykes
C. Jimmie Foxx
D. Al Simmons
E. Bob Johnson
F. Bill Lamar
G. Eddie Collins

310: 1-B, 2-D, 3-F, 4-A, 5-C, 6-E, 7-G

308: 1-G, 2-E, 3-C, 4-A, 5-F, 6-D, 7-B • **309:** 1-F, 2-D, 3-B, 4-G, 5-E, 6-C, 7-A •

Philadelphia A's (1901–1954) pitchers.

1. Most shutouts in a career—59

2. Most consecutive games lost—19

3. Most consecutive games won—16

4. Most strikeouts in a game (he did it twice)—18

5. Most complete games in a season—39

6. Most games lost in a season—25

7. Most 1–0 games won in a season—4

A. Lefty Grove

B. Harry Krause

C. Jack Coombs

D. Eddie Plank

E. Rube Waddell

F. Jack Nabors

G. Scott Perry

312

Kansas City A's (1955–1967) hitters.

1. Most games played in a career—726

2. Most home runs in a season—38

3. Highest batting average in a season—.319

4. Most RBIs in a season—117

5. Most hits in a season—193

6. Most extra-base hits in a season—67

7. Most stolen bases in a season—55

A. Jerry Lumpe

B. Rocky Colavito

C. Ed Charles

D. Bob Cerv

E. Vic Power

F. Norm Siebern

G. Bert Campaneris

313

Kansas City A's (1955–1967) pitchers.

1. Most games pitched in a career—292

2. Most games won in a season—16

3. Lowest ERA for a season—2.80

4. Most games lost in a season—22

5. Most strikeouts in a game (he did it twice and he's tied with Catfish Hunter)—12

6. Most strikeouts in a career—513

7. Most consecutive games lost—11

A. Troy Herriage

B. Art Ditmar

C. Catfish Hunter

D. Bud Daley

E. John Wyatt

F. Jim Nash

G. Diego Segui

313: 1-E, 2-D, 3-C, 4-B, 5-F, 6-G, 7-A

311: 1-D, 2-F, 3-A, 4-C, 5-E, 6-G, 7-B • **312:** 1-C, 2-D, 3-E, 4-F, 5-A, 6-B, 7-G •

Montreal Expos (1969–2004) hitters.

1. Most games played in a career—1,767
2. Most stolen bases in a season—97
3. Highest batting average in a season—.345
4. Most runs scored in a season—133
5. Most home runs in a season by a lefthander—36
6. Most grand slams in a career—7
7. Most home runs by a rookie—20

A. Vladimir Guerrero
B. Henry Rodriguez
C. Brad Wilkerson
D. Ron LeFlore
E. Tim Raines Sr.
F. Gary Carter
G. Tim Wallach

315

Montreal Expos (1969–2004) pitchers.

1. Most games pitched in a career—425
2. Most complete games in a season—20
3. Most games won in a season—20
4. Lowest ERA for a career—3.06
5. Most strikeouts in a game—18
6. Most losses in a season—22
7. Most consecutive games lost—10

A. Bill Gullickson
B. Dennis Martinez
C. Bill Stoneman
D. Tim Burke
E. Ross Grimsley
F. Steve Renko
G. Steve Rogers

316

Washington Senators (replacement team, 1961–1971) hitters.

1. Most hits in a season—175
2. Most stolen bases in a season—29
3. Most games played in a career—1,142
4. Highest batting average in a season—.310
5. Most consecutive games hit safely—19
6. Most grand slams in a season—2
7. Most doubles in a season—31

A. Ed Brinkman
B. Ed Stroud
C. Aurelio Rodriguez
D. Ken McMullen
E. Don Zimmer
F. Frank Howard
G. Chuck Hinton

316: 1-F, 2-B, 3-A, 4-G, 5-D, 6-E, 7-C

315: 1-D, 2-C, 3-E, 4-B, 5-A, 6-G, 7-F •

314: 1-G, 2-D, 3-A, 4-E, 5-B, 6-F, 7-C •

Washington Senators (replacement team, 1961–1971) pitchers.

1. Lowest ERA in a season—2.19

2. Most games lost in a season—22

3. Most strikeouts in a game (16 innings)—21

4. Most strikeouts in a career—561

5. Most complete games in a season—13

6. Most games pitched in a career—267

7. Most saves in a career—40

A. Claude Osteen

B. Dick Bosman

C. Darold Knowles

D. Casey Cox

E. Denny McLain

F. Tom Cheney

G. Joe Coleman

318

NAME THAT YEAR

Seven clues. One year. See how few clues it takes you to guess the year.

1. **Firpo Marberry of the Senators** becomes the first relief specialist in major league history as he collects 15 saves.

2. **Tony Boeckel becomes the first** major league player to die in an automobile crash.

3. **Brooklyn's 28-game winner, Dazzy Vance,** narrowly wins the NL MVP Award over Rogers Hornsby (.424, 25 HRs, 152 RBIs) when one voter leaves Hornsby completely off the ballot because he doesn't like Hornsby's attitude.

4. **John McGraw wins his tenth** and final NL pennant.

5. **The Giants and White Sox undertake a European barnstorming tour** in an effort to expand baseball's appeal to a worldwide audience.

6. **The Giants win their NL-record** fourth straight pennant.

7. **In one of the most exciting World Series of all time,** the Washington Senators defeat the New York Giants, 4–3.

ASSUME THE POSITION

319

How well do you know your shortstops? Try to match them with their feats.

1. Most hits in a season—221

2. Most games played in a career—2,581

3. Best single-season fielding average by a shortstop—.996

4. Highest batting average for a season—.401

5. Most home runs in a season—47

6. Once went three consecutive games without a fielding chance

7. Most stolen bases in a season—104

A. Cal Ripken Jr.

B. Hughie Jennings

C. Michael Young

D. Maury Wills

E. Ernie Banks

F. Tom Tresh

G. Luis Aparicio

320

How test your knowledge of these outfielders' all-time records.

1. Highest batting average in a season—.440

2. Most games played in a career—2,934

3. Highest career fielding average by an outfielder—.995

4. Most consecutive games played—897

5. Most RBIs in a season—191

6. Most runs scored in a season—198

7. Most stolen bases in a season—130

A. Hack Wilson

B. Rickey Henderson

C. Billy Williams

D. Ty Cobb

E. Darryl Hamilton

F. Hugh Duffy

G. Billy Hamilton

321

How let's see what your batting average is with these pitching records.

1. Most games pitched in a career—1,252

2. Most games pitched in a season—106

A. Walter Johnson

B. Whitey Ford

319: 1-C, 2-G, 3-A, 4-B, 5-E, 6-F, 7-D • **320:** 1-F, 2-D, 3-E, 4-C, 5-A, 6-G, 7-B

3. Most Opening Day victories—9

4. Tied for most grand slams allowed—10

5. Most games won by a rookie since 1900—28

6. Highest career winning percentage—.690

7. Most games lost in a career—313

C. **Jesse Orosco**

D. **Cy Young**

E. **Mike Marshall**

F. **Grover Alexander**

G. **Nolan Ryan**

322

Try your hand at some hot corner all-time records.

1. Most career games played at third base—2,870

2. Highest batting average in a season—.391

3. Most home runs in a season by a third baseman—48

4. Most hits in a season by a third sacker—240

5. Most doubles in a season—56

6. Most RBIs in a season—145

7. Highest slugging average in a season—.664

A. **John McGraw**

B. **Al Rosen**

C. **Wade Boggs**

D. **Mike Schmidt**

E. **George Brett**

F. **Brooks Robinson**

G. **George Kell**

323

See if you can match these first sackers and their feats.

1. Highest batting average in a season—.420

2. First player ever with three consecutive 50-homer seasons

3. Most RBIs in a season by a first baseman—184

4. Most stolen bases in a season by a first sacker—67

5. Most strikeouts in a season—185

6. Most games played at first in a career—2,413

7. Best fielding average for a career—.996

A. **Steve Garvey**

B. **Eddie Murray**

C. **Mark McGwire**

D. **Frank Chance**

E. **Lou Gehrig**

F. **Jim Thome**

G. **George Sisler**

323: 1-G; 2-C; 3-E; 4-D; 5-F; 6-B; 7-A

322: 1-F; 2-A; 3-D; 4-C; 5-G; 6-B; 7-E •

321: 1-C; 2-E; 3-A; 4-G; 5-F; 6-B; 7-D •

324

How it's time to get caught up on catchers' records.

1. Most innings caught in one game—25   **A. Carlton Fisk**

2. Most games caught in rookie season—154   **B. Dan Wilson**

3. Best fielding average for a career—.995   **C. Johnny Bench**

4. Most home runs in a season while playing catcher—42   **D. Randy Hundley**

5. Most consecutive errorless games—252   **E. Mike Matheny**

6. Most putouts in a career—11,785   **F. Gary Carter**

7. Most games caught in a season—160   **G. Javy Lopez**

325

Now some second basemen and their records.

1. Highest career fielding average by a second baseman—.9893   **A. Jeff Kent**

2. Holds the season record by any player at any position for highest percentage of a team's games with at least one hit (135 games of his team's 154, or 87.7%)   **B. Eddie Collins**

3. Only second baseman to reach 300 career home runs   **C. Joe Morgan**

4. Highest batting average in a season—.426   **D. Ryne Sandberg**

5. Most years spent playing as a second baseman—22   **E. Rogers Hornsby**

6. Most at bats in a season—701   **F. Juan Samuel**

7. Most games played at second base—2,650   **G. Napoleon Lajoie**

324: 1-A, 2-C, 3-B, 4-G, 5-E, 6-F, 7-D • **325:** 1-D, 2-E, 3-A, 4-G, 5-C, 6-F, 7-B

WHO, WHAT, WHEN, WHERE, AND WHY

1. Who is driving the car on the right?

2. Why is this automobile significant to baseball history?

3. When was this practice initiated?

4. Where was the automotive company based?

5. BONUS: Why was it discontinued?

326:

1. Hall of Famer Ty Cobb.

2. This was a Chalmers automobile; one was given to each league's batting champion, and later to each league's MVP, by Chalmers Automotive.

3. 1910 for batting champs, then 1911 for league MVPs.

4. Detroit.

5. The practice was discontinued after the 1915 season because of rumors of cheating among players for the award, and loss of public interest, due partly to the rule stating that no player could win more than one automobile.

NAME THAT YEAR

Seven clues. One year. See how few clues it takes you to guess the year.

1 **Babe Ruth defeats Walter Johnson,** 1–0, pitching a shutout and driving in the game's only run.

2 **Ernie Shore pitches a perfect game** in relief of Babe Ruth, who was ejected after walking the leadoff batter.

3 **Wally Pipp hits nine home runs** and repeats as the AL's home run king.

4 **Pitcher Eddie Cicotte, with 28 wins,** is ordered benched by owner Charles Comiskey so he won't trigger a $10,000 bonus clause in his contract if he reaches 30 wins.

5 **Manager John McGraw becomes the highest-paid person** in baseball when he signs an extension for $40,000 a year plus a percentage of the profits.

6 **Fred Toney of the Reds** and Hippo Vaughn of the Cubs pitch a double no-hitter on May 2, broken up in the tenth by pro football Hall of Famer Jim Thorpe.

7 **The White Sox win their second World Series** title by defeating the Giants, 4–2.

THE LEAGUE CHAMPIONSHIP SERIES

Baseball Trivia

(Note: LCS = League Championship Series; NLCS = National League Championship Series; ALCS = American League Championship Series.)

328

League Championship Series team trivia.

1. Highest batting average for a seven-game LCS—.309

2. Lowest batting average for a seven-game LCS—.204

3. Highest batting average in an LCS by a *losing* team—.303

4. Lowest batting average in an LCS by a *winning* team—.183

5. Most runs scored in an LCS—45

6. Fewest runs scored in an LCS (tied with the 1970 Pirates, although Pittsburgh played just three games in their LCS while this team played four)—3

7. One of only two teams ever to have 11 different players score at least one run in an LCS game (the 1993 Braves are the other)

A. 2001 Mariners

B. 1989 Cubs

C. 1983 White Sox

D. 1996 Cardinals

E. 1996 Braves

F. 2004 Yankees

G. 1974 A's

329

More League Championship Series team trivia.

1. Most runs scored in one inning of an LCS game—10

2. Fewest hits in an LCS—15

3. Most hits in an LCS—78

4. Only team in LCS history to collect seven consecutive hits in seven consecutive at bats in one inning (had one sacrifice fly during the streak)

5. One of only two teams (1996 Braves were the other) ever to collect 15 singles in one LCS game

6. The only National League team in history to play an LCS game without hitting a single (it's been done twice in the AL)

7. The only team in history to collect five doubles in one inning of an LCS game

A. 1981 Yankees

B. 2002 Angels

C. 1990 Pirates

D. 1970 Orioles

E. 1982 Braves

F. 2000 Mets

G. 2004 Yankees

328: 1-E, 2-D, 3-B, 4-G, 5-F, 6-C, 7-A • **329:** 1-B, 2-E, 3-G, 4-D, 5-A, 6-C, 7-F

Still more League Championship Series team trivia.

1. Only team in history to hit five triples in an LCS, and it was just a five-game series
   A. 1980 Astros

2. The only team ever to hit three triples in one LCS game
   B. 1993 Phillies

3. The only team ever to hit two grand slams in one LCS
   C. 2004 Astros

4. Only team ever to hit a home run in all seven games of an LCS
   D. 1984 Cubs

5. Of all the teams ever to play a six- or seven-game LCS, this is the only club to hit just one home run in its series
   E. 2004 Yankees

6. Only team ever to hit five home runs in one LCS game
   F. 1977 Dodgers

7. Team that got the most extra-base hits in one LCS game—13
   G. 1997 Marlins

331

Even more League Championship Series team trivia.

1. This team had 21 batters strike out in one LCS game (the next most is only 15!)
   A. 2005 White Sox

2. Only team ever not to have a single batter strike out in an LCS game
   B. 1974 Pirates

3. Most stolen bases in an LCS—16
   C. 1975 Reds

4. Most stolen bases in one LCS game—7
   D. 1992 A's

5. Had the most runners thrown out attempting to steal in one LCS—6
   E. 1985 Cardinals

6. Most runners left on base in one LCS game—19; incredibly, just the day before *in the same LCS,* this team also set the record as the only club in history to finish a game with *no* runners left on base!
   F. 1997 Indians

7. Only team in history with four complete games in one LCS, and it was just a five-game series
   G. 1999 Braves

330: 1-A, 2-B, 3-F, 4-C, 5-G, 6-D, 7-E • **331:** 1-F, 2-B, 3-D, 4-C, 5-E, 6-G, 7-A

Another game of League Championship Series team trivia.

1. Only team to record four saves in a four-game LCS   **A. 1984 Royals**

2. Only team to be shut out three times in one LCS   **B. 1997 Indians**

3. Winner of the largest shutout game in LCS history—15–0   **C. 1988 A's**

4. Most consecutive innings shutting out their opponent in one LCS—30   **D. 1974 A's**

5. Only National League team ever to maintain a perfect 1.000 fielding average for an entire LCS   **E. 1991 Pirates**

6. This team fielded an abysmal .940 for their LCS, the worst in history   **F. 1996 Braves**

7. Only team in history to win all four games of its LCS games by just one run   **G. 1979 Pirates**

333

We're not through yet.

1. Winner of the longest game in LCS history (16 innings)   **A. 2003 Yankees**

2. Committed the most errors in one LCS—10   **B. 1999 Red Sox**

3. One of only two teams to commit five errors in a single LCS game (1974 Dodgers were the other)   **C. 1987 Cardinals**

4. Turned the most double plays in one LCS—12   **D. 2003 Marlins**

5. The host team of the LCS game with the highest attendance ever—65,829   **E. 1986 Mets**

6. The only team ever to win the NLCS in four straight games   **F. 1995 Braves**

7. The winning team in the LCS with the highest attendance of all time—396,597 in seven games   **G. 1976 Yankees**

332: 1-C, 2-E, 3-F, 4-D, 5-G, 6-A, 7-B • **333:** 1-E, 2-B, 3-G, 4-A, 5-D, 6-F, 7-C

WHO, WHAT, WHEN, WHERE, AND WHY

1. Who is this player?

2. What all-time major league record did he set that still stands?

3. When did he do it?

4. Against which team did he extend this record further in the National League Championship Series?

334:

1. Orel Hershiser.

2. Most consecutive scoreless innings pitched—59.

3. 1988.

4. New York Mets, to 67 straight innings.

Not even close.

1. Only team to win their LCS after losing the first three games of the series

A. 1973 Reds

2. The host team of the LCS game with the lowest attendance of all time—24,265

B. 1990 A's

3. The team whose four-game sweep in the LCS made their franchise the only one to have done so twice

C. 1973 A's

4. Only American League team whose *smallest* LCS game attendance ever was still over 50,000 (50,135, to be exact)

D. 2002 Twins

5. Only team ever to have two outfield assists in one inning

E. 2004 Red Sox

6. Most outfield putouts in one game—18

F. 1972 Pirates

7. Fewest outfield putouts in one ALCS game—1

G. 1982 Brewers

336

Onward.

1. Most LCS games won—39

A. Yankees

2. Most LCS games lost—33

B. A's

3. Lost the most League Championship Series—7

C. Red Sox

4. Most consecutive LCS games won—10

D. Pirates

5. Most consecutive LCS games lost—10

E. Royals

6. Only team to lose the ALCS three straight years

F. Braves

7. Most stolen bases in LCS play—54

G. Orioles

And one more for good luck.

1. Most times caught stealing in LCS play—22
2. Most consecutive LCS games played without being shut out—36
3. Team that has lost the most extra-inning LCS games—5
4. American League team that has played the most extra-inning LCS games—8
5. No team has won more than four extra-inning LCS games, and this team is the only one to be undefeated at 4–0
6. National League team with the most consecutive wins in LCS play—6
7. The only ALCS team that has never lost a League Championship Series

A. Phillies

B. Royals

C. Brewers

D. Yankees

E. Reds

F. Orioles

G. Braves

338

In this game, see if you can match the player in the right column with his particular feat in the left column.

1. Played in more LCS than any other player—11
2. One of only two players (Tom Glavine is the other) in history to play nine LCS with the same club
3. Only player in history to play on seven losing LCS teams
4. Only player in history to play for five different LCS clubs
5. Youngest (19) player ever to play in an LCS
6. Oldest (43) player ever to play in an LCS
7. Player with the most years (16) between his first and second LCS

A. John Smoltz

B. Don Baylor

C. Chuck Finley

D. Andruw Jones

E. Reggie Jackson

F. Phil Niekro

G. Richie Hebner

337: 1-B, 2-D, 3-G, 4-F, 5-A, 6-E, 7-C • **338:** 1-E, 2-A, 3-G, 4-B, 5-D, 6-F, 7-C

More individual League Championship Series performances.

1. The player who has appeared in the most LCS games—46
2. The player who has appeared in the most ALCS games—45
3. The player who has appeared in the most NLCS games—38
4. The player with the highest career batting average in LCS play (minimum 50 at bats)—.468
5. The player with the most career plate appearances in LCS history—194
6. The player with the most career runs scored in LCS play—31
7. The only player in history with hits in 15 consecutive LCS games

A. Reggie Jackson

B. Derek Jeter

C. Bernie Williams

D. Will Clark

E. Terry Pendleton

F. Pete Rose

G. David Justice

340

Still more individual League Championship Series performances.

1. One of only two players in history with 14 hits in a single LCS (Hideki Matsui is the other)
2. The only player with four career triples in LCS play
3. One of only two players with nine career home runs in LCS play (George Brett is the other)
4. The only player ever to hit a home run in five different LCS
5. The only National Leaguer to hit three home runs in one NLCS game
6. One of only two American Leaguers (who doesn't appear as an answer elsewhere in this game) to hit three home runs in one ALCS game
7. Since LCS play began in 1969, he is the only player ever to hit a home run in a 1–0 extra-inning game

A. Albert Pujols

B. Adam Kennedy

C. Bob Robertson

D. George Brett

E. Bernie Williams

F. Tony Fernandez

G. Johnny Bench

339: 1-G, 2-A, 3-E, 4-D, 5-B, 6-C, 7-F • **340:** 1-A, 2-D, 3-E, 4-G, 5-C, 6-B, 7-F

Another round of individual League Championship Series performances.

1. One of only two players (Carlos Beltran is the other) in history to hit home runs in four consecutive games of one LCS

A. Gary Gaetti

2. Only player ever to homer in his first two LCS at bats

B. Hideki Matsui

3. Of his 12 extra-base hits in 22 games of LCS play, eight were home runs

C. Jeffrey Leonard

4. Only American League player in history to collect four extra-base hits in one LCS game

D. Mark McGwire

5. Holds the record for the most RBIs in one LCS—11

E. David Ortiz

6. Only American Leaguer with six RBIs in one LCS game

F. Steve Garvey

7. Only player in history to collect an RBI in six consecutive games in LCS play

G. Johnny Damon

342

Here are some more, but they're getting tougher.

1. He holds the career record for strikeouts in NLCS play—32

A. Jorge Posada

2. Only player in history to strike out 12 times in a seven-game LCS

B. Miguel Cairo

3. Only player in LCS history to strike out in seven consecutive official at bats

C. John Shelby

4. He holds the career record for grounding into the most double plays in LCS play—6

D. Reggie Sanders

5. He holds the record for being hit by a pitch the most times in one LCS—4

E. Cesar Geronimo

6. Only player in LCS history to strike out twice in the same inning

F. Ron Karkovice

7. He's received more career bases on balls than any other batter in LCS history

G. Manny Ramirez

341: 1-C, 2-A, 3-F, 4-B, 5-E, 6-G, 7-D • **342:** 1-D, 2-C, 3-E, 4-G, 5-B, 6-F, 7-A

This baserunning-related game should give you a run for your money.

1. He holds the career record for stolen bases in ALCS play—16

2. He holds the career record for stolen bases in NLCS play—9

3. He holds the record for most steals in a seven-game LCS—7

4. In the first 25 years of LCS play, he was the only player ever to steal home

5. He has been thrown out attempting to steal more times in his LCS career than any other player in history—6

6. Only player ever to be caught stealing four times in one LCS

7. Only player ever to be caught stealing twice in one LCS game

A. Trot Nixon

B. Rickey Henderson

C. Reggie Jackson

D. Ron Gant

E. Devon White

F. Davey Lopes

G. Hal McRae

344

Now for some League Championship Series pitching trivia.

1. He's appeared in the most games in ALCS history—25

2. He's appeared in the most games in NLCS history—18

3. Only five pitchers have ever appeared in six games in one LCS; he's the only one to do it in a six-game Series, and he did it twice

4. He has started more games in ALCS history than any other pitcher—11

5. He has the most career saves of any pitcher in LCS history—11

6. At 8–0, he easily has the best career record of any pitcher in LCS play

7. Only pitcher ever to win three games in a single LCS

A. John Rocker

B. Dennis Eckersley

C. Mark Wohlers

D. Dave Stewart

E. Mariano Rivera

F. Jesse Orosco

G. Roger Clemens

343: 1-B, 2-F, 3-D, 4-C, 5-G, 6-E, 7-A • **344:** 1-E, 2-C, 3-A, 4-G, 5-B, 6-D, 7-F

345

More League Championship Series pitching trivia.

1. The only National League pitcher with six career wins in LCS play

A. John Smoltz

2. Holds the record for games started in NLCS play with one team—15

B. Tom Glavine

3. Only pitcher ever to hurl four consecutive complete games in LCS play

C. Jim Palmer

4. Holds the record for most runs allowed in an LCS career—50

D. Phil Niekro

5. At 0–7, he easily holds the mark for worst career record in LCS play

E. Greg Maddux

6. Only pitcher ever to lose three games in one LCS

F. Jerry Reuss

7. Only pitcher ever to allow nine runs in one LCS game

F. Doug Drabek

346

And still more League Championship Series pitching trivia.

1. He allowed the most career home runs (12) in LCS play

A. Roger Clemens

2. Only pitcher ever to surrender five home runs in one LCS

B. Matt Morris

3. There has never been a no-hitter in LCS play. He has the only one-hitter.

C. Steve Avery

4. Holds the record for most consecutive hitless innings pitched in LCS play—10

D. Dave McNally

5. Only pitcher in LCS history to allow six consecutive hits in one inning

E. Mike Cuellar

6. Holds the record for most consecutive scoreless innings pitched in LCS play—22.1

F. Eric Show

7. Only pitcher ever to surrender nine walks in one LCS game

G. Catfish Hunter

345: 1-A, 2-B, 3-C, 4-E, 5-F, 6-G, 7-D • **346:** 1-G, 2-F, 3-A, 4-D, 5-B, 6-C, 7-E

WHO, WHAT, WHEN, WHERE, AND WHY

1. Who is this player?

2. What MVP accomplishment was he the first American Leaguer to attain?

3. When did he do it?

4. What position did he play during those years?

347:

1. Hall of Famer Robin Yount.

2. The first AL player to win an MVP Award for play at two different positions.

3. 1982 and 1989.

4. Shortstop and outfield.

And one final game of individual League Championship
Series pitching trivia.

1. The only pitcher ever to throw four wild pitches
   in one LCS

   A. Roger Clemens

2. The only pitcher ever to strike out the first five
   batters to come to the plate in an LCS game

   B. Jimmy Key

3. The only pitcher in history with two streaks of
   five consecutive strikeouts, though they both
   came in the middle of the games

   C. Rick Ankiel

4. The only pitcher to strike out 15 batters in
   an NLCS game

   D. Curt Schilling

5. One of only two pitchers to strike out 15 batters
   in an ALCS game (and who doesn't appear as
   an answer elsewhere in this game)

   E. Livan Hernandez

6. Only relief pitcher in NLCS history to strike out
   seven batters in one game

   F. Mike Mussina

7. Only pitcher ever to hit three batters in one inning

   G. Nolan Ryan

349

League Championship Series first basemen.

1. Most games played at first base in LCS history—38

   A. Glenn Davis

2. Most putouts in one LCS game—21

   B. Steve Garvey

3. Most assists in one LCS game—7

   C. Andres Galarraga

4. Most chances accepted in a nine-inning
   LCS game—18

   D. John Olerud

5. Only first baseman in LCS history to play a full
   nine-inning game and record only one putout

   E. Tino Martinez

6. Most errors made at first base in one LCS—4

   F. Bob Robertson

7. Most consecutive errorless games played at
   first base in an LCS career—24

   G. Keith Hernandez

348: 1-C, 2-D, 3-F, 4-E, 5-A, 6-G, 7-B • **349:** 1-D, 2-A, 3-G, 4-B, 5-F, 6-C, 7-E

League Championship Series second basemen.

1. Most games played at second base in LCS history—31

A. Mark Lemke

2. Most putouts in one LCS game—8

B. Joe Morgan

3. Most assists in one nine-inning LCS game—9

C. Bobby Grich

4. Most chances accepted in a nine-inning LCS game—13

D. Ryne Sandberg

5. Only second baseman in LCS history to play a full nine-inning game and not receive a single fielding chance

E. Manny Trillo

6. Most errors made at second base in an LCS career—5

F. Joey Cora

7. Most consecutive errorless games played at second base in an LCS career—27

G. Roberto Alomar

351

League Championship Series third basemen.

1. Most games played at third base in LCS history (he's tied with Terry Pendleton)—34

A. Ron Cey

2. By a wide margin, he holds the record for most chances accepted by a third baseman in one LCS—30

B. Jeff King

3. Most assists in one nine-inning LCS game—8

C. Mike Schmidt

4. The only American League third baseman to have three assists in one inning of an LCS game

D. Todd Cruz

5. Most assists by a third baseman in an LCS career—66

E. Chipper Jones

6. Most errors made at third base in an LCS career—8

F. Matt Williams

7. The only National League third baseman to commit three errors in one LCS

G. George Brett

League Championship Series shortstops.

1. Most games played at shortstop in LCS history—41
2. Most putouts in one nine-inning LCS game—7
3. Most assists (tied with Kiko Garcia) in one nine-inning LCS game—9
4. Only NLCS shortstop to make three putouts in one inning
5. Only shortstop in history to commit five errors in one LCS
6. One of only two shortstops in LCS history to make two errors in one inning (Kevin Elster was the other)
7. The NLCS shortstop who accepted the most chances without an error in one LCS—33

A. Bill Russell
B. Chris Speier
C. Edgar Renteria
D. Gene Alley
E. Spike Owen
F. Derek Jeter
G. Garry Templeton

353

League Championship Series outfielders.

1. Most games played in the outfield in LCS history—41
2. Most putouts in one LCS—28
3. The only left or right fielder in history to record nine putouts in one LCS game
4. Only outfielder in LCS history to have six career assists
5. Only American League outfielder in history with two assists in one LCS game
6. The only outfielder in LCS history with seven career errors. Ugh!
7. The only outfielder ever to record two double plays in one LCS game

A. Lonnie Smith
B. Bernie Williams
C. Rickey Henderson
D. Jesse Barfield
E. Bake McBride
F. Gary Pettis
G. Tony Oliva

League Championship Series catchers.

1. Most games played at catcher in LCS history—33

   A. Johnny Bench

2. Only catcher in LCS history to record 16 putouts in one game

   B. Manny Sanguillen

3. Only catcher in LCS history with three assists in one inning

   C. Jorge Posada

4. The catcher with the most career errors in LCS play—5

   D. Thurman Munson

5. The only catcher in history to have three passed balls in one inning

   E. Bengie Molina

6. No other catcher is even close to his LCS career record for most runners thrown out attempting to steal—12

   F. Mike Piazza

7. Holds the National League record for most career assists by a catcher—18

   G. Jason Varitek

355

League Championship Series pitchers.

1. Eight pitchers in history have recorded four putouts in an LCS. Amazingly, he did it in just one game!

   A. Don Gullett

2. Only pitcher in LCS history to record five assists in one game

   B. Juan Marichal

3. Holds the record for most assists in an LCS career—25

   C. Greg Maddux

4. Only pitcher in LCS history to record three assists in one inning

   D. Joaquin Andujar

5. The only pitcher in history to have two errors in one LCS

   E. Mariano Rivera

6. The only National League pitcher in history with six chances accepted in a single LCS game

   F. Charlie Leibrandt

7. Holds the record for most career putouts in LCS play—12

   G. Pat Zachry

354: 1-C, 2-F, 3-E, 4-B, 5-G, 6-D, 7-A • **355:** 1-A, 2-F, 3-C, 4-G, 5-D, 6-B, 7-E

WHO, WHAT, WHEN, WHERE, AND WHY

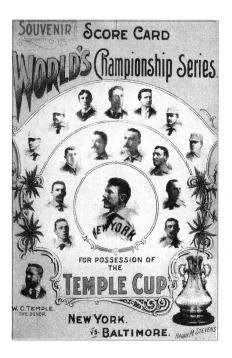

1. Who proposed the playing of the Temple Cup World's Championship Series, and why?

2. What did the first Temple Cup cost?

3. When did the first series take place?

4. Where did the award cup reside after it was discontinued in 1897?

5. BONUS: Where does it reside today?

5. The Hall of Fame in Cooperstown, New York.

4. Temporarily with Baltimore, the winner of the last Cup Series, but it was returned to Mr. Temple following the 1897 season because the series had been discontinued for lack of interest among both players and fans, and no team had won the three Series required to take permanent possession of the prize.

3. 1894.

2. Eight hundred dollars (it was made of silver).

1. William Chase Temple, a one-time minority owner of the Pittsburgh Pirates, because he felt the 1893 Pirates should have won the league championship.

356:

NAME THAT YEAR

Seven clues. One year. See how few clues it takes you to guess the year.

1   **Chuck Klein wins the NL Triple Crown,** hitting .368, with 20 home runs and 120 RBIs.

2   **Tom Yawkey inherits $7 million** on February 21, and purchases the Red Sox four days later for $1 million.

3   **Carl Hubbell pitches ten shutouts** for the Giants, more than seven the American League's eight teams managed to collect.

4   **Nick Altrock pinch-hits** for the Senators at the age of 57.

5   **Baseball Commissioner Kenesaw Mountain Landis** voluntarily takes a 40 percent cut in pay because of the conditions during the Depression.

6   **Jimmie Foxx wins** the AL Triple Crown, hitting .356 with 48 home runs and 163 RBIs.

7   **Babe Ruth hits the first home run** in an All-Star Game, a two-run shot that propels the American League to a 4–2 victory over the NL stars.

MEDIA

358

Let's see how well you know your baseball writers. The men in this game were the first seven writers to win the J. G. Taylor Spink Award for meritorious contributions to baseball writing. The award is presented at the annual Hall of Fame induction ceremony, leading many to think that the writers are being enshrined in the Hall, which is not the case.

1. Longtime editor and publisher of *The Sporting News*   **A. J. G. Taylor Spink**

2. Former editor of the *Atlanta Journal,* and friend of Ty Cobb's   **B. Ring Lardner**

3. One of the founding fathers of the Baseball Writers' Association, who doggedly pursued the Black Sox scandal   **C. Damon Runyon**

4. After a long career as a baseball writer, he became a famous short story writer; many of his stories became plays and musicals, including *Guys and Dolls* and *Little Miss Marker*   **D. Harry Salsinger**

5. Famous for his baseball humor and wit, he coined the phrase "Washington—first in war, first in peace, and last in the American League."   **E. Hugh Fullerton**

6. Achieved early fame for his series "You Know Me, Al," which appeared in the *Saturday Evening Post*   **F. Charles Dryden**

7. A president of the Baseball Writers' Association and the sports editor of the *Detroit News* for half a century   **G. Grantland Rice**

359

See if you can match up these famous home run calls with the announcers who made them famous.

1. "Hey, hey!"   **A. Harry Caray**

2. "Holy cow!"   **B. Harry Hartman**

3. "It could be . . . it might be . . . it IS! A home run!"   **C. Ernie Harwell**

358: 1-A, 2-G, 3-E, 4-C, 5-F, 6-B, 7-D

4. "It's going, going . . . Gone!"　　　D. Phil Rizzuto

5. "Kiss it good-bye!"　　　E. Rosey Roswell

6. "Long gone!"　　　F. Bob Prince

7. "Open the window, Aunt Minnie, here it comes!"　　　G. Jack Brickhouse

360

More famous home run calls.

1. "Back, back, back, back . . . Gone!"　　　A. Dave Neihaus

2. "Forget it!"　　　B. Leo Durocher

3. "Get out the rye bread and mustard, grandma, cuz it's GRAND SALAMI TIME!"　　　C. Chris Berman

4. "Get up . . . Get outta here . . . Gone!"　　　D. Michael Kay

5. "Going back . . . At the track . . . At the wall . . . SSSEEEYA!"　　　E. Dick Risenhoover

6. "Good-bye, baseball!"　　　F. Vin Scully

7. "Good-bye, Dolly Grey!"　　　G. Bob Uecker

361

Still more.

1. "Swing, and there it goes . . . Light tower power!"　　　A. Eric Nadel

2. "Tell it good-bye!"　　　B. Jon Miller

3. "That ball is going, and it ain't coming back!"　　　C. Ken Coleman

4. "That ball is history!"　　　D. Ken Harrelson

5. "They usually show movies on a flight like that!"　　　E. Jerry Trupiano

6. "Whattaya think about that?!"　　　F. Jeff Kingery

7. "You can put it on the board. Yesssssssss!"　　　G. Rob Faulds

361: 1-E, 2-B, 3-F, 4-A, 5-C, 6-G, 7-D

360: 1-C, 2-F, 3-A, 4-G, 5-D, 6-E, 7-B • **359:** 1-G, 2-D, 3-A, 4-B, 5-F, 6-C, 7-E •

WHO, WHAT, WHEN, WHERE, AND WHY

1. Who are these two guys?

2. What are they doing?

3. When?

4. Where?

5. BONUS: Who was the opposing team that day?

6. BETCHA-DIDN'T-KNOW BONUS: What was the combined record of all the home teams of all the major league games Reagan attended while in office as U.S. president?

362:

1. President Ronald Reagan and Chicago Cubs announcer Harry Caray.

2. Announcing the Cubs game over the radio. Reagan, a former baseball announcer, called the game for 1.5 innings.

3. September 30, 1988.

4. Wrigley Field in Chicago.

5. The Pittsburgh Pirates.

6. 0–4.

Now for the broadcasters. The Ford C. Frick Award is presented annually at the Hall of Fame induction ceremony to a broadcaster for his contributions to baseball. Like the Spink Award winners, recipients of the Frick Award are often mistakenly assumed to be Hall of Fame inductees, which they are not.

1. Broadcast Chicago baseball (both Cubs and White Sox) for more than 40 years, and was behind the mike for nine All-Star Games and 12 World Series

2. Longtime voice of the Dodgers and later the Yankees, he was also a lay preacher

3. Broadcaster who personally witnessed 631 of Willie Mays's first 633 home runs, and who announced Bobby Thomson's famous home run by telling listeners, "The Giants win the pennant! The Giants win the pennant!"

4. Longtime announcer of the Tigers, he was the only broadcaster ever involved in a baseball trade, when he was traded for a minor league manager

5. Longtime Dodger announcer whose voice and style are so friendly, smooth, knowledgeable, well-prepared, and colorful that he was once dubbed, "the Fordham Thrush with the .400 larynx"

6. He broadcast more than 5,000 Cubs and White Sox games, never criticizing and always taking a positive approach

7. Longtime voice of both the Yankees and the weekly highlight show, *This Week in Baseball*

A. Ernie Harwell

B. Red Barber

C. Russ Hodges

D. Bob Elson

E. Jack Brickhouse

F. Mel Allen

G. Vin Scully

363: 1-D, 2-B, 3-C, 4-A, 5-G, 6-E, 7-F

More broadcasters.

1. Longtime announcer for the Red Sox before joining NBC as its *Game of the Week* announcer, and who broadcast 13 World Series and 16 All-Star Games

   A. Jack Buck

2. Spanish-language broadcaster who announced 42 World Series

   B. Joe Garagiola

3. A shameless partisan announcer, he was affiliated with the Pirates for five decades

   C. Lindsey Nelson

4. Longtime Cardinals broadcaster whose versatility also allowed him to announce eight Super Bowls

   D. Harry Caray

5. Longtime Mets announcer who was known for his trademark psychedelic sports coats; at one time he owned 335 of them

   E. Curt Gowdy

6. In more than 8,300 games with the Cardinals, White Sox, and Cubs, he was a fearless announcer whose opinionated style was often controversial and sometimes outrageous

   F. Bob Prince

7. A former *Game of the Week* announcer known for his humor, he was a journeyman catcher from 1946 to 1954

   G. Buck Canel

365

See if you can match up these Frick Award winners with the teams they were most closely associated with.

1. Curt Gowdy   **A. Houston Astros**

2. By Saam   **B. Baltimore Orioles**

3. Milo Hamilton   **C. Philadelphia A's/Phillies**

4. Chuck Thompson   **D. Minnesota Twins**

5. Bob Murphy   **E. Boston Red Sox**

6. Bob Wolff   **F. Washington Senators**

7. Herb Carneal   **G. New York Mets**

364: 1-E, 2-G, 3-F, 4-A, 5-C, 6-D, 7-B • **365:** 1-E, 2-C, 3-A, 4-B, 5-G, 6-F, 7-D

366

More broadcasters and the teams they miked for.

1. Jimmy Dudley
2. Jaime Jarrin
3. Jerry Coleman
4. Lon Simmons
5. Harry Kalas
6. Bob Uecker
7. Marty Brennaman

A. San Diego Padres
B. Cleveland Indians
C. Philadelphia Phillies
D. San Francisco Giants/Oakland A's
E. Los Angeles Dodgers (Spanish)
F. Cincinnati Reds
G. Milwaukee Brewers

367

NAME THAT YEAR

Seven clues. One year. See how few clues it takes you to guess the year.

1 **Jim Palmer wins his third** Cy Young Award.

2 **The designated hitter** is used in the World Series for the first time.

3 **Wrigley Field hosts a Rick Monday Day** in honor of the outfielder's having stopped a flag burning in Dodger Stadium earlier in the year. Paying their respects are President Gerald Ford and Commissioner Bowie Kuhn.

4 **Atlanta owner Ted Turner signs Andy Messersmith** and nicknames him Channel. He then assigns him uniform number 17, thus promoting his television superstation on the player's back. NL president Chub Feeney quickly puts an end to the stunt.

5 **Yankee Stadium reopens** after a two-year renovation in which the team has played its regular-season games at the Mets' Shea Stadium.

6 **The National League** honors its centennial season.

7 **Cincinnati's Big Red Machine sweeps Philadelphia** in the NLCS, then sweeps the Yankees in the most one-sided World Series up to that point.

WHO, WHAT, WHEN, WHERE, AND WHY

1. Who is seated behind the microphones?

2. What shocking announcement had he just made to the world?

3. When did he make it?

4. Where did he play his last game?

5. How did he fare?

6. What infamous record was set in this game, though not by him?

368:

1. Hall of Famer Sandy Koufax.

2. He had just announced his premature retirement from baseball at the age of 30.

3. November 18, 1966.

4. Dodger Stadium in Los Angeles.

5. He lost to the Orioles in Game 2 of the 1966 World Series, 6–0.

6. Willie Davis made three errors in one inning, and the Dodgers made six in the game.

NOTABLE QUOTABLES

See if you can identify the source of these colorful quotes.

1. "I just got to be first—all the time."   A. Babe Ruth

2. "It don't take school stuff to help a fella play ball."   B. Ty Cobb

3. "I'd give a million dollars to undo what I've done."   C. Josh Gibson

4. "Pick a good one and sock it."   D. Joe Jackson

5. "A homer a day will boost my pay."   E. Dizzy Dean

6. "If you can do it, it ain't braggin'."   F. Lou Gehrig

7. "Today I consider myself the luckiest man on the face of the Earth."   G. Eddie Cicotte

370

More who-said-what.

1. "If it wasn't for baseball, I'd be in either the penitentiary or the cemetery."   A. Ty Cobb

2. "A ball bat is a wondrous weapon."   B. Johnny Bench

3. "A manager doesn't hear the cheers."   C. Pete Rose

4. "I can throw out any man alive."   D. Joe DiMaggio

5. "Above anything else, I hate to lose."   E. Jackie Robinson

6. "A ballplayer has to be kept hungry to become a big leaguer. That's why no boy from a rich family has ever made the big leagues."   F. Babe Ruth

7. "Brooks Robinson belongs in a higher league."   G. Alvin Dark

371

Easy, huh? Not so fast, hotshot. Here are more quotes for you to identify.

1. "It's a great day for a ball game. Let's play two!"   A. Frank Robinson

2. "The only reason I don't like playing in the World Series is I can't watch myself play."   B. Satchel Paige

3. "Fifty years from now I'll be just three inches of type in a record book."   C. Ernie Banks

4. "Close don't count in baseball. Close only counts in horseshoes and hand grenades."   D. Brooks Robinson

369: 1-B, 2-D, 3-G, 4-A, 5-C, 6-E, 7-F • **370:** 1-F, 2-A, 3-G, 4-B, 5-E, 6-D, 7-C

5. "Sporting goods companies pay me not to endorse their products."

E. Roberto Clemente

6. "If I could sleep, I could hit .400."

F. Reggie Jackson

7. "I ain't ever had a job, I just always played baseball."

G. Bob Uecker

372

One more.

1. "Rules are made to be broken, so there won't be any rules."

A. Earl Weaver

2. "I try not to break the rules, but merely to test their elasticity."

B. Billy Herman

3. "I made a game effort to argue, but two things were against me: the umpires and the rules."

C. John McGraw

4. "I think there should be bad blood between all clubs."

D. Bill Veeck Jr.

5. "Good pitching will always stop good hitting and vice-versa."

E. Bill Klem

6. "I think we can win if my brain holds out."

F. Leo Durocher

7. "Baseball is more than a game to me, it's a religion."

G. Casey Stengel

373

Just kidding.

1. "All I remember about my wedding day in 1967 is that the Cubs lost a doubleheader."

A. Harry Caray

2. "Every season has its peaks and valleys. What you have to try to do is eliminate the Grand Canyon."

B. Yogi Berra

3. "Booze, broads, and bullshit. If you got all that, what else do you need?"

C. Dizzy Dean

4. "I ain't what I used to be, but who the hell is?"

D. Nolan Ryan

5. "He hits from both sides of the plate. He's amphibious."

E. Warren Spahn

6. "Twenty wins is the magic figure for pitchers, and .300 is the magic figure for batters. It pays off in salary and reputation."

F. Andy Van Slyke

7. "It helps if the hitter thinks you're a little crazy."

G. George Will

373: 1-G, 2-F, 3-A, 4-C, 5-B, 6-E, 7-D
• **372:** 1-B, 2-D, 3-F, 4-A, 5-G, 6-C, 7-E • **371:** 1-C, 2-F, 3-D, 4-A, 5-G, 6-E, 7-B

This time, all the quotes are from managers.

1. "Are the Dodgers still in the league?" A. Bill Terry

2. "God watches over drunks and third basemen." B. Gene Mauch

3. "Baseball has been good to me since I quit trying to play it." C. Chuck Tanner

4. "Eighty percent of the people who hear your troubles don't care, and the other twenty percent are glad you're having them." D. Leo Durocher

5. "Losing streaks are funny. If you lose at the beginning you got off to a bad start. If you lose in the middle of the season, you're in a slump. If you lose at the end, you're choking." E. Whitey Herzog

6. "You can have money piled to the ceiling, but the size of your funeral is still going to depend on the weather." F. Billy Martin

7. "When I get through managing, I'm going to open up a kindergarten." G. Tommy Lasorda

375

Do you know which announcer said what?

1. "And Kansas is at Chicago tonight, or is it Chicago at Kansas City? Well, no matter, as Kansas leads in the eighth, four to four." A. Ron Fairly

2. "Last night I neglected to mention something that bears repeating." B. Harry Caray

3. "There never was any question about Enos Slaughter's courage. He proved it by getting married four times." C. Ken Harrelson

4. "Aw, how could he lose the ball in the sun, he's from Mexico." D. Jerry Coleman

5. "He slud into third." E. Bob Uecker

6. "The way to catch a knuckleball is to wait until it stops rolling and then pick it up." F. Jack Brickhouse

7. "Baseball is the only sport I know that when you're on offense, the other team controls the ball." G. Dizzy Dean

374: 1-A, 2-D, 3-E, 4-G, 5-B, 6-C, 7-F • **375:** 1-D, 2-A, 3-F, 4-B, 5-G, 6-E, 7-C

376

How about these players' quips—about fellow players.

1. "Cobb is a prick, but he sure can hit."

2. "Ruth has everybody else—including myself—hopelessly outclassed."

3. "Every time I look at my pocketbook, I see Jackie Robinson."

4. "After Jackie Robinson, the most important black in baseball history is Reggie Jackson. I really mean that."

5. "Does Pete Rose hustle? Before the All-Star Game he came into the clubhouse and took off his shoes and they ran another mile without him."

6. "If I had played my career hitting singles like Pete Rose, I'd wear a dress."

7. "Shoeless Joe Jackson was the finest natural hitter in the history of the game."

A. Reggie Jackson

B. Babe Ruth

C. Willie Mays

D. Mickey Mantle

E. Home Run Baker

F. Ty Cobb

G. Hank Aaron

377

Don't stop now.

1. "Of course the stories about Satchel Paige are legendary. Some of them are even true."

2. "The only thing Earl Weaver knows about big league pitching is that he couldn't hit it."

3. "Look at Bobby Richardson. He doesn't drink, he doesn't smoke, he doesn't chew, he doesn't stay out late, and he still can't hit .250."

4. "The only way to get a ball past Honus Wagner is to hit it eight feet over his head."

5. "I don't think Warren Spahn will ever get into the Hall of Fame. He'll never stop pitching."

6. "Leo Durocher had the ability of taking a bad situation and making it immediately worse."

7. "Tommy Lasorda will eat anything as long as you pay for it."

A. Joe Torre

B. John McGraw

C. Stan Musial

D. Buck O'Neil

E. Jim Palmer

F. Casey Stengel

G. Branch Rickey

376: 1-B, 2-E, 3-C, 4-A, 5-G, 6-D, 7-F • **377:** 1-D, 2-E, 3-F, 4-B, 5-C, 6-G, 7-A

Keep going, you're on a roll.

1. "Sandy Koufax throws a 'radio ball,' a pitch
   you hear, but you don't see."

   A. Bobby Murcer

2. "Ty Cobb lived off the field as though he wished
   to live forever. He lived on the field as though it
   was his last day."

   B. Branch Rickey

3. "Branch Rickey had both players and money.
   He just didn't like to see the two of them mix."

   C. Ray Kroc

4. "Bill Terry once hit a ball between my legs
   so hard that my center fielder caught it on
   the fly backing up against the wall."

   D. Gene Mauch

5. "I signed Oscar Gamble on the advice of my
   attorney. I no longer have Gamble and I no
   longer have my attorney."

   E. Dizzy Dean

6. "Trying to hit Phil Niekro is like trying to eat
   Jell-O with chopsticks. Sometimes you might
   get a piece, but most of the time you get hungry."

   F. Tommy Lasorda

7. "When Billy Martin reaches for a bar tab,
   his arm shrinks six inches."

   G. Chuck Connors

379

Try these pricelessly incoherent quotes.

1. "They X-rayed my head and found nothing."

   A. Casey Stengel

2. "One time I snuck a ball on me, and when I went
   to winding up, I threw one of them balls to first
   and one to second. I was so smooth, I picked off
   both runners and fanned the batter without that
   ump or the other team even knowing it."

   B. Yogi Berra

3. "There comes a time in every man's life, and I've
   had plenty of them."

   C. Dizzy Dean

4. "Baseball has no clock, no ties, and no liberal
   intrusions into the organized progression."

   D. Dale Berra

378: 1-D, 2-B, 3-G, 4-E, 5-C, 6-A, 7-F

5. "You should always go to other people's funerals, otherwise they won't come to yours."

E. Satchel Paige

6. "You can't compare me to my father. Our similarities are different."

F. Tug McGraw

7. "How will I spend my World Series share? Ninety percent of it I'll spend on whiskey, women, and other good times. The other ten percent I'll probably waste."

G. George Will

380

NAME THAT YEAR

Seven clues. One year. See how few clues it takes you to guess the year.

1 **John Kull of the A's** ends his major league career as the only player in history with a career average of 1.000 in batting (1 for 1), pitching (1–0), and fielding (cleanly fielded the only ball ever hit to him).

2 **Cleveland's Neal Ball** performs the first unassisted triple play in history.

3 **The Detroit Tigers** win their third straight pennant.

4 **Ty Cobb** wins the AL Triple Crown.

5 **Forbes Field** opens for play.

6 **The Cubs beat the Braves** 21 times during the season.

7 **Honus Wagner outhits Ty Cobb** in the World Series, .333 to .231.

WHO, WHAT, WHEN, WHERE, AND WHY

1. Who are these two men?

2. What is their claim to fame, at least according to one of them?

3. When did it occur?

4. Where did each of them finish the season?

5. Why had these two aging stars been brought together on the team?

381:

1. Hall of Famers Yogi Berra and Warren Spahn.

2. According to Yogi, they were the "ugliest battery ever."

3. 1965.

4. Spahn was sent to the Giants after going 4–12 for the Mets, and Berra retired as a player after catching only two games and stayed on with the Mets as a coach.

5. In an attempt to bolster attendance for a poor team by showcasing aging legendary players, after both the Dodgers and Giants left New York for the West Coast.

BEYOND THE COLOR LINE

The next five challenges feature "firsts" for black players.

1. Bud Fowler

A. First black pitcher to toss a perfect game (for the Cuban X-Giants in 1903)

2. Fleetwood Walker

B. First known professional black player to play on an integrated team when he joins the Lynn, Iowa, team for a series of exhibition games (1878)

3. Dan McClellan

C. First American black player to play in the Mexican League (1938)

4. Rube Foster

D. Formed the Negro National League, the first successful Negro league (1920)

5. Chet Brewer

E. First black pitcher to play in the major leagues (1947)

6. Dan Bankhead

F. First black player to play in the major leagues, with a 42-game stint for the Toledo Blue Stockings, of the American Association (1884)

7. Emmett Ashford

G. First black umpire in professional baseball when he calls a game in the Southwest International League (1951)

383

1. Larry Doby

A. First black player to win the AL MVP Award (1963)

2. Jackie Robinson

B. First black player to win back-to-back MVP Awards (1958 and 1959)

3. Ernie Banks

C. First black player to win a Triple Crown (1966)

4. Buck O'Neil

D. First black player to win an MVP Award (1949)

5. Elston Howard

E. First black coach in major league history (1962)

6. Willie Mays

F. First black player to be chosen as his team's captain (1964)

7. Frank Robinson

G. First black player to hit a home run in the World Series (1948)

382: 1-B, 2-F, 3-A, 4-D, 5-C, 6-E, 7-G • **383:** 1-G, 2-D, 3-B, 4-E, 5-A, 6-F, 7-C

384

1. Jackie Robinson	A. First black major league player of the modern era when he steps onto the field for Brooklyn on April 15, 1947
2. Larry Doby	B. First black player to lead a major league in RBIs (121 in 1951)
3. Dan Bankhead	C. First black pitcher in the American League as he shuts out the White Sox in his major league debut (August 13, 1948)
4. Satchel Paige	D. First black pitcher to win a World Series game (1952)
5. Don Newcombe	E. First black player in the American League when he takes the field for Cleveland (July 5, 1947)
6. Monte Irvin	F. First black pitcher to face a black batter in a major league game (against Hank Thompson, on July 8, 1949)
7. Joe Black	G. First black player to hit a home run in his first major league at bat

385

1. Dan Bankhead	A. First black player to lead either major league in home runs when he smacks 32 (1952)
2. Satchel Paige	B. First black player to be enshrined in the Hall of Fame (1962)
3. Larry Doby	C. First black pitcher to pitch in a World Series game (1948)
4. Sam Jones	D. First black player to win three MVP Awards (1951, 1953, 1955)
5. Roy Campanella	E. First black pitcher to *appear* in a World Series game (1947)
6. Don Newcombe	F. First black pitcher to lead his league in wins, when he racks up 27 victories (1956)
7. Jackie Robinson	G. First black pitcher to hurl a no-hitter in the majors (1955)

384: 1-A, 2-E, 3-G, 4-C, 5-F, 6-B, 7-D • **385:** 1-E, 2-C, 3-A, 4-G, 5-D, 6-F, 7-B

1. Sammy Drake

A. **First black manager in the major leagues**

2. Emmett Ashford

B. **First black manager to win a World Series**

3. Frank Robinson

C. **When he took the field for the Cubs in 1960, he became the second half of the first black brother duo to play in the major leagues. His brother Solly had played for Chicago as well, four years earlier.**

4. Bill Lucas

D. **First black player to hit four home runs in one game**

5. Cito Gaston

E. **The Atlanta Braves made him the first black GM in major league history (1977)**

6. Hank Thompson

F. **First black umpire in major league history (1966)**

7. Willie Mays

G. **First black player to play in both the American and National Leagues**

387

Some of the very first black players are closely associated with the teams they broke in with, but see if you can match the first black players to play for each of these other American League teams.

1. Jay Heard

A. **St. Louis Browns**

2. Ozzie Virgil

B. **Kansas City A's**

3. Bob Trice

C. **Washington Senators**

4. Julio Becquer

D. **Detroit Tigers**

5. Hank Thompson

E. **Baltimore Orioles**

6. Carlos Paula

F. **Chicago White Sox**

7. Minnie Minoso

G. **Los Angeles Angels**

386: 1-C, 2-F, 3-A, 4-E, 5-B, 6-G, 7-D • **387:** 1-E, 2-D, 3-B, 4-G, 5-A, 6-C, 7-F

WHO, WHAT, WHEN, WHERE, AND WHY

1. **Who's** the man in the suit?

2. **What** is his eternal claim to fame?

3. **When?**

4. **Where** did he send Jackie Robinson to play after signing him?

388:

1. Dodgers GM Branch Rickey, a Hall of Famer.

2. Signing Jackie Robinson and later tapping him to break baseball's color barrier.

3. He signed Robinson on October 23, 1945, and brought him to the majors in 1947 after Robinson played one year of minor league ball.

4. To Montreal of the International League.

Now identify the first black players on these National League teams (two NL teams took on more than one black player in a year).

1. Tom Alston

A. Houston Colt .45s

2. Curt Roberts

B. St. Louis Cardinals

3. John Kennedy

C. Boston Braves

4. Charlie Neal
   and Felix Mantilla

D. New York Mets

5. Roman Mejias,
   Jim Pendleton, and
   Johnny Weekly

E. Cincinnati Reds

6. Chuck Harmon
   and Nino Escalera

F. Pittsburgh Pirates

7. Sam Jethroe

G. Philadelphia Phillies

NAME
THAT TEAM

Baseball Trivia

390

1 **We have won** the most World Series after the Yankees: nine (we're tied with the Athletics).

2 **The 2006 season** was our 88th consecutive year finishing out of last place, a major league record.

3 **We hold the distinction** of being the first major league team to be owned by a woman and to have a woman president. And our first manager—though a man—was named Patsy.

4 **We were the first** major league team to travel by air. Also, before we settled on our present name, we were known as the Perfectos, although we are better known by one of our nicknames, the Gas House Gang.

391

1 **For the first 95 years** of our franchise's history, we never had a hitter who was a member of the 3,000-hit club. Then, from 1996 to 2005, we had three!

2 **Some things you can't explain.** For example, we once had a stretch where we beat Kansas City 23 straight times, a major league record for one team beating another.

3 **We lost the first night game** in World Series history to the Pirates, even though we were heavily favored.

4 **In 1971** we became the only pennant winner in history to have four 20-game winners.

392

1 **Joel Youngblood got two hits** for two different teams in two different cities on the same day when the New York Mets traded him to us in 1982.

2 **Our only Cy Young winner** captured the award in 1997.

3 **In one of the tightest pennant races in history,** in 1973, eventually we ended up in fourth place, 3.5 games out, but almost won it, thanks to Mike Marshall's record-breaking 92 pitching appearances (including 14 wins and 31 saves).

4 **From 1969 to 1988** we only opened a season at home once. What a bad bbbrrrrrreak.

390: St. Louis Cardinals • **391:** Baltimore Orioles • **392:** Montreal Expos

1 **Since divisional play began in 1969,** we are the only team to sweep our opponents in both the League Championship Series and the World Series in the same season.

2 **We were the first** major league home team to play a regular-season night game.

3 **Because of the long players' strike** and the ill-advised split-season format that followed, in 1981, we didn't make the playoffs, even though we had the best overall record on the season.

4 **Since the inception of the Cy Young Award** in 1956, we are the only National League team besides Colorado and Florida never to have had a pitcher capture the award. However, we are the only National League team since 1963 to win the World Series in four straight, and we've done it twice.

394

1 **On July 17, 1990,** we became the first team in major league history to make two triple plays in one game.

2 **Other than Arizona in 2001,** we are the only World Series winners to win all of our home games and lose all of our road games in a seven-game Series, and we've done it twice.

3 **We were the first team** in American League history to attract more than three million fans in a season, in 1988.

4 **On June 9, 1966,** we became the only team in major league history to hit five home runs in one inning, when Harmon Killebrew capped it off after homers by Rich Rollins, Zoilo Versalles, Tony Oliva, and Don Mincher.

395

1 **Ken Sanders** holds our team's record for most pitching appearances in a season, with 83.

2 **During the 1980s,** we had more players win the MVP Award than any other American League team.

3 **We are the only team** in the majors to have, at one time or another, spent time in the East, West, and Central divisions.

4 **When we joined the American League,** in 1970, it marked the fifth time our city has had a major league franchise. And we were especially pleased that Hank Aaron chose to end his career playing with us.

393: Cincinnati Reds • **394:** Minnesota Twins • **395:** Milwaukee Brewers

WHO, WHAT, WHEN, WHERE, AND WHY

1. Who are these two players?

2. What famous play is this?

3. When did it occur?

4. Where?

5. BONUS: Why was this such a significant play?

396:

1. Catcher Mickey Owen of the Dodgers and batter Tommy Henrich of the Yankees.

2. Mickey Owen's dropped third strike.

3. October 5, 1941, Game 4 of the World Series.

4. Ebbets Field in Brooklyn.

5. The Yankees were leading the Series two games to one, all games having been one-run affairs. Brooklyn was leading this game 4–3 with two out in the ninth inning when Owen (who led all major league catchers in fielding average in 1941) dropped what would have been the final strike of the game. The Yankees then rallied for four ninth-inning runs to win the game, 7–4, and took a 3–1 lead, eventually winning the Series in five games.

1 **We hold a strange record:** Through the 2006 season, we are the only team in the 20th century *never* to have lost a game by a score of 1–0.

2 **Our team record** for most stolen bases in a season, 73, was set by Tommy Harper.

3 **No manager has won** more games in our team's history than Joe Schultz.

4 **The 1969 season** was our inaugural and last in the major leagues. Just before the 1970 season was set to open, we packed up, moved to Milwaukee, and became the Brewers.

398

1 **The first time the All-Star Game** was played in a new stadium, 1962, we were the hosts.

2 **In 1957,** our team stole only 13 bases, a record major league low. Julio Becquer was the team leader, with three.

3 **We were the first team** in major league history to be honored by having a sitting U.S. president throw out the ceremonial first pitch.

4 **In the classic Broadway musical** (and later film) *Damn Yankees,* Shoeless Joe Hardy led us to the American League pennant.

399

1 **We've had 25 batting champions,** more than any other National League team.

2 **We are the only team** Connie Mack ever managed in 53 years besides the Athletics.

3 **We were the last National League team** to host a Sunday game after the repeal of our state's blue laws. We were also the last National League team to have two consecutive yet different MVPs until Jeff Kent and Barry Bonds of the Giants performed the feat in 2000 and 2001.

4 **We are the only National League team** to come back from a three-games-to-one deficit to win the World Series, and we've done it twice. The first time was in 1925, against the Senators, and the second in 1979, against the Orioles.

397: Seattle Pilots • **398:** Washington Senators • **399:** Pittsburgh Pirates

400

1 **On September 16, 1975,** Rennie Stennett of the Pirates went 7 for 7 against us as we suffered the worst shutout loss this century, 22–0.

2 **We've had more official and unofficial names** than any other team in the majors. Before we settled on our present name, some of our previous names were the Colts, Orphans, Babes, Rainmakers, Zephyrs, Panamas, Recruits, Rough Riders, Cowboys, and Broncos.

3 **We hold the record** for wins in a season by a National League team, 116.

4 **The 2006 season** marked our 61st consecutive year without a pennant. Holy cow!

401

1 **Since divisional play began,** in 1969, we are the only team to hit at least 100 home runs every year, *including* the strike-shortened season of 1981.

2 **From 1959 to 1971** we had a different manager every year!

3 **In 1927** we had seven regular players and four players off the bench who hit .300 or better. Despite our hitting prowess, we didn't even win the pennant.

4 **Not only was owner Charley Finley** quite colorful, he made sure we were, too, when he introduced tricolor uniforms to the major leagues and tried to get Major League Baseball to adopt a fluorescent yellow baseball and yellow bases.

402

1 **From 1901 to 1968,** before divisional play began, we ended up in last place only once, in 1952.

2 **Though we haven't had a player win** the batting title since 1961, we have had more batting champions (22) than any other American League team except the Red Sox.

3 **When the National Baseball Hall of Fame** was created, in 1936, one of our members was the leading vote getter in the first election to choose the first inductees.

4 **When we won the World Series in 1968** over the Cardinals, one of our pitchers won three games, but it wasn't Denny McLain, who racked up a 31–6 regular season, but Mickey Lolich.

402: Detroit Tigers

400: Chicago Cubs • **401: The Philadelphia/Kansas City/Oakland Athletics** •

1 **We held the record** for most consecutive seasons avoiding a last-place finish (86). It was broken by the Cardinals in 2005.

2 **In 1941** we became the first team to require all our batters to wear plastic batting helmets.

3 **Though we've maintained a tradition of success,** we're the only team in history to lose two consecutive pennants in the last inning of the last game of the season, and no other team has lost as many World Series as we have.

4 **In 1962** we became the first team ever to have two pitchers end up first and second for most strikeouts in the same season, when Sandy Koufax and Don Drysdale turned the trick.

404

1 **In 1979 we lost 109 games,** the most ever in the American League for a 162-game schedule, until Detroit eclipsed the mark with 119 in 2003.

2 **We finished last in our division** for the six years, from 1977 to 1982, but turned it around and finished first four times between 1989 and 1993.

3 **In 1993** we set an American League home attendance record by drawing 4,057,947 fans.

4 **We won our inaugural game** amid snow flurries on April 7, 1977, when Doug Ault hit two home runs in Exhibition Stadium, our home park that year.

405

1 **The new divisional format** was created in 1969 to (it was hoped) make more exciting pennant races. For most teams this was true, but not for us; from 1969 to 1974, we finished dead last in our division.

2 **Gaylord Perry** won 21 games in 1978, leading us to our first-ever winning season, and became the second of three Cy Young Award winners in our team's history.

3 **Down two games to none** in the 1984 playoffs, we rallied behind Steve Garvey to win the pennant and the right to play the Tigers in the World Series.

4 **We were all packed and ready to move** to Washington, D.C., in 1974, when a local buyer stepped in with mucho McCash and kept us in town.

405: San Diego Padres

403: Brooklyn/Los Angeles Dodgers • **404:** Toronto Blue Jays •

1 **Of all the teams in existence before 1961,** we were the last to have a black player on our roster, a full 12 years after Jackie Robinson broke the color barrier with the Dodgers.

2 **We hold the American League record** for most consecutive seasons avoiding a last-place finish, 74, from 1933 to 2006.

3 **Our ballpark** has one of the smallest seating capacities in the majors, yet we are consistently among the leaders in attendance each year.

4 **On June 18, 1953,** against the Detroit Tigers, we sent 23 batters to the plate in one inning, scoring 17 runs. It's nice having the Green Monster on our side.

407

1 **From 1969,** when divisional play began, through 1993, when the two-division format ended, we had only four winning seasons.

2 **In 1916** we became the first major league team to put numbers on the backs of player uniforms.

3 **In the heat of the 1954 pennant race,** we attracted nearly 85,000 fans for a September doubleheader against the Yankees.

4 **After Major League Baseball** switched to its divisional format in 1969, we were the last of the existing teams to win a divisional title, in 1995, whereupon we swept the Red Sox in the Division Series and took down Seattle in the ALCS before losing in the World Series to the Braves.

408

1 **In 1979** we became the first team ever to tear out its artificial turf and replace it with natural grass.

2 Although we had one tie game along the way, we still hold the major league record for the most consecutive games won, 26 (1916). Of course, maybe the fact that all these games were played at our home park had something to do with it.

3 In 1951, just four years after Jackie Robinson broke baseball's color line, we became the first team ever to have an all-black outfield.

4 For more than 120 years, we've had the same team name, longer than any other major league team. We didn't even change it when we moved from the East Coast to the West Coast in 1958 along with the Dodgers.

406: Boston Red Sox • **407:** Cleveland Indians • **408:** New York/San Francisco Giants

WHO, WHAT, WHEN, WHERE, AND WHY

1. What's going on?

2. When did it happen?

3. Who were the Giants' opponents?

4. BONUS: What was the score of the game?

409:

1. It was the last game played at the Polo Grounds by the Giants before their move to San Francisco and the players were racing off the field, just ahead of fans who wanted a piece of Giants history, be it a piece of sod or the uniform off a player's back.

2. September 29, 1957.

3. The Pittsburgh Pirates.

4. Pittsburgh 9, New York 1.

1 **In 1965** we won the first game ever played on artificial turf, 2–1, over Houston in the Astrodome. By the way, it was an exhibition game.

2 **We're the only team ever** to have five players with 100 or more RBIs in a season.

3 **In 1941** we clinched the pennant on September 4, the earliest date ever in major league history.

4 **We hold the record** for most home runs in a season by two teammates, 115, in 1961.

411

1 **Of all the franchises in existence** since the 1961–1962 expansion, we were the last team to play in a World Series.

2 **Dean Chance pitched** a team record 11 shutouts for us in 1964. Among them were five 1–0 victories.

3 **While playing for us in 1979,** Don Baylor became the first, and so far only, designated hitter to win the AL MVP Award.

4 **From 1973 to 1975,** while playing with us, Nolan Ryan became a superstar by hurling four no-hitters and setting the modern-era record with 383 strikeouts in one season.

412

1 **We set the modern** (since 1900) major league record for most consecutive losses with 23 in 1961.

2 **We're the only team in baseball history** to have three .400 hitters (our entire outfield) in the same season, and they all made it to the Hall of Fame. Tuck Turner, one of our backup outfielders that season, also hit .416, but he didn't have enough at bats (339) to qualify for the batting championship.

3 **Before Pittsburgh** in 1990 and 1991, we were the last National League East team to win back-to-back division titles, accomplishing the feat in 1977 and 1978.

4 **We had more MVP winners** in the 1980s than any other NL team, three—and Mike Schmidt was the winner all three times.

1 **We were the last major league team** to have an owner double as a manager.

2 **Baseball went through a chaotic period** during the 19th century with many franchise changes. By 1903, the shuffling of franchises ceased. It started again in 1953, when we relocated.

3 **Before settling on our present name,** we were known as the Bees, Rustlers, Doves, Beaneaters, and Red Caps.

4 **In 1973** we became the first team in history to have three players hit 40 or more home runs in the same season, when Hank Aaron hit 40, Dave Johnson 43, and Darrell Evans 41.

414

1 **In 1969** our pitching staff struck out a then-major-league-record 1,221 opposing batters.

2 **Of all the National League teams** in existence since the 1962 expansion, we are the only team who has never had a member of the 3,000-hit club play for them.

3 **In 1979** we became the last National League team to hit more triples (52) than home runs (49).

4 **Since 1965** we've only been rained out of one home game, but it wasn't because the field got wet. Rather, it was because the streets became so flooded that fans couldn't get to the stadium.

415

1 **Other than the Colorado Rockies,** we are the only major league team in history to have two players hit at least 30 homers and steal at least 30 bases in the same season (1987).

2 **Besides the Marlins and Astros,** we are the only National League team never to have a player win the batting championship.

3 **We once won the pennant** with a .509 winning percentage, the lowest in major league history.

4 **In 1968** we finished in ninth place, just a game out of last place. With essentially the same team in 1969, we won 100 games, swept the Braves in the NLCS, and went on to crush the heavily favored Orioles in the World Series, 4–1. That's why they call us "amazing."

415: New York Mets

413: Boston/Milwaukee/Atlanta Braves • **414:** Houston Astros

1 **As a team,** we once hit .212 for the season, the lowest team batting average in the majors since 1889.

2 **You want more frustration?** We're the only team ever to have four 20-game winners in the same season, yet fail to win the pennant.

3 **Of all the current major league teams,** we went the longest—53 years (1944–1996)—without a player winning the batting title. Of course, we were known for many years as the "Hitless Wonders."

4 **In 1933** we hosted the first-ever All-Star Game. Originally planned as a one-time added exhibition for the World's Fair, it was so popular with the fans that it was made a regular affair. It also helped reduce lingering bad feelings over our thrown World Series in 1919.

417

NAME THAT YEAR

Seven clues. One year. See how few clues it takes you to guess the year.

1 **For the first time in history,** pitchers sweep the NL and AL MVP Awards.

2 **Also for the first time in history,** two Cy Young Award winners face each other in the World Series, although they weren't yet announced at the time of the matchup.

3 **Catfish Hunter of the A's** pitches a perfect game against Minnesota.

4 **Bob Gibson sets a World Series record** with 17 strikeouts in one game.

5 **The first indoor All-Star Game** is played, and the NL prevails, 1–0.

6 **In what becomes known as the Year of the Pitcher,** Carl Yastrzemski is the only hitter in the AL to top .300, finishing at .301.

7 **Denny McLain goes 31–6** for the Detroit Tigers.

1 **Ted Williams** managed us for only one year before Whitey Herzog took over, making his managerial debut.

2 **Ferguson Jenkins** holds our team's record for most wins in a season, with 25.

3 **Our second best season ever** was 1977, when we won 94 games, yet we had four different managers—Frank Lucchesi, Eddie Stanky, Connie Ryan, and Billy Hunter.

4 **We haven't always been located** in our current city. We became a major league team in 1961, when the original Washington Senators moved to Minnesota and we replaced them.

419

1 **We were the only World Series team** in history to lose the first two games at home and still come back to win the Series, until the Yankees performed the same feat in 1996.

2 **Not only are we the most successful** of all the 1960s expansion teams from 1971 to 1989, but we were one of the most successful teams in all of baseball, finishing first or second in our division 15 times.

3 **The last time we won our division was 1985,** when we won the ALCS and the World Series.

4 **In 1980,** not only did we win our first pennant, but we also got to watch George Brett chase the .400 mark all year before he finally finished at .390.

420

1 **Until 1999,** we were the only team in major league history never to have played a home game outdoors.

2 **In 2006,** one of our former players hit a home run in St. Louis's new Busch Stadium, giving him a home run in 43 ballparks, including every one currently in use. This tied him with Fred McGriff as the only two players ever to do so.

3 **As a member of our team,** Floyd Bannister led the league with 209 strikeouts in 1982. When Harold Reynolds led the league with 60 stolen bases in 1987, it marked the first time in our team's history that one of our players led in an offensive category.

4 **1990 was an especially exciting year** for two of our players. For the first time in major league history, a father and son played in the same game for the same team.

418: Texas Rangers • **419:** Kansas City Royals • **420:** Seattle Mariners

WHO, WHAT, WHEN, WHERE, AND WHY

1. **Who** are these guys?

2. **What** miraculous feat did they accomplish?

3. **What** year?

4. **Where** were they in the National League standings
   on July 4 of that year?

4. Last place.

3. 1914.

2. Winning the NL pennant by 10.5 games after trailing at one point by 15.5.

1. The Boston Braves.

421:

218

TEAMS

MISCELLANEOUS

See if you can match the teams with their former ballparks.

1. St. Louis Cardinals   **A. Forbes Field**

2. Pittsburgh Pirates   **B. Navin Field**

3. Detroit Tigers   **C. Municipal Stadium**

4. Houston Astros   **D. Sportsman's Park**

5. Minnesota Twins   **E. Colt Stadium**

6. Cleveland Indians   **F. Jarry Park**

7. Montreal Expos   **G. Metropolitan Stadium**

Too easy, you say? Okay, try to pair these teams and the former names of one of their ballparks.

1. Boston Red Sox   **A. Bank Street Grounds**

2. Los Angeles Angels   **B. Wrigley Field**

3. Chicago Cubs   **C. National League Park**

4. Cincinnati Reds   **D. American League Park**

5. Washington Senators   **E. Huntington Avenue Grounds**

6. New York Yankees   **F. Shea Stadium**

7. Philadelphia Phillies   **G. Brotherhood Park**

424

Still not challenged? Match up this list of former major league teams with these former ballparks.

1. Wilmington Quick Steps   **A. Washington Park**

2. St. Paul Apostles   **B. Olympic Park**

3. Kansas City Cowboys   **C. Athletic Park**

4. Altoona Mountain Cities   **D. Columbia Park**

5. Buffalo Bisons   **E. Exposition Park**

6. Brooklyn Tip Tops   **F. Union Association Park**

7. Pittsburgh Rebels   **G. No park; played all their games on the road**

424: 1-F, 2-G, 3-C, 4-D, 5-B, 6-A, 7-E

423: 1-E, 2-B, 3-G, 4-A, 5-D, 6-F, 7-C •

422: 1-D, 2-A, 3-B, 4-E, 5-G, 6-C, 7-F •

Do you know which American League clubs are responsible for these feats?

1. Winner, 7–6, of longest-ever AL game, 25 innings

2. Most tie games played in one season—10

3. Hosted the first-ever Opening *Night* game

4. First AL team ever to suffer a shutout

5. Most consecutive wins at the start of a season—13

6. Most games lost in one month—29

7. Largest single-day attendance in AL history

A. Tigers

B. Red Sox

C. Senators

D. Indians

E. White Sox

F. Athletics

G. Brewers

426

This time match National League club with their feats.

1. Lost the most games in NL history

2. Most consecutive games won in a season—26

3. Won the most games in NL history

4. Hosted the first-ever Sunday game

5. Hosted the first-ever Ladies Day Promotion

6. Lost the NL's longest-ever *decided* game, 4–3, in 25 innings

7. Won the longest-ever 1–0 game, 24 innings, in 1968

A. Reds

B. Astros

C. Cubs

D. Cardinals

E. Giants

F. Phillies

G. Mets

Match these former major league teams with the city where each group of teams once played.

1. Potato Bugs, Stogies, Zulus, Innocents, Burghers   **A. Chicago**

2. Blue Jays, Keystones, Whites, Quakers, Athletics   **B. Boston**

3. Rustlers, Doves, Speedboys, Puritans, Pilgrims   **C. Cleveland**

4. Terriers, Miners, Perfectos, Maroons, Brown Stockings   **D. Pittsburgh**

5. Whales, Browns, Babes, Pirates, Orphans   **E. New York**

6. Highlanders, Hilltoppers, Mutuals, Metropolitans, Gothams   **F. St. Louis**

7. Naps, Infants, Spiders, Broncos, Bluebirds   **G. Philadelphia**

428

NAME THAT YEAR

Seven clues. One year. See how few clues it takes you to guess the year.

1 **For the only time in history,** two players tie for a league MVP Award.

2 **Rotisserie baseball is born** when Daniel Okrent pens the first rules of the now hugely popular pastime.

3 **The Cubs blow a 21–9 lead** in a May 17 game and lose to the Phillies, 23–22.

4 **Hall of Famer Bruce Sutter** wins the NL Cy Young Award.

5 **Shortly after the season ends,** Nolan Ryan becomes the first $1-million-a-year player.

6 **Manager Joe Torre of the Mets** ends up in the cellar for the third straight year.

7 **Willie Stargell and his "Pirate family"** defeat the Orioles in the World Series.

HE SAID
IT ALL

WHO, WHAT, WHEN, WHERE, AND WHY

1. **Who** is this man?

2. **What's** he about to embark upon?

3. **When?**

4. **Where's** he standing?

5. **BONUS:** What team did he manage the year before?

429:

1. Hall of Famer Casey Stengel.

2. His career as Yankee manager.

3. On the eve of the 1949 season.

4. In an empty Yankee Stadium.

5. The Oakland Oaks of the Pacific Coast League, for whom he was named Minor League Manager of the Year in 1948.

430

In these next twelve games, we'll show you a group of quotations all uttered by the same person. Try to guess who said them, using the fewest number of clues.

1 **"I regret to this day** that I never went to college. I feel I should have been a doctor."

2 **"To get along with me,** don't increase my tension."

3 **"When I began playing the game,** baseball was about as gentlemanly as a kick in the crotch."

4 **"That god-damned Dutchman** [Honus Wagner] is the only man in the game I can't scare."

431

1 **"All ballplayers should quit** when it starts to feel as if the baselines run uphill."

2 **"I won't be happy** until we have every boy in America between the ages of six and sixteen wearing a glove and swinging a bat."

3 **"Paris ain't much of a town."**

4 **"I'd play for half my salary** if I could hit in this dump [Wrigley Field] all the time."

5 **"Hot as hell,** ain't it, Prez?"

432

1 **"My speed's not bad.** I'm no Joe Morgan, but I'm pretty good for a white guy."

2 **"I'd walk through Hell** in a gasoline suit to play baseball."

3 **"Tony [Perez],** how can anyone as slow as you pull a muscle?"

4 **"Don Gullett** is the only guy I know who can throw a baseball through a car wash and not get the ball wet."

5 **"I slide headfirst** because it gets my picture in the paper."

430: Ty Cobb • **431:** Babe Ruth • **432:** Pete Rose

433

1 **"So many ideas** come to you when you're slumping, that you want to try them all, but you can't. You're like a mosquito in a nudist camp. You don't know where to start."

2 **"Please, God,** let me hit one. I'll tell everybody you did it."

3 **"When you've played this game** for ten years and gone to bat seven thousand times and gotten two thousand hits, do you know what that really means? It means you've gone zero for five thousand."

4 **"I didn't come to New York to be a star.** I brought my star with me."

5 **"I'm the straw** that stirs the drink."

434

1 **"Just take the ball** and throw it where you want to. Throw strikes. Home plate don't move."

2 **"I never threw an illegal pitch.** The trouble is, once in a while I toss one that ain't never been seen by this generation."

3 **"My pitching philosophy** is simple: keep the ball away from the bat."

4 **"One time,** Cool Papa Bell hit a line drive right past my ear. I turned around and saw the ball hit his ass sliding into second."

5 **"How old would you** be if you didn't know how old you were?"

435

1 **"Being with a woman** all night never hurt no professional baseball player. It's staying up all night looking for a woman that does him in."

2 **"I was such a dangerous hitter** I even got intentional walks during batting practice."

3 **"You have to go broke three times** to learn how to make a living."

4 **"Been in this game one hundred years,** but I see new ways to lose 'em I never knew existed before."

5 **"The Yankees** don't pay me to win every day, just two out of three."

433: Reggie Jackson • **434:** Satchel Paige • **435:** Casey Stengel

1. "**I can see how Koufax** won twenty-five games. What I don't understand is how he lost five."

2. "**All pitchers** are either liars or crybabies."

3. "**I never** said most of the things I said."

4. "**Nobody goes there** anymore because it's too crowded."

5. "**The game ain't over** till it's over."

437

1. "**Give me some scratching,** diving, hungry ballplayers who come to kill you."

2. "**If you don't win,** you're going to be fired. If you do win, you've only put off the day you're going to be fired."

3. "**I never questioned** the integrity of an umpire. Their eyesight, yes."

4. "**You don't save a pitcher for tomorrow.** Tomorrow it may rain."

5. "**Nice guys finish last.**"

438

1. "**The good Lord was good to me.** He gave me a strong body, a good right arm, and a weak mind."

2. "**The dumber a pitcher is,** the better. When he gets smart and begins to experiment with a lot of different pitches, he's in trouble."

3. "**Anyone who's ever had the privilege** of seeing me play knows that I am the greatest pitcher in the world."

4. "**Slud is something more than slid.** It means sliding with great effort."

1 "**About the only problem with success** is that it does not teach you how to deal with failure."

2 "**Darryl Strawberry is not a dog;** a dog is loyal and runs after balls."

3 "**I walk into the clubhouse** and it's like walking into the Mayo Clinic. We have four doctors, three therapists, and five trainers. Back when I broke in, we had one trainer who carried a bottle of rubbing alcohol, and by the seventh inning he had drunk it all."

4 "**When we win,** I'm so happy, I eat a lot. When we lose, I'm so depressed, I eat a lot. When we're rained out, I'm so disappointed, I eat a lot."

5 "**Say 'Dodgers'** and people know you're talking about baseball. Say 'Braves' and they ask, 'What reservation?' Say 'Reds' and they think of communism. Say 'Padres' and they look around for a priest."

440

1 "**You never ask why** you've been fired, because if you do, they're liable to tell you."

2 "**There's someone warming up** in the bullpen, but he's obscured by his number."

3 "**Graig Nettles leaped** up to make one of those diving stops only he can make."

4 "**He slides into second** with a stand-up double."

5 "**Those amateur umpires** are sure flexing their fangs tonight."

6 "**Winfield goes back to the wall,** he hits his head on the wall and it rolls off! It's rolling all the way back to second base. This is a terrible thing for the Padres."

441

1 "**I signed with the Milwaukee Braves** for three thousand dollars. That bothered my dad at the time because he didn't have that kind of dough. But he eventually scraped it up."

2 "**They said I was such a great prospect** that they were sending me to a winter league to sharpen up. When I stepped off the plane, I was in Greenland."

439: Tommy Lasorda • **440:** Jerry Coleman, longtime Padres announcer

3 **"Career highlights?** I had three. I got an intentional walk from Sandy Koufax, I got out of a rundown against the Mets, and in '67 with St. Louis, I walked with the bases loaded to drive in the winning run in an intersquad game in spring training."

4 **"In 1962** I was named Minor League Player of the Year. It was my second year in the bigs."

5 **"Baseball hasn't forgotten me.** I go to a lot of Old Timers games and I haven't lost a thing. I sit in the bullpen and let people throw things at me. Just like old times."

442

NAME THAT YEAR

Seven clues. One year. See how few clues it takes you to guess the year.

1 **Upset over losing his salary dispute** with the White Sox, bat-control artist Luke Appling decides to get even, and fouls off 400 balls into the stands through the first two weeks of the season, until manager Jimmy Dykes convinces him to stop.

2 **Lefty Grove's 20-game winning streak** comes to an end.

3 **Twenty-two-year-old Pete Reiser** becomes the youngest player ever to win a National League batting title when he hits .343.

4 **Dodgers lose Game 4** of the World Series when catcher Mickey Owen commits his famous missed third strike with two out in the ninth inning.

5 **Jimmie Foxx collects 100 RBIs** for a record-tying 13th straight season.

6 **Arky Vaughn becomes the first player** ever to hit two homers in an All-Star Game.

7 **Ted Williams hits .406** and Joe DiMaggio hits safely in 56 straight games.

WHO, WHAT, WHEN, WHERE, AND WHY

1. Who are these two players?

2. What is significant about this moment?

3. When did it take place?

4. Why was the player on the left in a Philadelphia A's uniform?

443:

1. Hall of Famers Ty Cobb and Babe Ruth.

2. It was the last year the two greats met on the field.

3. 1928.

4. Cobb was unceremoniously traded from the Tigers to the A's after the 1926 season, following allegations that he had taken part in game-fixing years before.

PLAYERS

MISCELLANEOUS

See if you can match up these players with the teams on which they ended their careers.

1. Enos Slaughter	**A. Braves**
2. Warren Spahn	**B. Senators**
3. Don Newcombe	**C. Giants**
4. Roger Maris	**D. Cardinals**
5. Curt Flood	**E. Mets**
6. Orlando Cepeda	**F. Royals**
7. Yogi Berra	**G. Indians**

445

1 **On July 23, 1964,** I became the second major league player in the 20th century to hit two home runs in my first major league game, including one on the very first pitch I saw.

2 **In 1968 I stole 62 bases,** an all-time record for American League shortstops.

3 **I was always a versatile player.** On September 9, 1965, in one of owner Charles O. Finley's numerous publicity stunts, I became the first player in major league history to play all nine positions in a nine-inning game.

4 **As the leadoff hitter** for the Oakland A's during the team's dynasty years, I led the American League in stolen bases six times, retiring with 649 career steals.

446

1 **I hold the career record** for the most runs batted in (1,314) without ever having had a 100-RBI season. In fact, my personal best was 82, in 1969.

2 **In 1975,** in more than 750 trips to the plate as my team's leadoff hitter, I failed to steal even one base, and that's still a record.

3 **Only one player in history,** Joe DiMaggio, has hit safely in more consecutive games than I have. I gave his 56-game hitting streak a run for its money in 1978 with my nice 44-game streak.

4 **On September 11, 1985,** I collected my 4,192nd career hit, eclipsing Ty Cobb's record—a record that baseball experts had been saying for decades would never be broken.

444: 1-A, 2-C, 3-G, 4-D, 5-B, 6-F, 7-E • **445:** Bert Campaneris • **446:** Pete Rose

1 **Even though I was tragically limited** in my ability to deal with others (especially my Philadelphia teammates), I was supremely gifted in baseball abilities. I could run, throw, hit, and hit with power. My .356 lifetime batting average is third best of all time.

2 **The best years of my career** were spent with Cleveland, and I still hold a number of Indians team records, including most hits in a season (233), most triples in a season (26), and highest batting average for a career (.375).

3 **Using my famous bat,** "Black Betsy," I hit .408 in my first full season in the majors, and that's a record that will likely never be broken.

4 **Some folks feel I was unfairly banished** from baseball for life by Judge Landis after the infamous Black Sox scandal broke late in 1920. After all, I hit .375 for the Chicago White Sox in the 1919 World Series, and committed no errors—and kept my shoes on, to boot.

448

1 **Billy Hatcher** and I are the only two players in major league history to collect seven consecutive hits in World Series play.

2 **Moving to the majors** after a very brief minor league career, I hit .302, and in the process won the American League's Rookie of the Year Award in 1970.

3 **Until the arrival of Ivan Rodriguez,** I was the only catcher since World War II to hit over .300 for five seasons. As an appreciation for my spirited leadership, my Yankee teammates voted me the team's first captain since Lou Gehrig.

4 **On August 2, 1979,** I died when the private plane I was piloting crashed in Canton, Ohio.

449

1 **Besides Mickey Mantle,** I am the only switch-hitter in American League history to win the Most Valuable Player Award.

2 **Just 22 years old** when I won my MVP Award in 1971, I am still the youngest player in history ever to capture the prize.

3 **Life was exciting** with the Oakland A's in those days. In 1976, Charley Finley tried to sell me outright to the Cincinnati Reds for a few million dollars, but Commissioner Bowie Kuhn stepped in and voided the deal. Crazy Charlie even offered me money to change my first name to "True."

4 **I guess Kuhn didn't want** to see the Big Red Machine pick up the first black American League pitcher to win a Cy Young Award and the only pitcher ever to start the All-Star Game for both leagues (1971 for the AL and 1978 for the NL).

447: Shoeless Joe Jackson • **448:** Thurman Munson • **449:** Vida Blue

1 **I share the record** for the most World Series losses by a pitcher without a win (0–4) with Ed Summers, Bill Sherdel, and Charlie Leibrandt, and my World Series ERA of 8.59 is the worst ever by a pitcher with at least 20 innings pitched.

2 **When Bobby Thomson** hit his famous "Shot Heard 'Round the World" home run to win the 1951 pennant for the Giants, I was the Dodger pitcher who took a 4–2 lead into the bottom of the ninth, only to see it slip away.

3 **I was the first pitcher** ever to win the Cy Young Award.

4 **I joined the Brooklyn Dodgers** in 1949 after playing in the Negro leagues. I'm still the only player ever to win all three of baseball's major awards—Rookie of the Year, Cy Young, and MVP.

451

When a ballplayer signs a contract that sets a new salary record, it always makes the news. See if you can match up the players with their record-setting salaries.

1. First to break $50,000 per year

2. First to break $100,000 per year

3. First to break $500,000 per year

4. First to break $1 million per year

5. First to break $2 million per year

6. First to break $3 million per year

7. First to break $4 million per year

A. Nolan Ryan

B. Hank Greenberg

C. Kirby Puckett

D. Mike Schmidt

E. Jose Canseco

F. Babe Ruth

G. George Foster

452

And now for the really big bucks . . .

1. First to break $5 million per year

2. First to break $6/$7 million per year

3. First to break $8 million per year

A. Ken Griffey Jr.

B. Carlos Delgado

C. Mike Piazza

450: Don Newcombe • 451: 1-F, 2-B, 3-D, 4-A, 5-G, 6-C, 7-E

4. First to break $9/$10/$11 million per year

5. First to break $12 million per year

6. First to break $13 million per year

7. First to break $14/$15 million per year

8. First to break $16/$17 million per year

9. First to break $18/$19/$20 million per year

10. First to break $21, $22, $23, $24, $25, $26, and $27 million per year

D. Alex Rodriguez

E. Ryne Sandberg

F. Albert Belle

G. Manny Ramirez

H. Kevin Brown

I. Roger Clemens

J. Pedro Martinez

453

NAME THAT YEAR

Seven clues. One year. See how few clues it takes you to guess the year.

1 **Commissioner Bowie Kuhn orders Mickey Mantle** to sever all ties to major league baseball because of his business connections to an Atlantic City casino.

2 **Steve Garvey's consecutive game streak ends** at 1,207 when he injures his thumb while trying to score on a wild pitch.

3 **In baseball's 50th All-Star Game,** the AL ends the NL's 11-game winning streak with an 11–3 pasting of the senior league stars.

4 **Fernando Valenzuela becomes the first player** in history to be awarded a $1-million-a-year contract through the arbitration process.

5 **Dale Murphy of the Braves** wins his second consecutive NL MVP Award.

6 **Dave Winfield accidentally kills a seagull** with a warm-up throw before a game in Toronto and is arrested for killing a Canadian endangered species.

7 **The Orioles defeat the Phillies** in a five-game World Series in which Pete Rose, 42, the oldest regular player in Fall Classic history, hits .313.

WHO, WHAT, WHEN, WHERE, AND WHY

1. Who is this player?

2. What was he the first National League player since 1930 to *almost* do?

3. When did he do *almost* do it?

4. Where can blame be laid for his falling short?

454:

1. Hall of Famer Tony Gwynn.

2. Hit .400 in a season. (He hit .394.)

3. 1994.

4. The players' strike, which ended the season prematurely.

TEAM BY TEAM

Keep in mind that franchises have moved around. Take, for example, the Atlanta Braves, who were at different times located in both Boston and Milwaukee. The clues could refer to any of the three cities.

455

Atlanta Braves.

1. Alvin Dark — **A. The only Brave in the last 110 years to win more than one batting championship**

2. Bob Elliott — **B. The only Brave to win a Triple Crown**

3. Hugh Duffy — **C. Of all Braves batting champs since 1900, his average was the highest—.387**

4. Fred McGriff — **D. First Brave to win the Rookie of the Year Award**

5. Hank Aaron — **E. The only Brave to be the MVP of the All-Star Game**

6. Rogers Hornsby — **F. The only Brave first baseman ever to win a Gold Glove**

7. Felix Milan — **G. First Brave to win the NL MVP Award**

456

1. Terry Pendleton — **A. Most extra-base hits in one season—92**

2. Billy Hamilton — **B. Highest batting average for a Braves career—.338**

3. Andruw Jones — **C. The only Brave since 1972 to win a Gold Glove at a position other than pitcher or outfielder**

4. Rabbit Maranville — **D. Struck out more times than any other Brave during his career—1,581**

5. Hank Aaron — **E. The only Brave with more than 100 career triples (103)**

6. Herman Long — **F. Most career stolen bases with the Braves—431**

7. Dale Murphy — **G. Most home runs in a season—51**

457

1. Warren Spahn — **A. First Braves pitcher to win a Gold Glove**

2. Greg Maddux — **B. Had the fewest wins (16) of any Braves Cy Young Award winner**

455: 1-D, 2-G, 3-B, 4-E, 5-A, 6-C, 7-F • **456:** 1-C, 2-B, 3-G, 4-E, 5-A, 6-F, 7-D

3. Tom Glavine   **C. First Brave to be a World Series MVP**

4. John Smoltz   **D. Had the most wins (24) during his Cy Young year**

5. Phil Niekro   **E. The only Brave with two career Cy Young Awards**

6. Lew Burdette   **F. The last Braves pitcher to toss a no-hitter**

7. Kent Mercker   **G. The only Brave to record some saves during his Cy Young year**

458

1. Mike Hampton   **A. The only Braves pitcher with two career *complete-game* no-hitters . . . and in consecutive seasons**

2. Greg Maddux   **B. Holds Braves record for career games pitched—740**

3. Warren Spahn   **C. Best career WHIP (ratio of walks plus hits per inning pitched) with the Braves—1.022**

4. Phil Niekro   **D. Holds Braves record for shutouts in a season—11**

5. Tommy Bond   **E. The only Braves pitcher ever to have two seasons with an ERA below 2.00 (1.56 and 1.63)**

6. John Clarkson   **F. The last Braves pitcher to win a Gold Glove**

7. Tom Hughes   **G. Most games won in a season—49**

459

1. 2000   **A. The last time the Braves lost 100 games in a season**

2. 1999   **B. The only year the Braves were swept in the World Series of the nine times they played in the Fall Classic**

3. 1989   **C. Of four All-Star Games hosted by the Braves, the only year the National League lost the game**

4. 1996   **D. The last time a Brave won a batting title**

5. 1991   **E. The year in which a second consecutive—but different—Braves pitcher won the Cy Young Award**

6. 1993   **F. The last time the Braves won the NL West title**

7. 2005   **G. The last time a Brave won the NL home run title**

459: 1-C, 2-B, 3-A, 4-E, 5-D, 6-F, 7-G

458: 1-F, 2-E, 3-A, 4-B, 5-D, 6-G, 7-C • **457:** 1-G, 2-B, 3-E, 4-D, 5-A, 6-C, 7-F •

1. 1914
2. 1957
3. 1983
4. 1998
5. 1935
6. 1953
7. 1906

A. The Braves set their team record for most consecutive losses—19

B. The Braves set their team record for wins in a season—106

C. The only year in which a Braves player won his second consecutive MVP Award

D. The only year in which the Braves featured eight .300 hitters

E. The only season in nine World Series appearances that the Braves swept their opponent four straight

F. Year the Braves set their team record for losses in a season—115

G. The only season in nine World Series appearances that the Braves won in seven games

461

Baltimore Orioles. (Note: The franchise was also located in Milwaukee and St. Louis.)

1. Brooks Robinson
2. Cal Ripken Jr.
3. George Sisler
4. Roy Sievers
5. Frank Robinson
6. Rick Dempsey
7. Bobby Wallace

A. First eventual Hall of Famer ever to manage the team

B. The only Oriole to win more than one MVP Award

C. The last Oriole to be a World Series MVP

D. The only Oriole to hit for the cycle *twice*

E. Team's first-ever Rookie of the Year

F. The only Oriole ever to win a Triple Crown

G. The first to win an AL MVP Award

Baseball Trivia

462

1. George Sisler	**A. The team's last batting champion**
2. Frank Robinson	**B. The team's last home run champion**
3. George Stone	**C. The only Oriole to be a two-time All-Star Game MVP**
4. Ken Williams	**D. The team's first batting champion**
5. Eddie Murray	**E. The team's first home run champion**
6. Brooks Robinson	**F. The team's only two-time batting champion**
7. Cal Ripken Jr.	**G. First Oriole to win a Gold Glove**

463

1. Jim Palmer	**A. The last Oriole to lead the AL in ERA for a season**
2. Steve Stone	**B. The last Oriole to pitch a *complete-game* no-hitter**
3. Mike Cuellar	**C. Pitched the team's first-ever no-hitter**
4. Gregg Olson	**D. The last Oriole to win the AL Cy Young Award**
5. Bob Turley	**E. First Oriole to win a Cy Young Award**
6. Mike Boddicker	**F. The last Oriole to lead the AL in strikeouts for a season**
7. Earl Hamilton	**G. Team's last Rookie of the Year**

464

1. Mike Boddicker	**A. The only Oriole to *lose* a no-hitter (pitched first 8.2 innings of combined no-hitter)**
2. Steve Barber	**B. The last 20-game winner for the Orioles**
3. Mike Mussina	**C. Holds team record with 17 consecutive wins**
4. Urban Shocker	**D. The last Orioles pitcher to win a Gold Glove**
5. Dave McNally	**E. First Orioles pitcher to win the AL ERA title—2.19**
6. Hoyt Wilhelm	**F. Holds team record for wins in a season—27**
7. Jim Palmer	**G. First Orioles pitcher ever to win a Gold Glove**

464: 1-B, 2-A, 3-D, 4-F, 5-C, 6-E, 7-G

463: 1-B, 2-D, 3-E, 4-G, 5-F, 6-A, 7-C • **462:** 1-F, 2-A, 3-D, 4-E, 5-B, 6-G, 7-C •

WHO, WHAT, WHEN, WHERE, AND WHY

1. Who are these guys?

2. What had they just done?

3. When?

4. Why?

5. What automobile dealer led a group to prevent what happened in question 4?

465:

1. Hall of Famers Eddie Mathews and Hank Aaron.

2. Played their last home game as Milwaukee Braves.

3. September 22, 1965.

4. The team relocated to Atlanta for the 1966 season.

5. Bud Selig, now the commissioner of Major League Baseball.

242

1. 1969	A. The last time the Orioles won 100 games in a season
2. 1980	B. The Orioles set their team record for most consecutive losses—21
3. 1944	C. The Orioles set their team record for losses in a season—111
4. 1983	D. The team won their first pennant
5. 1939	E. The year the team won the second of their three *consecutive* pennants
6. 1970	F. The Orioles set their team record for wins in a season—109
7. 1988	G. The team won their last pennant

467

1. 1922	A. The year one member of the team put together a 41-game hitting streak, still the team record
2. 1997	B. First season the Orioles featured four Gold Glove winners
3. 1910	C. The only year the Orioles won the Wild Card berth in the playoffs since division play began
4. 1969	D. The team hit .218, their worst average ever
5. 1996	E. The Orioles ended their season by shutting out their opponents in five straight games
6. 1980	F. The Orioles were in first place every day of the season
7. 1995	G. The year an Orioles pitcher won the Cy Young Award in his last full season in the major leagues

Boston Red Sox.

1. Ted Williams   **A. Last Triple Crown winner**

2. Carl Yastrzemski   **B. Boston's first Rookie of the Year**

3. Manny Ramirez   **C. Boston's last Rookie of the Year**

4. Nomar Garciaparra   **D. The only Red Sox outfielder to be Rookie of the Year**

5. Fred Lynn   **E. First Red Sox Gold Glove winner**

6. Frank Malzone   **F. A two-time Triple Crown winner for the Red Sox**

7. Walt Dropo   **G. Boston's only World Series MVP**

469

1. Jason Varitek   **A. The last Red Sox batting champion**

2. Dwight Evans   **B. The only Boston player besides David Ortiz to be a League Championship Series MVP**

3. Marty Barrett   **C. The last Red Sox batting champion to win back-to-back batting titles**

4. Tony Armas   **D. The only Red Sox Gold Glover between 1992 and 2005**

5. Dale Alexander   **E. First Red Sox batting champion**

6. Bill Mueller   **F. The only Red Sox player to win five straight Gold Gloves**

7. Nomar Garciaparra   **G. The last Red Sox AL home run champ before Manny Ramirez in 2004**

470

1. Pedro Martinez   **A. Retired all 27 batters he faced, but is not credited with a perfect game**

2. Dick Radatz   **B. Boston's first Cy Young Award winner**

3. Don Schwall   **C. Boston's last All-Star Game MVP**

4. Jim Lonborg   **D. The only Boston pitcher to win AL MVP Award**

5. Roger Clemens   E. The only 20-game winner for Boston during the 1950s (he was 21–8)

6. Mel Parnell   F. The only pitcher to win Rookie of the Year for Red Sox

7. Ernie Shore   G. Boston's only two-time Fireman of the Year

471

1. Cy Young   A. Of the three Boston pitchers in team history to win four ERA titles, he took the most years (seven) to win his

2. Babe Ruth   B. The first pitcher in major league history to appear in eight games in eight days

3. Roger Clemens   C. The only Red Sox pitcher from 1902 to 1966 to lead the AL in strikeouts for a season

4. Tex Hughson   D. The only Red Sox pitcher to lead the AL in ERA from 1950 to 1985

5. Luis Tiant   E. The Red Sox pitcher with the most 20-win seasons—6

6. Mike Fornieles   F. When he won his ERA title, he was the third consecutive Red Sox player to win the title

7. Ben Flowers   G. Boston's first Fireman of the Year Award winner

472

1. 1965   A. The Red Sox lost a team record 20 straight games

2. 1966   B. The last year the Red Sox won 100 games in a season

3. 1946   C. The last time the Red Sox were managed by either a Hall of Famer or someone who would become a Hall of Famer

4. 1932   D. The Red Sox sported a batting champion who didn't even have a regular position in the field

5. 1912   E. The Red Sox set their team record for most wins in a season—105

6. 1906   F. The Red Sox set their team record for losses in a season—111

7. 1950   G. The last year when the Red Sox lost 100 games in a season

472: 1-G, 2-C, 3-B, 4-F, 5-E, 6-A, 7-D

• **471:** 1-E, 2-F, 3-A, 4-C, 5-D, 6-G, 7-B •

470: 1-C, 2-G, 3-F, 4-B, 5-D, 6-E, 7-A

1. 1912

A. The last year the Red Sox finished with the worst record in the American League

2. 1941

B. A Red Sox pitcher became the only one in major league history to win 20 straight home games

3. 1918

C. The last year the Red Sox had the best regular-season record in the major leagues

4. 1932

D. Boston hurlers fired a team-record 26 shutouts

5. 1946

E. Boston became the first team in major league history to have all four infielders rack up back-to-back seasons of 20 or more home runs

6. 1950

F. The only year since 1904 that the Red Sox have featured three 20-game winners in the same season

7. 1940

G. Boston hit .302 as a team and had nine .300 hitters

Chicago Cubs.

1. Jimmy Ryan

A. The most recent Cub to win the NL MVP Award

2. Gabby Hartnett

B. The only Cubs player to hit for the cycle twice

3. Ernie Banks

C. The only Cub to win back-to-back batting titles

4. Sammy Sosa

D. The last batting champ before Derrek Lee in 2005

5. Billy Williams

E. The first Cub to win the NL MVP Award

6. Bill Buckner

F. The only Cubs player to win two MVP Awards

7. Bill Madlock

G. The first Cub to win a Rookie of the Year Award

473: 1-F, 2-B, 3-D, 4-A, 5-C, 6-G, 7-E • **474:** 1-B, 2-E, 3-F, 4-A, 5-G, 6-D, 7-C

WHO, WHAT, WHEN, WHERE, AND WHY

1. Who is this player?

2. Which major league record of his still stands today?

3. When did he accomplish it?

4. Why did his hometown fans pelt him with lemons throughout his record-breaking season?

475:

1. Hall of Famer Hack Wilson.

2. Most RBIs in a season—191.

3. 1930.

4. Because they were still angry with him over losing two fly balls in the sun during the 1929 World Series in which the Cubs were beaten by the A's.

476

1. King Kelly	**A. The first Cub to win back-to-back home run titles**
2. Ken Hubbs	**B. The first Cubs player to win an NL home run title**
3. Frank Chance	**C. The first two-time Cub batting champion**
4. Ned Williamson	**D. The only Cubs infielder to win a Rookie of the Year Award**
5. Hack Wilson	**E. The player-manager who led the Cubs to four 100-win seasons**
6. Frank Schulte	**F. The last Cubs infielder to win an NL home run title**
7. Ryne Sandberg	**G. The Cub who won the most home run titles—4**

477

1. Ferguson Jenkins	**A. The last Cubs pitcher to win the Cy Young Award**
2. Kerry Wood	**B. The last Cub to pitch a no-hitter**
3. Larry Corcoran	**C. The first Cub to win the NL Cy Young Award**
4. Milt Pappas	**D. Pitched three no-hitters for Chicago**
5. Greg Maddux	**E. The last Cub to both win and lose 20 games in the same year**
6. Ken Holtzman	**F. The only Cubs pitcher to win the NL Rookie of the Year Award**
7. Bill Hutchinson	**G. The only Cub with two 20th-century no-hitters**

478

1. Grover Alexander	**A. The only Cub to win two Fireman of the Year Awards**
2. Hank Borowy	**B. The first Cub to win the Fireman of the Year Award**
3. Kerry Wood	**C. Player who won the Cy Young Award while pitching for two teams in his Cy Young year (16–1 with the Cubs, 4–5 with the other team)**
4. Sam Jones	**D. The last Cubs pitcher to win back-to-back NL strikeout titles**

Baseball Trivia

5. Lindy McDaniel   **E. The last Cubs pitcher to win the NL strikeout crown**

6. Rick Sutcliffe   **F. The only Cubs pitcher to win two ERA titles (he won them in consecutive years)**

7. Randy Myers   **G. The last Cubs pitcher to win the NL ERA title**

479

1. 1935   **A. The last time the Cubs won at least 100 games**

2. 1966   **B. The only year a Cub won the All-Star Game MVP Award**

3. 1912   **C. The second of the only two years in which the Cubs skipper was named the Manager of the Year**

4. 1975   **D. The last time the Cubs lost at least 100 games**

5. 1989   **E. The only year the Cubs featured eight .300 hitters**

6. 1906   **F. The only year to feature a Cubs Triple Crown winner**

7. 1921   **G. The Cubs set the team record for wins in a season (116)**

480

1. 1945   **A. The team somehow stuffed 51,556 fans into a Wrigley Field game to set their one-game record**

2. 1876   **B. The last season the Cubs won the National League pennant**

3. 1908   **C. The Cubs' pitching staff set a new NL record for strikeouts in a season, 1,344, shattering the old record of 1,245 set by the Braves**

4. 1892   **D. The Cubs won their third straight NL pennant**

5. 1930   **E. The Cubs repeated as World Series champs**

6. 1906   **F. The Cubs were 26–3 in August (no second-half swoon here!)**

7. 2001   **G. The last time a Cubs pitcher won 30 games in a season**

480: 1-B, 2-E, 3-D, 4-G, 5-A, 6-F, 7-C

• **479:** 1-A, 2-D, 3-F, 4-B, 5-C, 6-G, 7-E • **478:** 1-F, 2-G, 3-E, 4-D, 5-B, 6-C, 7-A

Chicago White Sox.

1. Frank Thomas   **A. The only two-time batting champ in White Sox history**

2. Nellie Fox   **B. The first White Sox player to win the AL MVP Award**

3. Luis Aparicio   **C. The only White Sox player to hit for the cycle from 1901 to 1976**

4. Ozzie Guillen   **D. The only White Sox player ever to win back-to-back MVP Awards**

5. Luke Appling   **E. The first White Sox player to win the AL Rookie of the Year Award**

6. Ray Schalk   **F. The former player-manager who became a Hall of Famer**

7. Clark Griffith   **G. The most recent White Sox Rookie of the Year**

482

1. Frank Thomas   **A. The only White Sox player to be an LCS MVP**

2. Jermaine Dye   **B. The last White Sox batting champion**

3. Paul Konerko   **C. He set the AL record with RBIs in 13 straight games**

4. Carlos Lee   **D. He holds the White Sox record for longest hitting streak—28 games**

5. Joe Jackson   **E. The first major leaguer ever to lead his league in triples for four straight years**

6. Taffy Wright   **F. The only White Sox player to be a World Series MVP**

7. Lance Johnson   **G. He holds top two spots in the team record book for most triples in a season (21, 20)**

481: 1-D, 2-B, 3-E, 4-G, 5-A, 6-C, 7-F • **482:** 1-B, 2-F, 3-A, 4-D, 5-G, 6-C, 7-E

1. Gary Peters	**A.** The only White Sox hurler ever to pitch a perfect game
2. Early Wynn	**B.** The first White Sox pitcher to win a Cy Young Award
3. Jack McDowell	**C.** The only White Sox pitcher to be Rookie of the Year
4. Charlie Robertson	**D.** Pitched the most recent no-hitter in White Sox history
5. Eddie Cicotte	**E.** The only White Sox hurler to win the AL ERA crown in back-to-back seasons
6. Wilson Alvarez	**F.** The most recent White Sox Cy Young Award winner
7. Red Faber	**G.** The only White Sox pitcher to toss a no-hitter in the same season that the team won the AL pennant

484

1. Esteban Loaiza	**A.** First White Sox Fireman of the Year Award winner
2. Ed Walsh	**B.** The only White Sox pitcher to win two AL strikeout titles
3. Tom Seaver	**C.** White Sox pitcher who set the major league record by pitching in his 16th consecutive Opening Day game
4. LaMarr Hoyt	**D.** Most recent White Sox pitcher to win the Fireman of the Year Award
5. Eddie Fisher	**E.** The last White Sox pitcher to win the AL strikeout title
6. Wilbur Wood	**F.** The last White Sox pitcher to both win and lose at least 20 games in the same season (Hint: he won an AL Fireman of the Year Award earlier in his career)
7. Bobby Thigpen	**G.** The White Sox Cy Young Award winner who had the most victories in his big year—24

483: 1-C, 2-B, 3-F, 4-A, 5-G, 6-D, 7-E • **484:** 1-E, 2-B, 3-C, 4-G, 5-A, 6-F, 7-D

WHO, WHAT, WHEN, WHERE, AND WHY

1. **Who** instigated this baseball field stunt?

2. **Where** did the "aliens" land?

3. **When?**

4. **What** was the reason for their visit?

485:

1. Owner Bill Veeck.

2. Comiskey Park in Chicago.

3. June 1, 1959.

4. The little green men wanted to meet Chicago's two little middle infielders, Luis Aparicio and Nellie Fox.

486

1. 1917	A. The last year the White Sox lost the World Series
2. 1970	B. The last year the White Sox had the league's top home run hitter
3. 1974	C. The first year the White Sox had the league's top home run hitter
4. 1971	D. Year the White Sox set the team record for losses in a season—106
5. 1950	E. The only year the White Sox hosted the All-Star Game in which the American League lost (the AL won the other three)
6. 1919	F. First year the White Sox lost the World Series
7. 1959	G. The only year the White Sox ever won 100 games

487

1. 1906	A. The White Sox set their team record for consecutive wins—19
2. 1920	B. The White Sox had four 20-game winners
3. 1983	C. The White Sox opened a new ballpark with a 16–0 loss
4. 1997	D. The last year the White Sox had two 20-game winners
5. 1976	E. The first year the White Sox ever led the American League in home runs (they hit 135)
6. 1974	F. The White Sox featured the oldest player ever (54) to get a hit in a major league game (he singled)
7. 1991	G. The White Sox ended their 54-year drought without a batting champion

486: 1-G, 2-D, 3-B, 4-C, 5-E, 6-F, 7-A • 487: 1-A, 2-B, 3-D, 4-G, 5-F, 6-E, 7-C

Cincinnati Reds.

1. Pete Rose	**A.** The only Reds player to hit for the cycle from 1960 to 2005
2. Cy Seymour	**B.** The first Reds player to win two NL home run titles
3. George Foster	**C.** The first Red to win a batting title
4. Johnny Bench	**D.** The only Red to win back-to-back home run titles
5. Frank Robinson	**E.** The only Red to win a batting championship in the same year Cincinnati won the World Series
6. Edd Roush	**F.** The only Reds outfielder to have his number retired
7. Eric Davis	**G.** The first Red to win a World Series MVP Award

489

1. Pete Rose	**A.** The last Reds position player to win the NL Rookie of the Year Award
2. Ernie Lombardi	**B.** The first Reds player to win the NL MVP Award
3. Frank Robinson	**C.** The first Cincinnati player to win a home run title
4. Chris Sabo	**D.** The first designated hitter in NL history
5. Bug Holliday	**E.** The first Red to win the NL Rookie of the Year Award
6. Ted Kluszewski	**F.** The last Reds player to win an NL batting championship
7. Dan Driessen	**G.** The only Red between 1906 and 1969 to win the NL home run title

490

1. Jose Rijo	**A.** The only Reds pitcher ever to be a World Series MVP
2. Pat Zachry	**B.** The last Reds pitcher to win the NL ERA title
3. Scott Williamson	**C.** The last Red to win the NL Rookie of the Year Award
4. Tom Browning	**D.** He pitched two no-hitters for the Reds

488: 1-G, 2-C, 3-D, 4-B, 5-F, 6-E, 7-A • **489:** 1-F, 2-B, 3-E, 4-A, 5-C, 6-G, 7-D

5. Jim Maloney

E. The first Reds pitcher to win the NL's Rookie of the Year Award

6. Bucky Walters

F. He pitched the only perfect game in Reds history

7. Ed Heusser

G. The only Reds pitcher to win back-to-back ERA titles

491

1. Johnny Vander Meer

A. The only Reds pitcher to lead the NL in strikeouts from 1944 to 1992

2. Dolf Luque

B. The last Reds pitcher to be a 20-game winner in back-to-back seasons

3. Ewell Blackwell

C. The last Reds pitcher to lead the NL in strikeouts for three consecutive seasons

4. Noodles Hahn

D. The first Reds pitcher to win two NL ERA titles

5. Eppa Rixey

E. The last 20-game winner for the Reds

6. Danny Jackson

F. The first of only two Reds pitchers to lead the NL in strikeouts for three consecutive seasons

7. Joey Jay

G. He allowed only one home run in 301 innings, a major league record since the dead-ball era ended in 1919

492

1. 1940

A. The Reds set a major league record by losing 41 one-run games

2. 1919

B. The Reds lost 26 games in September

3. 1957

C. The first year the Reds won a National League pennant

4. 1946

D. The first year the Reds won 100 games in a season

5. 1939

E. The only World Series appearance (out of nine) in which the Reds were swept four straight

6. 1914

F. The year that fan voting elected eight members of the Reds to starting spots in the All-Star Game

7. 1976

G. The first year the Reds swept their opponent in the World Series

492: 1-D, 2-C, 3-F, 4-A, 5-E, 6-B, 7-G

490: 1-A, 2-E, 3-C, 4-F, 5-D, 6-G, 7-B • **491:** 1-C, 2-D, 3-A, 4-F, 5-G, 6-E, 7-B •

493

1. 1976	A. George Foster set the Reds home run record, with 52
2. 1982	B. The last year the Reds won 100 games in a season
3. 1995	C. The year the Reds set their team record for most wins in a season—108
4. 1978	D. The last year the Reds won a divisional title
5. 1977	E. The year of Pete Rose's 44-game hitting streak
6. 1975	F. The only year in Reds history they lost 100 games in a season
7. 1981	G. The year the Reds had the best record in baseball and didn't even make the playoffs

494

Cleveland Indians.

1. Travis Hafner	A. The last Indian to be the AL Rookie of the Year
2. Sandy Alomar Jr.	B. The last Indian to win the AL home run title
3. Chris Chambliss	C. The first Indian to win an AL batting title
4. Albert Belle	D. The only Indian infielder to have his number retired
5. Bobby Avila	E. The last Indian to win an AL batting title
6. Napoleon Lajoie	F. The first Indian position player to be AL Rookie of the Year
7. Lou Boudreau	G. Between 1979 and 2005, the only Indian to hit for the cycle

495

1. Napoleon Lajoie	A. The first Indian to win the AL MVP Award
2. Al Rosen	B. The last Indian to win two AL home run titles
3. Larry Doby	C. He lost the Triple Crown when he grounded out in his final at bat of the season
4. Lou Boudreau	D. The only Indian ever to win back-to-back batting titles

5. Vic Power   **E. The player-manager who hit an Opening Day home run**

6. Sandy Alomar Jr.   **F. The only Indian to be the MVP of an All-Star Game**

7. Frank Robinson   **G. The first Indian to win a Gold Glove Award**

496

1. Addie Joss   **A. Before Kevin Millwood, in 2005, he was the last Indians pitcher to win the AL ERA title**

2. Dennis Eckersley   **B. He pitched the first perfect game in Indians history**

3. Gaylord Perry   **C. He pitched the last no-hitter in Cleveland history that was *not* a perfect game**

4. Herb Score   **D. The only Cleveland pitcher ever to win a Cy Young Award**

5. Rick Sutcliffe   **E. The only Indians pitcher ever to be AL Rookie of the Year**

6. Bob Feller   **F. The last Indians pitcher to win back-to-back AL strikeout titles**

7. Len Barker   **G. The first Indians pitcher to win three straight AL strikeout titles**

497

1. Sam McDowell   **A. He won five AL strikeout titles in six seasons**

2. Len Barker   **B. The last Indians pitcher to lead the AL in ERA with a mark below 2.00—1.60**

3. Bob Feller   **C. He pitched the last perfect game in Indians history**

4. Stan Coveleski   **D. The only Indians pitcher ever to lead the AL in ERA with a mark above 3.00—3.20**

5. Luis Tiant   **E. He pitched three no-hitters for Cleveland**

6. Early Wynn   **F. He has the team record for career winning percentage—.667**

7. Vean Gregg   **G. The first Indians pitcher to win the AL strikeout title**

497: 1-A, 2-C, 3-E, 4-G, 5-B, 6-D, 7-F

496: 1-D, 2-C, 3-B, 4-A, 5-G, 6-F, 7-E • **496:** 1-B, 2-C, 3-D, 4-E, 5-A, 6-G, 7-F •

WHO, WHAT, WHEN, WHERE, AND WHY

1. Who is this player?

2. What is his famous trademark?

3. When did he have his best season for home runs and RBIs, and what was its result?

4. Where did he attempt to place many of his hits? Why?

498:

1. Heinie Groh.

2. His bottle bat.

3. 1919, when he led the Cincinnati Reds to a (tainted) World Series title.

4. Bunt hits to first and third because his famous bottle bat allowed him to be an excellent bunter.

1. 1987   **A.** Cleveland won its fifth-straight divisional title

2. 1995   **B.** Cleveland set its team record for losses in a season (105)

3. 1999   **C.** Three Indians pitchers tied for the staff lead in victories with (gulp!) just seven each, setting a 20th-century major league record for fewest wins by a staff leader

4. 1997   **D.** The last year Cleveland won the AL pennant

5. 1991   **E.** Cleveland became the first team in nearly 50 years to play two different opponents on the same day

6. 1996   **F.** Cleveland's closer had more saves than any other team in the major leagues

7. 2000   **G.** Cleveland's major league–record 455 consecutive sellouts began

500

1. 1948   **A.** The last time the Indians had three 20-game winners in the same season

2. 1954   **B.** Cleveland set its team record for wins in a season, with 111

3. 1956   **C.** Cleveland hit .308 as a team (they had nine .300 hitters)

4. 1921   **D.** Cleveland finished fourth in the AL with a 92–62 record, yet the NL pennant winner came in at 91–63!

5. 1920   **E.** First year Cleveland won the World Series

6. 1950   **F.** The last year Cleveland won the World Series

7. 1952   **G.** Cleveland had three 20-game winners and still failed to win the pennant

499: 1-C, 2-F, 3-A, 4-D, 5-B, 6-G, 7-E • **500:** 1-F, 2-B, 3-A, 4-C, 5-E, 6-D, 7-G

501

Detroit Tigers.

1. George Kell	**A.** The last Tigers Hall of Famer to win the AL batting title
2. Mickey Cochrane	**B.** The last Tigers Hall of Famer to hit for the cycle
3. Hank Greenberg	**C.** The first Tigers player to win the AL home run title
4. Al Kaline	**D.** The first Tigers player to win two AL MVP Awards
5. Ty Cobb	**E.** The only Tigers player besides Ty Cobb to win more than one batting title (he won four)
6. Harry Heilmann	**F.** The first Tigers player to win the AL MVP Award
7. Sam Crawford	**G.** First Tigers Hall of Famer to win the AL batting title

502

1. Cecil Fielder	**A.** The last Tiger to win back-to-back Gold Glove Awards
2. Harvey Kuenn	**B.** The first Tiger to win the AL Rookie of the Year Award
3. Norm Cash	**C.** The last Tigers player to win the AL batting title
4. Lou Whitaker	**D.** The only nonpitcher Tigers player to win the World Series MVP Award
5. Gary Pettis	**E.** The last Tiger to win back-to-back AL home run titles
6. Ty Cobb	**F.** The last Tiger to win the AL Rookie of the Year Award before Justin Verlander in 2006
7. Alan Trammell	**G.** The only Tiger ever to win a Triple Crown

503

1. Mark Fidrych	**A.** The only Tigers pitcher to win the World Series MVP Award
2. Mickey Lolich	**B.** The last Tigers pitcher to win the AL strikeout title
3. Hal Newhouser	**C.** The last 20-game winner for the Tigers

4. Jack Morris   **D. The first Tigers pitcher to win the AL Rookie of the Year**

5. Tommy Bridges   **E. The only Tigers pitcher ever to have his number retired**

6. Jim Bunning   **F. The last Tigers pitcher to win back-to-back strikeout titles**

7. Bill Gullickson   **G. The first Tigers pitcher to win back-to-back strikeout titles**

504

1. Mickey Lolich   **A. The last Tigers pitcher to win the AL ERA title**

2. Denny McLain   **B. He threw Detroit's first no-hitter**

3. Mark Fidrych   **C. The last Tigers pitcher to be a 20-game winner in back-to-back seasons**

4. Hal Newhouser   **D. Threw Detroit's last no-hitter**

5. Willie Hernandez   **E. Detroit's last AL MVP**

6. George Mullin   **F. He holds the Tigers record for most victories in two consecutive seasons—55**

7. Jack Morris   **G. The only Tigers pitcher to win back-to-back ERA titles**

505

1. 1952   **A. Denny McLain won his second straight Cy Young Award**

2. 1969   **B. The only year the Tigers ever had three 20-game winners**

3. 1984   **C. The Tigers set their team record for losses in a season—119**

4. 1909   **D. Virgil Trucks pitched two no-hitters for the Tigers**

5. 1915   **E. The last year a Tiger won the AL Cy Young Award**

6. 2003   **F. The Tigers won their third straight AL pennant**

7. 1907   **G. First time the Tigers ever won 100 games in a season**

505: 1-D, 2-A, 3-E, 4-F, 5-G, 6-C, 7-B

504: 1-C, 2-F, 3-A, 4-G, 5-E, 6-B, 7-D • **503:** 1-D, 2-A, 3-E, 4-B, 5-G, 6-F, 7-C •

1. 1921
2. 1984
3. 1975
4. 1907
5. 1935
6. 1968
7. 1971

A. A Tigers outfielder won a Gold Glove and then proceeded to play all seven games of that year's World Series at shortstop

B. The Tigers had a 25-game winner who did not win the Cy Young Award, the last time that's happened in major league history

C. The Tigers set their team record for most wins—104

D. The Tigers won their first World Series

E. The Tigers lost a team-record 19 straight games

F. The first year a Tiger other than Ty Cobb won the AL batting championship

G. The only World Series appearance (out of nine) in which the Tigers were swept four straight

507

Houston Astros.

1. Jeff Bagwell
2. Doug Rader
3. Jimmy Wynn
4. Cesar Cedeno
5. Craig Biggio
6. Bill Spiers
7. Buddy Bell

A. His 200th career home run made him and his father the first father-son duo in major league history to reach reach the 200-homer total

B. The first Astros hitter to have his number retired

C. The first player in major league history to play a 162-game season without grounding into a double play

D. The first Astro to win a Gold Glove Award

E. The only Astros outfielder to win five straight Gold Gloves

F. The only Astro to win the NL Rookie of the Year Award

G. He reached base 13 straight times, one short of the NL record

506: 1-F, 2-C, 3-E, 4-G, 5-D, 6-A, 7-B • **507:** 1-F, 2-D, 3-B, 4-E, 5-C, 6-G, 7-A

WHO, WHAT, WHEN, WHERE, AND WHY

1. Who is this player?

2. What's he standing under?

3. When was it given to him?

4. Why?

508:

1. Hall of Famer Napoleon Lajoie.

2. A giant horseshoe made up of more than 1,000 silver dollars.

3. 1912.

4. Cleveland fans presented it to him as a testament to their love and appreciation of his playing for their team. The fans had even renamed their team the Cleveland Naps in his honor in 1903.

509

1. Brad Ausmus	**A.** The last Astro to win back-to-back Gold Gloves
2. Denny Walling	**B.** The only Astro to win the NL MVP Award
3. Jeff Bagwell	**C.** He has been hit by pitches more times than any other player in major league history
4. Bob Aspromonte	**D.** The Astros career leader in grand slams, with six
5. Lance Berkman	**E.** The only Astro to hit for the cycle more than once
6. Cesar Cedeno	**F.** He led the Astros in home runs at home one season with just three (yikes!)
7. Craig Biggio	**G.** The only Astro with a career batting average over .300

510

1. John Hudek	**A.** The first Astros pitcher to win the NL Cy Young Award
2. Jim Umbricht	**B.** He started the season in the minors and made it to the All-Star Game, one of only five players in major league history up to that point to do so
3. Don Nottebart	**C.** The first Astro to have his number retired
4. Don Wilson	**D.** The only Astros pitcher with two NL ERA titles
5. Darryl Kile	**E.** The only Astros pitcher with two career no-hitters
6. Nolan Ryan	**F.** Pitched first no-hitter in Astros history
7. Mike Scott	**G.** The last Astro to pitch a complete game no-hitter

511

1. Roger Clemens	**A.** He holds the Astros record for wins in a season—22
2. J. R. Richard	**B.** The first Astros pitcher to win back-to-back NL strikeout titles
3. Mike Scott	**C.** The last Astros pitcher to win back-to-back NL strikeout titles
4. Nolan Ryan	**D.** The only Astros pitcher to strike out 300 batters in a season besides the answer to clue B, above

5. Larry Dierker	E. The only Astros pitcher to start 40 games in one season
6. Mike Hampton	F. The last Astros pitcher to win the NL Cy Young Award
7. Jerry Reuss	G. The only Astros pitcher to hurl more than 300 innings in a season

512

1. 1998	A. The only year the Astros featured two 20-game winners
2. 1999	B. The Astros set the record for errors committed in a season—174
3. 2003	C. The first year the Astros had an eventual Hall of Famer on their roster
4. 1988	D. The Astros set a team record for steals in a season—198
5. 1966	E. The last time the All-Star Game was held in Houston
6. 1963	F. The Astros used six pitchers to hurl a no-hitter
7. 2004	G. The only year the Astros ever won 100 games in a season

513

1. 1968	A. The team changed its name from the Colt .45s to the Astros
2. 1965	B. The umpires filed a complaint with the National League that the Astrodome's scoreboard operators were inciting the fans against the umps
3. 1962	C. The Astros won 11 one-run games during a streak in which they won 16 of 17 games
4. 1969	D. The Astros hit only 49 homers all season, one more than NL leader Dave Kingman's 48
5. 1979	E. The Astros and Mets played a 24-inning, 1–0 game
6. 1981	F. All five Astros starting pitchers finished with ERAs below 3.00
7. 1989	G. The Astros went 4–20 in April, closing out the month by being no-hit, then opened May with a no-hitter of their own before going 20–6 for the month

513: 1-E, 2-A, 3-B, 4-G, 5-D, 6-F, 7-C

• **511:** 1-F, 2-B, 3-D, 4-C, 5-G, 6-A, 7-E • **512:** 1-G, 2-A, 3-F, 4-D, 5-B, 6-C, 7-E •

Baseball Trivia

Kansas City Royals.

1. Bo Jackson   **A. The first of only four Royals players to hit for the cycle**

2. George Brett   **B. The first Royals player to be named the LCS MVP**

3. Lou Piniella   **C. The first Royals player to win a Gold Glove**

4. Frank White   **D. The only Royals player to win the AL batting title besides George Brett**

5. Amos Otis   **E. The only Royals player to be the All-Star Game MVP**

6. Willie Wilson   **F. The only Royals player to win the AL MVP**

7. Freddie Patek   **G. The first Royals player to be the AL Rookie of the Year**

515

1. Bob Hamelin   **A. He holds the Royals record for doubles in a season—54**

2. Angel Berroa   **B. Royals player with the highest career on-base percentage—.380**

3. Kevin Seitzer   **C. The last Royals player to be the AL Rookie of the Year**

4. Mike Sweeney   **D. Tied the AL record with RBIs in 13 straight games**

5. Hal McRae   **E. Won the AL Rookie of the Year Award as a DH**

6. Carlos Beltran   **F. The first rookie in major league history to have both 100 runs and 100 RBIs**

7. Mark Quinn   **G. Became the fourth player in major league history to hit two home runs in his debut game**

516

1. Bret Saberhagen   **A. The only Royals pitcher to be the World Series MVP**

2. Steve Busby   **B. The last Royals pitcher to win a Fireman of the Year Award**

3. David Cone   **C. The last Royals pitcher to win the AL Cy Young Award**

514: 1-E, 2-F, 3-G, 4-B, 5-C, 6-D, 7-A • 515: 1-E, 2-C, 3-B, 4-D, 5-A, 6-F, 7-G

266

4. Kevin Appier   D. The only Royals pitcher to win back-to-back Fireman of the Year Awards

5. Jeff Montgomery   E. The last Royals pitcher to win the AL ERA title

6. Dan Quisenberry   F. The only Royals pitcher with two no-hitters

7. Dennis Leonard   G. The winningest righthanded pitcher in the major leagues for a six-year period

517

1. Mark Gubicza   A. Holds the Royals career record for strikeouts (1,458)

2. Kevin Appier   B. The only Royals pitcher ever to win a Gold Glove

3. Paul Splittorff   C. The only Royals pitcher to toss six shutouts in one season

4. Roger Nelson   D. Holds the Royals record for career winning percentage—.593

5. Bret Saberhagen   E. Threw more wild pitches (107) and hit more batters (58) in his career than any other Royals pitcher

6. Dennis Leonard   F. Holds the Royals record for strikeouts in a season (244)

7. Al Fitzmorris   G. Holds the Royals career record for earned runs allowed—1,082

518

1. 1977   A. Willie Wilson became the first player in major league history to reach 700 at bats (he had 705)

2. 1979   B. The team's catcher stole 36 bases, a major league record

3. 1982   C. The team's catcher had more than 100 runs, 100 RBIs, and 100 walks, only the second time the feat had been accomplished in the American League

4. 1980   D. Four Royals players were sent to prison for violating federal drug laws

5. 1983   E. The Royals won their first division title

6. 1973   F. The Royals had a stretch in which they went 24–1

7. 1976   G. The team moved into Royals Stadium

518: 1-F, 2-C, 3-B, 4-A, 5-D, 6-G, 7-E

516: 1-A, 2-F, 3-C, 4-E, 5-B, 6-D, 7-G • **517:** 1-E, 2-A, 3-G, 4-C, 5-B, 6-F, 7-D •

1. 2000   **A.** The Royals finished in second place, but a whopping 30 games behind the division winner

2. 1995   **B.** The only year the Royals hosted the All-Star Game

3. 1998   **C.** The Royals won six straight games in their last at bat

4. 2005   **D.** The Royals set their team record for losses in a season—106

5. 1980   **E.** The last year the Royals made it to the World Series

6. 1985   **F.** The Royals had a winning record on the road (43–38), but were a dismal 29–51 at home

7. 1973   **G.** The first year the Royals ever made it to the World Series

520

Los Angeles Angels.

1. Jim Fregosi   **A.** The Angel who most recently won the AL MVP Award

2. Don Baylor   **B.** The first Angel to win the AL MVP Award

3. Vladimir Guerrero   **C.** The only Angel to win a batting championship

4. Tim Salmon   **D.** The last Angel to win the AL home run title

5. Alex Johnson   **E.** The only Angel to hit for the cycle twice

6. Bobby Grich   **F.** The first Angel to win the AL home run title

7. Troy Glaus   **G.** The only Angel to be an AL Rookie of the Year

521

1. Troy Glaus   **A.** The only Angel to win the World Series MVP Award

2. Reggie Jackson   **B.** He hit so poorly one April that he refused his paycheck for the month, and gave it to charity instead

3. Lyman Bostock   **C.** The most recent Angel to be the All-Star Game MVP

4. Fred Lynn   **D.** He holds the Angels career record for stolen bases—186

519: 1-C, 2-A, 3-F, 4-D, 5-G, 6-E, 7-B • **520:** 1-E, 2-B, 3-A, 4-G, 5-C, 6-F, 7-D

5. Garret Anderson   **E. The Angel who led the AL in home runs (39) and strikeouts (156) in 1982**

6. Gary Pettis   **F. The first Angel to win the All-Star Game MVP Award**

7. Darin Erstad   **G. He set the single-season major league record for RBIs by a leadoff hitter—100**

522

1. Bo Belinsky   **A. Pitched the most recent complete game no-hitter that wasn't a perfect game**

2. Nolan Ryan   **B. Pitched the only perfect game in Angels history**

3. Mark Langston   **C. The only Angels pitcher besides Nolan Ryan to win an AL strikeout title**

4. Clyde Wright   **D. Starting pitcher of Angels' last no-hitter (it was a combined effort with another pitcher)**

5. Mike Witt   **E. The first Angel to win the AL Cy Young Award**

6. Dean Chance   **F. Pitched the only no-hitter for the Angels between 1963 and 1983 besides Nolan Ryan**

7. Frank Tanana   **G. The first Angel to pitch a no-hitter**

523

1. Frank Tanana   **A. The last Angel to win the AL ERA title—2.54**

2. Dean Chance   **B. Holds the Angels career record for best walks per nine innings pitched ratio—1.74**

3. Nolan Ryan   **C. The first Angel to win the AL ERA title—1.65**

4. Bartolo Colon   **D. Has lowest career ERA of all Angels pitchers—2.78**

5. Chuck Finley   **E. Most recent Angel to win the AL Cy Young Award**

6. Andy Messersmith   **F. The only Angels pitcher to have his number retired**

7. Bert Blyleven   **G. Won more games than any other Angels pitcher (165)**

521: 1-A, 2-E, 3-B, 4-F, 5-C, 6-D, 7-G • **522:** 1-G, 2-A, 3-D (combined with Mike Witt), 4-F, 5-B, 6-E, 7-C • **523:** 1-A, 2-C, 3-F, 4-E, 5-G, 6-D, 7-B

WHO, WHAT, WHEN, WHERE, AND WHY

1. Who is the batter?

2. What has he just done?

3. When?

4. Where?

5. BONUS: What was the final score of the game?

524:
1. Bobby Thomson.
2. Hit a pennant-winning, walk-off home run during playoff series with Dodgers.
3. 1951.
4. The Polo Grounds.
5. 5–4.

525

1. 2002

A. The Angels began playing in Anaheim Stadium

2. 1979

B. The Angels won their first division title

3. 1971

C. The Angels stole 220 bases, the most in the majors since 1918

4. 1964

D. The Angels had four starters with ERAs below 3.00

5. 1975

E. The Angels set their team record for wins (99)

6. 1965

F. The team changed their name from the Los Angeles Angels to the California Angels

7. 1966

G. Dean Chance pitched an incredible 11 shutouts

526

1. 1997

A. The Angels changed their team name from the California Angels to the Anaheim Angels

2. 2003

B. The Angels broke the three million mark in attendance for the first time

3. 1999

C. The manager gave his whole regular team a day off and the replacements were no-hit by a 6–11 pitcher

4. 1990

D. The last year the Angels hosted the All-Star Game

5. 1986

E. The two-day players' strike likely cost the Angels the division title because two lost home games against the weak Mariners were shifted to Seattle and were made up as two back-to-back doubleheaders

6. 1985

F. The Angels were up three games to one in the LCS and were leading 5–2 with one out in the ninth inning of game 5 and still lost the series

7. 1989

G. The Angels used 93 different lineups in the first 94 games of the season

525: 1-E, 2-D, 3-D, 4-G, 5-C, 6-F, 7-A • **526:** 1-A, 2-B, 3-C, 4-G, 5-F, 6-E, 7-D

Los Angeles Dodgers. (Note: Includes previous franchise location in Brooklyn.)

1. Wes Parker

A. The only Dodger to win more than one NL MVP Award

2. Dolph Camilli

B. The last Dodger to win the NL Rookie of the Year Award

3. Kirk Gibson

C. Amazingly, the only Dodger to hit for the cycle between 1950 and 2005, and it required an extra-inning game

4. Roy Campanella

D. Most recent Dodger to win the NL MVP Award

5. Todd Hollandsworth

E. The first Dodger outfielder to win the NL Rookie of the Year Award

6. Babe Herman

F. The only Dodger to hit for the cycle twice (he did it in the same season)

7. Frank Howard

G. The first Dodger to win the NL MVP Award

528

1. Duke Snider

A. The first Dodger batting champion—.335

2. Dan Brouthers

B. The last Dodger batting champion—.326

3. Jake Daubert

C. The only Dodger home run champ between 1957 and 2006

4. Tommy Davis

D. The only two-time Dodger home run champion

5. Adrian Beltre

E. The Dodger who set an NL record by stealing home seven times in one season

6. Tim Jordan

F. The only Dodger outfielder to have his number retired

7. Pete Reiser

G. The first Dodger to win back-to-back batting titles

527: 1-C, 2-G, 3-D, 4-A, 5-B, 6-F, 7-E • **528:** 1-F, 2-A, 3-G, 4-B, 5-C, 6-D, 7-E

529

1. Eric Gagne	A. The first Dodger to win the NL strikeout title
2. Hideo Nomo	B. The third consecutive Los Angeles pitcher to win the NL Rookie of the Year Award
3. Fernando Valenzuela	C. Most recent Dodger Cy Young Award winner
4. Carl Erskine	D. The last Dodger pitcher to toss a no-hitter
5. Burleigh Grimes	E. The only Dodger pitcher besides Sandy Koufax to pitch more than one no-hitter
6. Kevin Brown	F. The last Dodger to win the NL ERA title
7. Ramon Martinez	G. The last 20-game winner for the Dodgers

530

1. Mike Marshall	A. The only Dodger Cy Young Award winner in the 1970s
2. Rick Sutcliffe	B. The only Dodger Rookie of the Year in the 1970s
3. Don Sutton	C. The last Dodger pitcher to be a World Series MVP
4. Andy Messersmith	D. The only Dodger pitcher to be an All-Star Game MVP
5. Johnny Podres	E. The only Dodger pitcher to win a Gold Glove in the 1970s
6. Don Newcombe	F. The first Dodger pitcher to win a World Series MVP
7. Orel Hershiser	G. The first Dodger to win a Cy Young Award

529: 1-C, 2-D, 3-B, 4-E, 5-A, 6-F, 7-G • **530:** 1-A, 2-B, 3-D, 4-E, 5-F, 6-G, 7-C

531

1. 1974   A. The last year the Dodgers won the NL pennant

2. 1988   B. The last 100-win season for the Dodgers (they won 102)

3. 1977   C. Of the Dodgers' 18 trips to the World Series, this was the only year they were swept four straight

4. 1981   D. Of the Dodgers' 18 trips to the World Series, this was the only year they swept their opponent in four straight

5. 1966   E. Year of first Dodgers pennant under Tommy Lasorda

6. 1963   F. The last year the Dodgers hosted the All-Star Game

7. 1980   G. Year the World Champion Dodgers had three players as co-MVPs

532

1. 1890   A. The only year the Dodgers won the NL pennant with two managers

2. 1900   B. The first year the Dodgers repeated as NL champions

3. 1947   C. The last year the Dodgers had two 20-game winners in the same season

4. 1899   D. The Dodgers won their first pennant

5. 1953   E. The Dodgers lost 27 games in September

6. 1908   F. The last year the Dodgers had three 20-game winners on their staff

7. 1969   G. The Dodgers set their team record for wins in a season—105

Milwaukee Brewers. (Note: Includes previous franchise location in Seattle.)

1. Pat Listach

2. George Scott

3. Robin Yount

4. Hank Aaron

5. Gorman Thomas

6. Paul Molitor

7. Cecil Cooper

A. The only Brewer besides George Scott to win more than one Gold Glove (he won two)

B. The first Brewers position player to win an AL MVP Award

C. The first Brewer to win the AL home run title

D. Once scored 114 runs in a season even though he missed 44 games

E. The only Brewer to win the AL Rookie of the Year Award

F. The last Brewer to win the AL home run title

G. The first Brewers outfielder to have his number retired

534

1. George Scott

2. Sixto Lezcano

3. Gorman Thomas

4. Robin Yount

5. Cecil Cooper

6. Tommy Harper

7. Richie Sexson

A. The last Brewers player to win an AL MVP Award

B. Holds the Brewers record for hits in a season—219

C. The only outfielder in Brewers history to win a Gold Glove

D. The first Brewer to win a Gold Glove

E. Holds Brewers career record for slugging percentage—.536

F. The first Brewer to hit 45 homers in a season (tied for the team record)

G. Holds Brewers record for stolen bases in a season (73)

533: 1-E, 2-C, 3-B, 4-G, 5-F, 6-D, 7-A • **534:** 1-D, 2-C, 3-F, 4-A, 5-B, 6-G, 7-E

WHO, WHAT, WHEN, WHERE, AND WHY

1. Who's on the right?

2. What had he just accomplished?

3. Where was he when his streak ended? Against which team?

4. BONUS: Which Hall of Fame opponent was on the mound for the last shutout?

535:

1. Hall of Famer Don Drysdale.

2. He had just set a new major league record by pitching 58.2 consecutive scoreless innings.

3. At Dodger Stadium. The Philadelphia Phillies ended Drysdale's shutout streak at six on June 8, although Drysdale did win the game, 5–3.

4. Jim Bunning of the Pirates was the victim of shutout number 6.

536

1. Rollie Fingers   A. Won 13 games in the team's inaugural year, setting a new record for expansion team pitchers

2. Juan Nieves   B. The only Brewers pitcher to throw a no-hitter

3. Pete Vukovich   C. Holds Brewers record for career games pitched—365

4. Gene Brabender   D. Most recent Brewer to win the AL Cy Young Award

5. Ben Sheets   E. The only Brewers pitcher to strike out 18 batters in a game

6. Ken Sanders   F. The first Brewers pitcher to win the AL Cy Young Award

7. Dan Plesac   G. Holds Brewers record for appearances in a season (83)

537

1. Jim Slaton   A. His 23 complete games in a season is a Brewers best

2. Mike Caldwell   B. Logged more innings than any other Brewers pitcher

3. Teddy Higuera   C. The first Brewers reliever to record 39 saves in a season, the team record he shares with Derrick Turnbow

4. Rollie Fingers   D. The first Brewer to win an AL MVP Award

5. Dan Plesac   E. Brewers season record holder with 77 games finished

6. Dan Kolb   F. Holds the Brewers record for career winning percentage (.595) and strikeouts (1,081)

7. Ken Sanders   G. Holds team record for career ERA—3.21

536: 1-F, 2-B, 3-D, 4-A, 5-E, 6-G, 7-C • **537:** 1-B, 2-A, 3-F, 4-D, 5-G, 6-C, 7-E

1. 2002   A. The Brewers earned first divisional title

2. 1982   B. The Brewers started the season with a 13–0 record

3. 1981   C. The Brewers lost 106 games, their team record

4. 1996   D. The last year that a Brewers player won a Gold Glove

5. 1992   E. The first year the Brewers played in the National League

6. 1987   F. The Brewers featured two pitchers who won ten straight games, the team record

7. 1998   G. The Brewers set a major league record for hits in an Opening Day game—22

539

1. 1976   A. The first season the Brewers passed the one million mark in attendance

2. 1971   B. Hank Aaron closed out his career with the Brewers

3. 1970   C. The Brewers staff pitched 23 shutouts after compiling just two the year before

4. 1982   D. The first year the team posted a winning record (93–69)

5. 1972   E. The team was nicknamed "Harvey's Wallbangers" for their hitting prowess under manager Harvey Kuenn

6. 1973   F. The Brewers moved from the AL West to the AL East

7. 1978   G. The first year the Brewers played in Milwaukee after moving from Seattle

540

Minnesota Twins. (Note: Includes previous franchise location in Washington, D.C.)

1. Kirby Puckett   A. The first Twin to win a Gold Glove

2. Albie Pearson   B. The first AL Rookie of the Year in team history

3. Marty Cordova   C. Batting champ with highest single season average—.388

4. Mickey Vernon   D. The only Twin from 1981 to 2005 to hit for the cycle

5. Rod Carew   E. The first player in team history to win two batting titles

6. John Castino   F. The only Twins Rookie of the Year from 1968 to 1990

7. Earl Battey   G. The last Twins batter to be the AL Rookie of the Year

541

1. Roy Sievers   A. The last Twin to win a home run title

2. Harmon Killebrew   B. The first Twin to win an LCS MVP Award

3. Rod Carew   C. The only Twin to be the All-Star Game MVP

4. Zoilo Versalles   D. The first home run champion in team history

5. Kirby Puckett   E. The last Twin to win the AL MVP Award before Justin Morneau in 2006

6. Gary Gaetti   F. The first Twin to win back-to-back batting titles

7. Tony Oliva   G. The first Twin to win the AL MVP Award

542

1. Frank Viola   A. Pitched the last no-hitter in the team's history

2. Jim Perry   B. The first Twin to win the AL Cy Young Award

3. Jack Morris   C. The first Twin to win a World Series MVP Award

4. Jim Kaat   D. The last Twin to win a World Series MVP Award

5. Walter Johnson   E. The first Twins pitcher to win a Gold Glove

6. Eric Milton   F. Pitched the first no-hitter in the team's history

7. Johan Santana   G. The team's most recent Cy Young Award winner

543

1. Scott Erickson   A. The only Twin from 1964 to 2003 to win the AL strikeout title

2. Frank Viola   B. The first Twin since Walter Johnson, in 1919, to win three straight strikeout titles

3. Allan Anderson   C. Won the team's only ERA title from 1929 to 2003

4. Camilo Pascual   D. Won the team's only Cy Young Award from 1971 to 2003

5. Bert Blyleven   E. Pitched the team's only no-hitter from 1968 to 1998

6. Bobo Newsom   F. The only pitcher in franchise history besides Walter Johnson to win a strikeout title from 1901 to 1960

7. Johan Santana   G. Holds franchise record for most consecutive wins—17

542: 1-C, 2-B, 3-D, 4-E, 5-F, 6-A, 7-G • **543:** 1-E, 2-D, 3-C, 4-B, 5-A, 6-F, 7-G

540: 1-D, 2-B, 3-G, 4-E, 5-C, 6-F, 7-A • **541:** 1-D, 2-A, 3-E, 4-G, 5-C, 6-B, 7-F •

544

1. 1933	**A.** The team sets their record for losses in a season (113)
2. 1924	**B.** The team's first appearance in the World Series
3. 1912	**C.** The team stole eight bases off Cleveland in the first inning
4. 1909	**D.** The only World Series of the six the team has played that did not go to seven games (it was 4–1)
5. 1915	**E.** Walter Johnson sets the major league record for batting average in a season by a pitcher (.433; 42 for 97)
6. 1925	**F.** The first year the team featured two 20-game winners
7. 1904	**G.** The staff ace lost ten games by shutouts

545

1. 1991	**A.** The last year the Twins featured three Gold Glove winners in the same season
2. 1985	**B.** The only year in the team's history they drew more than three million fans
3. 1963	**C.** The last year the team hosted the All-Star Game
4. 1969	**D.** The team's most recent World Series appearance
5. 1961	**E.** The only 100-win season in team's history—102
6. 1965	**F.** The last year the Twins featured two 20-game winners
7. 1988	**G.** The Twins began playing in Minnesota

546

New York Mets.

1. Darryl Strawberry	**A.** Played the most years with the team—18
2. Dave Kingman	**B.** Had 24 game-winning hits in one season to set a new major league record

544: 1-D, 2-B, 3-F, 4-G, 5-C, 6-E, 7-A • **545:** 1-D, 2-C, 3-A, 4-F, 5-G, 6-E, 7-B

3. Howard Johnson   **C. Tied the major league record with eight consecutive pinch-hits**

4. Ed Kranepool   **D. The first Met to win the NL home run title**

5. Rusty Staub   **E. Most recent Met to win the NL home run crown**

6. Keith Hernandez   **F. The only nonpitcher in Mets history to be voted the NL Rookie of the Year**

7. Todd Hundley   **G. Hit the most home runs in a season, 41, of any New York player, Met or Yankee, from 1962 to 1996**

547

1. Robin Ventura   **A. The first player in major league history to hit grand slams in both games of a doubleheader**

2. Hubie Brooks   **B. The last Met to be the World Series MVP**

3. Lenny Harris   **C. Set a new major league record for career pinch-hits in his last game as a member of the Mets—151**

4. Tommie Agee   **D. Met with the most hits in a season—227**

5. Keith Hernandez   **E. Hit in 24 straight games, setting a new team record (later tied by another player)**

6. Ray Knight   **F. Met who won the most Gold Gloves—6**

7. Lance Johnson   **G. The first Met to win a Gold Glove**

548

1. Tom Seaver   **A. The only Met ever to be the All-Star Game MVP**

2. Dwight Gooden   **B. The only Mets pitcher to win more than one NL Cy Young Award**

3. David Cone   **C. The only Mets pitcher ever to win a Gold Glove**

4. Craig Swan   **D. The only Mets pitcher besides Seaver and Gooden to win the National League's ERA title—2.43**

5. Jon Matlack   **E. The last Met to win the NL strikeout title**

6. Ron Darling   **F. The last 20-game winner for the Mets**

7. Frank Viola   **G. Most recent Met to win the NL Cy Young Award**

548: 1-B, 2-G, 3-E, 4-D, 5-A, 6-C, 7-F

547: 1-A, 2-E, 3-C, 4-G, 5-F, 6-B, 7-D • **546:** 1-F, 2-D, 3-E, 4-A, 5-C, 6-B, 7-G •

WHO, WHAT, WHEN, WHERE, AND WHY

1. Who are these two guys?

2. What are they doing?

3. When?

4. Where?

4. In the right-field bullpen.

3. 1980.

2. Tending their vegetable garden.

1. Pitcher Craig Swan and Coach Joe Pignatano of the Mets.

549:

550

1. Dwight Gooden	A. The only Mets pitcher ever to be an LCS MVP
2. Mike Stanton	B. The last Met to win the NL ERA title
3. John Franco	C. Mets record holder for most games pitched in a season—83
4. Tom Seaver	D. Mets record holder for most games pitched in a career—695
5. Mike Hampton	E. The first Met to win the NL Rookie of the Year Award
6. Armando Benitez	F. Mets record holder for most saves in a season—43
7. Al Leiter	G. Mets record holder for most hit batsmen in a career—63

551

1. 1985	A. The Mets had four starters finish in the NL's top 5 in strikeouts
2. 1990	B. Jim Bunning pitched a perfect game against the Mets on Father's Day in Shea Stadium
3. 1965	C. The Mets lost over 100 games for the fourth consecutive season
4. 1976	D. The Mets traded away their two biggest stars: Tom Seaver and Dave Kingman, initiating the biggest drop in attendance in major league history
5. 1977	E. The Mets pitched 53 complete games
6. 1980	F. The Mets collected a team record 28 hits in one game
7. 1964	G. The Mets' catchers failed to hit even one home run (now *that's* amazing!)

550: 1-B, 2-C, 3-D, 4-E, 5-A, 6-F, 7-G • **551:** 1-F, 2-A, 3-C, 4-E, 5-D, 6-G, 7-B

552

1. 1969	**A. The Mets set their team record for wins—108**
2. 1988	**B. The last year before 2006 the Mets won the division title**
3. 1964	**C. The last year the Mets lost 100 games in a season**
4. 1986	**D. The Mets lost their eighth straight Opening Day game**
5. 1993	**E. The Mets lost 26 games in August**
6. 1985	**F. The only year the All-Star Game has been hosted by the Mets**
7. 1962	**G. Dwight Gooden set a Mets record with 14 straight victories**

553

New York Yankees. (Note: Includes previous franchise location in Baltimore, from 1901 to 1902.)

1. Bob Meusel	**A. The first Yankee to win the Rookie of the Year Award**
2. Lou Gehrig	**B. The first Yankee to win the AL batting title**
3. Don Mattingly	**C. The first Yankee to win an MVP Award**
4. Gil McDougald	**D. The first Yankee to win the World Series MVP Award**
5. Derek Jeter	**E. The only Yankee to win an All-Star Game MVP Award**
6. Joe Page	**F. The only Yankee (and one of only three major leaguers) ever to hit for the cycle three times**
7. Babe Ruth	**G. The last Yankee before A-Rod in 2005 to win the AL MVP Award**

554

1. Joe DiMaggio	**A. The only Yankee to win back-to-back batting titles**
2. Wally Pipp	**B. The last Yankee to win a Triple Crown**

552: 1-D, 2-B, 3-F, 4-A, 5-C, 6-G, 7-E • **553:** 1-F, 2-C, 3-G, 4-A, 5-E, 6-D, 7-B

3. Lou Gehrig   **C. The last Yankee to win back-to-back MVP Awards**

4. Mickey Mantle   **D. Yankee record holder for highest batting average in a season (.393) and a career (.349)**

5. Roger Maris   **E. Owns the second-longest batting streak in Yankees history (33 games) after DiMaggio's 56 games**

6. Babe Ruth   **F. The first Yankee to win a Triple Crown**

7. Hal Chase   **G. The first Yankee to win back-to-back home run titles**

555

1. Spud Chandler   **A. The first Yankee pitcher to win the AL strikeout title**

2. Bob Turley   **B. The last Yankee pitcher to be the AL Rookie of the Year**

3. Bob Grim   **C. The first Yankee pitcher to win a Gold Glove**

4. Dave Righetti   **D. The first Yankee pitcher to win a Cy Young Award**

5. Bobby Shantz   **E. The only Yankee pitcher ever to win an MVP Award**

6. Ron Guidry   **F. The last Yankee pitcher to win a Gold Glove**

7. Red Ruffing   **G. The first Yankee pitcher to be the AL Rookie of the Year**

556

1. Al Downing   **A. The last Yankee to win the AL Cy Young Award**

2. Lefty Gomez   **B. The first Yankee pitcher to have his number retired**

3. Rudy May   **C. The only Yankee to win back-to-back ERA titles**

4. Ron Guidry   **D. The last Yankee to win the AL ERA title**

5. Whitey Ford   **E. The only Yankee to pitch two career no-hitters (he pitched them in the same season)**

6. Roger Clemens   **F. The only Yankee to win more than one AL strikeout title**

7. Allie Reynolds   **G. The last Yankee pitcher to win the AL strikeout title**

556: 1-G, 2-F, 3-D, 4-C, 5-B, 6-A, 7-E
554: 1-A, 2-G, 3-F, 4-B, 5-C, 6-D, 7-E • 555: 1-E, 2-D, 3-G, 4-B, 5-C, 6-F, 7-A •

1. 1921	A. The Yankees were 21–1 against St. Louis, their only loss coming in the two teams' last meeting of the season
2. 1959	B. The first year the Yankees won the World Series
3. 1964	C. The Yankees became the first team in history to feature five players with at least 100 RBIs in the same season
4. 1912	D. The last year the Yankees lost 100 games in a season
5. 1936	E. The first year the Yankees appeared in the World Series
6. 1927	F. The only year in a ten-year stretch that the Yankees did *not* play in the World Series
7. 1923	G. The last year the Yankees played in their fifth straight World Series

558

1. 1965	A. The last year the Yankees hosted the All-Star Game
2. 1978	B. The last year the Yankees were swept in the World Series
3. 1999	C. The first of only two years the Yankees featured three Gold Glove Award winners
4. 1976	D. The last year the Yankees had two 20-game winners in the same season
5. 1957	E. The last year the Yankees played a World Series against a non-expansion team
6. 1977	F. The last year the Yankees featured three Gold Glove Award winners
7. 1985	G. The first year the Yankees played a team in the World Series that had relocated from another city

557: 1-E, 2-F, 3-G, 4-D, 5-C, 6-A, 7-B • **558:** 1-C, 2-D, 3-E, 4-B, 5-G, 6-A, 7-F

WHO, WHAT, WHEN, WHERE, AND WHY

1. Who is the pitcher?

2. What's he in the process of doing?

3. When was it?

4. Where was he in the World Series rotation?

559:

1. Hall of Famer Whitey Ford.

2. Pitching one of his two shutouts in the World Series against Pittsburgh.

3. 1960.

4. Third, behind Art Ditmar and Bob Turley. Had Ford been given three starts in the World Series instead of two (he pitched Games 3 and 6, again, both shutouts), the Yankees might very well have avoided their big upset at the hands of the underdog Pirates.

Oakland Athletics. (Note: Includes previous franchise locations in Philadelphia and Kansas City.)

1. Jose Canseco   **A. The first A's player to win back-to-back batting titles**

2. Al Simmons   **B. The only A's player to win back-to-back MVP Awards**

3. Ferris Fain   **C. The last A's player to win four straight AL home run titles**

4. Jimmie Foxx   **D. The first A's position player to be AL Rookie of the Year**

5. Nap Lajoie   **E. The last A's player to win the AL home run title**

6. Mark McGwire   **F. The first A's player to win the AL home run title**

7. Home Run Baker   **G. The last A's player to win back-to-back batting titles**

561

1. Gene Tenace   **A. The only A's position player to have his number retired**

2. Terry Steinbach   **B. The last A's player to win a Triple Crown**

3. Jimmie Foxx   **C. The last A's outfielder to win the AL MVP Award**

4. Joe Rudi   **D. The last member of the A's to win the AL MVP**

5. Miguel Tejada   **E. The only A's player to be the All-Star Game MVP**

6. Reggie Jackson   **F. The first member of the A's to win a Gold Glove**

7. Rickey Henderson   **G. The first member of the A's to be a World Series MVP**

562

1. Dave Stewart   **A. The last A's pitcher to win the AL ERA title**

2. Catfish Hunter   **B. The last A's pitcher to throw a no-hitter**

3. Dennis Eckersley   **C. The first A's pitcher to win an MVP Award**

Baseball Trivia

4. Lefty Grove   **D. The only A's pitcher with a perfect game**

5. Steve Ontiveros   **E. The first A's pitcher to win the AL Cy Young Award**

6. Vida Blue   **F. The last A's pitcher to win the AL MVP Award**

7. Barry Zito   **G. The last A's pitcher to win the AL Cy Young Award**

563

1. Catfish Hunter   **A. The only A's starting pitcher to have his number retired**

2. Rube Waddell   **B. The first A's pitcher to win 20 games in a season seven times**

3. Lefty Grove   **C. Won the AL Cy Young Award and AL MVP Award in the same season**

4. Vida Blue   **D. Pitched the first no-hitter in A's history**

5. Weldon Henley   **E. A's pitcher who had a winning percentage of .850 one year (17–3), and then .200 the next (4–16) after taking big money to switch leagues**

6. Eddie Plank   **F. Won six straight AL strikeout titles**

7. Chief Bender   **G. Won seven straight AL strikeout titles**

564

1. 1990   **A. Year of first A's pennant in post–Connie Mack era**

2. 2002   **B. The A's set their team record for consecutive wins—20**

3. 1972   **C. Year of the A's last World Series title**

4. 1968   **D. The A's began play in Kansas City**

5. 1989   **E. Year of the A's last AL pennant**

6. 1974   **F. The A's began play in Oakland**

7. 1955   **G. The first time the A's won their third consecutive AL pennant**

565

1. 1910	**A.** Year of the first A's AL pennant
2. 1931	**B.** The A's won their fourth AL pennant in five years
3. 1902	**C.** The only year the A's ever swept their World Series opponent
4. 1951	**D.** Year of the A's first World Series title
5. 1914	**E.** The first year someone other than Connie Mack managed the A's
6. 1989	**F.** The A's lost 28 games in July
7. 1916	**G.** The A's set their team record for wins in a season with 107

566

Philadelphia Phillies.

1. Chuck Klein	**A.** Won six NL home run titles in seven-year period
2. Bobby Wine	**B.** The first Phillies player to win an NL Gold Glove Award
3. Richie Ashburn	**C.** The first Phillies player to win the NL Rookie of the Year Award
4. Gavvy Cravath	**D.** The first Phillies player to win the NL batting title—.340
5. Billy Hamilton	**E.** The only Phillies player to win two NL batting titles
6. Sam Thompson	**F.** The only Phillies player ever to win a Triple Crown and hit for the cycle twice
7. Dick Allen	**G.** The first Phillies player to win the NL home run title

567

1. Mike Schmidt	**A.** The only member of the Phillies to be a World Series MVP
2. Johnny Callison	**B.** The only Phillie to be the All-Star Game MVP
3. Cy Williams	**C.** The first member of the Phillies to join the 30-30 club when he hit 31 homers to go along with his 36 stolen bases
4. Chuck Klein	**D.** The first member of the Phillies to win the NL MVP Award

5. Danny Litwhiler   **E. At 40, the oldest major leaguer to lead both leagues in hits in one season**

6. Bobby Abreu   **F. The first of only two Phillies (Jim Thome is the other) to hit 15 home runs in one month**

7. Pete Rose   **G. The first full-time player on any team in major league history to field a perfect 1.000 for a season**

568

1. Jim Konstanty   **A. The only Phillies pitcher to strike out 300 batters in a season twice, and he did it in back-to-back years**

2. Jack Sanford   **B. The only Phillies pitcher to be a 20-game winner for six consecutive seasons**

3. Steve Carlton   **C. The only Phillies pitcher ever to win the NL MVP Award**

4. Curt Schilling   **D. The only Phillies pitcher ever to win the NL Rookie of the Year Award**

5. Grover Alexander   **E. The first Phillies pitcher to win five NL strikeout titles**

6. Steve Bedrosian   **F. The only Phillie to win the NL ERA title since 1917**

7. Robin Roberts   **G. The last Phillies pitcher to win the NL Cy Young Award**

569

1. Curt Schilling   **A. The last Phillies pitcher to win a Gold Glove Award**

2. Steve Carlton   **B. Won the 1983 Cy Young Award for leading the Phillies to a World Series berth with 19 wins and a 2.37 ERA**

3. Chris Short   **C. The only Phillies pitcher ever to win the LCS MVP Award**

4. Grover Alexander   **D. Pitched the last no-hitter for the Phillies**

5. John Denny   **E. Incredibly, the only Phillies pitcher to win 20 games in a season since 1917 besides Steve Carlton and Robin Roberts**

6. Kevin Millwood   **F. Of the four ERA titles won by Phillies pitchers, he won three of them—in consecutive seasons**

7. Jim Bunning   **G. Pitched the only perfect game in Phillies history**

569: 1-C, 2-A, 3-E, 4-F, 5-B, 6-D, 7-G

568: 1-C, 2-D, 3-F, 4-A, 5-E, 6-G, 7-B •

567: 1-A, 2-B, 3-F, 4-D, 5-G, 6-C, 7-E •

1. 1899	A. The first year the Phillies were in the World Series
2. 1981	B. The Phillies lost 23 straight games
3. 1980	C. The last year the Phillies featured four Gold Glove winners in the same season
4. 1915	D. The Phillies were swept by the Yankees in the World Series
5. 1952	E. The only year in five tries that the Phillies won the World Series
6. 1950	F. The last year the Phillies featured three 20-game winners in the same season
7. 1961	G. The first year the All-Star Game was hosted by the Phillies

571

1. 1894	A. Terry Mulholland picked off 16 runners for a major league record
2. 1992	B. The team changed its official nickname from the Phillies to the Blue Jays
3. 1971	C. Rick Wise pitched a no-hitter and belted two home runs in the same game
4. 1977	D. The Phillies lost a team record 111 games
5. 1976	E. The Phillies hit an astounding .343 as a team
6. 1943	F. The first year the Phillies won 100 games in a season
7. 1941	G. The last year the Phillies won 100 games in a season

572

Pittsburgh Pirates.

1. Dick Groat	A. The last Pirate to win the NL batting title before Freddy Sanchez in 2006
2. Barry Bonds	B. The first Pirate to win the NL MVP Award

3. Jason Bay   **C. Most recent Pirate to win the NL MVP Award**

4. Dave Parker   **D. The only Pirate to win the NL Rookie of the Year Award**

5. Willie Stargell   **E. The first Pirate to win the NL batting title**

6. Bill Madlock   **F. The last Pirate to win back-to-back batting titles**

7. Honus Wagner   **G. The last Pirate to win the NL home run title**

573

1. Tommy Leach   **A. The first Pirate to be the World Series MVP**

2. Roberto Clemente **B. The first Pirate to win a Gold Glove Award**

3. Bill Mazeroski   **C. Won three batting titles with Pittsburgh**

4. Dave Parker   **D. The first Pirate to win the NL home run title**

5. Willie Stargell   **E. The last Pirate to win back-to-back NL home run titles**

6. Paul Waner   **F. The only Pirate to be the MVP of the NLCS**

7. Ralph Kiner   **G. The only Pirate to be the MVP of the All-Star Game**

574

1. John Candelaria **A. Threw the only no-hitter for the Pirates from 1908 through 1968**

2. Rube Waddell   **B. The last Pirate to win the NL Cy Young Award**

3. Bob Veale   **C. The last Pirate to win the NL strikeout title**

4. Vern Law   **D. The last Pirate to win the NL ERA title**

5. Doug Drabek   **E. The first Pirate to win the NL ERA title**

6. Francisco Cordova **F. The first Pirate to win the NL Cy Young Award**

7. Cliff Chambers   **G. Starting pitcher who threw the first nine innings of a ten-inning no-hitter—the last no-hitter in Pirates history**

WHO, WHAT, WHEN, WHERE, AND WHY

1. Who is sliding home?

2. What did he just do?

3. Where does he stand on the all-time list for this feat?

4. How long did his career last?

5. BONUS: How many times did Ty Cobb perform this same feat?

575:
1. Hall of Famer Honus Wagner of the Pittsburgh Pirates.

2. Stole home after stealing second and third in the same at bat.

3. First, with five such successful second-to-home steals.

4. From 1897 to 1917.

5. Three.

576

1. Roy Face	A. Holds the top three spots in the Pirates record book for strikeouts in a season (his best being 326)
2. Dave Giusti	B. Pirates record holder for career strikeouts—1,682
3. John Smiley	C. The only Pirates pitcher to win the NL strikeout title from 1901 to 1963
4. Ray Kremer	D. The only Pirates pitcher to win back-to-back ERA titles
5. Preacher Roe	E. The last 20-game winner for the Pirates
6. Ed Morris	F. Holds Pirates record with 22 consecutive wins
7. Bob Friend	G. Pirates' most recent NL Fireman of the Year

577

1. 1890	A. The only year in the team's last six World Series appearances that the Pirates lost
2. 1903	B. The Pirates became the first team ever to come back from a three-games-to-one deficit to win the World Series
3. 1909	C. The United States Board of Geographic Names proclaimed that Pittsburgh had to drop the "h" in its name, which they did for 21 years, until city residents protested and the letter was reinstated
4. 1927	D. The first year the Pirates won the World Series
5. 1902	E. The first year the Pirates played in the World Series
6. 1925	F. The first year the Pirates won 100 games in a season
7. 1923	G. The first baseman Charlie Grimm set a new NL record by getting a hit in his first 23 games to start the season

1. 1909

A. Dale Long set a new major league record by hitting a home run in eight consecutive games

2. 1956

B. The Pirates were—amazingly—the only team in the NL to have three consecutive winning seasons

3. 1959

C. The Pirates set their team record for wins in a season with 109, which was also the last time they won 100 games

4. 1979

D. The Pirates whipped the Cubs, 22–0, the worst shutout one team has inflicted on another during the 20th century

5. 1975

E. Harvey Haddix pitched his 12-inning perfect game before losing in the 13th

6. 1974

F. Willie Stargell was the NL's co-MVP, the only year in history in which the award was a tie

7. 1992

G. Richie Zisk collected an incredible 21 RBIs in just ten games

579

St. Louis Cardinals.

1. Frankie Frisch

A. The first Cardinal to win back-to-back NL batting titles

2. Stan Musial

B. The last Cardinal to win the NL Rookie of the Year Award

3. Wally Moon

C. The first Cardinal to win an NL batting title

4. Albert Pujols

D. The first Cardinal to win the NL Rookie of the Year Award

5. Willie McGee

E. The only Cardinal to win more than one MVP Award

6. Rogers Hornsby

F. The first Cardinal to win the NL MVP Award

7. Jesse Burkett

G. The last Cardinal (before 2005) to win the NL MVP Award

580

1. Joe Torre

A. The first Cardinal to win an NL Gold Glove

2. Joe Medwick

B. The first Cardinal to win two NL home run titles

578: 1-C, 2-A, 3-E, 4-F (with Keith Hernandez), 5-D, 6-G, 7-B • **579:** 1-F, 2-E, 3-D, 4-B, 5-G, 6-A, 7-C

3. Darrell Porter   **C. The last Cardinal to win the NL batting title who wasn't a first baseman or outfielder**

4. Ken Boyer   **D. The first batting champion to wear glasses**

5. Rogers Hornsby   **E. The last Cardinal to win a Triple Crown**

6. Johnny Mize   **F. The first Cardinal to win back-to-back NL home run titles**

7. Chick Hafey   **G. The last Cardinal to be the MVP of the World Series before David Eckstein in 2006**

581

1. Bud Smith   **A. The only Cardinals pitcher to win the NL Rookie of the Year Award**

2. Bob Forsch   **B. The last Cardinal to win the NL Cy Young Award**

3. Chris Carpenter   **C. Pitched last no-hitter for the Cardinals**

4. Bob Gibson   **D. The first Cardinals pitcher to win the NL MVP Award**

5. Jesse Haines   **E. The only Cardinal to pitch two no-hitters**

6. Dizzy Dean   **F. The only Cardinals pitcher to be the World Series MVP**

7. Todd Worrell   **G. Pitched the first no-hitter ever for the Cardinals**

582

1. Bob Gibson   **A. The first of only two Cardinals pitchers to win two NL ERA titles**

2. Jose DeLeon   **B. The first Cardinals pitcher to win back-to-back NL strikeout titles**

3. Bill Hallahan   **C. The last Cardinals pitcher to win the NL strikeout title**

4. Dizzy Dean   **D. The only Cardinal to win more than one Cy Young Award**

5. Joe Magrane   **E. Second of only two Cardinals pitchers to win two NL ERA titles**

6. Bill Doak   **F. The last Cardinal to win the NL ERA title**

7. Howie Pollet   **G. The only Cardinal to win four straight NL strikeout titles**

582: 1-D, 2-C, 3-B, 4-G, 5-F, 6-A, 7-E

• **581:** 1-C, 2-E, 3-B, 4-F, 5-G, 6-D, 7-A • **580:** 1-C, 2-E, 3-G, 4-A, 5-B, 6-F, 7-D

1. 1926   A. The first year the Cardinals appeared in the World Series

2. 1944   B. Outfielder George Watkins hit .373 for St. Louis, still the National League record for rookies

3. 1888   C. The Cardinals defeated their crosstown rivals the St. Louis Browns in the World Series

4. 1928   D. The only year besides 2004 in the Cardinals' 16 trips to the World Series that they were swept in four straight

5. 1909   E. The last year the Cardinals lost 100 games in a season

6. 1930   F. St. Louis won their fourth straight American Association pennant

7. 1908   G. The Cardinals made 17 errors in a doubleheader against Cincinnati

584

1. 1964   A. The last year the Cardinals had two 20-game winners in the same season

2. 1982   B. The Cardinals stormed back from 8.5 games behind and fourth place in mid-September to win the pennant when Philadelphia collapsed

3. 1963   C. The Cardinals lost 27 games in September

4. 1985   D. The last year the Cardinals won the World Series before 2006

5. 1942   E. The Cardinals set their team record for wins in a season—106

6. 1930   F. The first of only three years in which the Cardinals had four Gold Glove Award winners

7. 1908   G. The Cardinals had 11 players hit over .300

583: 1-A, 2-C, 3-F, 4-D, 5-G, 6-B, 7-E • **584:** 1-B, 2-D, 3-F, 4-A, 5-E, 6-G, 7-C

WHO, WHAT, WHEN, WHERE, AND WHY

1. **Who** are these guys?

2. **What** is the group's nickname, and why?

3. **When** did they earn it?

4. **Where** was their home?

585:

1. Several members of the St. Louis Cardinals.

2. The Gas House Gang, because they were always clowning around.

3. 1934, primarily. The name stuck for a few more years, but is generally attributed to the Series-winning team of 1934.

4. Sportsman's Park.

San Diego Padres.

1. Ken Caminiti
2. Tony Gwynn
3. Steve Garvey
4. Benito Santiago
5. Dave Winfield
6. Fred McGriff
7. Nate Colbert

A. The only Padre ever to win the NL MVP Award
B. The only Padre ever to win the NL home run title
C. The first Padre to win an NL Gold Glove Award
D. The first Padre to win the NLCS MVP Award
E. The last Padre to win the NL Rookie of the Year Award
F. Padre with the most home runs in a rookie season (24)
G. The first Padre to win a batting title

587

1. Gary Sheffield
2. Steve Garvey
3. Ken Caminiti
4. Tony Gwynn
5. Phil Nevin
6. Steve Finley
7. Jack Clark

A. The last Padre to win a Gold Glove before Mike Cameron in 2006
B. Padres record holder for most walks in a season (132)
C. The only member of the Padres to win an NL batting title besides Tony Gwynn
D. Holds Padres record for most extra-base hits in one season—84
E. Padre who owns the most Gold Gloves—5
F. The only Padres infielder to have his number retired
G. Holds the Padres record for most career grand slams—6

588

1. Sterling Hitchcock
2. LaMarr Hoyt
3. Randy Jones
4. Gaylord Perry

A. The first Padres pitcher to win the NL strikeout title
B. The only Padres pitcher to win the NLCS MVP Award
C. The only Padres pitcher to win the NL Rookie of the Year Award
D. The only Padres pitcher to be the MVP of the All-Star Game

586: 1-A, 2-G, 3-D, 4-E, 5-C, 6-B, 7-F • **587:** 1-C, 2-F, 3-A, 4-E, 5-G, 6-D, 7-B

5. Butch Metzger   **E. The only Padres pitcher since 1975 to win an NL ERA title**

6. Jake Peavy   **F. The only Padres pitcher to have his number retired**

7. Andy Benes   **G. Most recent Padres starting pitcher to win an NL Cy Young Award**

589

1. Randy Jones   **A. The last Padres pitcher to win the NL strikeout title**

2. Mark Davis   **B. The last Padres pitcher to win the NL Cy Young Award**

3. Trevor Hoffman   **C. The first Padres pitcher to win the NL Cy Young Award**

4. Rollie Fingers   **D. Padres record holder for most games pitched in a season—83**

5. Gaylord Perry   **E. The last Padre to win an NL Fireman of the Year Award**

6. Jake Peavy   **F. The last 20-game winner for the Padres**

7. Craig Lefferts   **G. Padres reliever with the most NL Fireman of the Year Awards—3**

590

1. 1998   **A. Andy Hawkins and LaMarr Hoyt both won 11 straight games to set the Padres record (since tied by Kevin Brown)**

2. 1969   **B. Steve Arlin pitched two one-hitters and three two-hitters in one month, yet won only three of the five games**

3. 1999   **C. Padres set their team record for consecutive wins—14**

4. 1994   **D. Dave Roberts was 14–17 despite having the second-best ERA among National League starters—2.10**

5. 1985   **E. Padres set their team record for consecutive losses—13**

6. 1971   **F. Padres set their team record for wins in a season—98**

7. 1972   **G. Padres set their team record for losses in a season—110**

590: 1-F, 2-G, 3-C, 4-E, 5-A, 6-D, 7-B

589: 1-C, 2-B, 3-E, 4-G, 5-F, 6-A, 7-D • **588:** 1-B, 2-D, 3-F, 4-G, 5-C, 6-E, 7-A •

1. 1971	A. The year only nine Padres were hit by pitches all season!
2. 1984	B. The first year the Padres won a division title
3. 1998	C. The last year the Padres won the NL pennant
4. 1993	D. The last time the Padres lost 100 games in a season
5. 1972	E. Shortstop Enzo Hernandez had 549 at bats but only 12 RBIs
6. 1989	F. Fred Norman won only nine games, but six of them were shutouts and four were against the NL champ Reds
7. 1980	G. The Padres were managed for one season by the team's radio announcer from the year before who had no prior managing experience

592

San Francisco Giants. (Note: Includes previous franchise location in New York.)

1. Roger Connor	A. The only Giant ever to win three straight NL home run titles
2. Barry Bonds	B. The last Giants position player to win the NL Rookie of the Year Award
3. Willie Mays	C. The only Giant to win more than one batting title
4. Gary Mathews	D. The first Giant to win an NL home run title
5. Buck Ewing	E. The first Giant to win an NL batting title
6. Mike Tiernan	F. The only Giant to win a batting title from 1931 to 2001
7. Mel Ott	G. The first Giant to win back-to-back NL home run titles

593

1. Willie Mays	A. The first Giant to win the NL Rookie of the Year Award
2. Willie McCovey	B. Won a Gold Glove one year and then led the National League in errors at his position the next year

591: 1-E, 2-B, 3-C, 4-D, 5-F, 6-A, 7-G • **592:** 1-E, 2-C, 3-F, 4-B, 5-D, 6-G, 7-A

3. Bobby Bonds   **C. Hit the first-ever grand slam by a National Leaguer in the World Series**

4. Dusty Rhodes   **D. The last Giant to be the All-Star Game MVP**

5. George Davis   **E. The only Giant to win the All-Star Game MVP Award and the NL MVP Award in the same season**

6. Chuck Hiller   **F. Holds the Giants batting streak record—33 games**

7. Matt Williams   **G. The only Giant to win a World Series MVP Award**

594

1. Mike McCormick   **A. The only Giants pitcher to win an MVP Award**

2. John Montefusco   **B. The only Cy Young Award winner in Giants history**

3. Rick Reuschel   **C. The only Giants pitcher to throw more than one no-hitter**

4. Carl Hubbell   **D. The only Giants pitcher to win a Gold Glove Award**

5. Juan Marichal   **E. The only Giants pitcher to be the All-Star Game MVP**

6. Amos Rusie   **F. The only Giants pitcher to be NL Rookie of the Year**

7. Christy Mathewson   **G. The first Giants pitcher to toss a no-hitter**

595

1. John Montefusco   **A. The last Giants pitcher to throw a no-hitter**

2. Jason Schmidt   **B. Giants pitcher with the most NL ERA titles—5**

3. Joe McGinnity   **C. The last Giants pitcher to win the NL ERA title**

4. Bill Voiselle   **D. Giants record holder for most consecutive wins in one season—19**

5. Tim Keefe   **E. The only Giant since 1937 to win an NL strikeout title**

6. Christy Mathewson   **F. The first Giants pitcher to win the NL ERA title**

7. Rube Marquard   **G. The first Giants pitcher to win the NL strikeout crown**

595: 1-A, 2-C, 3-F, 4-E, 5-G, 6-B, 7-D

594: 1-B, 2-F, 3-D, 4-A, 5-E, 6-G, 7-C • **593:** 1-A, 2-E, 3-D, 4-G, 5-F, 6-C, 7-B •

WHO, WHAT, WHEN, WHERE, AND WHY

1. Who are these three guys?

2. Why is their appearance together significant?

3. When was this taken?

4. Where?

5. BONUS: Who won the game?

6. BETCHA-DIDN'T-KNOW BONUS: What positions did each play in this game?

6. Felipe played right field while Jesus and Matty were both pinch hitters.

5. The Mets, 4–2.

4. At the Polo Grounds in New York, home of the New York Mets.

3. September 10, 1963.

2. For the first time ever, three brothers appeared in the same game playing for the same team (the San Francisco Giants).

1. Jesus, Matty, and Felipe Alou.

596:

1. 1954

    A. The Giants won their fourth straight NL pennant, still the National League record for consecutive titles

2. 1937

    B. Mel Ott was the NL runner-up in home runs, and all 18 of his homers were hit at home

3. 1924

    C. The last year the Giants repeated as National League champions

4. 1916

    D. The only year in Giants history the team had the NL batting champ and the NL ERA champ

5. 1953

    E. The Giants lost 25 games in August

6. 1904

    F. The Giants won 29 games in September

7. 1943

    G. The Giants set their team record for wins in a season—106

598

1. 1920

    A. The only year in 17 trips to the World Series that the Giants were swept in four straight

2. 1930

    B. The last year the Giants hosted the All-Star Game

3. 1906

    C. Bill Terry hit .401 for the Giants, the last time a National League player topped the mark

4. 1993

    D. The only year in the Giants' 124-year history (through 2006) that the team lost 100 games in a season

5. 1984

    E. The last year the Giants had three 20-game winners in the same season

6. 1989

    F. The only year in Giants history they had four Gold Glove winners

7. 1985

    G. The Giants suffered their worst shutout loss, 19–0, to the Chicago Cubs

597: 1-D, 2-C, 3-A, 4-F, 5-E, 6-G, 7-B • **598:** 1-E, 2-C, 3-G, 4-F, 5-B, 6-A, 7-D

Seattle Mariners.

1. Ken Griffey Jr.   **A. The first Mariner to win the AL Rookie of the Year Award**

2. Ichiro Suzuki   **B. The first Mariner to win the AL MVP Award**

3. Alvin Davis   **C. Holds the Mariners record for the most strikeouts in one season—176**

4. Jay Buhner   **D. Won the AL Rookie of the Year Award, AL MVP Award, and AL batting title all in the same season**

5. Edgar Martinez   **E. The only Mariner batting champ with just one title; all the others have at least two**

6. Alex Rodriguez   **F. The first Mariner to win the AL batting title**

7. Mike Cameron   **G. The first of only three Mariners ever to hit for the cycle**

600

1. Ichiro Suzuki   **A. Holds Mariners record for most times hit by a pitch in one season—17**

2. Ken Griffey Jr.   **B. The only Mariner to win back-to-back AL home run titles**

3. Edgar Martinez   **C. The only Mariner with a 6-for-6 game, tied for the AL best**

4. Alex Rodriguez   **D. The only Mariner with more than 2,000 career hits—2,247**

5. Dan Wilson   **E. The last Mariner to win the AL MVP Award**

6. Dave Valle   **F. Holds Mariners record for runs scored in a season—141**

7. Raul Ibanez   **G. Holds the Mariners career record for sacrifice hits—85**

601

1. Randy Johnson   **A. The last Mariners pitcher to win the AL ERA title**

2. Chris Bosio   **B. The first Mariner to win back-to-back AL strikeout titles**

599: 1-B, 2-D, 3-A, 4-G, 5-F, 6-E, 7-C • **600:** 1-E, 2-B, 3-D, 4-F, 5-G, 6-A, 7-C

3. Freddy Garcia   **C. The only Mariners pitcher to win the AL Cy Young Award**

4. Floyd Bannister   **D. The last Mariners pitcher to throw a perfect game**

5. Mark Langston   **E. Holds the Mariners record for wins in a season—21**

6. Kazuhiro Sasaki   **F. The first Mariners pitcher to win the AL strikeout title**

7. Jamie Moyer   **G. The only Mariners pitcher to win the AL Rookie of the Year Award**

602

1. Randy Johnson   **A. Seattle record holder for games finished in a season—64**

2. Mike Parrott   **B. Lost his first game as a rookie, then set a Seattle record by winning his next nine consecutive decisions**

3. Mark Langston   **C. Had one season in which he got the win on Opening Day and then lost his next 16 straight games**

4. Dave Fleming   **D. Seattle record holder for saves in a season—45**

5. Jamie Moyer   **E. The first Mariners pitcher to throw a perfect game**

6. Bill Caudill   **F. The first rookie to lead the AL in strikeouts since Herb Score in 1955**

7. Kazuhiro Sasaki   **G. Mariners record holder for career wins—145**

603

1. 1978   **A. Year that only one player in the major leagues hit three home runs in one game—the Mariners' Jeff Burroughs**

2. 1999   **B. The Mariners set the AL record for most wins in a season (116) and tied the major league record**

3. 2001   **C. The first year the Mariners won a division title**

4. 1977   **D. The Mariners moved into Safeco Field**

5. 1983   **E. The first year the Mariners lost 100 games in a season (they lost 104, the team record)**

6. 1995   **F. The Mariners began play in the AL**

7. 1981   **G. The last year the Mariners lost 100 games in a season**

603: 1-E, 2-D, 3-B, 4-F, 5-G, 6-C, 7-A
• **602:** 1-E, 2-C, 3-F, 4-B, 5-G, 6-A, 7-D • **601:** 1-C, 2-D, 3-A, 4-F, 5-B, 6-G, 7-E

Baseball Trivia

604

1. 1994	A. The first year the All-Star Game was hosted by the Mariners
2. 2001	B. The Mariners played 30 of their last 35 games of the season on the road
3. 1993	C. Ken Griffey Jr. homered in eight consecutive games to tie the major league record
4. 2003	D. The first year the Mariners had a 20-game winner
5. 1979	E. The Mariners led the majors in batting average, earned run average, and fielding average, the first team to win the "team Triple Crown" since the 1948 Cleveland Indians
6. 1997	F. The first year the Mariners had a skipper who won the AL Manager of the Year Award
7. 1995	G. The Mariners featured four Gold Glove winners

605

Texas Rangers. (Note: Includes previous franchise location in Washington, D.C., as the replacement Senators team.)

1. Frank Howard	A. The only Ranger to be the AL Rookie of the Year
2. Jeff Burroughs	B. The only Ranger to win more than one AL MVP Award
3. Juan Gonzalez	C. Most recent Ranger to win the AL batting title
4. Alex Rodriguez	D. The first Ranger to win the AL MVP Award
5. Mike Hargrove	E. Most recent Ranger to win the AL MVP Award
6. Julio Franco	F. The first Ranger to win two AL home run titles
7. Michael Young	G. The first Ranger to win the AL batting title

WHO, WHAT, WHEN, WHERE, AND WHY

1. Who are these two players?

2. What did they do to achieve notoriety?

3. When?

4. Which two teams did both pitchers eventually play for after leaving the Yankees?

606:
1. Fritz Peterson and Mike Kekich of the Yankees.

2. They swapped wives, families, and even pets.

3. 1973.

4. Cleveland and Texas.

607

1. Frank Howard	**A. Hit three grand slams in one week**
2. Larry Parrish	**B. The only Ranger to win three consecutive AL home run titles**
3. Juan Gonzalez	**C. Upset over his lack of playing time, he attacked the manager and sent him to the hospital with a shattered cheekbone**
4. Alex Rodriguez	**D. Once hit ten home runs in a stretch of 20 at bats**
5. Michael Young	**E. The first Ranger to win an AL Gold Glove Award**
6. Jim Sundberg	**F. The first Ranger to win back-to-back AL home run titles**
7. Lenny Randle	**G. Most recent Ranger to be the All-Star Game MVP**

608

1. Jim Bibby	**A. Pitched first no-hitter in Rangers history**
2. Kenny Rogers	**B. The first Ranger to win the AL ERA title**
3. Nolan Ryan	**C. Pitched only perfect game in Rangers history**
4. Rick Honeycutt	**D. The last Ranger to win 20 games in a season**
5. Dick Donovan	**E. Most wins in a season by a Rangers pitcher—25**
6. Ferguson Jenkins	**F. The only Ranger with more than one no-hitter**
7. Rick Helling	**G. The last Ranger to win the AL ERA title**

609

1. Kenny Rogers	**A. Once struck out 21 batters in one 16-inning game**
2. Tom Cheney	**B. 21-game winner in 1992, and one of only three 20-game winners in team history**
3. Bennie Daniels	**C. The only Rangers pitcher to win a Gold Glove**
4. Bert Blyleven	**D. Went on the DL after injuring his arm flicking sunflower seeds**
5. Kevin Brown	**E. Holds team record for most consecutive losses—10**
6. Nolan Ryan	**F. Pitched a no-hitter in 1977**
7. Greg Harris	**G. The only Rangers player at any position to have his number retired**

609: 1-C, 2-A, 3-E, 4-F, 5-B, 6-G, 7-D

607: 1-D, 2-A, 3-F, 4-B, 5-G, 6-E, 7-C • **608:** 1-A, 2-C, 3-F, 4-G, 5-B, 6-E, 7-D •

610

1. 1970	A. Billy Martin became the team's manager
2. 1969	B. Ted Williams became the team's manager
3. 1971	C. The first time the team hosted the All-Star Game
4. 1973	D. The team lost 106 games, the franchise record
5. 1962	E. The team lost their last 14 games of the season
6. 1963	F. The last year the team played in Griffith Stadium
7. 1961	G. The team's last year in Washington

611

1. 1999	A. The fourth straight season the team lost 100 games in a season
2. 1973	B. The team's owner publicly called his players, "Dogs on the field, and dogs off the field," and promptly put the team up for sale (that year the team had four managers in six days)
3. 1964	C. The last year when the team lost 100 games in a season
4. 1994	D. The team scored 16 runs in the eighth inning of a 26–7 game
5. 1996	E. The team won 95 games, the franchise record
6. 1980	F. The first year the team ever won a divisional title
7. 1977	G. Ferguson Jenkins was arrested in Toronto for possession of narcotics and suspended by Commissioner Bowie Kuhn

612

Toronto Blue Jays.

1. Alfredo Griffin	A. Most recent AL Rookie of the Year
2. John Olerud	B. The only AL MVP in Blue Jays history
3. George Bell	C. The only batting champion in Blue Jays hist
4. Eric Hinske	D. The first Blue Jays infielder to win a Gold Glove
5. Jesse Barfield	E. The first Blue Jay to win the AL home run title
6. Fred McGriff	F. The last Blue Jay to win the AL home run title
7. Tony Fernandez	G. The first AL Rookie of the Year in Blue Jays history

612: 1-G, 2-C, 3-B, 4-A, 5-E, 6-F, 7-D

611: 1-E, 2-C, 3-A, 4-F, 5-D, 6-G, 7-B

610: 1-E, 2-B, 3-G, 4-A, 5-C, 6-D, 7-F

613

1. Pat Borders
2. Devon White
3. Paul Molitor
4. Roberto Alomar
5. Carlos Delgado
6. Glenallen Hill
7. Dave Collins

A. The first Blue Jay to be the World Series MVP

B. Spent time on the DL from severe cuts and scrapes sustained while having a nightmare about spiders

C. The only Blue Jays outfielder to win five consecutive AL Gold Glove Awards

D. The only Blue Jays infielder to win five consecutive AL Gold Glove Awards

E. Holds the team record for stolen bases in a season—60

F. The last Blue Jay to be the World Series MVP

G. Once hit eight home runs in six games

614

1. Pat Hentgen
2. Roy Halladay
3. Roger Clemens
4. Dave Stieb
5. Dave Stewart
6. Jack Morris
7. Dennis Lamp

A. Most recent Blue Jay to win the AL Cy Young Award

B. The only Blue Jays pitcher ever to be an ALCS MVP

C. The first 20-game winner in Blue Jays history

D. Had a perfect 11–0 record one season

E. The first Blue Jay to win the AL Cy Young Award

F. The only Blue Jay ever to win back-to-back AL Cy Young Awards

G. The first Blue Jay to win the AL ERA title

613: 1-A, 2-C, 3-F, 4-D, 5-G, 6-B, 7-E • **614:** 1-E, 2-A, 3-F, 4-G, 5-B, 6-C, 7-D

WHO, WHAT, WHEN, WHERE, AND WHY

1. **Who** is this pitcher?

2. **What** had he just done?

3. **When** did he do it?

4. **Where?**

615:
1. Hall of Famer Phil Niekro.

2. Win his 300th career game.

3. October 6, 1985, the last day of the season.

4. Exhibition Stadium in Toronto.

1. Dave Stieb	**A. The last Blue Jay to win 20 games in a season**
2. Roger Clemens	**B. The only Blue Jay to average more than ten strikeouts per nine innings pitched for his career with the team**
3. Roy Halladay	**C. The only Blue Jays pitcher to throw a no-hitter**
4. Duane Ward	**D. Holds Blue Jays record for highest winning percentage (.824) in a season (he was 14–3)**
5. Jim Clancy	**E. The only Blue Jays pitcher to be a 20-game winner more than once**
6. Tom Henke	**F. The only Blue Jay ever to start 40 games in a season**
7. Juan Guzman	**G. Holds team record for career games pitched—452**

617

1. 1979	**A. The last year the Blue Jays won the AL pennant**
2. 1977	**B. The first year the Blue Jays lost 100 games in a season**
3. 1985	**C. The first year the Blue Jays appeared in the World Series**
4. 1992	**D. The Blue Jays set their team record for losses (109)**
5. 1991	**E. The first year the Blue Jays finished anywhere except the AL East's cellar**
6. 1983	**F. The first year the Blue Jays won a division title**
7. 1993	**G. The only year the All-Star Game was played in Toronto**

1. 1985
2. 1989
3. 1991
4. 1993
5. 1981
6. 2001
7. 2000

A. The Blue Jays began playing in Toronto's SkyDome

B. The Blue Jays set their team record for wins—99

C. The last year the Blue Jays drew more than four million fans

D. The only year in team history the Blue Jays failed to draw at least one million fans

E. The Blue Jays homered in 23 consecutive games

F. The first year the Blue Jays drew more than four million fans

G. The Blue Jays had seven players who hit 20 or more homers

619

NAME THAT YEAR

Seven clues. One year. See how few clues it takes you to guess the year.

1 Cincinnati's **Ted Kluszewski** completes a three-year stretch in which he clubs 136 home runs, yet, amazingly, strikes out just 109 times.

2 **The Yankees lose a seven-game** World Series for the first time since 1926.

3 **Jimmy Piersall's autobiography,** *Fear Strikes Out,* is released.

4 **Mickey Mantle leads the American League** in homers *and* triples.

5 **Roy Campanella wins** his third NL MVP Award.

6 **Herb Score wins** the AL Rookie of the Year Award.

7 **The Dodgers win** their first World Championship.

618: 1-B, 2-A, 3-F, 4-C, 5-D, 6-E, 7-G • **619:** 1955

WHO, WHAT, WHEN, WHERE, AND WHY

1. Who is this player?

2. What's his claim to fame?

3. When was the spitball declared illegal, and when did he
pitch his last one?

4. What team did he end his career with?

620:

1. Hall of Famer Burleigh Grimes.

2. He was the last of the legal spitball pitchers.

3. When the spitball was declared illegal in 1920, Grimes and 16 other spitball
pitchers were allowed to continue throwing the pitch until the end of their
careers. Grimes played until 1934, longer than any of the other
"grandfathered" spitballers.

4. The longtime Dodger finished his career with the Pittsburgh Pirates, the
same team he broke in with in 1916.

BASEBALL IN THE MOVIES

Match the movie title and release year with its plot.

1. *Headin' Home* (1920)

2. *The Pride of the Yankees* (1942)

3. *It Happens Every Spring* (1949)

4. *Take Me Out to the Ball Game* (1949)

5. *Angels in the Outfield* (1951)

6. *The Pride of St. Louis* (1952)

7. *Fear Strikes Out* (1957)

A. The life and career of Lou Gehrig

B. A hard-hearted, foul-mouthed manager agrees to clean up his act in exchange for divine help with his lowly Pirates team

C. The life and career of Jimmy Piersall

D. The star of the hometown team competes with a rival for the affection of the banker's daughter and first place in the hearts of the townsfolk

E. The life and career of Dizzy Dean

F. Team's second baseman falls in love with the new woman owner of the ballclub

G. A chemistry professor takes a leave of absence to pitch in the major leagues when he discovers a chemical that makes baseballs avoid bats

622

1. *Damn Yankees* (1958)

2. *Bang the Drum Slowly* (1973)

3. *It's Good to Be Alive* (1974)

4. *Bad News Bears* (1976)

A. A washed-up minor leaguer finds himself reinvigorated after he begins coaching a team of underprivileged kids

B. The life and career of Roy Campanella

C. The life and career of Satchel Paige

D. The life and career of Ron LeFlore

621: 1-D, 2-A, 3-G, 4-F, 5-B, 6-E, 7-C

5. *One in a Million* (1978)

E. A pitcher befriends the team's dimwitted rookie catcher, who is afflicted with Hodgkin's disease

6. *The Comeback Kid* (1980)

F. A Washington Senators fan makes a deal with the devil in order to help his team

7. *Don't Look Back* (1981)

G. Story of a pathetic California Little League team coached by a drunken swimming pool cleaner

623

1. *The Natural* (1984)

A. The life and career of Pete Gray

2. *The Slugger's Wife* (1985)

B. A washed-up pitcher attempts a comeback with the aid of a second-rate lounge singer and her baseball-fanatic daughter

3. *Brewster's Millions* (1985)

C. Story about a couple's conflicting careers, which undermines the superstar husband's play

4. *A Winner Never Quits* (1986)

D. A minor league player inherits a fortune but has to give it away in order to inherit even more

5. *Long Gone* (1987)

E. Story of a minor league baseball team battling for the league title amidst the corruption and racism of the American South

6. *Amazing Grace and Chuck* (1987)

F. A star Little League pitcher creates a national movement when he refuses to pitch again until all nuclear weapons are disarmed

7. *Trading Hearts* (1987)

G. A mysterious middle-aged player arrives out of nowhere to lead a losing team to the pennant

622: 1-F, 2-E, 3-B, 4-G, 5-D, 6-A, 7-C • **623:** 1-G, 2-C, 3-D, 4-A, 5-E, 6-F, 7-B

Baseball Trivia

1. *Bull Durham* (1988)

2. *Eight Men Out* (1988)

3. *Field of Dreams* (1989)

4. *Major League* (1989)

5. *Night Game* (1989)

6. *Talent for the Game* (1991)

7. *The Babe* (1992)

A. Story of the Black Sox Scandal of 1919

B. An exotic dancer inherits a baseball team and does everything she can to make the team lose so she can exercise her escape clause and move

C. A serial killer strikes every time a certain Astros pitcher wins a game

D. A baseball scout is ethically torn when he discovers a new star that the owners want to exploit

E. A baseball groupie romances two minor league players, the rookie pitcher and the veteran catcher who is hired to teach him the ropes

F. The life story of a legend, from his tumultuous childhood to his iconic moments on the field

G. A farmer plows under his cornfield in order to build a baseball field to satisfy the command of a strange voice

625

1. *A League of Their Own* (1992)

2. *Mr. Baseball* (1992)

3. *The Sandlot* (1993)

4. *Rookie of the Year* (1993)

A. A homeless man finds renewed strength to live his life after coaching a Little League team

B. Divine intervention helps a boy realize his wish of getting a family

C. A disgraced talent scout risks a new find's mental health in order to jumpstart his own career

D. A boy recovers from an arm injury with a supernatural strength that allows him to become a pitcher for the Chicago Cubs

624: 1-E, 2-A, 3-G, 4-B, 5-C, 6-D, 7-F

5. *The Man from Left Field* (1993)

E. A fading baseball star is traded to a Japanese team and has trouble fitting into Japanese society

6. *The Scout* (1994)

F. A group of kids must devise a way to recover a Babe Ruth–autographed ball from The Beast, a legendary canine with a penchant for eating both baseballs and people

7. *Angels in the Outfield* (1994)

G. Two sisters become rivals in the first women's professional baseball league

626

1. *Soul of the Game* (1996)

A. A boy suffering from stunted growth is convinced God has a plan for him

2. *The Fan* (1996)

B. Story, told in flashback, of a pitcher at the end of his career who struggles with his love for a woman

3. *Simon Birch* (1998)

C. An 11-year-old boy, wishing to be a great ballplayer like his father, rallies his not-so-talented teammates and their curmudgeon of a coach in order to beat the team that rejected them

4. *For Love of the Game* (1999)

D. Negro league greats Satchel Paige and Josh Gibson vie to become the first black player in the majors, only to lose out to Jackie Robinson

5. *A Little Inside* (1999)

E. A superstar baseball player is tormented by a disturbed down-on-his-luck salesman

6. *Perfect Game* (2000)

F. A professional baseball player (and single father) tries to raise his daughter and live his own dream

7. *61** (2001)

G. Story of Roger Maris's pursuit of Babe Ruth's home run record amid hostile fans and indifferent teammates

WHO, WHAT, WHEN, WHERE, AND WHY

1. Who played the lead in this movie?

2. What bad habit prompted the love interest to meet the hero?

3. When was it released?

4. Where were the movie's ballpark scenes filmed?

627:

1. Babe Ruth.

2. Ruth's extreme sloppiness with chewing tobacco prompted Vernie, a laundress, to attend a game just to see how one man could be so messy.

3. 1927.

4. Wrigley Field in Chicago, which proved to be such an effective backdrop that it was used in many baseball movies over the next few decades.

628

1. *Hard Ball* (2001)

A. An aimless young ticket scalper agrees to coach a team from the projects in return for a loan

2. *Summer Catch* (2001)

B. Romance of a rich girl and her poor minor league boyfriend

3. *Bleacher Bums* (2002)

C. A long-retired player makes a comeback in order to set a record he erroneously thought he had already set

4. *The Rookie* (2002)

D. Three buddies try to make up for their lost childhood by forming a three-man team to compete against Little League teams

5. *Mr. 3000* (2004)

E. A slice-of-life story about a handful of minor league baseball fans watching a game from the stands

6. *Fever Pitch* (2005)

F. The life and career of Jimmy Morris

7. *The Benchwarmers* (2006)

G. Story of a young woman stuck between her relationship with her boyfriend and his passion for the Boston Red Sox

629

Now that you've been properly warmed up with the movie plots, let's put you in the game of naming each of the actors who starred in these movies.

1. *Headin' Home*

A. Jimmy Stewart

2. *The Babe Ruth Story*

B. Gary Cooper

3. *It Happens Every Spring*

C. Frank Sinatra

4. *The Stratton Story*

D. Babe Ruth

5. *The Jackie Robinson Story*

E. Ray Milland

6. *Take Me Out to the Ball Game*

F. William Bendix

7. *The Pride of the Yankees*

G. Jackie Robinson

628: 1-A, 2-B, 3-E, 4-F, 5-C, 6-G, 7-D • **629:** 1-D, 2-F, 3-E, 4-A, 5-G, 6-C, 7-B

630

1. *Angels in the Outfield* (1951)   **A. Walter Matthau**

2. *The Pride of St. Louis*   **B. Dan Dailey**

3. *Fear Strikes Out*   **C. Robert De Niro**

4. *Damn Yankees*   **D. Anthony Perkins**

5. *Bang the Drum Slowly*   **E. Paul Winfield**

6. *It's Good to Be Alive*   **F. Tab Hunter**

7. *The Bad News Bears*   **G. Paul Douglas**

631

1. *One in a Million*   **A. Louis Gossett Jr.**

2. *The Comeback Kid*   **B. Keith Carradine**

3. *Don't Look Back*   **C. LaVar Burton**

4. *The Natural*   **D. Richard Pryor**

5. *The Slugger's Wife*   **E. John Ritter**

6. *Brewster's Millions*   **F. Robert Redford**

7. *A Winner Never Quits*   **G. Michael O'Keefe**

632

1. *Long Gone*   **A. Kevin Costner**

2. *Amazing Grace and Chuck*   **B. John Cusack**

3. *Trading Hearts*   **C. Roy Scheider**

4. *Bull Durham*   **D. Charlie Sheen**

5. *Eight Men Out*   **E. William Petersen**

6. *Major League*   **F. Raul Julia**

7. *Night Game*   **G. Joshua Zuehike**

632: 1-E, 2-G, 3-F, 4-A, 5-B, 6-D, 7-C
631: 1-C, 2-E, 3-A, 4-F, 5-G, 6-D, 7-B •
• **630:** 1-G, 2-B, 3-D, 4-F, 5-C, 6-E, 7-A

324

633

1. *Field of Dreams*	A. Kevin Costner
2. *Talent for the Game*	B. Tom Selleck
3. *The Babe*	C. Tom Hanks
4. *A League of Their Own*	D. John Goodman
5. *Mr. Baseball*	E. Thomas Ian Nicholas
6. *The Sandlot*	F. Tom Guiry
7. *Rookie of the Year*	G. Edward James Olmos

634

1. *The Man from Left Field*	A. Albert Brooks
2. *The Scout*	B. Burt Reynolds
3. *Angels in the Outfield* (1994)	C. Ian Michael Smith
4. *Cobb*	D. Tommy Lee Jones
5. *Mr. 3000*	E. Bernie Mac
6. *The Fan*	F. Danny Glover
7. *Simon Birch*	G. Robert De Niro

635

1. *For Love of the Game*	A. Dennis Quaid
2. *Fever Pitch*	B. Edward Asner
3. *Perfect Game*	C. Kevin Costner
4. *61**	D. Drew Barrymore
5. *Hard Ball*	E. Barry Pepper
6. *Summer Catch*	F. Freddie Prinze Jr.
7. *The Rookie*	G. Keanu Reeves

635: 1-C, 2-D, 3-B, 4-E, 5-G, 6-F, 7-A

633: 1-A, 2-G, 3-D, 4-C, 5-B, 6-F, 7-E • **634:** 1-B, 2-A, 3-F, 4-D, 5-E, 6-G, 7-C •

636

And now, a couple of games of movie costars . . . just from the classics. Can you match the movie character to the actor who played the part?

1. Mr. Applegate
2. Henry "Author" Wiggen
3. Jake Taylor
4. Shoeless Joe Jackson
5. Al Stump
6. Mickey Mantle
7. Terence Mann

A. Ray Liotta
B. Michael Moriarty
C. James Earl Jones
D. Tom Berenger
E. Robert Wuhl
F. Ray Walston
G. Thomas Jane

637

1. Amanda Whurlitzer
2. Dixie Lee Boxx
3. Lola
4. Annie Savoy
5. Annie Kinsella
6. Clare Hodgson Ruth
7. Dottie Hinson

A. Gwen Verdon
B. Kelly McGillis
C. Susan Sarandon
D. Geena Davis
E. Virginia Madsen
F. Amy Madigan
G. Tatum O'Neal

638

Now some baseball movie quotations. Can you name the movie that all of the following lines came from?

1 "Quit trying to strike everybody out. Strikeouts are boring, and besides that, they're fascist. Throw some ground balls. They're more democratic."

636: 1-F, 2-B, 3-D, 4-A, 5-E, 6-G, 7-C • 637: 1-G, 2-E, 3-A, 4-C, 5-F, 6-B, 7-D

Baseball Trivia

2 "You guys . . . You lollygag the ball around the infield. You lollygag your way down to first. You lollygag in and out of the dugout. You know what that makes you? LOLLYGAGGERS!"

3 "There are 108 beads in a Catholic rosary. And there are 108 stitches in a baseball. When I learned that, I gave Jesus a chance."

4 Pitcher: "God, the sucker teed off on that like he knew I was gonna throw a fastball."
Catcher: "He did know."
Pitcher: "How?"
Catcher: "I told him. I'm your new catcher and you just got lesson number one: don't think, it can only hurt the ballclub."

639

Now, see if you can match these to the movies from which they come.

1. "If you build it, he will come."   **A. Damn Yankees**

2. "Are you trying to say Jesus   **B. The Rookie**
   can't hit a curveball?"

3. "Do you know what we get to   **C. Major League**
   do today, Brooks? We get to
   play baseball."

4. "Pick me out a winner, Bobby."   **D. The Pride of the Yankees**

5. "People say that I've had a bad   **E. Taking Care of Business**
   break. But today, I consider
   myself the luckiest man on the
   face of the Earth."

6. "I see cannibals munchin' a   **F. Field of Dreams**
   missionary luncheon."

7. "I broke out of prison to see the   **G. The Natural**
   Cubs play in the World Series."

NAME THAT YEAR

Seven clues. One year. See how few clues it takes you to guess the year.

1 **Charlie Root leads the major leagues** in wins, with 26.

2 **Three baseball movies hit the theaters:** *Casey at the Bat; Slide, Kelly, Slide;* and *The Babe Comes Home.*

3 **By himself,** Babe Ruth hits more home runs than every team in the league except the Yankees.

4 **Jimmy Cooney of the Cubs** executes an unassisted triple play against Pittsburgh.

5 **Lloyd Waner** collects a rookie-record 223 hits.

6 **Jesse and Virgil Barnes** become the first brothers in major league history to oppose each other as starting pitchers.

7 **The Murderer's Row Yankees** romp to a record 110 victories.

THE
BALLPARKS

See how well you know the specs of some of the current National League ballparks.

1. AT&T Park, San Francisco	A. Largest seating capacity—56,500
2. RFK Stadium, Washington	B. Smallest seating capacity—38,127
3. PNC Park, Pittsburgh	C. Shortest right field distance—307 feet
4. PETCO Park, San Diego	D. Deepest right field distance (382 feet) and left field distance (367 feet)
5. Minute Maid Park, Houston	E. The league's newest ballpark
6. Dodger Stadium, Los Angeles	F. Deepest center field distance (435 feet) and shortest left field distance (315 feet)
7. Busch Stadium, St. Louis	G. Shortest center field distance (395 feet)

642

Now for the current American League ballparks.

1. Comerica Park, Detroit	A. Deepest left and right field distances—347 feet
2. Fenway Park, Boston	B. The league's newest ballpark
3. Rogers Centre, Toronto	C. League's largest seating capacity—57,545
4. U.S. Cellular Field, Chicago	D. Besides Fenway Park and Yankee Stadium, the oldest ballpark in the American League
5. Yankee Stadium, New York	E. Shortest left field distance (310 feet) and shortest right field distance (302 feet)
6. Angel Stadium, Anaheim	F. Has second largest seating capacity in AL, and is the only other park besides the answer to clue C that can hold over 50,000 fans
7. SAFECO Field, Seattle	G. Of only two AL ballparks to open in midseason, this one opened later—July 15

641: 1-C, 2-A, 3-B, 4-D, 5-F, 6-G, 7-E • **642:** 1-B, 2-E, 3-F, 4-A, 5-C, 6-D, 7-G

WHO, WHAT, WHEN, WHERE, AND WHY

1. Who is the player acknowledging the fans?

2. What has he just done?

3. When did he do it?

4. Where did he do it, and where did the ball land?

5. BONUS: Who was the pitcher?

6. BETCHA-DIDN'T-KNOW BONUS: What did the Yankee
players do after the player crossed home plate?

643:
1. Roger Maris.

2. Hit his 61st home run of the season, establishing a new major league record.

3. October 1, 1961, the last day of the season.

4. Yankee Stadium, the sixth row back in the lower right-field stands.

5. Tracy Stallard of the Red Sox.

6. Formed a human wall four separate times to prevent Maris from entering
the dugout so he could receive his proper due from the fans.

Baseball Trivia

644

Baseball's ballparks are as much a part of its history as the players. Each has witnessed some of the game's greatest performances and historic contests. See if you can connect these green cathedrals to the unforgettable feats and distinctions they hosted.

1. Fenway Park
2. Yankee Stadium
3. Anaheim Stadium
4. County Stadium
5. Oakland Coliseum
6. Royals Stadium
7. The Metrodome

A. Hosted the longest All-Star Game (15 innings)

B. Where Catfish Hunter pitched his perfect game

C. Host to the first playoff game in AL history in which Lou Boudreau hit two home runs, to lead Cleveland to the pennant

D. Where Dave Winfield joined the 3,000-hit club

E. Where Tom Seaver earned his 300th career victory

F. Site of umpire Don Denkinger's infamous World Series call

G. Where Robin Yount joined the 3,000-hit club

645

1. Olympic Stadium
2. Turner Field
3. Coors Field
4. Pro Player Stadium
5. Candlestick Park
6. Dodger Stadium
7. Jack Murphy Stadium

A. Where Cal Ripken Jr. went 6 for 6 with two home runs in a 22–1 interleague win

B. Where Barry Bonds became the first 400-400 player in major league history

C. Site of Dennis Martinez's perfect game

D. Where Willie Mays joined the 600-home run club

E. Where Tony Gwynn joined the 3,000-hit club

F. Site of the highest-scoring All-Star Game in history, a 13–8 American League victory

G. Site of major league baseball's only back-to-back no-hitters

644: 1-C, 2-E, 3-A, 4-G, 5-B, 6-F, 7-D • **645:** 1-E, 2-A, 3-F, 4-B, 5-G, 6-C, 7-D

332

1. Shea Stadium	**A. Site of Jim Bunning's perfect game**
2. Riverfront Stadium	**B. Where Willie Mays joined the 500-home run club**
3. Fulton County Stadium	**C. Where Paul Waner joined the 3,000-hit club**
4. Crosley Field	**D. Site of major league baseball's only double no-hitters**
5. The Astrodome	**E. Where Pete Rose's NL-record 44-game hitting streak came to an end**
6. Wrigley Field	**F. Where Hank Aaron joined the 3,000-hit club**
7. Braves Field	**G. Where Hank Aaron hit his 714th career home run**

647

1. Comiskey Park	**A. Where Mike Witt pitched his perfect game**
2. Municipal Stadium	**B. Where Joe DiMaggio's 56-game hitting streak ended**
3. Yankee Stadium	**C. Where Larry Doby broke the AL's color barrier**
4. Tropicana Field	**D. Where Harmon Killebrew joined the 500-home run club**
5. Ballpark in Arlington	**E. Where Mickey Mantle joined the 500-home run club**
6. Arlington Stadium	**F. Where Kenny Rogers pitched his perfect game**
7. Metropolitan Stadium	**G. Where Wade Boggs joined the 3,000-hit club**

1. Tiger Stadium
2. Municipal Stadium
3. Yankee Stadium
4. Memorial Stadium
5. Shibe Park
6. Fenway Park
7. Anaheim Stadium

A. Where Al Kaline joined the 3,000-hit club

B. Where Don Sutton joined the 300-win club

C. Where Lou Gehrig's 2,130-consecutive game streak came to an end

D. Where David Wells pitched his perfect game

E. Where Bucky Dent hit his dramatic playoff home run

F. Site of the All-Star Game with the highest attendance—72,086

G. Where Ted Williams finished the 1941 season by going 6 for 8 on the final day, to hit .406 for the year

649

1. Wrigley Field
2. Ebbets Field
3. Crosley Field
4. Polo Grounds
5. Forbes Field
6. Three Rivers Stadium
7. Busch Stadium

A. Site of major league baseball's first night game

B. Where Lou Brock stole his 105th base of the season, breaking Maury Wills's record

C. Site of two unassisted triple plays in just three seasons

D. Where Stan Musial joined the 3,000-hit club

E. Where Mickey Morandini made his unassisted triple play

F. Where Johnny Vander Meer pitched his second straight no-hitter

G. Where Ray Chapman was struck by a pitch that later claimed his life

650

1. Three Rivers Stadium
2. Fulton County Stadium

A. Where the midget Eddie Gaedel made his famous one and only pinch-hit appearance

B. Where Pete Rose tied Ty Cobb's record for career hits

648: 1-C, 2-F, 3-D, 4-A, 5-G, 6-E, 7-B • **649:** 1-D, 2-F, 3-A, 4-G, 5-C, 6-E, 7-B

3. The Astrodome

C. Where Bob Watson scored baseball's one millionth run

4. Candlestick Park

D. Where Nolan Ryan joined the 4,000-strikeout club

5. Sportsman's Park

E. Where Tom Browning pitched his perfect game

6. Wrigley Field

F. Where Willie McCovey joined the 500-home run club

7. Riverfront Stadium

G. Where Ted Turner managed his team for a day

651

1. Royals Stadium

A. Where Paul Molitor joined the 3,000-hit club

2. Yankee Stadium

B. Where pitcher Stu Miller was blown off the mound during the 1961 All-Star Game

3. Anaheim Stadium

C. Where Harvey Haddix pitched his 12 perfect innings before losing in the 13th

4. County Stadium

D. Where Willie Mays made his over-the-shoulder catch of Vic Wertz's World Series drive

5. Forbes Field

E. Site of the famous "Pine Tar Game"

6. Candlestick Park

F. Where Babe Ruth hit home runs 712, 713, and 714, all in the same game

7. Polo Grounds

G. Where Rod Carew joined the 3,000-hit club

652

1. Municipal Stadium

A. Where Rickey Henderson broke Lou Brock's career record for stolen bases

2. Fenway Park

B. Where Carl Yastrzemski joined the 3,000-hit club

3. Yankee Stadium

C. Where Ted Williams joined the 500-home run club

4. Anaheim Stadium

D. Hosted the first-ever regular-season interleague game

5. County Stadium

E. Where David Cone pitched his perfect game

6. Oakland Coliseum

F. Where Nolan Ryan joined the 300-win club

7. Ballpark in Arlington

G. Where George Brett joined the 3,000-hit club

652: 1-C, 2-B, 3-E, 4-G, 5-F, 6-A, 7-D

• **650:** 1-G, 2-F, 3-D, 4-C, 5-A, 6-B, 7-E • **651:** 1-A, 2-E, 3-G, 4-C, 5-F, 6-B, 7-D •

WHO, WHAT, WHEN, WHERE, AND WHY

1. Who participated in this, the first night game in major league history?

2. What was the score?

3. When did it take place?

4. Where?

653:
1. The Cincinnati Reds and Philadelphia Phillies.
2. 2–1, Cincinnati.
3. May 24, 1935.
4. Crosley Field in Cincinnati.

654

1. Olympic Stadium	A. Where Bill Buckner made his infamous error
2. Bank One Ballpark	B. Where Rennie Stennett became the only 20th-century player to go 7 for 7 in a nine-inning game
3. Shea Stadium	C. The only stadium with a dirt track between home plate and the pitcher's mound
4. Dodger Stadium	D. Where Mark McGwire joined the 500-home run club
5. Wrigley Field	E. Where Pete Rose joined the 4,000-hit club
6. Jack Murphy Stadium	F. Where Sandy Koufax pitched his perfect game
7. Busch Stadium	G. Where Lou Brock stole the 893rd base of his career, eclipsing Ty Cobb's record

655

1. Three Rivers Stadium	A. Where Dave Dravecky collapsed with a gruesomely broken arm
2. Busch Stadium	B. Where Bobby Thomson hit his famous "Shot Heard 'Round the World"
3. Olympic Stadium	C. Where Mike Schmidt joined the 500-home run club
4. Fulton County Stadium	D. Where Lou Brock joined the 3,000-hit club
5. Polo Grounds	E. Where Jimmie Foxx joined the 500-home run club
6. Forbes Field	F. Where Hank Aaron joined the 600-home run club
7. Shibe Park	G. Site of baseball's first game to be broadcast over the radio

This game's got you covered—it's all about baseball's domed stadiums.

1. The Kingdome

2. Harris County Domed Stadium

3. The Metrodome

4. The Astrodome

5. The SkyDome

6. Tropicana Field

7. Olympic Stadium

A. Site of the first indoor World Series game

B. Site of the first indoor All-Star Game

C. The only major league baseball stadium ever to have served as a hockey or basketball arena

D. Site where network television accidentally caught and televised a couple engaging in sex during a game

E. Where Gaylord Perry joined the 300-win club

F. Roof was completely removed one year for repair work, making this stadium an outdoor park for one season

G. The first stadium to feature artificial turf

657

1. Yankee Stadium

2. Memorial Stadium

3. Fulton County Stadium

4. Ebbets Field

5. Exhibition Stadium

6. Griffith Stadium

7. Three Rivers Stadium

A. Where Hoyt Wilhelm pitched his 1,000th career game

B. Site of first World Series night game

C. Site of Don Larsen's perfect game

D. Where Frank Robinson joined the 500-home run club

E. Where Mickey Mantle hit baseball's longest measured home run—565 feet

F. Where Phil Niekro joined the 300-win club

G. Where Jim Bottomley got 12 RBIs in one game

656: 1-E, 2-G, 3-A, 4-B, 5-D, 6-C, 7-F • **657:** 1-C, 2-D, 3-A, 4-G, 5-F, 6-E, 7-B

658

1. League Park	**A. Site of baseball's highest-scoring game ever, 26–23**
2. Tiger Stadium	**B. Site of baseball's last tripleheader**
3. Polo Grounds	**C. Where Lou Gehrig hit four home runs in one game**
4. Shibe Park	**D. Where Walter Johnson joined the 300-win club**
5. Forbes Field	**E. Site of Merkle's Boner game**
6. Griffith Stadium	**F. Where Babe Ruth joined the 500-home run club**
7. Wrigley Field	**G. Where Babe Ruth hit his 626-foot "rolling home run"**

659

1. Wrigley Field	**A. Where Chuck Klein hit four homers in one game**
2. Yankee Stadium	**B. Where Gabby Hartnett hit his homer in the gloamin'**
3. League Park	**C. Where both Napoleon Lajoie and Tris Speaker joined the 3,000-hit club**
4. Ebbets Field	**D. Where Jackie Robinson broke major league baseball's color barrier**
5. Polo Grounds	**E. Where Mel Ott joined the 500-home run club**
6. Shibe Park	**F. Where Reggie Jackson hit three home runs on three first pitches**
7. Forbes Field	**G. Site of the first American League night game**

660

1. Griffith Stadium	**A. Where Johnny Burnett got nine hits in one game (18 innings)**
2. Candlestick Park	**B. Where Dizzy Dean's toe was smashed in the 1937 All-Star Game**
3. Shibe Park	**C. Site of baseball's most dramatic World Series Game 7 home run**
4. Municipal Stadium	**D. Where Len Barker pitched his perfect game**
5. League Park	**E. Where Ernie Banks joined the 500-home run club**
6. Wrigley Field	**F. Where Pat Seerey hit four homers in one game**
7. Forbes Field	**G. Where Willie Mays joined the 3,000-hit club**

661

1. Riverfront Stadium	**A. Where Pete Rose broke Ty Cobb's record for career base hits (Cobb's total was later corrected to 4,189)—4,191**
2. Three Rivers Stadium	**B. Site of the only combined, extra-inning no-hitter in baseball history**
3. Camden Yards	**C. Site of baseball's most dramatic World Series Game 6 home run**
4. Fulton County Stadium	**D. Where Cal Ripken Jr. broke Lou Gehrig's record for consecutive games played—2,131**
5. Exhibition Stadium	**E. Where Hank Aaron broke Babe Ruth's record for career home runs—715**
6. County Stadium	**F. Where Hank Aaron hit his last career home run**
7. Fenway Park	**G. Where Dave Winfield was arrested after the game for killing a seagull with a warm-up throw**

660: 1-B, 2-G, 3-F, 4-D, 5-A, 6-E, 7-C • **661:** 1-A, 2-B, 3-D, 4-E, 5-G, 6-F, 7-C

WHO, WHAT, WHEN, WHERE, AND WHY

1. Why are these people sitting atop the buildings?

2. Where is this?

3. When?

4. Who was the team owner?

5. BONUS: How did he respond?

662:

1. These baseball fans were watching a game for free from across the street.

2. Shibe Park in Philadelphia.

3. 1929.

4. Connie Mack.

5. He built a metal fence atop the right-field wall called the "Spite Fence," in order to keep fans from watching games for free.

NAME THAT YEAR

Seven clues. One year. See how few clues it takes you to guess the year.

1 **The Pirates unveil** a statue of the late Roberto Clemente outside Three Rivers Stadium.

2 **Superstar basketball player Michael Jordan** signs with the White Sox.

3 **Ryne Sandberg shocks the baseball world** when he announces his retirement in June.

4 **Hall of Famer Dennis Eckersley ends the season** with a combined 482 career wins and saves, more than any other pitcher in history except Cy Young.

5 **A second suspension for substance abuse** in midseason forces Dwight Gooden to sit out the entire next season.

6 **Two construction workers are killed** when they fall 250 feet to their deaths in Seattle's Kingdome while making repairs.

7 **A players' strike ends the season** on August 12, and no World Series is held for the first time since 1904.

663: 1994

NOW
BATTING

1. Lloyd Waner
2. Ichiro Suzuki
3. Steve Sax
4. Johnny Pesky
5. Napoleon Lajoie
6. Joe Jackson
7. Juan Pierre

A. The last NL player to collect 200 hits in his rookie season

B. The last player to collect 200 hits in both leagues

C. Player with the fewest extra-base hits (25) in a season in which he had at least 200 hits (he had 223)

D. The first player to collect 200 hits in both leagues

E. The only AL player in the 20th century to collect at least 200 hits in each of his first three seasons

F. The first player ever to have more than 200 singles in a season—225

G. The first major league rookie since 1900 to collect over 200 hits in a season

665

1. John Olerud
2. Robin Yount
3. Ty Cobb
4. Mel Ott
5. Freddie Lindstrom
6. Keith Hernandez
7. Bill Buckner

A. The last NL player to collect 1,000 hits before his 25th birthday

B. The first AL player to collect 1,000 hits before his 25th birthday

C. The last AL player to finish second to one of his teammates in base hits for the season

D. The last player in the major leagues to collect 200 or more hits and hit less than .300

E. The last player in either league to collect 1,000 hits before his 25th birthday

F. The first NL player to collect 1,000 hits before his 25th birthday

G. The last NL player to finish second to one of his teammates in base hits for the season

666

1. George Watkins	**A.** Hall of Famer who had the highest batting average as a rookie—.355
2. Lloyd Waner	**B.** Had the most career singles (2,513) by a player who did not make the 3,000-hit club
3. Rogers Hornsby	**C.** Of all players with at least 2,500 hits, his season's best of 158 hits is the lowest
4. Sam Rice	**D.** NL rookie with the highest batting average (.373)
5. Willie Keeler	**E.** Had the highest batting average (.424) by a player on a losing team (65–89)
6. Reggie Jackson	**F.** Had the highest career batting average by a player who never hit below .290—.322
7. Frankie Frisch	**G.** Had the most career hits of all switch-hitters who didn't make the 3,000-hit club—2,880

667

1. Ralph Garr	**A.** The last NL player to collect 200 hits in a season and hit less than .300
2. Brooks Robinson	**B.** The first post-1900 major leaguer who played for at least five seasons to hit over .300 in both his rookie and final seasons
3. Rick Dempsey	**C.** NL player who hit for the highest average over the age of 40—.388
4. Joe Jackson	**D.** Had the lowest career batting average of all players with at least 20 years of major league service—.233
5. Wade Boggs	**E.** Player with most career at bats who didn't make the 3,000-hit club—10,654
6. Ty Cobb	**F.** The last post-1900 major leaguer who played for at least five seasons who hit over .300 in both his rookie *and* final seasons
7. Cap Anson	**G.** AL player who hit for the highest average over the age of 40—.357

666: 1-D, 2-A, 3-E, 4-F, 5-B, 6-C, 7-G • **667:** 1-A, 2-E, 3-D, 4-B, 5-F, 6-G, 7-C

WHO, WHAT, WHEN, WHERE, AND WHY

1. Who is this player?

2. What record did he set in his third major league season?

3. When did he accomplish it?

4. Where did he play minor league ball?

668:

1. Hall of Famer Al Kaline.

2. He was and still is the youngest player ever (20) to win a batting title.

3. 1955.

4. Nowhere—he never played in the minors. He went straight from the sandlots to the majors.

669

1. Todd Helton	**A. The first post-1900 NL player to win a batting title without hitting a home run**
2. Don Mueller	**B. The first post-1900 NL player to win a batting title (.320) while playing for a last-place team**
3. Terry Pendleton	**C. The only NL player since 1937 to finish second in the batting race to a teammate—.342 and .354**
4. Pete Rose	**D. The first post-1900 switch-hitter to win the NL batting title**
5. Larry Doyle	**E. The last switch-hitter to win the NL batting title**
6. Ginger Beaumont	**F. The last post-1900 NL player to win a batting title without hitting a home run**
7. Zack Wheat	**G. Lost the closest batting average race in NL history—.3587 to .3585**

670

1. Bill Mueller	**A. The last AL player to lose a batting title by .0001 point—.3429 to .3428**
2. Dale Alexander	**B. The first AL player to finish second in the batting race to a teammate**
3. Edgar Martinez	**C. The first switch-hitter to win the AL batting title, with .353**
4. Willie Wilson	**D. The first AL player to win the batting title while playing for a last-place team—.367**
5. Sam Crawford	**E. The only AL switch-hitter to win the batting title while playing for an expansion team (.332)**
6. Ted Williams	**F. The last switch-hitter to win the AL batting title—.326**
7. Mickey Mantle	**G. The last AL player to win the batting title while playing for a last-place team—.343**

1. Joe Jackson	**A.** Had the highest batting average in either league that did not win the batting title—.408
2. Ty Cobb	**B.** Had the highest average in NL history that did not win a batting title—.393
3. Babe Herman	**C.** The only player in history to be the batting title runner-up in back-to-back seasons in *both* leagues
4. Al Oliver	**D.** The first post-1900 player to win a batting title after going to a new club
5. Mike Donlin	**E.** Once hit .401, but didn't win the batting title because George Sisler hit .420
6. Willie Keeler	**F.** The last player to be the runner-up for the batting title in both leagues
7. Napoleon Lajoie	**G.** A batting title runner-up four times in an eight-year stretch, once in the AL, three times in the NL

672

1. Napoleon Lajoie	**A.** Had lowest lifetime batting average of any NL batting champion—.270
2. Chick Hafey	**B.** NL batting champ whose next season average declined the most—.097 points, .353 to .256
3. Hal Chase	**C.** The first post-1900 NL batting champ to change teams the next year
4. Rogers Hornsby	**D.** The first two-time NL batting champ to retire with a career batting average below .300
5. Willie McGee	**E.** The first post-1900 NL player to win a batting title after joining a new team
6. Terry Pendleton	**F.** The first AL batting champ to change teams the next year
7. Tommy Davis	**G.** NL batting champ to win by the widest margin—.049 points

671: 1-A, 2-E, 3-B, 4-F, 5-G, 6-C, 7-D • **672:** 1-F, 2-C, 3-E, 4-G, 5-B, 6-A, 7-D

673

1. Norm Cash	A. The only three-time batting champ to retire with a career average below .300
2. Snuffy Stirnweiss	B. AL batting champ to win by the widest margin—.081 points
3. Carl Yastrzemski	C. AL record holder for most home runs hit in one ballpark during his career—266
4. Harmon Killebrew	D. Had lowest lifetime batting average of any AL batting champion—.268
5. Jimmy Piersall	E. AL batting champ whose next season average declined the most—.118 points, .361 to .243
6. Mickey Mantle	F. AL record holder for lowest batting average in a season (.242) by the league's home run champ
7. Napoleon Lajoie	G. Increased his home run production in seven straight years

674

1. Matty Alou	A. The first batting champ with more than 100 strikeouts
2. Roberto Clemente	B. The last batting champ with more than 100 strikeouts
3. Derrek Lee	C. The only batting champ from 1968 to 2004 to have more than 100 strikeouts
4. Tony Gwynn	D. Holds the NL record for most home runs in the month of October (regular season only)—5
5. Dave Parker	E. NL batting champ with the fewest RBIs—27
6. Vinny Castilla	F. Lowest batting average to win the NL batting title after 1900—.313
7. Sammy Sosa	G. Holds the major league record for most home runs in the month of March—2

1. Pete Runnels	**A.** The last of five AL players to hit four home runs in the month of October, the league record (regular season only)
2. Carl Yastrzemski	**B.** AL batting champ with the fewest RBIs—35
3. Manny Ramirez	**C.** Youngest player ever to hit a grand slam—19 years, five months
4. Jose Cruz Jr.	**D.** The last AL player to finish second in the batting race to one of his teammates—.325 to .326
5. Frank White	**E.** The only AL player ever to have both 30 homers and 30 errors in the same season
6. Tony Conigliaro	**F.** Lowest batting average to win the AL batting title—.301
7. Harmon Killebrew	**G.** The last AL player to hit 20 or more homers for the first time *after* the age of 35

676

1. Jose Canseco	**A.** Most career home runs by a player in his forties—72
2. Tony Conigliaro	**B.** Age of oldest AL player to win a home run title—38
3. Carlton Fisk	**C.** Most career home runs by a teenager—24
4. Babe Ruth	**D.** The first player in history to hit 30 or more home runs in his first three seasons
5. Minnie Minoso	**E.** Most career home runs by a player during his 30s—434
6. Jimmie Foxx	**F.** Most career home runs by a player during his 20s—376
7. Darrell Evans	**G.** Oldest AL player to hit a grand slam—41

WHO, WHAT, WHEN, WHERE, AND WHY

1. Who is this?

2. What's he doing?

3. Where did he serve?

4. Where does he rank on baseball's all-time home run list?

677:

1. Baseball Hall of Famer and war hero Ted Williams.

2. Climbing into his fighter jet.

3. He flew 39 combat missions during two tours in the Korean War. He also spent three years as a Marine flight instructor during World War II, even though he could have sat out the war because of his status as his mother's sole support.

4. Currently tied for 15th with Willie McCovey with 521, but he might have challenged Babe Ruth's career record of 714 had he not lost five of his prime years to military service.

1. Albert Pujols

A. The last NL player to have both 30 homers and 30 errors in the same season

2. Pedro Guerrero

B. Oldest NL player to win a home run title—39

3. Tony Perez

C. The only player in history to hit grand slams in nine consecutive seasons

4. Tim McCarver

D. The first NL player to hit 30 or more homers in his first three seasons

5. Willie McCovey

E. Oldest eventual Hall of Famer to win a home run title in either league—37

6. Cy Williams

F. The only player in history to have 30 homers and 30 errors in back-to-back seasons

7. Mike Schmidt

G. The last player in major league history to increase his home run totals in seven consecutive seasons

679

1. Gary Gaetti

A. Has the most career homers of all players who hit four in one game but are not in the Hall of Fame

2. Eddie Murray

B. Once hit 51 percent (50 of 98) of his team's home runs for the season

3. Jimmie Foxx

C. Most home runs by a player in his last season—35

4. Reggie Jackson

D. Most career home runs by a player who hit a home run on the first pitch he saw in the major leagues—360

5. Rocky Colavito

E. The first player to hit 40 or more home runs in a season before his 25th birthday

6. Lou Gehrig

F. The last Hall of Famer to hit at least 100 home runs in both leagues

7. Dave Kingman

G. The only AL player to hit 100 or more homers for three different teams

678: 1-D, 2-A, 3-F, 4-G, 5-C, 6-B, 7-E • **679:** 1-D, 2-F, 3-B, 4-G, 5-A, 6-E, 7-C

680

1. Frank Robinson	**A. Youngest player in history (20) to hit 40 or more home runs in a season**
2. Wally Berger	**B. Most home runs by an NL player in his last season—29**
3. Will Clark	**C. The first Hall of Famer to hit at least 100 home runs in both leagues**
4. Darrell Evans	**D. Has the fewest career homers of all players who hit four in one game but are not in the Hall of Fame**
5. Bobby Lowe	**E. Most career home runs (284) by an NL player who hit a home run on the first pitch he saw in the major leagues**
6. Mel Ott	**F. The only player in this game to hit 100 or more homers for three different teams**
7. Mark McGwire	**G. Once hit 58 percent (38 of 66) of his team's home runs for the season**

681

Those were too easy, right? Time for a few games of obscure records and oddities.

1. Nick Etten	**A. Most career at bats without hitting a home run—2,335**
2. Johnny Ray	**B. Hit the fewest career homers by a player who once won the NL home run title—88**
3. Kevin McReynolds	**C. Went the last 8½ seasons of his career (more than 3,000 at bats) without hitting a home run**
4. Bill Holbert	**D. Player who hit the fewest career homers (89) after once winning the AL home run title**
5. Jack McCarthy	**E. The only AL batting champ (.318) who didn't hit a home run in his batting title year**
6. Rod Carew	**F. Set the major league record when he had the game-winning RBI in six straight games**
7. Tommy Holmes	**G. The only player in major league history to have 95-plus RBIs in three consecutive seasons, but never had 100 in any year of his career**

680: 1-C, 2-G, 3-E, 4-F, 5-D, 6-A, 7-B • **681:** 1-D, 2-F, 3-G, 4-A, 5-C, 6-E, 7-B

Baseball Trivia

682

1. Honus Wagner
2. Tim Raines
3. Stan Musial
4. Pete Rose
5. Vince DiMaggio
6. Jimmy Sheckard
7. Max Carey

A. The only player to lead the NL in hits seven times

B. NL record holder for most stolen bases in a season by a home run champion—67

C. The first Hall of Famer to have 50 steals and 100 RBIs in the same season

D. The last NL Hall of Famer to steal second, third, and home in the same inning

E. The only player to lead the NL in triples five times

F. The only player in this game to steal a base in four different decades

G. The only player to lead the NL in strikeouts six times

683

NAME THAT YEAR

Seven clues. One year. See how few clues it takes you to guess the year.

1 **Don Schwall of the Red Sox** wins the AL Rookie of the Year Award.

2 **The Yankees set a record** with 240 home runs in one year.

3 **The year's second All-Star Game** ends in a 1–1 tie after being called because of rain.

4 **Ty Cobb's funeral** takes place, and only three former players are in attendance.

5 **Roberto Clemente hits .351** to claim his first batting title.

6 **Cincinnati wins** its first pennant since 1940.

7 **Roger Maris sets a new home run record** when he clouts his 61st on the last day of the season.

684

1. Rickey Henderson	**A.** The last player in the major leagues to steal second, third, and home in the same inning
2. Luis Aparicio	**B.** Had the most stolen bases (76) in a season by a league home run champion
3. Paul Molitor	**C.** The only player in major league history to hit at least one home run in 25 consecutive seasons
4. Barry Bonds	**D.** The first player to steal a base in four different decades
5. Ty Cobb	**E.** The last player in the major leagues to steal at least 50 bases and have at least 100 RBIs in the same season
6. Ted Williams	**F.** The only player to lead his league in singles eight times
7. Nellie Fox	**G.** The only player in major league history to lead his league in stolen bases in nine consecutive seasons

685

1. Don Kolloway	**A.** The first AL player ever to have 200 hits, 20 homers, and 20 stolen bases in the same season
2. Alan Trammell	**B.** The last AL player to lead the league in doubles and triples in the same season
3. Ben Chapman	**C.** The only player in AL history to have ten doubles, triples, homers, and steals in each of his first three seasons
4. Snuffy Stirnweiss	**D.** Holds the AL record for triples in a season—26
5. Cesar Tovar	**E.** The only player in either league from 1929 through 1968 to steal second, third, and home in the same inning
6. Ty Cobb	**F.** The only AL player ever to lead the league in doubles and triples in the same season more than once
7. Joe Jackson	**G.** The only player in AL history besides **Ty Cobb** to lead the league in stolen bases (33) and total bases (301) in the same season

WHO, WHAT, WHEN, WHERE, AND WHY

1. Who are these two players?

2. What exciting race were they involved in?

3. When did it take place?

4. Who eventually won the race?

686:

1. Hall of Famers Ralph Kiner of the Pittsburgh Pirates and Johnny Mize of the New York Giants.

2. One of the first great individual home run races in baseball history.

3. 1947.

4. They ended the season tied with 51 homers apiece.

1. Phil Cavaretta	**A.** The only *entirely* 20th-century player who played during seven different presidential administrations
2. Brooks Robinson	**B.** The only major leaguer who was on the U.S. Olympic shooting team
3. Jim Kaat	**C.** The only player to have the same uniform number retired by two different American League teams
4. Rod Carew	**D.** Played the most seasons in the city of his birth—22
5. Nick Altrock	**E.** The only full-time middle infielder to be a four-decade player
6. Al Spalding	**F.** The first AL player to play 23 seasons with the same team
7. Eddie Collins	**G.** Age of oldest player in major league history to hit a triple—48

688

1. Albert Belle	**A.** The only player in history to exceed 450 total bases in a year
2. Babe Ruth	**B.** The only AL player to hit 40 home runs and 40 doubles in the same season *three times*
3. Jim Rice	**C.** The first of only two players to lead the AL in triples (11) and home runs (37) in the same season
4. Lou Gehrig	**D.** The only player to lead the AL in strikeouts seven times
5. George Brett	**E.** The only player in history to have 50 or more doubles and home runs in the same season
6. Jimmie Foxx	**F.** The last AL player to have 20 doubles, 20 triples, and 20 home runs in the same season
7. Mickey Mantle	**G.** The last AL player to break 400 total bases in a season

687: 1-D, 2-F, 3-A, 4-C, 5-G, 6-B, 7-E • **688:** 1-E, 2-A, 3-G, 4-B, 5-F, 6-D, 7-C

Always the bridesmaid, never the bride—
National League only.

1. Stan Musial

2. Eddie Mathews

3. Tony Perez

4. Willie Mays

5. Lou Brock

6. Pete Rose

7. Riggs Stephenson

A. Most career home runs (475) by an NL player who never led the league in homers

B. Most career hits (3,023) by an NL player who never led the league in hits

C. Most career runs scored (1,491) by an NL player who never led the league in runs scored

D. Highest career batting average (.336) by an NL player who never led the league in batting average

E. Most career doubles (523) by an NL player who never led the league in doubles

F. Most career strikeouts (1,660) by an NL player who never led the league in strikeouts

G. Most career walks (1,566) by an NL player who never led the league in walks

690

American League bridesmaids.

1. Al Kaline

2. Carl Yastrzemski

3. Eddie Collins

4. Al Simmons

5. Joe Jackson

6. Tris Speaker

7. Reggie Jackson

A. Most career home runs (399) by an AL player who never led the league in home runs

B. Most career singles (2,262) by an AL player who never led the league in singles

C. Most career hits (3,311) by an AL player who never led the league in hits

D. Highest career batting average (.356) by an AL player who never led the league in batting average

E. Most career total bases (4,834) by an AL player who never led the league in total bases

F. Most career stolen bases (433) by an AL player who never led the league in stolen bases

G. Most career doubles (534) by an AL player who never led the league in doubles

689: 1-A, 2-C, 3-F, 4-E, 5-B, 6-G, 7-D • 690: 1-A, 2-B, 3-C, 4-G, 5-D, 6-F, 7-E

Each of the players listed was the runner-up by the widest margin ever in an offensive category. First ones up are American League players.

1. Ty Cobb

2. Lou Gehrig

3. Mike Donlin

4. Damaso Garcia

5. George Sisler

6. Jack Tobin

7. Michael Young

A. Runner-up in batting average at .340, trailing the league leader by 86 points

B. Runner-up in hits with 216, trailing the league leader by 46 hits

C. Runner-up in doubles with 36, trailing the league leader by 15 doubles

D. Runner-up in home runs with 19, trailing the league leader by 35 homers

E. Runner-up in RBIs with 119, trailing the league leader by 51 RBIs

F. Runner-up in stolen bases with 54, trailing the league leader by 76 steals

G. Runner-up in runs scored with 132, trailing the league leader by 45 runs

692

Now try it for the National League.

1. Dixie Walker

2. Jack Fournier

3. Zack Wheat

4. Todd Helton

5. Frank Demaree

6. Honus Wagner

7. Fred Charles

A. Runner-up in hits with 184, trailing the league leader by 44 hits

B. Runner-up in batting average at .375, trailing the league leader by 49 points

C. Runner-up in triples with 20, trailing the league leader by 16 triples

D. Runner-up in home runs with 22, trailing the league leader by 19 homers

E. Runner-up in walks with 127, trailing the league leader by 105 walks

F. Runner-up in runs scored with 97, trailing the league leader by 29 runs

G. Runner-up in RBIs with 115, trailing the league leader by 39 RBIs

691: 1-C, 2-E, 3-A, 4-F, 5-D, 6-G, 7-B • **692:** 1-A, 2-D, 3-B, 4-E, 5-G, 6-C, 7-F

Match up these hitters with the age at which each became the all-time major league leader in home runs.

1. Eddie Mathews		A. 611 homers at 37
2. Alex Rodriguez		B. 322 homers at 28
3. Ken Griffey Jr. (tied)		C. 713 homers at 40
4. Jimmie Foxx		D. 438 homers at 31
5. Sammy Sosa		E. 190 homers at 25
6. Babe Ruth		F. 539 homers at 35
7. Hank Aaron		G. 464 homers at 32

694

Ruth, Aaron, and Bonds are baseball's "Big 3" right now in career home runs. See if you can identify some of their lesser-known feats.

1. Babe Ruth	A. Hit the fewest homers off righthanded pitchers—499
2. Hank Aaron	B. Hit the most home runs in April—109
3. Barry Bonds	C. Hit the most ninth-inning homers—56
	D. Had the fewest multihomer games—62
	E. Hit the fewest grand slams—11
	F. Hit the most home runs off one Hall of Fame pitcher—17
	G. Hit the most home runs in extra innings—16

WHO, WHAT, WHEN, WHERE, AND WHY

1. Who are these two Hall of Famers?

2. What year did these two greats meet on the field for the first time?

3. The year was notable for both men. Do you know why?

4. Where does the batter rank on the all-time home run list for switch-hitters?

4. First with 536.

3. It was the last year Feller would win 20 games in a season (22–8) and the year Mantle would hit the fewest home runs (13) of any year of his career.

2. 1951.

695:
1. Mickey Mantle and Bob Feller.

NAME THAT YEAR

Seven clues. One year. See how few clues it takes you to guess the year.

1 **Roger Clemens wins** his second consecutive AL Cy Young Award.

2 **San Diego's Benito Santiago puts together** a 34-game batting streak, and is voted the NL Rookie of the Year.

3 **Andre Dawson wins** the NL MVP Award.

4 **LaMarr Hoyt, 1983 Cy Young Award winner,** is banned for the season by Commissioner Peter Ueberroth for illegal possession of narcotics.

5 **The Cardinals win** their third pennant of the decade.

6 **Milwaukee's Paul Molitor has the longest batting streak** in the American League (39 games) since Joe DiMaggio's 56-game streak in 1941.

7 **The Twins win the World Series** in seven games, each game being won by the home team.

696: 1987

362

NOW
PITCHING

697

Do you know which pitchers accomplished these feats?

1. HOF pitcher with most career wins who never led the league in wins—361

   A. Jim Palmer

2. HOF pitcher who recorded at least one victory in the most consecutive years—26

   B. Tom Seaver

3. The only HOF pitcher since 1903 to become a 20-game winner while pitching for more than one team that year (21–6)

   C. Nolan Ryan

4. HOF pitcher with the most consecutive seasons of 20 or more wins—12

   D. Cy Young

5. The first HOF pitcher to be a 100-game winner in both the American and National leagues

   E. Sandy Koufax

6. HOF pitcher with the most wins in the 1970s—186

   F. Pud Galvin

7. The only HOF pitcher to be a 20-game winner (27–6) in the last season of his career

   G. Christy Mathewson

698

Let's try some bits of magnificence on the mound.

1. HOF pitcher with most combined career wins and base hits—2,284 (161 wins, 2,123 hits)

   A. Christy Mathewson

2. At 5' 8" tall, he was the shortest 300-game winner in major league history

   B. Bob Grim

3. He was the last American League pitcher to win 20 games in his rookie season (20–6)

   C. John Ward

4. Only three rookie pitchers have ever won 20 games and struck out 200-plus batters in a season. He was the first.

D. Pud Galvin

5. This Hall of Famer was the first of 27 pitchers to lead the league in wins while pitching for a losing team

E. Whitey Ford

6. The only Hall of Famer to be a 20-game winner for a last-place American League team

F. Nolan Ryan

7. The last American League pitcher to win at least 20 more games than he lost in the same season (25–4)

G. Grover Alexander

699

I've been taking it easy on you. See if you can identify these lefthanded pitchers who've won 20 or more games more than once since World War II.

1. Only five Hall of Famers can lay claim to this feat. He is the only one to have done it in consecutive years while pitching for two different teams.

A. Whitey Ford

2. The only pitcher in this category to be a 20-game winner for six consecutive seasons

B. Hal Newhouser

3. The first pitcher to qualify for this category (Hint: he is a Hall of Famer)

C. Dave McNally

4. The first American Leaguer to accomplish this feat in four consecutive years

D. Andy Pettitte

5. The only other American Leaguer besides the answer to question 4 to accomplish this feat in four consecutive years

E. Steve Carlton

6. His two 20-win seasons for the Yankees were seven years apart

F. Wilbur Wood

7. This Yankee won a Cy Young Award in one of his two 20-win seasons

G. Warren Spahn

698: 1-C, 2-D, 3-B, 4-A, 5-G, 6-F, 7-E • **699:** 1-E, 2-G, 3-B, 4-C, 5-F, 6-D, 7-A

WHO, WHAT, WHEN, WHERE, AND WHY

1. Who is this player?

2. What exclusive record did he set in this uniform?

3. When?

4. Where was he playing when he set the first half of the record?

700:

1. Hall of Famer Gaylord Perry.

2. First pitcher to win the Cy Young Award in both leagues.

3. 1978.

4. Cleveland.

701

Now some miscellaneous memorable mound monuments.
Mmm . . . .

1. He once won 23 games in a season
without pitching a single shutout

   A. Rube Marquard

2. The only pitcher in this game to lead the league
in wins in back-to-back seasons . . . *twice*

   B. Denny McLain

3. He won 25 or more games three times
since the inception of the Cy Young Award,
and never received a single vote!

   C. Joe McGinnity

4. Since 1935, of all the pitchers to lead the league
in wins in back-to-back seasons, this pitcher has
the most combined wins for the two seasons—55

   D. Christy Mathewson

5. He won 23 games one season, then lost
22 the next

   E. Dennis Martinez

6. Before Dwight Gooden eclipsed his record
in 1985, he was the youngest National League
pitcher ever to win 20 games in a season

   F. Al Mamaux

7. He's the pitcher with the most career wins
who never won 20 in a season—245

   G. Juan Marichal

702

A potpourri of pitching performances positioned for
posterity.

1. Most career wins by a pitcher whose last
name starts with the letter *P*—326

   A. Gaylord Perry

2. Won the Cy Young Award . . . in *both* leagues

   B. Jim Perry

3. Won 20 games in his rookie season

   C. Scott Perry

4. Led the American League in wins, with 18,
while pitching for a losing team (Cleveland)

   D. Roy Patterson

5. Holds the major league record for worst
career winning percentage (.376) by a pitcher
who had a 20-win season during his career

   E. Jim Palmer

6. Won 27 games one year, then lost 22 games
the next

   F. Togie Pittinger

7. Led the American League in wins three
straight years

   G. Eddie Plank

701: 1-D, 2-C, 3-G, 4-B, 5-A, 6-F, 7-E • **702:** 1-G, 2-A, 3-D, 4-B, 5-C, 6-F, 7-E

Some substantially scintillating spherical spectacles.

1. Most career wins by a pitcher whose last name starts with the letter *S*—363

    A. Mel Stottlemyre

2. Had 324 career victories, but never once led his league in wins for a season

    B. Henry Schmidt

3. Became a 20-game winner (21–9) for the first time at the age of 36

    C. Rip Sewell

4. Won 21 games in his rookie season, then didn't win another game

    D. Karl Spooner

5. Won 20 games one season, then lost 20 the next

    E. Don Sutton

6. One of only two pitchers in history to have a season where he finished exactly 20–20

    F. Warren Spahn

7. Pitched only two games one season, and they were both complete-game shutouts!

    G. Jim Scott

704

Strictly Hall of Famers.

1. Most career shutouts without ever leading the league in the category—50

    A. Rube Waddell

2. Holds the major league record for highest percentage of games that were shutouts to games started in a career (threw 57 shutouts in his 315 games started)— 18.1 percent

    B. Jack Chesbro

3. Lost the most games in the decade of the 1900s—171

    C. Warren Spahn

4. Holds the American League record for highest percentage of a team's total wins in a season (41 of the team's 92 wins)— 45.6 percent

    D. Ed Walsh

703: 1-F, 2-E, 3-C, 4-B, 5-A, 6-G, 7-D

5. Holds the major league record for highest percentage of a team's total wins in a season (27 of the team's 59 wins)— 45.8 percent

E. Walter Johnson

6. The only pitcher ever to lead the American League in wins for four consecutive seasons

F. Vic Willis

7. The only pitcher ever to lead the National League in wins for five consecutive seasons

G. Steve Carlton

705

NAME THAT YEAR

Seven clues. One year. See how few clues it takes you to guess the year.

1 **The Giants defeat** the A's in a five-game World Series.

2 **Roger Bresnahan of the Giants** experiments with the first batting helmet after being hit in the head with a pitch.

3 **Detroit pays its rent** for its spring training facilities in Augusta, Georgia, by reassigning pitcher Eddie Cicotte to play for the local minor league team.

4 **Cleveland renames its team** from the Bluebirds to the Naps in honor of its star player, Napoleon Lajoie.

5 **Moonlight Graham, later portrayed by Burt Lancaster** in the movie *Field of Dreams,* plays the only inning of his career in the field without receiving a chance or coming to bat for the Giants.

6 **The Braves have four 20-game losers,** led by the future Hall of Famer Vic Willis, who lost 29.

7 **Christy Mathewson becomes the only pitcher** ever to hurl three shutouts in one World Series.

Strictly non–Hall of Famers.

1. Holds the major league record for most wins in a season without pitching a complete game—20

    A. Jerry Koosman

2. Holds the National League record for most wins in a season without pitching a complete game—19

    B. Noodles Hahn

3. Most wins in the decade of the 1990s—176

    C. Roy Oswalt

4. Pitcher with the most career victories (288) who never led the league in wins

    D. Tom Glavine

5. The only non-HOF pitcher ever to be a 20-game winner for a last-place National League team

    E. Tommy John

6. The last pitcher in either league to win 20 games one year and then lose 20 the next

    F. Greg Maddux

7. The only 20th-century non-HOF pitcher in either league to lead the league in wins three straight seasons

    G. Roger Clemens

707

You'll be lucky to get any of these right!

1. Had a losing record for ten consecutive major league seasons in three different major leagues

    A. Rick Wise

2. Holds the major league record for most career wins while still compiling a losing record (246–255)

    B. Bill Bailey

3. The last pitcher to play for a winning team (91–71) yet to lead the league in losses—17

    C. Jim Maloney

4. Holds the American League record for highest percentage of walks to innings pitched in a season (.979; walked 140 batters in 143 innings)

    D. Sam Jones

5. Holds the major league record for most walks given up while pitching a no-hitter—10

    E. Jack Powell

6. The last pitcher in either league to hit a home run in a game in which he pitched a no-hitter

    F. Bobby Witt

7. The last pitcher to throw a no-hitter in the same season he lost at least 20 games

    G. Bert Blyleven

706: 1-G, 2-C, 3-F, 4-E, 5-B, 6-A, 7-D • **707:** 1-B, 2-E, 3-G, 4-F, 5-C, 6-A, 7-D

WHEN DID
IT OCCUR?

Baseball Trivia

708

Match the events with the year they occurred.

1. The last year before 2000 the World Series was played in one city	**A.** 1918
2. The first black players appeared in the All-Star Game	**B.** 1968
3. The only All-Star Game with no extra-base hits	**C.** 1945
4. The only player strike ever during the World Series	**D.** 1949
5. The first indoor All-Star Game was played	**E.** 1958
6. Largest World Series attendance (420,000+)	**F.** 1959
7. The last year the Cubs were in the World Series	**G.** 1956

709

The 1990s.

1. Pete Rose reports to federal prison to begin serving his five-month sentence for income tax evasion	**A.** 1992
2. Nolan Ryan pitches his seventh and final no-hitter, defeating the Blue Jays, 3–0	**B.** 1997
3. Baseball welcomes two new ballparks to the major leagues: Jacobs Field in Cleveland and The Ballpark in Arlington, Texas	**C.** 1991
4. Cal Ripken Jr. breaks Lou Gehrig's all-time record for most consecutive games played, in a 4–2 win over the Angels at Camden Yards, by playing in his 2,131st straight	**D.** 1999
5. Major league baseball announces that all teams will retire uniform number 42 in honor of Jackie Robinson	**E.** 1995
6. The San Diego Padres begin the season by playing their home opener in Monterrey, Mexico, losing 8–2 to the Colorado Rockies in front of 27,104 Mexican fans	**F.** 1990
7. Robin Yount and George Brett both join the 3,000-hit club	**G.** 1994

708: 1-G, 2-D, 3-E, 4-A, 5-B, 6-F, 7-C • 709: 1-F, 2-C, 3-G, 4-E, 5-B, 6-D, 7-A

More 1990s.

1. For the first time in major league history, two no-hitters are pitched on the same day. Dave Stewart of the A's and Fernando Valenzuela of the Dodgers perform the unique feat

A. 1993

2. Dennis Martinez of the Expos pitches the 14th perfect game in baseball history, defeating the Dodgers, 2–0

B. 1990

3. In a famous altercation, Roberto Alomar of the Orioles spits in the face of umpire John Hirshbeck

C. 1996

4. Kevin Brown becomes baseball's first player to crack the $100 million mark when he inks a seven-year, $105 million contract with the Dodgers

D. 1999

5. The Tigers (Tiger Stadium), Giants (3Com Park, formerly Candlestick Park), and Astros (the Astrodome) all play their final games in their longtime home stadiums

E. 1991

6. Kenny Rogers of the Rangers pitches the 15th perfect game in baseball history when he defeats the Twins, 4–0

F. 1998

7. Steve Olin and Tim Crews of the Indians are killed in a boating accident while at spring training

G. 1994

711

Still more 1990s.

1. Rickey Henderson of the A's steals his 939th career base, replacing Lou Brock as the all-time base-stealing king

A. 1993

2. Mickey Mantle dies of lung cancer at the age of 63

B. 1992

3. Roger Clemens of the Red Sox ties his own major league record when he strikes out 20 Tigers in a nine-inning game

C. 1990

4. Cecil Fielder of the Tigers becomes the first player in 13 years to break the 50-homer mark when he clubs numbers 50 and 51 on the last day of the season

D. 1996

5. Ken Griffey Jr. homers in eight straight games, tying Dale Long's record

E. 1998

6. The Milwaukee Brewers become the first team in the 20th century to switch leagues, moving from the American to the National

F. 1991

7. Phillies second baseman Mickey Morandini becomes the ninth player in major league history to perform an unassisted triple play when he pulls the trick against the Pirates

G. 1995

710: 1-B, 2-E, 3-C, 4-F, 5-D, 6-G, 7-A • 711: 1-F, 2-G, 3-D, 4-C, 5-A, 6-E, 7-B

WHO, WHAT, WHEN, WHERE, AND WHY

1. **Who** are the two men?

2. **What** are they doing?

3. **When** did this ceremony take place?

4. **Where?**

712:
1. Muhammad Ali and Hall of Famer Joe DiMaggio.

2. Receiving the Ellis Island Medal of Honor.

3. May 1986.

4. Ellis Island.

374

The last of the 1990s.

1. Tony Gwynn and Wade Boggs join the 3,000-hit club   **A. 1997**

2. Houston and San Diego make a 12-player   **B. 1999**
trade, the largest in the majors since 1957

3. Randy Johnson strikes out 19 batters in a game—twice!   **C. 1992**

4. Camden Yards opens in Baltimore   **D. 1995**

5. Andy Hawkins of the Yankees becomes the second   **E. 1998**
pitcher in major league history to pitch a complete-game
no-hitter and lose, suffering a 4–0 loss to the White Sox

6. With 100 wins, the Indians win their division by 30 games,   **F. 1990**
the widest margin since divisional play began in 1969. The
wins are even more impressive, considering it's a strike-
shortened season.

7. Bud Selig becomes baseball's ninth commissioner   **G. 1994**

714

The 1980s.

1. The SkyDome is christened as the Blue Jays lose to   **A. 1982**
Milwaukee, 5–3

2. The Baltimore Orioles start the season by losing their   **B. 1988**
first 21 games

3. Mickey Mantle is ordered to sever all ties with major league   **C. 1985**
baseball after taking a job with an Atlantic City casino

4. Atlanta opens the season by winning their first   **D. 1981**
13 straight games

5. Boston's Roger Clemens sets a new single-game strikeout   **E. 1989**
record when he fans 20 Seattle Mariners en route to a 3–1
win at Fenway Park

6. Nolan Ryan of the Astros becomes the first pitcher   **F. 1983**
to hurl five no-hitters when he blanks the Dodgers, 5–0

7. Tom Seaver gets his 300th career win and Rod Carew   **G. 1986**
his 3,000th career hit on the same day

713: 1-B, 2-G, 3-A, 4-C, 5-F, 6-D, 7-E • **714:** 1-E, 2-B, 3-F, 4-A, 5-G, 6-D, 7-C

More 1980s.

1. Baseball Commissioner A. Bartlett Giamatti bans Pete Rose from the game for life, then dies eight days later	**A. 1989**
2. Mike Scott of the Astros pitches the first playoff-clinching no-hitter as Houston stops San Francisco, 2–0	**B. 1984**
3. Steve Garvey's NL-record consecutive-games-played streak ends at 1,207 games after he injures his thumb in a home-plate collision against Atlanta	**C. 1982**
4. Rickey Henderson smashes the single-season stolen-base record by swiping 130 bags for the Oakland A's	**D. 1986**
5. Peter Ueberroth becomes baseball's sixth commissioner	**E. 1980**
6. George Brett of the Royals makes a strong run at .400, finishing at .390, the highest average in the majors since Ted Williams broke the .400 mark in 1941	**F. 1983**
7. Orel Hershiser sets a new record for consecutive scoreless innings pitched, 59, by shutting out San Diego for ten innings in his last start of the regular season	**G. 1988**

716

Still more 1980s.

1. Pitcher Dave Dravecky, recovering from cancer surgery, breaks his arm while making a pitch in a game at Montreal	**A. 1987**
2. Pete Rose passes Ty Cobb as baseball's all-time hits leader when he collects career hit number 4,192, a single off San Diego's Eric Show	**B. 1981**
3. George Brett hits his famous "pine tar" home run	**C. 1984**
4. Bo Jackson of the Royals signs a five-year contract with the Oakland Raiders, becoming a two-sport star	**D. 1989**
5. Major league baseball fans suffered through a 50-day players' strike, the longest in American sports history up to that time	**E. 1980**
6. Detroit's Willie Hernandez cops both the AL Cy Young Award and AL MVP Award in the same season	**F. 1985**
7. Rickey Henderson breaks Ty Cobb's AL record for stolen bases in a season (96) when he becomes the first AL player ever to reach 100 steals in a season	**G. 1983**

715: 1-A, 2-D, 3-F, 4-C, 5-B, 6-E, 7-G • **716:** 1-D, 2-F, 3-G, 4-A, 5-B, 6-C, 7-E

1. The Cubs knock off the Mets, 6–4, in the first official night game in Wrigley Field's 74-year history — **A. 1985**

2. Denny McLain, a former 31-game winner, is sentenced to 23 years in prison for racketeering, extortion, and possession of cocaine — **B. 1980**

3. Catcher Benito Santiago puts together a rookie-record 34-game batting streak — **C. 1987**

4. Len Barker of the Indians pitches a perfect game, a 3–0 whitewash of the Toronto Blue Jays — **D. 1981**

5. The Astros win their first-ever NL West division title — **E. 1988**

6. Mike Witt of the Angels pitches baseball's 11th perfect game on the season's last day, a 1–0 gem over Texas — **F. 1984**

718

NAME THAT YEAR

Seven clues. One year. See how few clues it takes you to guess the year.

1 **After Ferguson Jenkins's arrest** for possession of narcotics, Commissioner Bowie Kuhn announces that all major league teams will have to begin drug abuse programs by the start of the season.

2 **Rollie Fingers wins** both the AL Cy Young and the MVP awards.

3 **Steve Carlton becomes the first lefthander** in history to record 3,000 career strikeouts.

4 **The Yankees sign John Elway** to a minor league contract, but he later decides to play football.

5 **Rochester and Pawtucket, of the International League,** play a 33-inning game, the longest in organized baseball history.

6 **The Dodgers defeat the Yankees** in a six-game World Series.

7 **Cincinnati has the best record** in either league, but doesn't make the playoffs because of the two-half system employed this year only because of a long players' strike.

The 1970s.

1. A six-week strike by major league umpires forces the two major leagues to utilize umpires from the minor and amateur leagues

A. 1978

2. Lyman Bostock of the Angels is killed by a shotgun blast while riding in a car in Indiana. The murderer is acquitted by reason of insanity.

B. 1973

3. George Steinbrenner purchases the Yankees from CBS for $10 million

C. 1976

4. Baseball's antitrust exemption is upheld by the U.S. Supreme Court, and puts an end to Curt Flood's frustrating odyssey of testing the game's reserve clause

D. 1972

5. Center fielder Rick Monday of the Cubs sprints to left field and takes an American flag away from two protesters who had rushed onto the field in Dodger Stadium and were trying to burn it

E. 1975

6. The Orioles became the second team in major league history to sport four 20-game winners on their pitching staff in the same season. Jim Palmer, Dave McNally, Mike Cuellar, and Pat Dobson combined for the ultra-rare feat.

F. 1979

7. Four Oakland A's pitchers (Vida Blue, Glenn Abbott, Paul Lindblad, and Rollie Fingers) combine to pitch baseball's first-ever multipitcher no-hitter, a 5–0 final-day win over the Angels

G. 1971

720

More 1970s.

1. Pete Rose hits safely in 44 straight games, tying the NL record

A. 1976

2. George Brett wins a controversial batting title on the last day of the season (.3333 to .3326 over his teammate Hal McRae) when he collects three hits. McRae accuses Twins outfielder Steve Brye of racism when, according to McRae, Brye lets a routine fly ball hit by Brett drop for a hit on Brett's last at bat of the season

B. 1972

719: 1-F, 2-A, 3-B, 4-D, 5-C, 6-G, 7-E

3. Baseball's first-ever arbitration hearing is held, and the winner is pitcher Dick Woodson of the Minnesota Twins

    C. 1979

4. The American League begins using the designated hitter

    D. 1974

5. "Disco Demolition Night" at Comiskey Park turns into a riot as fans storm onto the field, throwing disco albums around the stadium and starting fires, forcing the umpires to declare a forfeit in the second game of a doubleheader in favor of visiting Detroit

    E. 1970

6. All-Star voting is returned to the fans, who will use computerized punch cards to make their selections

    F. 1973

7. Roberto Clemente of the Pirates dies when the cargo plane he has chartered to take relief supplies to victims of a Nicaraguan earthquake crashes into the ocean shortly after takeoff from Puerto Rico

    G. 1978

721

Still more 1970s.

1. Second baseman Lenny Randle of the Rangers, upset over losing his starting job, beats manager Frank Lucchesi so severely prior to a spring training game that Lucchesi is sent to the hospital

    A. 1979

2. Thurman Munson of the Yankees dies when his small plane crashes in Ohio

    B. 1974

3. Pitcher Don Wilson of the Astros dies by his own hand in the garage of his home, from carbon monoxide poisoning

    C. 1970

4. Hank Aaron becomes baseball's all-time home run leader when he hits his 715th clout off Al Downing of the Dodgers in Atlanta

    D. 1975

5. The New York Mets win the National League East division title with an 82–79 record

    E. 1971

6. The Washington Senators play their final season in the nation's capital

    F. 1973

7. The first-ever major league umpires strike takes place, lasting just one day before a settlement is reached on a new four-year contract

    G. 1977

The last of the 1970s.

1. Larry Doby, the second black player to make it to the major leagues in 1947, becomes the second black manager as well, taking over the helm of the Chicago White Sox   **A. 1975**

2. Lou Brock of the Cardinals passes Ty Cobb on the all-time stolen-bases list when he swipes his 893rd career base   **B. 1972**

3. The baseball world is rocked when arbitrator Peter Seitz declares Andy Messersmith and Dave McNally winners of their free agency claims   **C. 1970**

4. Al Kaline joins the 3,000-hit club   **D. 1978**

5. Harmon Killebrew of the Twins and Frank Robinson of the Orioles both join the 500-home run club   **E. 1977**

6. Hank Aaron and Willie Mays both join the 3,000-hit club   **F. 1971**

7. The first regular-season players' strike in major league history lasts 13 days and wipes 86 games from the schedule   **G. 1974**

723

The 1960s.

1. Catfish Hunter pitches the ninth perfect game in major league history, a 4–0 gem against the Twins in Oakland   **A. 1969**

2. Major league baseball's first black umpire, Emmett Ashford, takes the field in Washington, breaking another color barrier   **B. 1965**

3. Ken Johnson of the Astros becomes the first pitcher in major league history to lose a complete-game no-hitter when the Reds spoil his big day, 1–0   **C. 1964**

4. Bowie Kuhn becomes the fifth commissioner in baseball history   **D. 1961**

5. Tom Cheney of the Senators strikes out a major league–record 21 batters in one game, though the 2–1 win over the Orioles takes 16 innings to resolve   **E. 1966**

6. Juan Marichal of the Giants clubs Dodger catcher John Roseboro with his bat, setting off one of the most famous brawls—it lasts 14 minutes—in all of baseball history   **F. 1962**

7. The Philadelphia Phillies establish a modern-era record by losing 23 straight games   **G. 1968**

722: 1-D, 2-E, 3-A, 4-G, 5-F, 6-C, 7-B • **723:** 1-G, 2-E, 3-C, 4-A, 5-F, 6-B, 7-D

WHO, WHAT, WHEN, WHERE, AND WHY

1. Who is this player?

2. Why is he in so much pain?

3. When did it happen?

4. Where?

5. BONUS: Who else was involved?

724:
1. Hall of Famer Bob Gibson.
2. A line drive fractured his leg just above the ankle while he was on the mound.
3. July 1967.
4. Busch Stadium in St. Louis.
5. Roberto Clemente hit the ball that fractured Gibson's leg.

More 1960s.

1. Ron Hansen of the Senators accomplishes the eighth unassisted triple play in major league history, though Cleveland wins, 10–1		**A. 1968**
2. Sandy Koufax's record fourth career no-hitter is also a perfect game, a 1–0 sparkler against the Cubs		**B. 1966**
3. After finishing the season in a dead heat with 101 wins apiece, the Giants and Dodgers square off in a three-game playoff to determine the National League championship. San Francisco wins, two games to one.		**C. 1962**
4. Elston Howard becomes the first black MVP in American League history		**D. 1960**
5. In one of the strangest trades in baseball history, the Indians and Tigers swap managers in midseason		**E. 1969**
6. Sandy Koufax stuns not only the Dodgers but the whole baseball world when he announces his retirement from the game at the age of 30 because of an arthritic elbow		**F. 1963**
7. Baseball's four new expansion teams all win their Opening Day games		**G. 1965**

726

Still more 1960s.

1. Mickey Mantle of the Yankees and Eddie Mathews of the Astros join the 500-home run club in the same season		**A. 1967**
2. Steve Carlton of the Cardinals sets a new major league record with 19 strikeouts in one game, but loses 4–3 when the Mets' Ron Swoboda hits a pair of two-run homers		**B. 1964**
3. Shea Stadium opens for business. The Mets, of course, lose, 4–3 to the Pittsburgh Pirates		**C. 1963**
4. The Cubs eliminate the position of manager on their club, choosing instead to run their team with a college of coaches—a system of rotating nine different coaches into the top spot for several weeks at a time during the season		**D. 1960**

725: 1-A, 2-G, 3-C, 4-F, 5-D, 6-B, 7-E

5. The Washington Senators play their last season in D.C. **E. 1961**
before relocating to Minnesota. To stave off pressure
from Congress, the American League quickly replaces
the team with a replacement Washington Senators team
the following year.

6. Frank Robinson of the Orioles becomes baseball's **F. 1969**
13th Triple Crown winner, and in the process becomes
the first player ever to win the MVP Award in both leagues

7. Early Wynn battles through five tough innings, but holds **G. 1966**
on to win his 300th—and last—career game, 7–4, over
the Athletics

727

NAME THAT YEAR

Seven clues. One year. See how few clues it takes you to
guess the year.

1 **Jim Maloney twice pitches** a no-hitter for ten innings, but comes
away with only one victory.

2 **Reliever Denny McLain enters the game** and strikes out the first
seven Red Sox hitters he faces in a June 15 game in Detroit.

3 **In a September 8 game** against the Angels, Bert Campaneris of the
A's plays all nine positions.

4 **Major League Baseball conducts its first-ever free agent draft;** Rick
Monday is the first player selected.

5 **Helicopters and blowtorches** are used in an effort to dry out a soggy
playing field in a World Series game.

6 **The era of indoor baseball begins** as the Astrodome opens for play
in Houston.

7 **Walter Alston becomes the first NL manager** to win four World Series
when his Dodgers come back from an 0–2 deficit against the Twins to
win in seven games.

The last of the 1960s.

1. In an effort to increase the scoring in baseball, Major League Baseball's Rules Committee lowers the height of the pitching mound, decreases the size of the strike zone, and promises to crack down on illegal pitches	**A. 1964**
2. The Astrodome opens in Houston with an exhibition game between the Astros and Yankees	**B. 1967**
3. Dodger Stadium opens in Los Angeles and D.C. Stadium opens in Washington	**C. 1962**
4. The Athletics play their last season in Kansas City before moving to Oakland	**D. 1965**
5. Ted Williams hits the 521st home run of his career in his last at bat of the season and immediately announces his retirement	**E. 1960**
6. Jim Bunning of the Phillies pitches a perfect game against the Mets on Father's Day, the first regular-season perfecto in the big leagues in 42 years	**F. 1961**
7. The Mets and Colt .45s participate in the National League's first-ever expansion draft	**G. 1968**

729

More events from 1951 to 1961.

1. Roger Maris breaks Babe Ruth's season record for home runs	**A. 1956**
2. Boston Braves relocate to Milwaukee	**B. 1955**
3. Don Larsen pitches a perfect game in the World Series	**C. 1961**
4. Bill Mazeroski hits a walk-off, Series-ending home run	**D. 1951**
5. Harvey Haddix pitches 12 perfect innings, then loses in 13th	**E. 1960**
6. Philadelphia Athletics relocate to Kansas City	**F. 1953**
7. Bobby Thomson hits his "Shot Heard 'Round the World"	**G. 1959**

730

Let's see how well you know your 1950s baseball.

1. The Red Sox become the last team in baseball to break the color barrier when they send Pumpsie Green onto the field in a game against the White Sox	**A. 1955**

728: 1-G, 2-D, 3-C, 4-B, 5-E, 6-A, 7-F • **729:** 1-C, 2-F, 3-A, 4-E, 5-G, 6-B, 7-D

2. Al Kaline, the 20-year-old outfielder of the Tigers, becomes the youngest batting champ in major league history when he finishes the season at .340 — **B. 1953**

3. The Browns play their final season in St. Louis — **C. 1959**

4. The Giants defeat the Dodgers, 8–0, in the first-ever West Coast game — **D. 1956**

5. The Dodgers erupt for a major league–record 15 first-inning runs on their way to a 19–1 rout of the Reds in Brooklyn's Ebbets Field — **E. 1951**

6. Bobby Thomson hits his famous "Shot Heard 'Round the World," giving the Giants one of the most dramatic pennant wins ever — **F. 1952**

7. The Brooklyn Dodgers play seven of their "home" games at Jersey City's Roosevelt Stadium in an effort to expand their fan base — **G. 1958**

731

More 1950s.

1. The Phillies become the last National League team to break the color barrier when John Kennedy pinch-hits in a game against the Brooklyn Dodgers — **A. 1956**

2. The Major League Baseball Players Association is formed and J. Norman Lewis is hired to represent the body in all negotiations with the owners — **B. 1959**

3. Don Newcombe of the Dodgers wins baseball's first-ever Cy Young Award after a 27–7 season in which he also won the NL MVP Award — **C. 1953**

4. Eighteen-year-old Paul Pettit of the Pirates becomes baseball's first $100,000 bonus baby — **D. 1950**

5. The U.S. Supreme Court rules that professional baseball is a sport, not an interstate business, thereby exempting the organization from federal antitrust laws — **E. 1954**

6. Virgil Trucks of the Tigers becomes the third pitcher in major league history to toss two no-hitters in one season — **F. 1957**

7. After ending the season tied for first, the Dodgers and Braves play a best-of-three playoff series to determine the NL champion. The Dodgers win in two straight. — **G. 1952**

WHO, WHAT, WHEN, WHERE, AND WHY

1. Who is this player?

2. What was his trademark?

3. What were the best four years of his career?

4. Where did this tremendous power hitter suffer an injury that ended his ability to hit monstrous home runs?

732:
1. Ted Kluszewski.

2. Going bare-armed by cutting off his uniform sleeves to display his massive upper arms.

3. 1953 to 1956.

4. In the clubhouse in a fistfight with a teammate, he suffered a slipped disc, which affected his powerful swing for the rest of his career.

Still more 1950s.

1. Dodger catcher Roy Campanella is left paralyzed from his shoulders down after an automobile accident on a slippery road in Long Island, New York — **A. 1954**

2. The Orioles and Yankees pull off the largest trade in major league history when 17 players switch teams — **B. 1957**

3. In perhaps the most famous promotional stunt in history, Bill Veeck of the Browns sends in a midget, Eddie Gaedel, to pinch-hit in a game against Detroit — **C. 1950**

4. Elston Howard becomes the first black player to appear in a game for the New York Yankees — **D. 1951**

5. Bobo Holloman of the St. Louis Browns accomplishes a first in major league history when he pitches a no-hitter in his first big league start. He never pitches another complete game in his career. — **E. 1953**

6. The Red Sox set a new major league record for runs scored in a game when they pound the Browns, 29–4, at Fenway Park — **F. 1958**

7. Cincinnati fans successfully stuff the All-Star Game ballot boxes, giving their beloved Reds eight starters in the annual Summer Classic. Commissioner Ford Frick sets off a firestorm of controversy when he later replaces three of the Reds with players from other teams. — **G. 1955**

734

The last of the 1950s.

1. The Athletics begin play in Kansas City after 54 years in Philadelphia — **A. 1955**

2. Ted Williams, Willie Mays, and others give up their major league careers and head for the front lines of the war in Korea — **B. 1950**

3. The All-Star voting is taken away from the fans and returned to the players, managers, and coaches — **C. 1957**

4. The Phillies win their first National League pennant in 35 years — **D. 1952**

5. Cleveland pitching phenom Herb Score suffers one of the most grisly on-field injuries in baseball history when he is hit in the eye by a line drive off the bat of New York's Gil McDougald, which effectively ends his once promising career — **E. 1958**

6. Ford Frick becomes baseball's third commissioner — **F. 1954**

7. The Orioles begin their inaugural season in Baltimore with a 3–1 victory over the White Sox at Memorial Stadium — **G. 1951**

733: 1-F, 2-A, 3-D, 4-G, 5-E, 6-C, 7-B • **734:** 1-A, 2-D, 3-E, 4-B, 5-C, 6-G, 7-F

The 1940s.

1. The Dodgers become the first team to travel by air when the team flies from St. Louis to Chicago in two planes	**A. 1941**
2. Baseball Commissioner Kenesaw Mountain Landis dies suddenly of a heart attack at the age of 78	**B. 1945**
3. Baseball's color barrier is finally broken when Jackie Robinson takes the field for the Dodgers against the Braves	**C. 1948**
4. Joe DiMaggio puts together his 56-game hitting streak and Ted Williams hits .406	**D. 1942**
5. In the most incredible race between two dominant teams in baseball history, the Cardinals edge out the Dodgers by two games, finishing with 106 victories to Brooklyn's 104	**E. 1947**
6. Babe Ruth dies of throat cancer at the age of 53. Tens of thousands of mourners pass by his open casket.	**F. 1944**
7. Baseball's All-Star Game is canceled for the first time ever due to wartime travel restrictions	**G. 1940**

736

More 1940s.

1. The Yankees clinch the AL pennant on the earliest calendar date in major league history—September 4	**A. 1944**
2. Joe Nuxhall, a 15-year-old pitcher for the Reds, becomes the youngest player ever to appear in a major league game when he works two-thirds of an inning against St. Louis	**B. 1940**
3. Ewell Blackwell of the Reds nearly duplicates Johnny Vander Meer's feat of pitching back-to-back no-hitters. With one out in the ninth of what would have been his second no-hitter, Eddie Stanky of the Dodgers laces a single.	**C. 1943**
4. Bob Feller of the Indians pitches the first and only Opening Day no-hitter when he blanks the White Sox, 1–0, in Chicago	**D. 1948**
5. After a great three-team pennant race, the American League title is settled with a one-game playoff between Cleveland and Boston. The Indians win, 8–3, then go on to beat the other Boston team, the Braves, in the World Series.	**E. 1947**

735: 1-G, 2-F, 3-E, 4-A, 5-D, 6-C, 7-B

6. In a wartime concession, Major League Baseball decides to open the season a week late and conduct its spring training games in northern cities to save on travel

F. 1941

7. Pete Gray, a one-armed outfielder for the Browns, makes his major league debut, collecting one hit in a 7–1 St. Louis win over Detroit

G. 1945

737

Still more 1940s.

1. Major league baseball's owners consider shutting down operations in support of the war, but President Franklin Roosevelt tells them to keep playing for the good of the country

A. 1946

2. Jimmie Foxx of the Red Sox joins Babe Ruth as just the second member of the 500-home run club

B. 1942

3. Danny Gardella of the Giants becomes the first of 18 players to jump to the Mexican League after receiving a big-money offer. Baseball Commissioner Happy Chandler levies five-year suspensions on all of them in order to stem the increasing tide of jumping players.

C. 1947

4. The St. Louis Browns win their only American League pennant by one game when they defeat the Yankees 5–2 on the season's final day

D. 1944

5. Mort Cooper of the Cardinals puts on one of the most dominant performances in major league history when he pitches back-to-back complete-game one-hitters

E. 1949

6. In the greatest home run battle up to that time, Ralph Kiner of the Pirates and Johnny Mize of the Giants enter the final day of the season tied at 51 homers each, but neither man hits another one, so they end up sharing the title

F. 1940

7. Joe DiMaggio of the Yankees becomes baseball's first player to crack the $100,000 per year level when he signs a new contract

G. 1943

Baseball Trivia

The last of the 1940s.

1. Paul Waner of the Braves becomes the seventh member of the 3,000-hit club when he hits a single against his longtime former teammates, the Pirates   **A. 1941**

2. Yankee great Lou Gehrig dies at the age of 37   **B. 1944**

3. Albert (Happy) Chandler becomes the second commissioner in baseball history   **C. 1948**

4. In the first pennant playoff ever, the St. Louis Cardinals defeat the Brooklyn Dodgers two straight in a best-of-three series to win the National League pennant   **D. 1949**

5. In a touching ceremony at Yankee Stadium, the team unveils three granite statues in honor of Babe Ruth, Lou Gehrig, and Miller Huggins. The statues rest permanently in deep center field.   **E. 1942**

6. The Tigers become the last American League team to host a night game when they defeat the A's, 4–1, under the lights at Briggs Stadium   **F. 1945**

7. Baseball cancels its schedule for June 5 and June 6 in honor of the impending D-day invasion, which involves many major league players who enlisted after the outbreak of the war   **G. 1946**

The 1930s.

1. Babe Ruth, Ty Cobb, Honus Wagner, Christy Mathewson, and Walter Johnson are selected as the first group of Hall of Fame inductees   **A. 1938**

2. Pennsylvania voters pass a referendum on November 7, legalizing the playing of baseball on Sunday in the state. Pittsburgh and Philadelphia are the last two teams to observe the original blue law that prohibited working on Sunday.   **B. 1932**

3. The Baseball Hall of Fame is opened and its first four classes of inductees are honored   **C. 1936**

738: 1-E, 2-A, 3-F, 4-G, 5-D, 6-C, 7-B

4. On June 3, Lou Gehrig smacks four homers in a game against Philadelphia and the Yankees' manager of 31 years, John McGraw, retires

D. 1931

5. Johnny Vander Meer pitches back-to-back no-hitters for the Reds, the second of which is the first night game ever in Brooklyn

E. 1935

6. Lou Gehrig homers in six straight games, including three grand slams, and finishes the season with an AL-record 184 RBIs

F. 1939

7. The Cubs win 21 straight games in September to cop the NL flag by just four games over the Cardinals

G. 1933

740

More 1930s.

1. The legendary Red Barber calls the play-by-play as baseball's first televised game takes place at Ebbets Field between the Dodgers and the Reds

A. 1938

2. Babe Ruth becomes the first member of the 700-home run club with a shot against the Tigers in July

B. 1933

3. Jimmie Foxx falls two home runs short of Babe Ruth's record of 60 home runs in a season when he connects for number 58 on the last day of the season

C. 1934

4. Bob Feller of the Indians sets a new major league record by striking out 18 batters in a game, but still loses, 4–1, to the Tigers

D. 1936

5. Yankee first baseman Lou Gehrig breaks Everett Scott's major league record for consecutive games played when he appears in the 1,308th straight game of his career

E. 1939

6. Bob Feller, a 17-year-old phenom pitcher for the Cleveland Indians, ties the major league record for strikeouts in a game when he fans 17 Athletics in a 5–2 win

F. 1930

7. Babe Ruth sets a new salary record when he signs a new two-year deal with the Yankees for $80,000 per season

G. 1932

WHO, WHAT, WHEN, WHERE, AND WHY

1. **Who's** the big guy?

2. **What** was he doing?

3. **When?**

4. **Where?**

4. Barnstorming in Japan with a team of American baseball greats.

3. 1934.

2. Greeting fans while on a barnstorming tour overseas.

1. Hall of Famer Babe Ruth.

741:

Still more 1930s.

1. Carl Hubbell of the Giants makes a rare relief appearance, and wins for the 24th straight time, 3–2, over the Reds **A. 1937**

2. Babe Ruth ends his tenure with the Yankees and signs with the Boston Braves. After little more than a month with Boston, he retires. **B. 1933**

3. Former AL president Ban Johnson and White Sox owner Charles Comiskey, bitter rivals and personal enemies (particularly during the era of the Black Sox scandal), both die in the same year **C. 1930**

4. Lou Gehrig, disabled with a life-threatening disease, is honored in a July 4 ceremony at Yankee Stadium **D. 1934**

5. The city of Philadelphia has much to be proud of when Jimmie Foxx of the A's and Chuck Klein of the Phillies each win his league's Triple Crown Award—in the same season! **E. 1935**

6. In a significant rule change that will take place the next season, balls that bounce into the stands will now be considered ground-rule doubles instead of home runs **F. 1931**

7. Rookie pitcher Schoolboy Rowe of the Detroit Tigers reels off 16 wins in a row to tie the all-time AL mark **G. 1939**

743

The last of the 1930s.

1. Cincinnati defeats Philadelphia, 2–1, at Crosley Field in the first night game in major league history **A. 1935**

2. The National League grants permission to the Reds to officially christen each season with the league's first home opener beginning the following year **B. 1930**

3. At long last the National League finally approves the use of identifying numbers on the backs of players' uniforms **C. 1938**

4. After Dizzy Dean of the Cardinals shuts out Brooklyn on three hits in the first game of a doubleheader, his brother, Paul, trumps him, pitching a no-hitter against the Dodgers in the second game **D. 1931**

5. For the first time ever, the Baseball Writers Association of America selects the two league MVPs: Frank Frisch of the Cardinals and Lefty Grove of the Athletics **E. 1932**

6. Hack Wilson establishes a new National League home run record when he slams 56 round-trippers on his way to 191 RBIs—still the major league record **F. 1934**

742: 1-A, 2-E, 3-F, 4-G, 5-B, 6-C, 7-D • **743:** 1-A, 2-C, 3-E, 4-F, 5-D, 6-B

The 1920s.

1. Rogers Hornsby wins his second NL Triple Crown in four years when he hits .403 with 39 homers and 143 RBIs

   A. 1929

2. Shortstop Jimmy Cooney of the Cubs and first baseman Johnny Neun of the Tigers pull off unassisted triple plays on back-to-back days on May 30 and 31

   B. 1923

3. The Cubs defeat the Phillies, 26–23, in Wrigley Field, a game featuring 51 hits. Both the runs and hits are new records. Apparently the wind was blowing out.

   C. 1921

4. The New York Yankees announce a new innovation: beginning this season, all players will wear uniform numbers on their backs that will show their position in the batting order

   D. 1925

5. Former Tigers pitcher Dutch Leonard comes forward and accuses Ty Cobb and Tris Speaker of throwing games for money back in 1919

   E. 1927

6. Yankee Stadium opens with a 4–1 victory over the Red Sox, and, perhaps appropriately, Babe Ruth hits a three-run homer to provide the margin of victory before a record crowd of 74,217

   F. 1922

7. Ty Cobb joins the 3,000-hit club with a hit against the Red Sox

   G. 1926

745

More 1920s.

1. Philadelphia's Ty Cobb collects his 4,000th career hit in a game against his former Tigers teammates

   A. 1927

2. Walter Johnson becomes the second 400-game winner in major league history, joining Cy Young, when he defeats St. Louis, 7–4

   B. 1920

3. A fight in Navin Field between the Yankees and Tigers escalates into a full-fledged riot among the fans, threatening the lives of players, coaches, and the police. The Yankees are awarded a forfeit win.

   C. 1923

4. Rogers Hornsby puts together baseball's third Triple Crown season when he hits .401 with 42 homers and 152 RBIs

   D. 1929

744: 1-D, 2-E, 3-F, 4-A, 5-G, 6-B, 7-C

Baseball Trivia

5. With five strikeouts against Cleveland, Walter Johnson of the Senators becomes the first pitcher in history to record 3,000 strikeouts in his career

E. 1922

6. Third baseman Joe Sewell of the Indians strikes out only four times in 578 official at bats

F. 1924

7. Red Sox owner Harry Frazee sells pitcher-outfielder Babe Ruth to the Yankees for $125,000

G. 1926

746

Still more 1920s.

1. Christy Mathewson dies at the age of 45 after a five-year struggle with tuberculosis brought on after being gassed during a training exercise in the First World War

A. 1923

2. The Philadelphia A's suffer their second no-hit loss at home in just three days when Howard Ehmke of the Red Sox mirrors the Yankee Sam Jones's earlier gem

B. 1925

3. National League president John Heydler proposes the use of a designated hitter in place of the pitcher so fans don't have to watch weak-hitting pitchers bat. The measure is voted down.

C. 1924

4. Judge Kenesaw Mountain Landis becomes the first commissioner in baseball history when a group of panicky owners hires him to restore baseball's image after the Black Sox scandal erupts

D. 1920

5. Babe Ruth breaks his own season record when he connects for 60 home runs

E. 1921

6. Jim Bottomley of the Cardinals has six hits, including two home runs, as he sets a major league record with 12 RBIs in one game, in a 17–3 thrashing of the Dodgers

F. 1928

7. Eight members of the Chicago White Sox are indicted by a grand jury for their alleged involvement in fixing the 1919 World Series, against the Cincinnati Reds

G. 1927

747

The last of the 1920s.

1. Ty Cobb of the Athletics collects career hit number 4,191, a double, in a game against the Senators on September 3   **A. 1926**

2. Charlie Robertson of the White Sox pitches baseball's third perfect game when he dusts the Tigers, 2–0, in Detroit   **B. 1921**

3. Tris Speaker of the Indians and Eddie Collins of the White Sox both become members of the 3,000-hit club   **C. 1922**

4. Second baseman Rogers Hornsby of the Cardinals finishes the season with a .424 batting average, the highest in baseball history   **D. 1925**

5. Shortstop Ray Chapman of the Indians dies a day after being beaned by Yankee pitcher Carl Mays   **E. 1924**

6. In the biggest trade in baseball history up to that point, the Giants send Frank Frisch to the Cardinals for Rogers Hornsby   **F. 1920**

7. Radio station KDKA in Pittsburgh provides the first-ever broadcast of a major league game when it airs the Pirates-Phillies contest on August 5. Two months later the station broadcasts the first game of the World Series, between the Yankees and Giants.   **G. 1928**

748

The 1910s.

1. Babe Ruth defeats the A's, 7–1, on Opening Day, and then again two days before the season ends, 6–1, to clinch the AL pennant for Boston   **A. 1916**

2. Baseball's ruling officials change the World Series series from a best-of-seven format to best-of-nine   **B. 1914**

3. The Philadelphia Athletics defeat the Detroit Tigers, 7–1, putting an end to their dismal 20-game losing streak   **C. 1918**

747: 1-G, 2-C, 3-D, 4-E, 5-F, 6-A, 7-B

4. Rube Marquard of the Giants wins 19 consecutive games   **D. 1911**

5. Major league baseball's first MVP Award winners,   **E. 1915**
Ty Cobb in the American League and Frank Schulte
in the National League, both receive new Chalmers
automobiles for their efforts

6. After decades of frustration, the Phillies finally win   **F. 1919**
their first pennant ever when Grover Cleveland
Alexander pitches a pennant-clinching 5–0 shutout
(his 12th of the season) over the Braves

7. Boston defeats the Chicago Cubs, 3–2, to clinch its first-   **G. 1912**
ever NL pennant. The "Miracle Braves," as they come to
be known, finish the season with a 68–19 flurry to romp
to a 10.5 game margin.

749

More 1910s.

1. Ty Cobb hits .369 to win his ninth consecutive batting title   **A. 1919**

2. In a season that will become known for its many   **B. 1912**
no-hitters, Eddie Cicotte of the White Sox begins the
no-hit parade with an 11–0 win over St. Louis on April 14

3. The Yankees join the Giants as co-tenants of the Polo Grounds   **C. 1916**

4. Babe Ruth sets a new single-season record when he   **D. 1915**
clubs 29 home runs

5. The New York Giants put together baseball's all-time   **E. 1911**
winning streak, 26 games, but play under .500 the rest
of the time (60–66), to finish in fourth place

6. Ty Cobb is suspended indefinitely for jumping into the   **F. 1917**
stands and severely beating a crippled heckler

7. Cy Young wins his last game in the majors, a 1–0   **G. 1913**
shutout of the Pirates, for career win number 511

748: 1-C, 2-F, 3-A, 4-G, 5-D, 6-E, 7-B • **749:** 1-D, 2-F, 3-G, 4-A, 5-C, 6-B, 7-E

Still more 1910s.

1. Grover Cleveland Alexander, one of the greatest pitchers in baseball history, is drafted into the army and heads for Europe to fight the forces of the Kaiser

A. 1914

2. Indianapolis nips Chicago by a game and a half to win the first Federal League championship

B. 1917

3. Grover Cleveland Alexander sets a modern-era record when he tosses 16 shutouts in one season

C. 1913

4. The National League joins the American League in approving a new 154-game schedule

D. 1918

5. On back-to-back days in early May, St. Louis Browns pitchers Bob Groom and Ernie Koob toss no-hitters against the White Sox

E. 1912

6. Fenway Park in Boston and Redland Field in Cincinnati open for play

F. 1910

7. The Phillies edge the Dodgers, 1–0, in the debut game of Ebbets Field

G. 1916

751

The last of the 1910s.

1. When Babe Ruth is ejected for arguing with the ump after walking the first batter of the game, Ernie Shore replaces him and records 27 outs in a row. For more than half a century, Major League Baseball considers this a perfect game for Shore, but later reverses the decision.

A. 1918

2. The Federal League suspends play when a peace treaty is worked out with the other two leagues

B. 1910

3. After New York's Polo Grounds burn down, the Giants play a large part of their remaining schedule at Hilltop Park, home of the American League's Highlanders (later renamed the Yankees)

C. 1915

4. Making his major league debut, Babe Ruth pitches the Red Sox to a 4–3 victory over the Cleveland Indians

D. 1913

5. William Howard Taft becomes the first U.S. president to throw out the ceremonial first pitch in a game at Washington, D.C.

E. 1917

6. Walter Johnson sets a new major league record that will stand for more than 50 years when he puts together a streak of 56 consecutive scoreless innings. Don Drysdale breaks the record in 1968.

F. 1911

7. Baseball officials vote to end the season by Labor Day and to play the World Series immediately after because of the ongoing war

G. 1914

752

The 1900s.

1. Fred Merkle commits his famous "Merkle's Boner" play, a base-running gaff that ultimately costs the Giants the pennant

A. 1906

2. In one of the strangest deaths in baseball history, future Hall of Famer Ed Delahanty of Washington is found drowned in the Niagara River after being swept over Niagara Falls. He either fell or was pushed off a railroad trestle that spanned the river after being kicked off a train for being drunk and disorderly.

B. 1902

3. Socks Seybold of the Athletics sets a new major league home run record when he finishes the season with 16

C. 1908

4. Both Pennsylvania teams—the Pirates and Phillies—christen new concrete and steel ballparks in the same year, a response to all the wooden parks that had burned down over the years

D. 1901

5. Jack Taylor of the Cubs had his record string of consecutive complete games pitched end at an incredible 187

E. 1903

6. Future Hall of Famer Ty Cobb makes his major league debut with a double off another future Hall of Famer, Jack Chesbro

F. 1905

7. Detroit, in the first game of its history, beats Milwaukee, 14–13, after trailing 13–4 going into the ninth inning. The ten-run rally in the ninth inning is still the greatest comeback in major league history.

G. 1909

More 1900s.

1. NL president Harry Pulliam commits suicide by shooting himself	**A. 1903**
2. The Pirates finish the season with a 103–36 record, 27.5 games in front of Brooklyn, still the record for the widest margin between a league's best and second best teams	**B. 1904**
3. The Cubs set an all-time record for wins that has never been beaten, 116, while losing just 36. (Seattle tied the record in 2001.)	**C. 1909**
4. New York Giants owner John T. Brush and manager John McGraw refuse to play the second World Series against the American League's Red Sox, calling the AL a "minor circuit"	**D. 1900**
5. In a tragic accident, 12 people are killed and 282 injured when a bleacher overhang collapses at Philadelphia's Baker Bowl	**E. 1908**
6. The National League declares war on the newly named American League, calling it an outlaw league outside the National Agreement. The AL, named the Western League the year before, is not considered a major league until the following season.	**F. 1902**
7. Addie Joss of the Indians pitches the second perfect game in modern times, a 1–0 gem against the White Sox	**G. 1906**

754

Still more 1900s.

1. The Red Sox endure a 20-game losing streak	**A. 1904**
2. Catcher Roger Bresnahan of the Giants unveils his latest invention—wooden shin guards	**B. 1909**
3. In mid-September, the team presidents of Boston and Pittsburgh agree to play a best-of-nine championship playoff, calling it the World Series	**C. 1901**

753: 1-C, 2-F, 3-G, 4-B, 5-A, 6-D, 7-E

Baseball Trivia

4. Baseball cancels its games for September 19 out of respect for the assassinated President William McKinley, who was being buried on that day — **D. 1906**

5. Shortstop Neal Ball of the Indians performed the first unassisted triple play of the century in a game against Boston — **E. 1900**

6. The first perfect game of the 20th century was pitched by—appropriately—Cy Young, a 3–0 game against the A's — **F. 1903**

7. In the single worst trade in baseball history, the Reds trade rookie pitcher Christy Mathewson to the Giants for an over-the-hill Amos Rusie. Rusie goes 0–1 in the rest of his career, while Mathewson goes on to win 373 more games, 372 of them for the Giants. — **G. 1907**

755

The last of the 1900s.

1. Future Hall of Famer Christy Mathewson pitches the second no-hitter of his career, a 1–0 beauty against Mordecai Brown, himself a future Hall of Famer — **A. 1908**

2. Baltimore manager John McGraw jumps to the National League and becomes manager of the Giants, taking five of his star players with him — **B. 1904**

3. Cy Young of the Red Sox becomes the first pitcher to throw three career no-hitters when he shuts down New York, 8–0 — **C. 1900**

4. With one of the most famous wild pitches in history, 41-game-winner Jack Chesbro of the Yankees allows the winning run to score in the ninth inning of the season's final game—against the Red Sox, no less—to give Boston its second straight AL pennant — **D. 1901**

5. Kid Nichols of the Braves joins the 300-victory club with an 11–4 win over the Cubs — **E. 1905**

6. The American League (now recognized as a major league) begins play with an 8–2 victory by Chicago over Cleveland — **F. 1902**

7. The Giants reel off 17 straight wins — **G. 1907**

The 1890s.

1. John McGraw makes his managerial debut piloting Baltimore to a win over New York — **A. 1898**

2. Pitcher Bill Duggleby of Philadelphia smashes a grand slam in his first major league at bat, something that has not been done since — **B. 1895**

3. Cleveland, the NL's regular-season runner-up, wins the Temple Cup, four games to one over regular-season champ Baltimore — **C. 1896**

4. In a major rule change, the pitcher's box is eliminated, replaced with a pitching rubber, and moved back more than ten feet to its present-day distance of 60 feet 6 inches — **D. 1892**

5. Catcher Wilbert Robinson of Baltimore becomes the first player in major league history to collect seven hits in a nine-inning game. The feat will not be duplicated until Rennie Stennett of the Pirates does it in 1975 against the Cubs. — **E. 1893**

6. The Pittsburgh Alleghenys are renamed the Pirates by competing teams after they "pirate away" the other teams' stars. Pittsburgh's owners like the new moniker and decide to keep it. — **F. 1899**

7. Jesse Burkett of Cleveland finishes with a .410 average, his second straight .400 campaign — **G. 1891**

757

More 1890s.

1. Baseball's postseason championship, the Temple Cup, is played for the final time due to lack of fan interest, as second-place Baltimore knocks off regular-season champion Boston, 4–1 — **A. 1896**

2. Second baseman Bobby Lowe of Boston becomes the first player in history to sock four home runs in one game — **B. 1899**

3. The Cleveland Spiders suffer through a 24-game losing streak — **C. 1893**

756: 1-F, 2-A, 3-B, 4-E, 5-D, 6-G, 7-C

4. Boston wins its third straight National League pennant, finishing the season at 86–43, five games ahead of Pittsburgh in a season that has been shortened to 132 games from 154 the year before

D. 1890

5. Bumpus Jones of Cincinnati pitches a no-hitter against Pittsburgh in his major league debut

E. 1892

6. Brooklyn jumps from the American Association and wins the NL pennant in its first season in the league

F. 1897

7. Ed Delahanty of Philadelphia ties the record of four home runs in one game—all of them inside-the-park jobs—though the Phillies still lose to Chicago

G. 1894

758

Still more 1890s.

1. Wee Willie Keeler of Baltimore compiles a 44-game hitting streak, still the National League record (although Pete Rose later tied it)

A. 1894

2. After the peace treaty of the year before, the National League—with its newly absorbed American Association teams—begins play as a 12-team league with a 154-game schedule

B. 1891

3. In a major rule change, all teams are required to have one or more replacement players available for each game

C. 1897

4. Baltimore wins its third straight National League pennant

D. 1890

5. Speedster Billy Hamilton of Philadelphia ties a major league record against Washington by stealing seven bases in one game

E. 1896

6. American Association champ Louisville and National League champ Brooklyn meet in the World Series, playing to a draw. Each team wins three games and there is one tie in the seven-game Series—which is more of an exhibition series than a championship series.

F. 1892

7. Cleveland finishes with a 20–134 record for a .130 winning percentage, the worst in baseball history

G. 1899

WHO, WHAT, WHEN, WHERE, AND WHY

1. Who are these three players?

2. What was their claim to fame?

3. When was this photograph taken?

4. What team did they play for?

759:
1. Duffy Lewis, Hall of Famer Tris Speaker, and Hall of Famer Harry Hooper.
2. They are considered to be one of the best outfields ever assembled on one team.
3. At a 1930 Old Timers game.
4. The Boston Red Sox, from 1910 to 1915.

The last of the 1890s.

1. For the first time in history, two pitchers hurl no-hitters on the same day. Jim Hughes of Baltimore and Ted Breitenstein of Cincinnati turn the trick.

2. In reaction to many player complaints, baseball officials decide to restrict the size of player gloves, allowing only first basemen and catchers to wear oversize mitts

3. The National League institutes a new postseason playoff called the Temple Cup, which will be played between the season's top two finishers. Second-place New York sweeps league champ Baltimore in four straight.

4. Cincinnati defeats St. Louis, 5–1, in the first-ever Sunday game, a radical departure from the nationwide blue laws, which prohibited working on Sunday

5. The American Association folds after ten seasons as a major league. Four of its teams (Baltimore, Louisville, St. Louis, and Washington) are absorbed into the National League under terms of a peace treaty.

6. Chicago sets the all-time scoring record with a 36–7 pasting of Louisville

7. A third major league, the Players League, begins play in an atmosphere of all-out war as player defections among the three leagues are common. The record high player salaries cause all three leagues to lose huge money, and the Players League folds after its inaugural season.

A. 1895

B. 1892

C. 1898

D. 1890

E. 1894

F. 1891

G. 1897

760: 1-C, 2-A, 3-E, 4-B, 5-F, 6-G, 7-D

The 1880s.

1. The American Association's Louisville Colonels lose a major league–record 26 straight games
   A. 1886

2. Batters are credited with a stolen base anytime they advance an extra base on their own volition, such as going from first to third on a single, or second to home on a single
   B. 1882

3. All pitching restrictions are removed, thereby allowing pitchers to pitch overhand for the first time
   C. 1881

4. The Philadelphia Phillies shut out the Providence Grays, 28–0, for the most one-sided shutout ever
   D. 1884

5. The Pirates defeat the Giants, 4–2, at the Polo Grounds, ending pitcher Tim Keefe's winning streak at 19 games
   E. 1889

6. In its first season of major league play, the American Association allows Sunday games and liquor sales, both of which are banned by the National League
   F. 1883

7. The National League passes a rule that no team may put in a substitute player except in the case of illness or injury. All players, including pitchers, are expected to go all nine innings.
   G. 1888

762

More 1880s.

1. In a nine-game postseason playoff, the National League's New York Giants defeat the American Association's Brooklyn Bridegrooms, 6–3, to grab the "World Series" title
   A. 1888

2. In the American Association, the number of balls needed for a walk is lowered from seven to six, while in the National League it is increased from six to seven
   B. 1885

3. In the American Association, home team captains are given the option of batting either first or last
   C. 1883

4. For the first time, umpires become salaried employees of major league baseball
   D. 1889

761: 1-E, 2-A, 3-D, 4-F, 5-G, 6-B, 7-C

5. The National League implements several rules changes
   this year: the home team is required to supply a 12-foot-
   long players' bench that is attached to the ground, and
   a bat rack capable of holding at least 20 bats. In addition,
   spectators who boo or hiss at the umpire will be
   ejected from the ballpark.

   E. 1880

6. The St. Louis Browns win their fourth straight
   American Association championship

   F. 1882

7. Lee Richmond of Worcester pitches the first perfect
   game in major league history, a 1–0 gem over Cleveland.
   Five days later, John Ward of Providence pitches the
   second, a 5–0 win over Buffalo.

   G. 1886

763

Still more 1880s.

1. The St. Louis Browns forfeit a late-season game
   against the Brooklyn Bridegrooms for fear of personal
   injury at the hands of unruly fans. Brooklyn ends up
   winning the league title, just one game ahead of the
   Browns in the loss column.

   A. 1885

2. The National League's Detroit Wolverines win the
   best-of-15 World Series against the St. Louis Browns,
   10–5

   B. 1889

3. John Clarkson, who goes on to win 53 games that year,
   pitches a no-hitter against Providence, 4–0

   C. 1883

4. The Union Association begins play as a third major
   league, but folds after just one season when a number
   of teams don't even play the full schedule

   D. 1884

5. In a February meeting that holds great significance,
   officials of both major leagues and many minor leagues
   draft the first National Agreement, a pact that ensures
   the peaceful coexistence of all teams, recognizes the
   reserve clause, and respects each team's player contracts

   E. 1880

6. Roger Connor of Troy hits the first grand slam in major
   league history, a bottom-of-the-ninth walk-off clout that
   gives his team an 8–7 win over visiting Worcester

   F. 1887

7. The National League decides that walks will occur after
   only eight balls instead of nine

   G. 1881

The last of the 1880s.

1. For the first time, players are allowed to use bats that have one flat side

A. 1888

2. The National League's Providence Grays sweep the New York Metropolitans of the American Association in three straight games to win the postseason playoff between the two established leagues

B. 1880

3. The National League votes to make it four balls for a walk and three strikes for a strikeout, a change that lasts to this day

C. 1885

4. The American Association begins play, and, after the season, the first postseason playoff in major league history takes place when the AA champ Cincinnati Red Stockings split a two-game series with the NL champ Chicago White Stockings

D. 1881

5. Athletics third baseman Denny Lyons establishes a new major league record by getting a hit in 52 straight games. MLB later disallows the streak, since in two of the games Lyons got on base only by walks, which for this year only are counted as base hits.

E. 1882

6. The front line of the pitcher's box is moved from 45 feet back to 50 feet from home plate

F. 1887

7. The Chicago White Stockings win the National League pennant with a 67–17 record, a 15-game margin over second place Providence. Along the way, Chicago sets a record by winning 21 straight games.

G. 1884

765

The 1870s.

1. For the second time in three years, the Cincinnati franchise folds in midseason, failing this time to pay its players for the final month

A. 1876

2. Pitcher Tommy Bonds wins 40 of Boston's 41 games to lead the Red Caps to the National League title

B. 1878

3. This year's strike zone rule requires batters to ask the umpire to tell the pitcher to deliver either a high or low pitch, the batter's choice, and the umpire must base his calls on the batter's preference

C. 1871

4. Four future major Hall of Famers are born this year: Honus Wagner, Napoleon Lajoie, Jack Chesbro, and umpire Bill Klem

D. 1875

764: 1-C, 2-G, 3-E, 4-A, 5-F, 6-D, 7-B

5. Deacon White of the Boston Red Stockings becomes the first catcher ever to play the position as we know it today (directly behind the batter) instead of 30 feet or so behind the plate   **E. 1879**

6. The National League changes its "fair-foul" rule because too many players are abusing it. Now, when a ball that starts off in fair ground goes foul before passing first or third base, it is ruled a foul ball.   **F. 1874**

7. Pete Norton of the Washington Olympics becomes the first pinch hitter in history when he hits for the injured Doug Allison, and he strikes out   **G. 1877**

766

NAME THAT YEAR

Seven clues. One year. See how few clues it takes you to guess the year.

1 **The Philadelphia Phillies change** their name to the Blue Jays—for just two years.

2 **The St. Louis Cardinals win** their third straight NL pennant.

3 **Hal Newhouser wins 29 games** for the second-place Tigers while his teammate Dizzy Trout wins 27, the most combined wins (56) by a pair of teammates in the post-dead-ball era.

4 **Cincinnati's Joe Nuxhall** makes his major league debut at the age of 15.

5 **Cardinal Marty Marion wins** the NL MVP Award by one vote, over Bill Nicholson of the Cubs.

6 **Dixie Walker of the Dodgers** leads the majors in batting at .357.

7 **The St. Louis Browns win** their only pennant by defeating the Yankees 5–2 on the last day of the season.

WHO, WHAT, WHEN, WHERE, AND WHY

1. Who is the player on the left?

2. What is his particular claim to fame?

3. When did he accomplish this feat?

4. Where did he spend most of his time, after his playing career ended?

5. BONUS: What did he do that AL President Ban Johnson so enjoyed, but banned him from doing anyway?

767:

1. Nick Altrock.

2. He was baseball's first five-decade player and he pinch-hit in a game at the age of 57 (1933).

3. 1890s to 1930s.

4. The coaching box, usually third base.

5. In order to distract the opposing pitcher, Altrock would engage in a one-man wrestling match that had fans and players alike howling with laughter. Johnson ordered baseball's first comedian to cease his act during the playing of the game.

More 1870s.

1. John Ward of Providence pitches every inning of 73 consecutive games before being knocked out in a 9–0 loss to Cincinnati

    A. 1876

2. The lineups, once submitted, can now no longer be changed

    B. 1874

3. The Boston Red Stockings win their fourth straight National Association title with a 71–8 record

    C. 1879

4. The baseball historian Henry Chadwick publishes his classic, *Chadwick's Base Ball Manual,* which includes definitions of baseball terminology and rules of the game

    D. 1872

5. The New York Mutuals and Philadelphia Athletics both announce that, due to lack of funds, they will not be making their final western trip of the season. Many games have to be canceled, and, after the season, both clubs are expelled from the National League.

    E. 1871

6. To resolve the confusing issue of amateur versus professional clubs, ten of the top professional teams band together to form their own new association, called the National Association of Professional Baseball Players; nine of them compete in a new league called the National Association

    F. 1875

7. After three teams drop out of the league, the National Association offers expansion teams interested in playing in their new league the opportunity to join for a $10 expansion fee. Five teams—from Washington, Baltimore, two teams from Brooklyn, and Middletown, Connecticut— take the new league up on its offer.

    G. 1878

768: 1-C, 2-G, 3-F, 4-B, 5-A, 6-E, 7-D

Still more 1870s.

1. The National League's Hartford club decides to play all its "home"games in Brooklyn while maintaining its official team office in Connecticut

   A. 1877

2. In a December meeting, William Hulbert and Albert Spalding create a constitution for a new league that will begin play the following year. The National League bans drinking, gambling, and disorderly conduct, and will charge a 50 cents admission per game.

   B. 1872

3. Will White of Cincinnati pitches 75 complete games and 680 innings, both still major league records

   C. 1874

4. Boston captures the first of four straight National Association titles with a 39–8 record on the season

   D. 1875

5. Chicago's Ross Barnes, the National League's first batting champion, at .403, is also the first player to hit a home run

   E. 1876

6. Al Spalding interrupts National Association league play to take two teams to England for the expressed purpose of introducing the game of baseball to the European continent

   F. 1871

7. The Philadelphia Athletics win the National Association title with a 21–7 record and become the only team besides the Boston Red Stockings to win an NA pennant

   G. 1879

770

The last of the 1870s.

1. Boston becomes the first National League team to repeat as league champion when they finish 41–17, four games ahead of Cincinnati

   A. 1875

2. Louisville boots four of its players off the team after discovering they were involved in game-fixing

   B. 1872

3. The Washington Nationals become the first team ever to go through a season without a victory, finishing 0–11

   C. 1871

769: 1-A, 2-D, 3-G, 4-B, 5-E, 6-C, 7-F

4. Ross Barnes hits .425 and scores 125 runs in just
59 games for the Boston Red Stockings
    D. 1878

5. Joe Borden of the Philadelphia Athletics pitches the
only no-hitter in the five-year history of the National
Association when he blanks Chicago, 4–0
    E. 1876

6. The only year in the five-year history of the National
Association that the Boston Red Stockings did *not*
win the pennant
    F. 1873

7. George Bradley of St. Louis pitches the first no-hitter in
National League history, defeating the Hartford club, 2–0
    G. 1877

771

NAME THAT YEAR

Seven clues. One year. See how few clues it takes you to
guess the year.

1 **Bobby Bonds dies** of cancer.

2 **Barry Bonds wins** his third straight NL MVP Award, and
sixth overall.

3 **Roger Clemens wins** his 300th career game, and collects his
4,000th career strikeout in the same game against the Cardinals.

4 **Detroit loses an American League–record** 119 games.

5 **Texas' Alex Rodriguez becomes the first player**
to win the AL MVP Award while playing for a last-place team.

6 **Albert Pujols nips Todd Helton** for the NL batting crown,
.359 to .358.

7 **The Florida Marlins win** their second World Series title in just
the 11th year of their existence.

772

And of course you remember the 1860s.

1. The Union Baseball Grounds opens for business in Brooklyn. It is the first enclosed park that charges an admission to the games.

A. 1864

2. Three New York Mutuals players conspire with a New York gambler in what could be baseball's first fixed game as the Brooklyn Eckfords defeat the Mutuals 23–11 after trailing 5–4 midway in the game

B. 1868

3. The National Association of Baseball Players approves the use of professional players, previously considered taboo

C. May 1862

4. The Brooklyn Excelsiors undertake the first baseball tour, taking on and beating all comers

D. Dec. 1862

5. A. J. Reach becomes baseball's first paid player when he leaves the Athletics of Philadelphia after five years and joins the Brooklyn team

E. 1869

6. A crowd of 40,000 watches two teams of Union soldiers play a game of baseball at Hilton Head, South Carolina

F. 1865

7. The Cincinnati Red Stockings, baseball's first all-professional team, tour the country and compile a perfect 57–0 record with one tie

G. 1860

773

And the pre-1860s.

1. Alexander Cartwright, the father of baseball, creates and publishes his set of 20 baseball rules

A. 1834

2. Baseball's first box scores appear in *The New York Clipper*

B. 1849

3. *Book of Sports,* by Robin Carver, the first book with printed rules for baseball, is published

C. 1858

4. The Knickerbockers of New York become the first baseball team to wear uniforms

D. 1853

5. New York City plays host to the first formal baseball convention. Two months later the National Association of Baseball Players is formed.

E. 1839

6. According to legend (and later proved false), Abner Doubleday invents baseball at Cooperstown, New York, in this year

F. 1845

7. Two All-Star teams from New York and Brooklyn square off in the first-ever game played for admission (50 cents)

G. 1857

772: 1-C, 2-F, 3-B, 4-G, 5-A, 6-D, 7-E • **773:** 1-F, 2-D, 3-A, 4-B, 5-G, 6-E, 7-C

414

WHO, WHAT, WHEN, WHERE, AND WHY

1. Who is the player on the right?

2. What was his nickname, and why?

3. When did he first fail to win 20 games in a season?

4. Where did he go after leaving the majors in 1908 at the age of 37?

4. He played minor league ball until well into his fifties.

3. 1907, his ninth year in the majors.

2. "Iron Man," because he worked in an iron foundry during the offseason.

1. Hall of Famer Joe McGinnity.

774:

775

NAME THAT YEAR

Seven clues. One year. See how few clues it takes you to guess the year.

1 **The Oakland A's become the first team** to employ ball girls instead of ball boys when they hire 13-year-old Debbie Sivyer, later to become the entrepreneur behind Mrs. Fields Cookies.

2 **Braves shortstop Leo Foster hits** into a double play in his first major league at bat, commits an error on the first ball ever hit to him, and, later in the same game, hits into a triple play.

3 **Houston plays a major league–record** 75 one-run games.

4 **Rick Wise of the Phillies** homers in four consecutive games in which he pitches.

5 **For the first time,** batting helmets are now mandatory in both major leagues.

6 **The World Series is played** at night for the first time.

7 **Oakland's Vida Blue wins** both the AL MVP and Cy Young awards.

FIRST
THINGS
FIRST

PLAYER AND
TEAM POTPOURRI

776

1. Derek Jeter

A. The first player to hit a home run with three different teams in the World Series

2. Ichiro Suzuki

B. The first rookie to be the leading vote getter for the All-Star Game

3. Scott Hatteberg

C. The first player to get a hit in an All-Star Game in which the stadium had the same name as his last name

4. Matt Williams

D. The first to hit a grand slam on two different continents

5. Benny Agbayani

E. The first player to win the All-Star Game MVP Award and World Series MVP Award in the same season

6. Marcus Thames

F. The first player to hit a home run in his first at bat off a defending Cy Young Award winner

7. Damian Miller

G. The first player to hit a grand slam and hit into a triple play in the same game

777

1. Nomar Garciaparra

A. The first player to hit three home runs on his birthday

2. Alex Rodriguez

B. The first player to hit a grand slam from both sides of the plate in the same game

3. Dave Kingman

C. The first player to hit a walk-off grand slam on his birthday

4. Todd Zeile

D. The first National Leaguer to have two hits in the same inning in his major league debut

5. Bill Mueller

E. The first player to play for teams in four different divisions in the same season

6. Adam LaRoche

F. The only National Leaguer to hit three home runs on Opening Day

7. Karl Rhodes

G. The first to hit home runs for ten different teams

776: 1-E, 2-B, 3-G, 4-A, 5-D, 6-F, 7-C • **777:** 1-A, 2-C, 3-E, 4-G, 5-B, 6-D, 7-F

WHO, WHAT, WHEN, WHERE, AND WHY

1. Who are these guys?

2. What is their claim to fame?

3. When did it first happen?

4. What positions did the two players play?

4. Cal Jr. played short and Billy played second.

3. 1987.

2. Cal Sr. was the first manager to manage two sons at the same time in the majors.

1. Billy Ripken, Cal Ripken Sr., and Hall of Famer Cal Ripken Jr.

778:

Baseball Trivia

779

1. Jason Jennings	A. The first pitcher to play for teams in four different divisions in the same season
2. Al Leiter	B. The first AL pitcher to start a game as the team's DH
3. Francisco Rodriguez	C. The first pitcher to defeat all 30 teams currently playing in the major leagues
4. Dan Miceli	D. The first pitcher since 1900 to hit a home run and pitch a shutout in his major league debut
5. Derek Lowe	E. The first pitcher to collect a save in each of the first four consecutive games to start a team's season
6. Derrick Turnbow	F. The first pitcher in major league history to collect his first two career wins in the postseason
7. Rick Rhoden	G. The first pitcher in history to win the final game of a League Division Series, League Championship Series, and World Series all in the same season

780

1. Dwight Evans	A. The first second baseman to join the 30-30 club
2. Andre Dawson	B. The first AL player to be hit by a pitch twice in the same inning
3. Doug Dascenzo	C. The first player to hit the first pitch of the first game of the season (including all teams scheduled to play) for a home run
4. Carlos Baerga	D. The first player in major league history to hit a home run from both sides of the plate in the same inning
5. Mark Lewis	E. The first player to win his league's MVP Award while playing for the last-place team
6. Brady Anderson	F. Started his career with 242 consecutive errorless games, a National League record
7. Alfonso Soriano	G. Hit the first pinch-hit grand slam in playoff history

779: 1-D, 2-C, 3-F, 4-A, 5-G, 6-E, 7-B • 780: 1-C, 2-E, 3-F, 4-D, 5-G, 6-B, 7-A

781

1. Davey Johnson	A. The first player to hit for the cycle in both leagues
2. Bob Watson	B. The first player to hit a home run in three different no-hitters
3. Keith Hernandez	C. One of the first two co-MVPs in a season
4. Paul Molitor	D. The first player to be *intentionally* walked five times in one game
5. Cal Ripken Jr.	E. The first player to get five hits in one World Series game
6. Andre Dawson	F. The first player to hit two game-winning pinch-hit grand slams in one season
7. Terry Pendleton	G. The first player to play every inning of every game from Opening Day through the playoffs and World Series

782

1. Dennis Eckersley	A. Pitched the first no-hitter in Coors Field
2. Bill Singer	B. Reliever who recorded the first officially recognized save
3. Larry Gowell	C. Participated in the first combined no-hitter in the National League
4. Hideo Nomo	D. The first relief pitcher ever to have more saves in a season (48) than base runners allowed (45)
5. Chan Ho Park	E. Bowed to the umpire before he played his first game in the major leagues
6. Kent Mercker	F. Pitched the first no-hitter that clinched a division title
7. Mike Scott	G. The last AL pitcher to get a hit before the implementation of the designated-hitter rule

781: 1-F, 2-A, 3-C, 4-E, 5-G, 6-D, 7-B • **782:** 1-D, 2-B, 3-G, 4-A, 5-E, 6-C, 7-F

Baseball Trivia

1. Cal Hubbard	**A.** The first major leaguer to play in a game umpired by his brother
2. Wes Fisler	**B.** Scored the first run in major league history
3. Bob Watson	**C.** The first player to hit at least 30 homers in a season and have more intentional walks (40) than homers (39)
4. Tom Haller	**D.** The first player to win a Gold Glove in each league
5. Tommie Agee	**E.** Scored the millionth run in baseball history
6. Willie McCovey	**F.** The first player in history to have three 3-homer games in the same season
7. Sammy Sosa	**G.** The first player to be elected into both the Football Hall of Fame and Baseball Hall of Fame

784

1. Alex Sanchez	**A.** Homered in his first at bat of the season for three consecutive years
2. Ichiro Suzuki	**B.** The first manager ever thrown out of both games of a doubleheader
3. Kaz Matsui	**C.** The first manager ever to resign and then be named Manager of the Year in the same day
4. George Sisler	**D.** The only player in major league history to collect at least 200 hits in his first six seasons
5. Mel Ott	**E.** The first player ever to be suspended for violating Major League Baseball's new steroids policy
6. Davey Johnson	**F.** The first player to have his birthday sewn onto his uniform
7. Carlos May	**G.** Half of the first-ever father-son managing combo

This game is a tough one. If you get all seven, you might just be my hero.

1. Steve Chilcott

A. The first umpire to wear glasses in a regular-season game

2. Spec Shea

B. The first number 1 pick not to make it to the major leagues

3. Phil Paine

C. The first player ever to hit a home run on the first pitch he saw in the major leagues

4. Ed Rommell

D. The first rookie to win an All-Star Game

5. Clint Courtney

E. The first catcher to use an oversized glove in order to catch the knuckleball

6. Elmer Smith

F. Hit the first grand slam in World Series history

7. Clise Dudley

G. The first ex–major leaguer to play in Japan

786

1. Willie Kamm

A. The first major leaguer to play all 154 scheduled games and not hit into a double play

2. Jack Graney

B. The first pitcher ever to throw a no-hitter the first game after being traded

3. Augie Galan

C. The first former player to become a play-by-play announcer

4. Bill Lefebvre

D. The first major leaguer to leave baseball and fight in World War I

5. Hank Gowdy

E. The first American League player to hit a home run on the first pitch he ever saw in the majors

6. George Kelly

F. The first minor league player to be purchased for more than $100,000

7. Don Cardwell

G. The first player to hit home runs in six consecutive games

785: 1-B, 2-D, 3-G, 4-A, 5-E, 6-F, 7-C • **786:** 1-F, 2-C, 3-A, 4-E, 5-D, 6-G, 7-B

WHO, WHAT, WHEN, WHERE, AND WHY

1. **Who** is wearing the black uniform?

2. **What** was he doing?

3. **When?**

4. **Where** did his team first unveil these new uniforms?

5. **BONUS:** Why did they switch to the black uniforms?

787:

1. Hall of Fame Giants manager John McGraw.

2. He was discussing the ground rules with the umpires and opposing manager prior to Game 1 of the World Series.

3. 1911.

4. The Polo Grounds in New York.

5. The Giants' last World Series triumph had come in 1905 while they were wearing their black uniforms, so the superstitious McGraw reverted to these uniforms for the 1911 World Series, though the Philadelphia A's went on to defeat the Giants anyway, four games to two.

788

Let's shift gears with some team trivia.

1. White Sox   A. The first team to turn two triple plays in the same game (1990)

2. Twins   B. The first AL team ever to feature four players with 30 or more homers in the same season—2000

3. Brewers   C. The only team in major league history to have two players hit two home runs in the same inning in the same game—2002

4. Angels   D. The first team ever to finish a season with more strikeouts, 1,399, than hits, 1,378—2001

5. Mariners   E. The first team ever to hit back-to-back home runs with two outs in the ninth inning—2002

6. Dodgers   F. The first team to employ a woman as its play-by-play announcer—1977

7. Braves   G. The first team ever to win a game by the score of 3–0 when the runs scored on back-to-back-to-back home runs (2003)

789

1. Dodgers   A. The first major league team to take the field with an all-black lineup—1971

2. Pirates   B. The first team to broadcast every one of its season's games on the radio—1935

3. Red Sox   C. The first team to win a modern-era World Series—1903

4. Indians   D. The first team to permanently put numbers on its uniform backs—1929

5. Yankees   E. The first team to take the field with a majority of black players (five of the nine)

6. Giants   F. The first team to make use of a public address system at its ballpark—1929

7. Cubs   G. The first team to temporarily put numbers on the backs of its uniforms—1929

788: 1-F, 2-A, 3-D, 4-B, 5-C, 6-E, 7-G • **789:** 1-E, 2-A, 3-C, 4-G, 5-D, 6-F, 7-B

1. Dodgers

A. The first organization to purchase its own team airplane—1957

2. Brewers

B. The first team ever to feature the major league debuts of four pitchers in the same game—2003

3. Rangers

C. Losers of the first coast-to-coast televised game (1951)

4. Devil Rays

D. Winners of major league baseball's first Opening *Day* night game—1950

5. Tigers

E. The first team to feature two players who hit three home runs in the same game—2001

6. Cardinals

F. The first team ever to be 18 games under .500 at one point in the season and eventually climb back above .500—2004

7. Giants

G. The first team in major league history to feature three active players with career home run totals over 300, 400, and 500—2003

791

See if you can figure out who the first designated hitter was for each of the listed teams. We'll start with the American League teams. (Note: Milwaukee was in the American League at the time the designated-hitter rule was adopted.)

1. Baltimore Orioles

A. Mike Andrews

2. Boston Red Sox

B. Ollie Brown

3. California Angels

C. Tommy McCraw

4. Chicago White Sox

D. Gates Brown

5. Cleveland Indians

E. Ed Kirkpatrick

6. Detroit Tigers

F. Terry Crowley

7. Kansas City Royals

G. John Ellis

8. Milwaukee Brewers

H. Orlando Cepeda

790: 1-A, 2-E, 3-G, 4-F, 5-B, 6-D, 7-C • **791:** 1-F, 2-H, 3-C, 4-A, 5-G, 6-D, 7-E, 8-B

1. Minnesota Twins	**A. Dave Collins**
2. New York Yankees	**B. Tony Oliva**
3. Oakland A's	**C. Billy North**
4. Seattle Mariners	**D. Paul Sorrento**
5. Texas Rangers	**E. Otto Velez**
6. Tampa Bay Devil Rays	**F. Ron Blomberg**
7. Toronto Blue Jays	**G. Rico Carty**

793

Now for each National League team's first designated hitter.

1. Atlanta Braves	**A. Eddie Taubensee**
2. Arizona Diamondbacks	**B. Mike Piazza**
3. Chicago Cubs	**C. Jim Eisenreich**
4. Cincinnati Reds	**D. Sean Berry**
5. Colorado Rockies	**E. Keith Lockhart**
6. Florida Marlins	**F. Kelly Stinnett**
7. Houston Astros	**G. Dave Clark**
8. Los Angeles Dodgers	**H. Dante Bichette**

794

1. Montreal Expos	**A. Mark Smith**
2. New York Mets	**B. Butch Huskey**
3. Philadelphia Phillies	**C. Glenallen Hill**
4. Pittsburgh Pirates	**D. Jose Vidro**
5. St. Louis Cardinals	**E. Dmitri Young**
6. San Diego Padres	**F. Darren Daulton**
7. San Francisco Giants	**G. Rickey Henderson**

794: 1-D, 2-B, 3-F, 4-A, 5-E, 6-G, 7-C

• **792:** 1-B, 2-F, 3-C, 4-A, 5-G, 6-D, 7-E • **793:** 1-E, 2-F, 3-G, 4-A, 5-H, 6-C, 7-D, 8-B

How about some home run firsts?

1. Babe Herman	A. The first to hit two grand slams in a game, one from each side of the plate
2. Tony Lazzeri	B. The first to hit three homers in one game
3. Bobby Lowe	C. The first to hit two grand slams in one game
4. Ned Williamson	D. The first to hit 30 homers in a season
5. Babe Ruth	E. The first to hit a home run in a night game
6. Bill Mueller	F. The first to hit four homers in one game
7. Pop Snyder	G. The first to hit an extra-inning home run

796

These home run firsts date back to baseball's early days.

1. George Hall	A. The first to hit 20 home runs in a season
2. Wally Schang	B. Hit the first home run in American League history
3. Buck Ewing	C. The first switch-hitter to homer from both sides of the plate in the same game
4. Erve Beck	D. The first to hit two homers in one game
5. Ross Barnes	E. The first player in major league history to hit a home run in his first at bat in the majors
6. Ned Williamson	F. The first to hit ten home runs in a season
7. Joe Harrington	G. Hit the first home run in National League history (he was tied later that same day by Charley Jones)

WHO, WHAT, WHEN, WHERE, AND WHY

1. **Who** is this player?

2. **What** award is he receiving?

3. **When** did he receive it?

4. **Where** did he finish in the Rookie of the Year race in 1954?

5. **BONUS:** What was so significant about this award?

797:
1. Hall of Famer Ernie Banks.
2. The NL MVP Award.
3. Early in the 1960 season for his 1959 performance.
4. Second to Wally Moon.
5. It was his second consecutive NL MVP Award, making him the first National League player ever to win back-to-back MVP Awards.

Every major league player remembers whom he hit his first home run off, even these members of the 500-home run club. Do you?

1. Hank Aaron	A. Billy Hoeft
2. Ernie Banks	B. Ron Kline
3. Harmon Killebrew	C. Ken Heintzelman
4. Mickey Mantle	D. Gerry Staley
5. Eddie Mathews	E. Vic Raschi
6. Willie Mays	F. Warren Spahn
7. Willie McCovey	G. Randy Gumpert

799

Try these 500-home run club members and the pitchers who served up their first round-trippers.

1. Barry Bonds	A. Kevin Gross
2. Reggie Jackson	B. Jim Weaver
3. Mark McGwire	C. Craig McMurtry
4. Eddie Murray	D. Walt Terrell
5. Rafael Palmeiro	E. Roger Clemens
6. Mike Schmidt	F. Pat Dobson
7. Sammy Sosa	G. Balor Moore

800

Even these 3,000-hit club members hit their first home run off somebody.

1. Wade Boggs	A. Dennis Leonard
2. George Brett	B. Steve Comer
3. Tony Gwynn	C. Bill Campbell

798: 1-E, 2-D, 3-A, 4-G, 5-C, 6-F, 7-B • **799:** 1-C, 2-B, 3-D, 4-F, 5-A, 6-G, 7-E

Baseball Trivia

4. Rickey Henderson   D. Ross Grimsley

5. Cal Ripken Jr.   E. Ken Forsch

6. Dave Winfield   F. Ferguson Jenkins

7. Robin Yount   G. Dave Tobik

801

A few more members of the 3,000-hit club and the pitchers who served up their first gopher balls.

1. Lou Brock   A. Jerry Casale

2. Roberto Clemente   B. Rip Sewell

3. Al Kaline   C. Joe Kerrigan

4. Paul Molitor   D. Ray Washburn

5. Stan Musial   E. Don Liddle

6. Pete Rose   F. Ernie Broglio

7. Carl Yastrzemski   G. Dave Hoskins

802

One more round, this time with some of the game's earliest stars—all 3,000-hit club members—and the pitchers who served up their first home runs.

1. Cap Anson   A. Skinny Graham

2. Ty Cobb   B. George Bradley

3. Eddie Collins   C. Jack Ryan

4. Napoleon Lajoie   D. Jack Dunn

5. Tris Speaker   E. Cy Falkenberg

6. Honus Wagner   F. Art Herman

7. Paul Waner   G. Dolly Gray

802: 1-B, 2-E, 3-C, 4-F, 5-G, 6-D, 7-A

801: 1-D, 2-E, 3-G, 4-C, 5-B, 6-F, 7-A • **800:** 1-G, 2-F, 3-C, 4-B, 5-A, 6-E, 7-D •

431

NAME THAT YEAR

Seven clues. One year. See how few clues it takes you to guess the year.

1 **Dave Winfield, 41,** becomes the oldest player to hit a home run in World Series play.

2 **Eric Karros wins** the NL Rookie of the Year Award.

3 **Kenny Lofton sets a new** American League rookie record by swiping 66 bases.

4 **Edgar Martinez hits .343** to become the first Mariner to win a batting title.

5 **The Tigers' Cecil Fielder** becomes just the second player in history to lead the majors in RBIs three consecutive years.

6 **Fay Vincent resigns** as commissioner.

7 **Canada takes home** its first World Series title as the Blue Jays defeat the Braves in six games.

DREAM
TEAMS BY THE
NUMBERS

While it would be possible to compile a team for almost all numbers up to the low 50s, I have listed my choices for dream teams with uniform numbers 1 to 9 and 21 (because of all numbers, it's the strongest team). All of the answers are players who wore the required uniform number at some point in their careers. Besides each uniform number, I'll provide the position to be filled and some clues about the player. Several players appear on more than one team because they wore several different numbers during their careers and were the best at their position for both numbers. Some players might be listed at positions at which they played fewer games than at their primary one. (Note: I didn't differentiate between the three outfield positions.) Answers are on page 553.

Uniform number 1 dream team.

Catcher (Played 1949–1966, mostly with Braves)

First base (HOFer, pre-WWII, Cardinals, Reds)

Second base (HOFer, Red Sox for whole career)

Third base (HOFer, Tigers, Red Sox, A's)

Shortstop (HOFer, Cardinals, Padres)

First outfielder (HOFer, mostly Phillies, pre-WWII)

Second outfielder (HOFer, mostly Phillies, post-WWII)

Third outfielder (Speedster, 1991–present, mostly Indians)

Starting pitcher (55–95 record, mostly with Seattle in 1980s)

Manager (HOFer, pre-WWII, Reds, Pirates, Braves)

805

Uniform number 2 dream team.

Catcher (HOFer, A's and Tigers)

First base (1931–1942, three-time All-Star, mostly Cardinals)

Second base (HOFer, 19 years, with Detroit)

Third base (Yankees for whole career, 1931–1942)

Shortstop (1996 AL Rookie of the Year)

First outfielder (HOFer, 1920s–1930s, Senators, Tigers)

Second outfielder (1981–1997, mostly Dodgers, Indians)

Third outfielder (1985–2001, mostly Angels, Blue Jays)

Starting pitcher (63–87, mostly with Detroit in 1930s)

Manager (HOFer, Dodgers)

806

Uniform number 3 dream team.

Catcher (HOFer, won AL MVP in 1928 and 1934)

First base (HOFer, 1925–1945, 534 homers)

Second base (HOFer, Giants, Cardinals, 1931 NL MVP)

Third base (Won six straight Gold Gloves, 2001–2006)

Shortstop (Ahead of Aaron's career home run pace)

First outfielder (HOFer, almost bigger than the game)

Second outfielder (HOFer, Triple Crown winner in 1937)

Third outfielder (HOFer, six-time All-Star with Cleveland)

Starting pitcher (225-plus wins, pitched perfect game)

Manager (HOFer, all Giants, .341 career average)

807

Uniform number 4 dream team.

Catcher (HOFer, Reds, one of slowest players ever)

First base (HOFer, AL Triple Crown in 1934)

Second base (HOFer, mostly Cubs, 1931–1947)

Third base (HOFer, Brewers, Jays, Twins)

Shortstop (A's, O's, long consecutive game streak)

First outfielder (HOFer, all Giants, 511 homers)

Second outfielder (HOFer, Dodgers, Boys of Summer)

Third outfielder (HOFer, led NL in homers his first seven years)

Starting pitcher (Gave up Ruth's "called shot" home run)

Manager (HOFer, Orioles)

808

Uniform number 5 dream team.

Catcher (HOFer, All-Star every year in the 1970s)

First base (Biggest offensive threat in game, 2001–2006)

Second base (HOFer, Murderer's Row)

Third base (HOFer, 23 years with same team)

Shortstop (HOFer, Pirates, Dodgers, 1932–1948)

First outfielder (HOFer, received many death threats in 1974)

Second outfielder (HOFer, *"Where have you gone?"*)

Third outfielder (HOFer, Jewish slugger)

Starting pitcher (211-game winner, mostly Chicago White Sox, 1945–1964)

Manager (One of three Braves to hit 40-plus home runs in 1973)

809

Uniform number 6 dream team.

Catcher (245 homers, debuted with A's in 1984)

First base (HOFer, he's the man)

Second base (Yanks, Indians, 1938–1950, nine times All-Star)

Third base (Debuted with Phillies in 1996)

Shortstop (38-game hitting streak ended in 2006)

First outfielder (HOFer, 536 homers as a switch-hitter)

Second outfielder (HOFer, everything is just "Ducky")

Third outfielder (HOFer, joined Detroit at 18 in 1953)

Starting pitcher (HOFer who spent first two seasons at third base)

Manager (Hit .363 for 1971 Cardinals with 137 RBIs)

810

Uniform number 7 dream team.

Catcher (Hit over .300 in nine of ten years, 1995–2004)

First base (200-plus home runs with Indians, 1933–1941)

Second base (HOFer, with Cardinals for nearly 50 years)

Third base (HOFer, Braves, 500-HR club member)

Shortstop (Mostly Tigers and Giants, 1952–1966)

First outfielder (Balco Bad Boy from the Bay)

Second outfielder (HOFer, lost the great homer race in 1961)

Third outfielder (HOFer, won NL Triple Crown in 1937)

Starting pitcher (127 wins from 1928 to 1936, mostly with A's)

Manager (Managed Cubs and Braves 1932–1960)

811

Uniform number 8 dream team

Catcher (HOFer, 11 time All-Star with Yanks, 1928–1946)

First base (HOFer, *We are family)*

Second base (HOFer, Astros, Reds)

Third base (15 years, mostly Pirates and Dodgers, 1939–1953)

Shortstop (HOFer, a *Streak* performer)

First outfielder (HOFer, Phillies, won Triple Crown in 1933)

Second outfielder (HOFer, all 23 years in Beantown)

Third outfielder (21 years, Expos and Cubs, won 1987 NL MVP)

Starting pitcher (211 wins with nine teams from 1929 to 1953)

Manager (HOFer, played 14 World Series with Yanks)

812

Uniform number 9 dream team.

Catcher (HOFer, 19 of 20 years with Cubs, 1922–1941)

First base (17 years with Toronto/ Mets/Seattle)

Second base (HOFer, nine-time All-Star with Red Sox)

Third base (Played in five different decades)

Shortstop (Giants, Diamondbacks, moved to third base in second year)

First outfielder (HOFer, hit a home run in last at bat of career)

Second outfielder (HOFer, married to a movie star)

Third outfielder (HOFer, his candy bar struck out a lot, too)

Starting pitcher (HOFer, all Indians, 1936–1956)

Manager (Current; in top 10 all time for wins)

WHO, WHAT, WHEN, WHERE, AND WHY

1. **Who** are these three guys?

2. **Why** is this photograph significant?

3. **When** was this photograph taken?

4. **Where** was the man on the right playing the next year?

813:

1. Hall of Famer Lou Gehrig, Hall of Fame manager Joe McCarthy, and Hall of Famer Babe Ruth.

2. It is the last year the three of them would be together on the same team.

3. 1934.

4. Boston, for the Braves.

Uniform number 21 dream team (the best of the bunch!).

Catcher (Four-time Gold Glover with Marlins in 1990s)

First base (1930s slugger for Indians)

Second base (HOFer, hit .402 over 1921–1925 seasons)

Third base (HOFer, struck out only 114 times in 7,132 AB!)

Shortstop (HOFer, died at 40 in fishing accident)

First outfielder (HOFer, star of 1971 World Series)

Second outfielder (HOFer, fourth time on this list with different number!)

Third outfielder (Was half of great home run duo of 1998)

Starting pitcher (HOFer, 363 wins with Braves, Mets, and Giants)

Manager (Played 1974–1985 with Texas and Cleveland)

PRESIDENTS

Baseball Trivia

815

1. Harry S. Truman	**A. The first president to attend an exhibition game**
2. Woodrow Wilson	**B. The first president to attend an All-Star Game**
3. Franklin Roosevelt	**C. The first president to watch a game from the dugout**
4. Lyndon Johnson	**D. The first lefthanded president to throw out the first pitch**
5. William H. Taft	**E. The first president to attend a game in his home city**
6. Richard Nixon	**F. The first president to attend a World Series game**
7. Ronald Reagan	**G. The first president to witness a triple play**

816

1. Ulysses S. Grant	**A. The first president to invite any team of any kind to the White House**
2. Chester A. Arthur	**B. The first president to attend a major league game somewhere other than Washington (Pittsburgh)**
3. Theodore Roosevelt	**C. The first president to attend three consecutive games of a series**
4. Andrew Johnson	**D. The first president to bring a major league team into the White House**
5. William H. Taft	**E. The first president to be issued a lifetime pass by the National Association of Professional Baseball Leagues**
6. Woodrow Wilson	**F. The first president to attend a major league game**
7. Benjamin Harrison	**G. The first president to invite a professional team into the White House**

815: 1-D, 2-F, 3-B, 4-A, 5-E, 6-G, 7-C • **816:** 1-G, 2-D, 3-E, 4-F, 5-A, 6-B, 7-C

1. Benjamin Harrison	A. The first president to call a portion of the play-by-play for a game while in office
2. Harry S. Truman	B. The first president to attend two major league games while in office
3. William H. Taft	C. The first president to attend a game with his vice-president
4. Ronald Reagan	D. The first president to attend a night game
5. Richard Nixon	E. The first president to throw out the first pitch of a game in Canada
6. Bill Clinton	F. The first president to toss out the first pitch of an Opening Day game outside of Washington
7. George H. W. Bush	G. The first president to throw out an Opening Day pitch

818

1. William H. Taft	A. The first president to attend a game cut short by rain
2. Harry S. Truman	B. The first president who threw out a first pitch while he was a governor
3. Calvin Coolidge	C. The first president to award an MVP trophy to a player
4. Richard Nixon	D. The first president to attend a night All-Star Game
5. Bill Clinton	E. The first president to throw out a first pitch from the pitcher's mound and make it to the catcher
6. George Bush	F. The first president to attend a game on the Fourth of July
7. William McKinley	G. The first president to have been a managing general partner of a major league team before he became president

NAME THAT YEAR

Seven clues. One year. See how few clues it takes you to guess the year.

1 **Steve Bedrosian of Atlanta** sets a record when he starts 37 games and fails to complete any of them.

2 **The League Championship Series** are expanded from a best-of-five to a best-of-seven format.

3 **Dwight Gooden, age 20,** becomes the youngest ever Cy Young Award winner.

4 **Star Cardinals outfielder Vince Coleman** is knocked out of the post-season after an automatic tarpaulin machine runs over his leg before game 4 of the NLCS.

5 **Ex-president Richard Nixon** mediates a dispute between the umpires and owners regarding postseason pay.

6 **Pete Rose breaks Ty Cobb's record** for career hits.

7 **The Kansas City Royals defeat the St. Louis Cardinals** in a seven-game World Series, thanks in large part to Don Denkinger's umpiring mistake in Game 6 that allows the Royals to score both their runs in a 2–1 victory.

VICTIMS

1. Pirates
2. Cubs
3. Braves
4. Dodgers
5. Reds
6. Padres
7. Astros

A. Giants opponents in the famous "Merkle Boner" game

B. Victims of Carlton Fisk's dramatic Game 6 home run

C. Lost the first modern World Series to Boston in 1903

D. Pete Rose's opponents when he set the all-time hits record

E. Opponents when Johnny Vander Meer pitched the second of his two consecutive no-hitters

F. Kerry Wood's victims when the rookie pitcher struck out 20 batters in one game

G. Dodgers opponents when Jackie Robinson broke the color barrier in 1947

821

1. Senators
2. Tigers
3. Indians
4. Orioles
5. Red Sox
6. Angels
7. Royals

A. Bob Feller's opponents when he set a new major league record with 18 strikeouts in one game

B. Red Sox opponents when Ted Williams hit a home run in the final at bat of his career

C. Rickey Henderson's opponents when he pilfered his 130th stolen base of the season to establish the all-time record

D. Yankees opponents when Joe DiMaggio got a hit in his 56th consecutive game

E. Victims of Cy Young's 500th career win

F. Yankees opponents when Roger Maris hit homer number 61

G. Oakland's victims in the first multipitcher no-hitter in major league history

822

1. Cubs
2. Dodgers
3. Padres
4. Expos
5. Reds

A. Orel Hershiser's victims when he set the new major league record of 59 consecutive scoreless innings pitched

B. Philadelphia's opponents when Rick Wise made history by pitching a no-hitter and hitting two homers in same game

C. Victims of Mark McGwire's 70th home run of 1998 season

D. The last team Babe Ruth ever played against

E. Victims of Babe Ruth's "called shot" home run

820: 1-C, 2-A, 3-G, 4-E, 5-B, 6-D, 7-F • **821:** 1-E, 2-A, 3-D, 4-B, 5-F, 6-G, 7-C

6. Giants   **F. Victims of Bobby Thomson's "Shot Heard 'Round the World"**

7. Phillies   **G. Dodgers opponent when Sandy Koufax tied Bob Feller's record of 18 strikeouts in one game**

823

1. Senators   **A. Dodgers opponents when Kirk Gibson hit his "fist pumping" home run**

2. Indians   **B. Babe Ruth's opponents when he set the new home run record with 60 in a season**

3. Yankees   **C. Tom Cheney's opponents when the Washington pitcher struck out 21 batters in a 16-inning game**

4. Orioles   **D. Nolan Ryan's victims for his seventh and final no-hitter**

5. Mariners   **E. Opponents when Willie Mays made his memorable over-the-shoulder catch, considered by many to be the greatest defensive play ever made**

6. Athletics   **F. Boston's opponents when Roger Clemens set a new record for strikeouts in a game with 20**

7. Blue Jays   **G. Pirates opponents when Bill Mazeroski hit the most dramatic home run in World Series history**

824

During Joe DiMaggio's 56-game hitting streak, he collected 91 hits, scored 56 runs, and had 55 RBIs. He had 16 doubles, four triples, and 15 home runs. Do you know what roles each of the other seven American League teams played in his streak?

1. Chicago   **A. Team he scored the fewest runs against—5**

2. St. Louis   **B. Team that ended his streak**

3. Detroit   **C. Team he started his streak against**

4. Boston   **D. Team he had the highest ratio of multiple-hit games against—80 percent**

5. Washington   **E. Team he had the most hits against—22**

6. Cleveland   **F. Team he had the fewest hits against—8**

7. Philadelphia   **G. Team whose future HOF pitcher gave up a double, triple, and homer to DiMaggio during the streak**

824: 1-C, 2-E, 3-G, 4-A, 5-F, 6-B, 7-D

823: 1-B, 2-E, 3-G, 4-C, 5-F, 6-A, 7-D • **822:** 1-E, 2-F, 3-A, 4-C, 5-B, 6-G, 7-D •

How well do you know your perfect game opponents? Each team on the left was the victim of one of the pitchers on the right.

1. Expos	**A. Mike Witt**
2. Twins	**B. Dennis Martinez**
3. Braves	**C. David Cone**
4. Dodgers	**D. Randy Johnson**
5. Angels	**E. Sandy Koufax**
6. Rangers	**F. David Wells**
7. Cubs	**G. Kenny Rogers**

826

Now try these perfect-game pitchers and their victims.

1. Dodgers	**A. Charlie Robertson**
2. Mets	**B. Tom Browning**
3. Blue Jays	**C. Addie Joss**
4. Twins	**D. Jim Bunning**
5. Tigers	**E. Catfish Hunter**
6. White Sox	**F. Cy Young**
7. Athletics	**G. Len Barker**

827

There have been even fewer unassisted triple plays in major league history than perfect games. Each of the teams listed at the right was the victim of an unassisted triple play executed by one of the players listed at the left. (Note: Some teams will be the answer to more than one clue.)

1. Neal Ball	**A. Red Sox**
2. Bill Wambsganss	**B. Dodgers**
3. George Burns	**C. Indians**

825: 1-C, 2-F, 3-D, 4-B, 5-G, 6-A, 7-E • **826:** 1-B, 2-D, 3-G, 4-E, 5-A, 6-C, 7-F

4. Jimmy Cooney

5. Ron Hansen

6. John Valentin

7. Randy Velarde

8. Ernie Padgett

9. Glenn Wright

10. Johnny Neun

11. Mickey Morandini

12. Rafael Furcal

D. Phillies

E. Mariners

F. Cardinals

G. Yankees

H. Pirates

828

NAME THAT YEAR

Seven clues. One year. See how few clues it takes you to guess the year.

1 **Babe Ruth's** uniform number, 3, is retired by the Yankees.

2 **The Braves win** their first pennant since 1914.

3 **Cleveland defeats the Red Sox** in the AL's first-ever pennant playoff game.

4 **Lou Boudreau becomes the last player-manager** to win an MVP Award.

5 **The Negro National League disbands,** having lost most of its players to the two major leagues.

6 **Bob Lemon pitches the first-ever night game no-hitter,** defeating Detroit, 2–0.

7 **Babe Ruth dies** of throat cancer.

WHO, WHAT, WHEN, WHERE, AND WHY

1. Who is this player?

2. What had he just done?

3. When did he do it?

4. Where?

5. BONUS: Who was the opposing team and the pitcher?

829:

1. Hall of Famer Ted Williams.

2. Hit a home run in the final at bat of his career.

3. September 28, 1960, in the bottom of the eighth inning.

4. Fenway Park.

5. Jack Fisher of the Baltimore Orioles served it up on a 1-1 pitch.

Hitting four home runs in one game is as rare a baseball feat as pitching a perfect game or making an unassisted triple play. See if you can match up these four-homers-in-one-game sluggers with the unfortunate team they were playing against. (Note: One team will be the answer for two players.)

1. Lou Gehrig	A. Orioles
2. Mike Cameron	B. Devil Rays
3. Rocky Colavito	C. Athletics
4. Pat Seerey	D. White Sox
5. Carlos Delgado	E. Reds
6. Bobby Lowe	F. Cubs
7. Ed Delahanty	

831

Now try these four-homer men and their opponents. (Note: One team will be the answer for two players.)

1. Chuck Klein	A. Reds
2. Gil Hodges	B. Dodgers
3. Joe Adcock	C. Brewers
4. Willie Mays	D. Braves
5. Mike Schmidt	E. Expos
6. Bob Horner	F. Pirates
7. Mark Whiten	G. Cubs
8. Shawn Green	

830: 1-C, 2-D, 3-A, 4-C, 5-B, 6-E, 7-F • **831:** 1-F, 2-D, 3-B, 4-D, 5-G, 6-E, 7-A, 8-C

832

Winning 300 games in a career is another extreme rarity. In the next three games, your job is to identify which team each of the pitchers won his milestone game against. (Note: One team will be the answer for two players.)

1. Cy Young
2. Pud Galvin
3. Kid Nichols
4. Tim Keefe
5. John Clarkson
6. Eddie Plank
7. Charles Radbourn
8. Mickey Welch

A. Pittsburgh Pirates
B. Brooklyn Bridegrooms (now the Dodgers)
C. Chicago Cubs
D. Kansas City Packers (Federal League)
E. Boston Reds (Players League)
F. Indianapolis Hoosiers (National League)
G. 1901 Baltimore Orioles

833

1. Walter Johnson
2. Warren Spahn
3. Gaylord Perry
4. Grover Alexander
5. Lefty Grove
6. Early Wynn
7. Christy Mathewson

A. Boston Braves
B. New York Giants
C. Detroit Tigers
D. Kansas City Athletics
E. New York Yankees
F. Chicago Cubs
G. Cleveland Indians

834

(Note: One team will be the answer for two players.)

1. Roger Clemens
2. Phil Niekro
3. Greg Maddux
4. Steve Carlton

A. Texas Rangers
B. Toronto Blue Jays
C. New York Yankees
D. St. Louis Cardinals

832: 1-G, 2-F, 3-C, 4-E, 5-A, 6-D, 7-B, 8-B • **833:** 1-C, 2-F, 3-E, 4-B, 5-G, 6-D, 7-A

5. Nolan Ryan

6. Don Sutton

7. Tom Seaver

E. Milwaukee Brewers

F. San Francisco Giants

835

Only 26 players have ever reached the 3,000-hit plateau. (Craig Biggio is set to join the club in 2007.) See if you can match up the 3,000-hit club members with the team they reached that milestone against. (Note: One team will be the answer for two players.)

1. Ty Cobb

2. Tris Speaker

3. Carl Yastrzemski

4. Eddie Collins

5. Robin Yount

6. Cap Anson

7. Rafael Palmeiro

8. Nap Lajoie

9. Cal Ripken Jr.

A. Cleveland Indians

B. Baltimore Orioles (National League)

C. Washington Senators

D. Detroit Tigers

E. Boston Red Sox

F. Minnesota Twins

G. New York Yankees

H. Seattle Mariners

836

Try another round of 3,000-hit club members and their opposing teams. (Note: One team will be the answer for three players.)

1. Pete Rose

2. Hank Aaron

3. Stan Musial

4. Honus Wagner

5. Paul Waner

6. Rickey Henderson

7. Roberto Clemente

8. Tony Gwynn

9. Willie Mays

A. Philadelphia Phillies

B. Colorado Rockies

C. Chicago Cubs

D. Montreal Expos

E. New York Mets

F. Pittsburgh Pirates

G. Cincinnati Reds

834: 1-D, 2-B, 3-F, 4-D, 5-E, 6-A, 7-C • **835:** 1-E, 2-C, 3-G, 4-D, 5-A, 6-B, 7-H, 8-G, 9-F • **836:** 1-D, 2-G, 3-C, 4-A, 5-F, 6-B, 7-E, 8-D, 9-D

837

One last game of 3,000-hit clubbers and their opponents.
(Note: One team name is the answer for two players.)

1. Paul Molitor
2. Eddie Murray
3. Al Kaline
4. George Brett
5. Dave Winfield
6. Rod Carew
7. Lou Brock
8. Wade Boggs

A. Minnesota Twins

B. Oakland A's

C. Kansas City Royals

D. Baltimore Orioles

E. California Angels

F. Chicago Cubs

G. Cleveland Indians

838

Nine pitchers in history have thrown a shutout in Game 7 of
the World Series. See if you can match them with their
opponents.

1. Jack Morris
2. Bret Saberhagen
3. Sandy Koufax
4. Ralph Terry
5. Lew Burdette
6. Johnny Kucks
7. Johnny Podres
8. Dizzy Dean
9. Babe Adams

A. Shut out the Twins, 2–0

B. Shut out the Dodgers, 9–0

C. Shut out the Giants, 1–0

D. Shut out the Tigers, 8–0

E. Shut out the Braves, 1–0

F. Shut out the Yankees, 2–0

G. Shut out the Tigers, 11–0

H. Shut out the Cardinals, 11–0

I. Shut out the Yankees, 5–0

837: 1-C, 2-A, 3-D, 4-E, 5-B, 6-A, 7-F, 8-G • **838:** 1-E, 2-H, 3-A, 4-C, 5-I, 6-B, 7-F, 8-G, 9-D

WHO, WHAT, WHEN, WHERE, AND WHY

1. **Who** is this player?

2. **What's** he doing?

3. **When** was this photograph taken?

4. **Where?**

5. **BONUS:** Who was the opposing team that day?

839:

1. Hall of Famer Jackie Robinson.

2. Signing autographs before his first game in the major leagues.

3. April 15, 1947.

4. Ebbets Field in Brooklyn.

5. The Boston Braves.

Eleven teams have won the World Series in the bottom of the last inning. How well do you know the circumstances?

1. Boston Red Sox

A. A two-out, one-run double in the ninth provided a 3–2 victory over the Cubs in the Game 5 clincher

2. Washington Senators

B. A three-run homer in the ninth inning of Game 6 sent the Phillies home unhappy

3. New York Yankees (1927)

C. A sacrifice fly with one out to defeat the Giants, 3–2, in a ten-inning Game 7

4. Philadelphia A's

D. A two-out, one-run single in the ninth inning of Game 6 provided the 4–3 win that finished off the Cubs

5. Detroit Tigers

E. A one-out, one-run single in the tenth inning provided the only run in a 1–0 Game 7 win over the Braves

6. New York Yankees (1953)

F. A two-out, one-run single in the 11th inning sent the Indians home with a 3–2 loss in Game 7

7. Pittsburgh Pirates

G. A one-out, one-run single in the 12th inning defeated the Giants, 4–3, in Game 7

8. Minnesota Twins

H. A one-out, one-run single in the ninth inning of Game 7 made the final score 3–2 and ended the Yankees' hopes

9. Toronto Blue Jays

I. A one-out, one-run single in the ninth inning of Game 6 made the final score 4–3, killing the Dodgers' chances

10. Florida Marlins

J. A leadoff home run in the ninth inning of Game 7 dashed the Yankees' hopes, 10–9

11. Arizona Diamondbacks

K. A runner scored on a two-out wild pitch in the ninth inning to defeat the Pirates, 4–3, in Game 4 of a sweep

Each of the teams in this game made one of the greatest comebacks in baseball history to win the pennant. See if you can identify which team each of them overtook for the pennant. (Note: One team will be the answer for two clues.)

1. The 1914 Boston Braves, 15.0 games behind on July 5 with a 26–40 record, tore through the NL with a 68–19 record the rest of the way, finishing 10.5 games ahead of . . .

   A. Brooklyn Dodgers

2. 1978 Yankees, 14.0 games behind on July 19 with a 48–42 record, went 52–21 the rest of the way and won a one-game playoff to beat . . .

   B. Phillies and Reds

3. 1951 New York Giants were 13.5 games behind on August 11 with a 59–51 record. They then went on a 38–9 tear to force a tie at the top, and then in a best-of-three playoff, they won by shocking the . . .

   C. Chicago Cubs

4. 1930 St. Louis Cardinals were 12.0 games behind the Brooklyn Dodgers on August 8 with a 53–52 record. Their 39–10 finish allowed them to finish just two games ahead of . . .

   D. New York Giants

5. 1964 St. Louis Cardinals were 11.0 games behind on August 23 with a 65–58 record. They went 28–11 the rest of the way to finish a single game ahead of . . .

   E. Boston Red Sox

6. 1935 Chicago Cubs were 10.5 games behind on July 5 with a 38–32 record before finishing 62–22 to win the pennant by 4.0 games over . . .

   F. St. Louis Cardinals

7. 1942 St. Louis Cardinals were 10.0 games behind on August 5, even though they had a great record at 63–39. Thereafter they were almost unbeatable as they turned it up a notch, finishing 43–9 to finish just two games in front of . . .

Only 13 pitchers have ever won three games in a World Series. In the next two games, see if you can correctly match the pitchers to their frustrated opponents.

1. Deacon Phillippe   **A. Yankees**

2. Randy Johnson   **B. Cardinals**

3. Christy Mathewson   **C. Pirates**

4. Mickey Lolich   **D. Tigers**

5. Bill Dineen   **E. Giants**

6. Red Faber   **F. Red Sox**

7. Babe Adams   **G. Athletics**

843

(Note: One team will be the answer for two players.)

1. Lew Burdette   **A. Red Sox**

2. Harry Brecheen   **B. Giants**

3. Stan Coveleski   **C. Yankees**

4. Smoky Joe Wood   **D. Dodgers**

5. John Coombs   **E. Cubs**

6. Bob Gibson

BY THE
DECADE

1990s pitching records.

1. Most wins—176
2. Most losses—116
3. Most strikeouts—2,538
4. Best winning percentage—.682
5. Most wins in a season without pitching a shutout—21
6. Most wins in a season without pitching a complete game—18
7. The only pitcher to lead his league in wins for three consecutive seasons

A. Tom Glavine
B. Andy Benes
C. Pedro Martinez
D. Kent Bottenfield
E. Greg Maddux
F. Jose Lima
G. Randy Johnson

845

1990s hitting records.

1. Most RBIs—1,099
2. Highest batting average—.344
3. Most runs scored—1,091
4. Most stolen bases—478
5. Most home runs—405
6. Most hits—1,754
7. The only hitter to win a Gold Glove all ten years of the decade

A. Barry Bonds
B. Ken Griffey Jr.
C. Mark McGwire
D. Tony Gwynn
E. Otis Nixon
F. Albert Belle
G. Mark Grace

846

1980s pitching records.

1. Lowest ERA—2.64
2. Most strikeouts—2,167
3. Most losses—126

A. Mark Langston
B. Jack Morris
C. Don Sutton

844: 1-E, 2-B, 3-G, 4-C, 5-F, 6-D, 7-A • **845:** 1-F, 2-D, 3-A, 4-E, 5-C, 6-G, 7-B

4. The only rookie to win 20 games in either league since 1954

D. Dwight Gooden

5. Most wins during the decade—162

E. Nolan Ryan

6. The only rookie to lead the AL in strikeouts (204) since 1955

F. Tom Browning

7. 1986 winner of first matchup between 300-game winners since 1892

G. Jim Clancy

847

1980s hitting records.

1. Most hits during the decade—1,731

A. Wade Boggs

2. Most home runs—313

B. Eddie Murray

3. Most runs scored—1,122

C. Rickey Henderson

4. Highest batting average—.352

D. Robin Yount

5. The only hitter to win a Gold Glove Award all ten years of the decade

E. Mike Schmidt

6. Most RBIs

F. Keith Hernandez

7. Most stolen bases—838

G. Ozzie Smith

848

1970s pitching records.

1. Pitched in the most games during the decade—640

A. Don Gullett

2. Started the most games—376

B. Jim Palmer

3. Most wins (186) and shutouts (44) during the 1970s

C. Tom Seaver

4. Most strikeouts—2,678

D. Nolan Ryan

5. Highest winning percentage—589

E. Rollie Fingers

6. Had the best ratio of walks and hits per nine innings pitched—9.66

F. Phil Niekro

7. Had the most innings pitched (2,905) and complete games (197)

G. Gaylord Perry

848: 1-E, 2-F, 3-B, 4-D, 5-A, 6-C, 7-G

• **847:** 1-D, 2-E, 3-F, 4-A, 5-G, 6-B, 7-C •

846: 1-D, 2-E, 3-G, 4-F, 5-B, 6-A, 7-C

WHO, WHAT, WHEN, WHERE, AND WHY

1. Who is this player?

2. What Ruthian feat keeps him in the record books?

3. When did he accomplish this feat?

4. Where did he finish in the home run race that year?

849:

1. Rudy York.

2. He hit 18 home runs in one month, still the American League record. Sammy Sosa eclipsed York for the major league record when he slammed 20 home runs in June 1998.

3. August 1937.

4. Fifth, with 35 homers.

850

1970s hitting records.

1. Most games played during the decade—1,604

2. Most triples—80

3. Most home runs—296

4. Most RBIs—1,013

5. Most stolen bases—551

6. Struck out the most times—1,368

7. One of two players with 586 extra-base hits during the 1970s and who is *not* the answer to another question in this game

A. Bobby Bonds

B. Rod Carew

C. Reggie Jackson

D. Pete Rose

E. Johnny Bench

F. Lou Brock

G. Willie Stargell

851

1960s pitching records.

1. Most games started during the decade—360

2. Most wins—191

3. Most saves—152

4. Most innings pitched—2,629.2

5. Most games pitched—589

6. Most strikeouts—2,071

7. Highest winning percentage of the decade—.695

A. Bob Gibson

B. Hoyt Wilhelm

C. Sandy Koufax

D. Ron Perranoski

E. Jim Bunning

F. Juan Marichal

G. Don Drysdale

852

1960s hitting records.

1. Most games played—1,578

2. Most runs scored—1,091

3. Most hits—1,877

4. Most doubles—318

5. Most home runs—393

6. Most stolen bases—535

7. Struck out the most times during the decade—1,103

A. Frank Howard

B. Brooks Robinson

C. Hank Aaron

D. Roberto Clemente

E. Maury Wills

F. Carl Yastrzemski

G. Harmon Killebrew

852: 1-B, 2-C, 3-D, 4-F, 5-G, 6-E, 7-A

850: 1-D, 2-B, 3-G, 4-E, 5-F, 6-A, 7-C • **851:** 1-E, 2-F, 3-B, 4-G, 5-D, 6-A, 7-C •

1950s pitching records.

1. Most wins during the decade—202	**A. Hoyt Wilhelm**
2. Most innings pitched—3,011.2	**B. Billy Pierce**
3. Most saves—96	**C. Robin Roberts**
4. One of three pitchers with 33 shutouts, and the only non–Hall of Famer	**D. Warren Spahn**
5. Most games pitched—432	**E. Whitey Ford**
6. Most strikeouts—1,544	**F. Ellis Kinder**
7. Highest winning percentage—.708	**G. Early Wynn**

854

1950s hitting records.

1. Highest batting average for the decade—.336	**A. Ted Williams**
2. Most stolen bases—179	**B. Willie Mays**
3. Most RBIs—1,031	**C. Duke Snider**
4. Most runs scored—994	**D. Eddie Yost**
5. Most hits—1,875	**E. Stan Musial**
6. Most doubles—356	**F. Mickey Mantle**
7. Most walks received—1,185	**G. Richie Ashburn**

855

1940s pitching records.

1. Pitched in the most games during the decade—377	**A. Bill Voiselle**
2. Collected the most saves—63	**B. Tiny Bonham**
3. Lowest ERA—2.67	**C. Hal Newhouser**
4. The only pitcher to have a perfect 1.000 fielding average	**D. Joe Page**

853: 1-D, 2-C, 3-F, 4-B, 5-A, 6-G, 7-E • **854:** 1-A, 2-B, 3-C, 4-F, 5-G, 6-E, 7-D

5. Best ratio of hits and walks per nine innings pitched—10.38

    E. Harry Brecheen

6. In 1944 he became the last rookie in major league history to break the 300-inning mark, finishing the season with 312.2

    F. Spud Chandler

7. The only pitcher during the decade to win three games in one World Series

    G. Lon Warneke

856

1940s hitting records.

1. Most games played during the decade—1,455   **A. Bob Elliott**

2. Most hits (1,578) and doubles (339)   **B. Bill Nicholson**

3. Most triples—108   **C. Jeff Heath**

4. Most home runs—234   **D. George Case**

5. Most stolen bases—285   **E. Ted Williams**

6. Struck out the most times—708   **F. Stan Musial**

7. The only player in this game to have a season in the 1940s with at least 20 doubles, 20 triples, and 20 home runs   **G. Lou Boudreau**

857

1930s pitching records.

1. Pitched in the most games—430   **A. Lefty Grove**

2. Had the most complete games—207   **B. Carl Hubbell**

3. Collected the most saves—54   **C. Wes Ferrell**

4. Won the most games—199   **D. Larry French**

5. Pitched the most innings—2,596.2   **E. Lefty Gomez**

6. Had the most strikeouts—1,337   **F. Johnny Murphy**

7. Had the best walk ratio per nine innings pitched—1.46   **G. Red Lucas**

857: 1-D, 2-C, 3-F, 4-A, 5-B, 6-E, 7-G

855: 1-C, 2-D, 3-F, 4-G, 5-B, 6-A, 7-E • **856:** 1-A, 2-G, 3-F, 4-E, 5-D, 6-B, 7-C •

1930s hitting records.

1. Most games played—1,473
2. Most runs scored—1,257
3. Most hits—1,959
4. Most doubles—400
5. Most home runs—415
6. Most stolen bases—269
7. Highest batting average for the decade—.352

A. Charlie Gehringer

B. Jimmie Foxx

C. Lou Gehrig

D. Paul Waner

E. Bill Terry

F. Ben Chapman

G. Mel Ott

859

1920s pitching records.

1. Pitched in the most games during the 1920s—423
2. Won the most games—190
3. Recorded the most saves—75
4. Had the most shutouts—24
5. Had far and away (446 more than his closest rival) the most strikeouts during the 1920s—1,464
6. Had the best winning percentage—.660
7. Had the lowest ERA of the decade—3.04

A. Burleigh Grimes

B. Grover Alexander

C. Walter Johnson

D. Ray Kremer

E. Eddie Rommel

F. Firpo Marberry

G. Dazzy Vance

858: 1-G, 2-C, 3-D, 4-A, 5-B, 6-F, 7-E • **859:** 1-E, 2-A, 3-F, 4-C, 5-G, 6-D, 7-B

860

1920s hitting records.

1. Most games played during the decade—1,496   **A. Harry Heilmann**

2. Most hits—2,085   **B. Sam Rice**

3. Most home runs—467   **C. Babe Ruth**

4. Most stolen bases—346   **D. Milt Stock**

5. Had 257 hits in 1920, a major league record that stood for more than 80 years   **E. Rogers Hornsby**

6. Had four hits in a game on four consecutive days in 1925   **F. Max Carey**

7. Hit a composite .380 from 1921 to 1927, winning four batting titles with averages of .393, .394, .398, and .403   **G. George Sisler**

861

1910s pitching records.

1. Had the most wins (265), games pitched (454), complete games (327), shutouts (74), innings pitched (3,434), strikeouts (2,219), and the lowest ERA   **A. Slim Sallee**

2. Had the most saves—32   **B. Eddie Cicotte**

3. Best winning percentage of the decade—.680   **C. Smoky Joe Wood**

4. Had the best single-season ERA in the 20th century in 1914—0.96   **D. Bill Bailey**

5. Besides the answer to number 1, he pitched the most games—396   **E. Dutch Leonard**

6. Besides the answer to number 1, he had the most complete games (243), wins (208), shutouts (70), innings pitched (2,752.1), and strikeouts (1,539)   **F. Walter Johnson**

7. After compiling an 0–17 record as a starter in 1910, the St. Louis Browns asked, "Won't you please *go home?*"   **G. Grover Alexander**

860: 1-B, 2-E, 3-C, 4-F, 5-G, 6-D, 7-A • **861:** 1-F, 2-A, 3-C, 4-E, 5-B, 6-G, 7-D

467

1910s hitting records.

1. Most games played—1,450
2. Most runs scored—1,050
3. Most doubles—367
4. Most home runs—116
5. Hit .408 and .395 in his first two full seasons in the majors, but didn't win a batting title!
6. Winner of the National League's first official MVP Award in 1911
7. Won both Federal League batting titles during the league's two-year existence in 1914 and 1915

A. Ty Cobb

B. Donie Bush

C. Benny Kauff

D. Gavvy Cravath

E. Frank Schulte

F. Tris Speaker

G. Joe Jackson

863

1900s pitching records.

1. Pitched in the most games—417
2. Started the most games—372
3. Had the most complete games—337
4. Most shutouts—61
5. Recorded the most strikeouts—2,251
6. Lowest ERA—1.63
7. Best winning percentage—.713

A. Christy Mathewson

B. Cy Young

C. Vic Willis

D. Joe McGinnity

E. Rube Waddell

F. Mordecai Brown

G. Ed Reulbach

864

1900s hitting records.

1. Most games played—1,410
2. Scored the most runs (1,014), had the most hits (1,847), doubles (372), total bases (2,668), RBIs (956), stolen bases (487), extra-base hits (571), and the highest averages—batting (.352), slugging (.508), and on-base (.412)

A. Honus Wagner

B. Jimmy Sebring

862: 1-B, 2-A, 3-F, 4-D, 5-G, 6-E, 7-C • **863:** 1-D, 2-C, 3-B, 4-A, 5-E, 6-F, 7-G

3. Most home runs—67   **C. Frank Chance**

4. Besides the answer to number 2, he had the most stolen bases during the decade—357   **D. Ed Delahanty**

5. Besides the answer to number 2, he had the highest batting average—.346   **E. Nap Lajoie**

6. When he won the American League batting title in 1902 with a .376 average, he became the first player in history to win the batting title in both the AL and NL   **F. Roy Thomas**

7. Hit the first home run in modern World Series history   **G. Sam Crawford**

865

NAME THAT YEAR

Seven clues. One year. See how few clues it takes you to guess the year.

1 **Ted Williams becomes the highest-paid player** in history when he inks a contract with Boston for $150,000.

2 **The film version** of *Damn Yankees* is released.

3 **Richie Ashburn of the Phillies** leads the majors in hitting at .350.

4 **The New York Yankees win their fourth** straight pennant.

5 **Roy Campanella is paralyzed** in an automobile accident.

6 **Second baseman Nellie Fox** sets a major league record by playing in 98 consecutive games without striking out.

7 **The Yankees are the only major league team left** in New York after the Dodgers and the Giants relocate to the West Coast.

WHO, WHAT, WHEN, WHERE, AND WHY

1. Who, collectively, are the men in this photograph?

2. What brought them together?

3. When?

4. Where?

5. BONUS: Who was missing and why?

866:

1. All of the living members, except one, of the Baseball Hall of Fame at the time the photograph was taken, in 1939. First row, l. to r.: Eddie Collins, Babe Ruth, Connie Mack, Cy Young; second row: Honus Wagner, Pete Alexander, Tris Speaker, Nap Lajoie, George Sisler, Walter Johnson.

2. The opening of the Hall of Fame Museum and Library.

3. 1939, baseball's supposed centennial.

4. Cooperstown, New York.

5. Ty Cobb arrived a few minutes late, after the photograph was taken.

BATTING
RECORDS

UNSURPASSED AND SURPASSED

Extra-base hits (doubles, triples, and home runs combined).

1. George Wright **A. Upon the founding of the National League in 1876 through 1907, he was the only player to lead the majors in extra-base hits in back-to-back seasons**

2. Roger Connor **B. Held the single-season record for extra-base hits (44) until he was passed by Dan Brouthers in 1883 (61)**

3. Tip O'Neill **C. Was the National Association's career leader in extra-base hits (135) when the league folded in 1875**

4. Cap Anson **D. Held the career record for extra-base hits (195) until he was surpassed by Jim O'Rourke in 1880**

5. Ross Barnes **E. Became the career leader in extra-base hits in 1886 and held it until Roger Connor passed him in 1896**

6. Buck Freeman **F. Led the National Association in extra-base hits in three of the league's five years of existence, and the National League in its first year (1876)**

7. Lip Pike **G. Smashed the former single-season record of 66 extra-base hits with 85 in 1887**

868

More extra-base hits.

1. Dan Brouthers **A. The first player in history with 1,000 career extra-base hits**

2. Honus Wagner **B. Presented the only real challenge to the all-time record of 119 extra-base hits in a season when he got 117**

3. Ty Cobb **C. Became the active leader in extra-base hits in 1898 after Cap Anson retired**

4. Babe Ruth **D. The first player to reach 100 extra-base hits in a season (he reached 119), a record that has never been broken**

5. Rogers Hornsby **E. The only 20th-century NL player with more than one season of 100 extra-base hits**

6. Lou Gehrig **F. With his 821st career extra-base hit in 1912, he surpassed Cap Anson as the all-time leader**

7. Chuck Klein **G. The second player to reach 100 extra-base hits in a season**

867: 1-D, 2-B, 3-G, 4-E, 5-F, 6-A, 7-C • **868:** 1-C, 2-F, 3-A, 4-D, 5-G, 6-B, 7-E

Still more extra-base-hit achievements.

1. Stan Musial   **A. The only player to lead the major leagues in extra-base hits in four consecutive seasons**

2. Babe Ruth   **B. The only player in major league history to record 100 or more extra-base hits in back-to-back seasons**

3. Ty Cobb   **C. Became the career leader in extra-base hits when he passed Honus Wagner in 1925**

4. Hank Greenberg   **D. Became the active leader in extra-base hits in 1940 when Lou Gehrig retired**

5. Jimmie Foxx   **E. The only player to lead the major leagues in extra-base hits seven times**

6. Albert Belle   **F. The only player from 1938 to 1999 besides Stan Musial to reach 100 extra-base hits in a season**

7. Todd Helton   **G. The last player before World War II to lead the majors in extra-base hits in back-to-back seasons**

870

One last game of extra-base hits.

1. Don Mattingly   **A. The last 20th-century player to lead the major leagues in extra-base hits in back-to-back seasons**

2. Albert Pujols   **B. Became the active leader in extra-base hits upon the retirement of Hank Aaron in 1976**

3. Barry Bonds   **C. From 1963 to 1994, he was the only major league player to collect at least 90 extra-base hits in a season**

4. Willie Stargell   **D. The last National Leaguer to lead the major leagues in extra-base hits in back-to-back seasons**

5. Mike Schmidt   **E. Major league leader who hit the fewest extra-base hits in a season (52) since Babe Ruth's 48 in 1918**

6. Carl Yastrzemski   **F. Became the active leader in extra-base hits upon the retirement of Pete Rose in 1985**

7. Reggie Jackson   **G. The last American Leaguer to lead the major leagues in extra-base hits in back-to-back seasons**

869: 1-E, 2-A, 3-C, 4-G, 5-D, 6-F, 7-B • **870:** 1-G, 2-D, 3-A, 4-C, 5-E, 6-B, 7-F

WHO, WHAT, WHEN, WHERE, AND WHY

1. Who are these two players?

2. What were they both after?

3. When?

4. Where was the loser when the winner ultimately won?

871:

1. Roger Maris and Hall of Famer Mickey Mantle.

2. They were both trying to break Babe Ruth's record of 60 home runs in a season.

3. 1961.

4. In the hospital, recovering from various injuries that forced him out of the chase, leaving it for Maris to pursue alone.

Try to match these singles hitters to their records and accomplishments.

1. Deacon White

A. The first player (since 1876) to lead the league in singles in back-to-back seasons

2. Ross Barnes

B. Although he never led the league in singles, he was the active career leader from 1913 to 1917

3. Cap Anson

C. The first player in history (1873) to collect 100 singles in a season

4. Willie Keeler

D. He broke Cap Anson's 44-year hold on the record for career singles

5. Jesse Burkett

E. The first player to collect 200 singles in one season

6. Ty Cobb

F. Had the most career singles when the National Association folded in 1875

7. Honus Wagner

G. Became the first player to reach 2,000 career singles *after* the retirement of Cap Anson

873

Strictly singles-hitting Hall of Famers in this game.

1. Nellie Fox

A. This Hall of Famer was the active career leader in singles from 1991 to 1993

2. Cap Anson

B. The last National Leaguer Hall of Famer to be the major leagues' career leader in singles

3. Paul Molitor

C. Never led the major leagues in singles in any season, but was the active career leader for five straight years

4. Robin Yount

D. The last Hall of Famer in either league to lead the major leagues in singles in a season (through 2006 season)

5. Wade Boggs

E. The last Hall of Fame outfielder to lead the major leagues in singles for a season

6. Roberto Clemente

F. The only 20th-century Hall of Famer to lead the major leagues in singles four consecutive seasons

7. Kirby Puckett

G. His 187 singles in one season was the most in the majors for any season from 1928 to 2000

872: 1-C, 2-F, 3-A, 4-E, 5-G, 6-D, 7-B • **873:** 1-F, 2-B, 3-D, 4-A, 5-G, 6-C, 7-E

Double your pleasure, double your fun with these next three games. Time for two-bagger records, accomplishments, and progressions.

1. Cal McVey   A. Set a new major league record for doubles in a season in 1899 with 55, a record that stood for 24 years

2. Ross Barnes   B. The first player in NL history to break the 40-double mark in a season—49

3. Ned Williamson   C. Holds the all-time record for fewest doubles to lead the major leagues in a season—19

4. Tip O'Neill   D. Holds the National Association record for doubles in a season—36

5. Jim O'Rourke   E. Held the career record for doubles (159) until he was passed by Cap Anson

6. Cap Anson   F. The first player in NL history to break the 50-double mark in a season—52

7. Ed Delahanty   G. National Association career leader in doubles—99

875

1. Nap Lajoie   A. The first player to lead the major leagues in doubles in back-to-back seasons

2. Tris Speaker   B. Set a new mark for doubles in a season with 59 in 1923

3. Ed Delahanty   C. Set a new mark for doubles in a season with 64 in 1926

4. Honus Wagner   D. Set the current mark for doubles in a season with 67 in 1931

5. George Burns   E. Passed Cap Anson for the top spot on the career doubles list when he hit number 582 in 1913

6. Sherry Magee   F. The first player to lead the major leagues in doubles for three consecutive seasons

7. Earl Webb   G. Became the active leader in career doubles upon the retirement of Honus Wagner in 1917

874: 1-D, 2-G, 3-B, 4-F, 5-E, 6-C, 7-A • **875:** 1-E, 2-B, 3-A, 4-F, 5-C, 6-G, 7-D

1. Pete Rose

A. Became the active leader in career doubles with George Brett's retirement in 1993

2. Don Mattingly

B. The last player to lead the major leagues in doubles in a season with a total less than 50 (45)

3. Chuck Knoblauch

C. The only NL player since 1909 to lead the major leagues in doubles three consecutive years

4. Hal McRae

D. The only player in history to lead the major leagues in doubles for four consecutive seasons

5. Tris Speaker

E. The last player to lead the major leagues in doubles in back-to-back seasons with more than 50 each season

6. Dave Winfield

F. The only AL player since 1923 to lead the major leagues in doubles three consecutive years

7. Craig Biggio

G. Became the active leader in career doubles with the retirement of Pete Rose in 1986

877

Now let's try triples records and accomplishments.

1. Harry Stovey

A. The first player to reach 20 triples in a season—23

2. Dave Orr

B. The first player to lead the major leagues in triples in back-to-back seasons

3. Tom York

C. The first player to reach 250 career triples

4. Sam Crawford

D. Holds the National Association record for career triples—41

5. George Wright

E. The career leader in triples until he was passed by Jim O'Rourke in 1885

6. Ross Barnes

F. Won the NL's first triples title in 1876 with 14

7. Chief Wilson

G. Set a new record with 36 triples in a season in 1912, a record that still stands to this day

876: 1-C, 2-F, 3-B, 4-G, 5-D, 6-A, 7-E • 877: 1-A, 2-B, 3-E, 4-C, 5-D, 6-F, 7-G

More triples.

1. Dave Orr	**A.** Holds the major league record for most consecutive years as the active leader in career triples—12
2. Sam Crawford	**B.** The only righthanded batter in history to collect more than 200 career triples
3. Stan Musial	**C.** The only player from 1915 to 1975 to lead the major leagues in triples in back-to-back seasons
4. Honus Wagner	**D.** The first player in history to reach 30 triples in a season—he got 31
5. Ty Cobb	**E.** The only player in history to collect more than 300 career triples—309
6. Elmer Flick	**F.** Became the active leader in career triples with the retirement of Sam Crawford in 1917
7. Earle Combs	**G.** The first 20th-century player to lead the major leagues in triples in back-to-back seasons without being tied for the title

879

One last game of triples.

1. Dale Mitchell	**A.** The only player in the 1990s to hit 20 triples in a season
2. Lance Johnson	**B.** The last player to lead the major leagues in triples for three consecutive seasons
3. George Brett	**C.** The only 20th-century player to lead the major leagues (and be untied) with as few as 11 triples in a season, just one short of the all-time low mark of ten set in 1878
4. Willie Wilson	**D.** The only player in the 1980s to hit 20 triples in a season
5. Carl Crawford	**E.** Hit the most triples in a season since the end of World War II—23
6. Brett Butler	**F.** Became the active leader in career triples when Willie Wilson retired in 1994
7. Johnny Damon	**G.** The only player in the 1970s to hit 20 triples in a season

878: 1-D, 2-E, 3-A, 4-B, 5-F, 6-G, 7-C • **879:** 1-E, 2-A, 3-G, 4-D, 5-B, 6-F, 7-C

WHO, WHAT, WHEN, WHERE, AND WHY

1. Who is with Babe Ruth?

2. What promise did Ruth make to him?

3. When?

4. Where?

5. BONUS: What did Ruth actually do in the next day's game?

880:

1. Johnny Sylvester.

2. That he would hit a home run for him in the next day's game.

3. On the day before Game 4 of the 1926 World Series.

4. In Sylvester's hospital room. Ruth promised he would hit a home run for the gravely ill Johnny if he promised to get better and get out of the hospital.

5. He became the first player ever to hit three home runs in one World Series game.

All right, home run hitters now and their records.

1. Lip Pike	**A.** His nine home runs to lead the major leagues in 1905 was the first time since 1882 a leader had less than ten
2. Harry Stovey	**B.** The first player to lead the National League in home runs when he hit five in 1876
3. Roger Connor	**C.** The last player to hit less than ten home runs in a season (9) and still lead the major leagues
4. George Hall	**D.** Holds the National Association record for career home runs—15
5. Fred Odwell	**E.** The first player to lead the majors in home runs with at least 20 in a season—27
6. Ty Cobb	**F.** Became the career leader in home runs in 1895 and held the title for 26 years
7. Ned Williamson	**G.** The first player to reach ten home runs in a season—14

882

Going, going, gone.

1. Gavvy Cravath	**A.** The first player in history to lead the major leagues in home runs three consecutive seasons
2. Frank Schulte	**B.** Broke Ned Williamson's single-season record of 27 home runs by hitting 29
3. Honus Wagner	**C.** Became the active leader in career home runs in 1912 when he hit number 85
4. Babe Ruth	**D.** The only one from 1918 to 1929 (besides Babe Ruth) to lead the major leagues in home runs in a season without being tied for the lead
5. Lou Gehrig	**E.** Second player in history to join the 500-home run club
6. Jimmie Foxx	**F.** Became the active leader in career home when Babe Ruth retired in 1935
7. Rogers Hornsby	**G.** The first 20th-century player to reach 20 homers in a season

881: 1-D, 2-G, 3-F, 4-B, 5-A, 6-C, 7-E • **882:** 1-A, 2-G, 3-C, 4-B, 5-F, 6-E, 7-D

Holy cow.

1. Mel Ott	A. The first player ever to lead the major leagues in home runs for four consecutive seasons
2. Jimmie Foxx	B. Third member of the 500-home run club
3. Joe DiMaggio	C. The only player to lead the major leagues in home runs for six consecutive seasons
4. Babe Ruth	D. The first player since Babe Ruth to lead the major leagues in home runs in back-to-back seasons
5. Ralph Kiner	E. The only player from 1953 to 1974 to lead the major leagues in homers in back-to-back seasons
6. Ted Williams	F. Became the active leader in career home runs when Mel Ott retired in 1947
7. Harmon Killebrew	G. Became the active leader in career home runs when Johnny Mize retired in 1953

884

That baby's out of here.

1. Mark McGwire	A. Hit the most homers in a season during the 1950s (52)
2. Albert Belle	B. Became the active leader in career home runs upon the retirement of Hank Aaron in 1976
3. Mickey Mantle	C. The last player before Mark McGwire to hit 50 or more home runs in a season
4. Mike Schmidt	D. Hit the most homers in a season during the 1970s—52
5. Willie McCovey	E. Player most recently to lead the major leagues in home runs for four consecutive seasons
6. Willie Mays	F. Except for the great home run race year of 1961, he hit the most homers in a season during the 1960s—52
7. George Foster	G. Of the four lowest yearly home run totals to lead the major leagues from 1953 to 2006, he had them all

Baseball Trivia

The next three games feature stellar base stealers.

1. Hugh Nicol   **A. The first player to reach 500 career stolen bases**

2. Billy Hamilton   **B. The first player in major league history to steal more than 100 bases in a season—138**

3. Arlie Latham   **C. Holds the National Association record for stolen bases in a season—30**

4. Ross Barnes   **D. The first player to lead the major leagues in stolen bases for three consecutive seasons**

5. Honus Wagner   **E. The first 20th-century player to lead the major leagues in stolen bases in back-to-back seasons**

6. Tim Murnane   **F. Professional baseball's career stolen base leader from 1875 to 1886**

7. Ty Cobb   **G. The first 20th-century player to lead the major leagues in stolen bases in three consecutive seasons**

1. Arlie Latham   **A. Became the active leader in career stolen bases with Ty Cobb's retirement in 1928**

2. Honus Wagner   **B. The first player after Ty Cobb to lead the major leagues in stolen bases for three consecutive seasons**

3. Eddie Collins   **C. The first player in history to reach 800 stolen bases**

4. Max Carey   **D. The only player from 1896 to 1982 to lead the major leagues in stolen bases in back-to-back years with at least 75 steals in both seasons**

5. George Case   **E. Became the active leader in career stolen bases with Arlie Latham's retirement in 1909**

6. Clyde Milan   **F. The first player in history to reach 700 stolen bases**

7. Billy Hamilton   **G. The only player in history to lead the major leagues in stolen bases for five consecutive seasons**

1. Bill Bruton	A. The second player to reach the 900-stolen-base mark in the 20th century
2. Billy Hamilton	B. Had the fewest stolen bases (48) of any major league leader between 1964 and 2006
3. Marquis Grissom	C. Led the majors in stolen bases three consecutive seasons, and two of them were the two lowest totals ever to lead the major leagues (25 and 26)
4. Rickey Henderson	D. The last player to lead the major leagues in back-to-back years with at least 75 steals in both seasons
5. Kenny Lofton	E. Third player to reach the 900-stolen-base mark in the 20th century
6. Luis Castillo	F. Became the active leader in career stolen bases when Rickey Henderson retired in 2003
7. Lou Brock	G. The first player to reach the 900-stolen-base mark in the 20th century

888

Now for the batting average records, surpassed and unsurpassed.

1. Cap Anson	A. The career batting average leader through the 1886 season at .347
2. Paul Hines	B. Holds the National Association record for batting average in a season (.492) in 1871
3. Ross Barnes	C. Set a new batting average record in 1894 (.440), a record that stands today
4. Levi Meyerle	D. The first National League hitter to win back-to-back batting titles
5. Tip O'Neill	E. Ended the 19th century as baseball's career batting average leader at .381
6. Hugh Duffy	F. Won the first National League batting title in 1876 with an average of .429, a record that stood for 11 years
7. Willie Keeler	G. Established a new batting average record (.435) in 1887

887: 1-C, 2-G, 3-D, 4-E, 5-F, 6-B, 7-A • **888:** 1-A, 2-D, 3-F, 4-B, 5-G, 6-C, 7-E

WHO, WHAT, WHEN, WHERE, AND WHY

1. Who's sliding into second base?

2. What modern season record did he just set?

3. When did he do it?

4. Where?

5. BONUS: Who was the catcher?

More batting average accomplishments.

1. Jesse Burkett

A. The only Federal League player to lead the majors in batting average for a season (.370 in 1914)

2. Ty Cobb

B. The first of only two players to lead the major leagues in batting average for three consecutive seasons

3. Napoleon Lajoie

C. Became the active leader in career batting average (.343) when Rogers Hornsby retired in 1937

4. Rogers Hornsby

D. Player who hit over .400 in both 1920 and 1922 to lead the major leagues

5. Benny Kauff

E. The first player to lead the major leagues in batting average in back-to-back seasons in which he hit over .400 in both seasons

6. George Sisler

F. Became the active leader in career batting average (.363) when Ty Cobb retired in 1928

7. Paul Waner

G. Baseball's new career leader in batting average from 1905 to 1910, and the last player to hold the top spot before Ty Cobb took over for good in 1911

891

Let's see if you can get good wood on these.

1. Rod Carew

A. The first of three players to lead the major leagues in batting average in back-to-back seasons in the 1960s

2. Stan Musial

B. The only player in the 1960s to lead the major leagues in batting average three times

3. Pete Rose

C. His .330 average one season was the lowest to lead the major leagues between the years 1966 and 2006

4. Tommy Davis

D. Became the active leader in career batting average with Stan Musial's retirement in 1963

5. Roberto Clemente

E. Became the active leader in career batting average with Roberto Clemente's death in 1972

6. Hank Aaron

F. The first player since World War II to lead the major leagues in batting average in back-to-back seasons

7. Eddie Murray

G. Of the three players to lead the major leagues in batting average in back-to-back seasons in the 1960s, his combined average for the two seasons was the highest

890: 1-E, 2-B, 3-G, 4-F, 5-A, 6-D, 7-C • **891:** 1-E, 2-F, 3-G, 4-A, 5-B, 6-D, 7-C

One last game of batting average records and accomplishments.

1. Larry Walker

A. The only player besides Ty Cobb to lead the major leagues in batting average for three consecutive seasons

2. Rod Carew

B. The first player to hit at least .390 in a season since Ted Williams his .406 in 1941 (he hit exactly .390)

3. Wade Boggs

C. Became the active leader in career batting average upon Rod Carew's retirement in 1985

4. Ted Williams

D. The last player to lead the major leagues in batting average who *wasn't* a first baseman or outfielder

5. Tony Gwynn

E. The first player to hit at least .385 (he hit .388) in a season since Ted Williams hit .406 in 1941

6. Alex Rodriguez

F. Player who came the closest to batting .400 (.394) since Ted Williams last accomplished it in 1941

7. George Brett

G. The last player to lead the major leagues in batting average in back-to-back seasons

893

The next four games honor records in run scoring.

1. Fred Dunlap

A. The career leader in runs scored until he was passed by Cap Anson in 1894

2. Jim O'Rourke

B. Set a new major league record for runs scored in a season in 1891—177

3. Tip O'Neill

C. Set a new major league record for runs scored in a season in 1884, 160, smashing the old record of 126

4. Ross Barnes

D. The first player to lead the major leagues in runs scored in back-to-back seasons

5. George Gore

E. Set a new major league record for runs scored in a season in 1887—167

6. Harry Stovey

F. Holds the National Association record for career runs scored—459

7. Tom Brown

G. The first player to score more than 100 runs in a season twice

894

1. Billy Hamilton

A. Became the active leader in career runs scored when Honus Wagner retired in 1917

2. Babe Ruth

B. Scored 192 runs in a season, a record that has never been broken

3. Eddie Collins

C. Became the active leader in career runs scored when Willie Keeler retired in 1910

4. Fred Clarke

D. The first 20th-century player to reach 150 runs scored in a season

5. KiKi Cuyler

E. Between 1919 and 1929, he scored the third most runs in the major leagues, after Babe Ruth and Rogers Hornsby

6. Ty Cobb

F. The first player to reach 2,000 career runs scored

7. Tommy Leach

G. The first player to lead the major leagues in runs scored for three consecutive seasons

895

1. Lou Gehrig

A. The only player in the 1930s and 1940s to lead the major leagues in runs scored three consecutive seasons

2. Ted Williams

B. Passed Jimmie Foxx in 1944 as the active leader in career runs scored

3. Mel Ott

C. Became the active leader in career runs scored when Luke Appling retired in 1950

4. Doc Cramer

D. The only player from 1883 to 1967 to lead the major leagues with less than 100 runs scored in a season—86

5. Joe DiMaggio

E. Became the active leader in career runs scored when Babe Ruth retired in 1935

6. Mickey Mantle

F. The only player between 1943 and 1975 to lead the major leagues in runs scored three consecutive seasons

7. Heinie Groh

G. The active leader in career runs scored in 1948, with 1,357, though he never once led the majors in runs scored for a single season

One last game of runs scored records, accomplishments, and progressions.

1. Jeff Bagwell

A. The only player between 1959 and 2004 to lead the major leagues in runs scored three consecutive seasons

2. Albert Pujols

B. Became the active leader in career runs scored when Stan Musial retired in 1963

3. Mickey Mantle

C. His 152 runs scored to lead the majors one season was the most by any player between 1936 and 2006

4. Hank Aaron

D. Became the active leader in career runs scored when Pete Rose retired, in 1986

5. Pete Rose

E. Became the active leader in career runs scored when Willie Mays retired, in 1973

6. Reggie Jackson

F. The last player to lead the major leagues in runs scored for three consecutive seasons

7. Rickey Henderson

G. Overtook Dave Winfield as the active leader in career runs scored in 1995

897

Okay—RBI records.

1. Deacon White

A. The only player between 1887 and 1917 to lead the major leagues in RBIs in back-to-back seasons

2. Cap Anson

B. Led the NL in RBIs in its first season, 1876, with 60

3. Dave Orr

C. The first player ever to reach 100 RBIs in a season

4. Buck Freeman

D. Holds the National Association record for career RBIs—276

5. Harry Davis

E. Established a new record with 166 RBIs, a mark that stood for 34 years

6. Sam Thompson

F. The only player between 1884 and 1917 to lead the major leagues with less than 100 RBIs—96

7. Cal McVey

G. The first player to lead the major leagues in RBIs for three consecutive seasons

896: 1-C, 2-F, 3-B, 4-E, 5-A, 6-D, 7-G • **897:** 1-B, 2-G, 3-C, 4-A, 5-F, 6-E, 7-D

WHO, WHAT, WHEN, WHERE, AND WHY

1. Who is being congratulated at home plate?

2. Why?

3. When?

4. Where?

5. BONUS: What was the final score?

898:

1. Bucky Dent.

2. He hit a three-run homer in the AL's second-ever playoff game to determine the AL East Division winner.

3. October 2, 1978.

4. Fenway Park in Boston.

5. 5–4.

More RBI records.

1. Cap Anson

2. Babe Ruth

3. Ed Delahanty

4. Honus Wagner

5. Lou Gehrig

6. Ken Williams

7. Hack Wilson

A. The first player to reach 1,000 career RBIs

B. Became the active leader in career RBIs with George Davis's retirement in 1909

C. Became the active leader in career RBIs in 1901, when he passed both Sam Thompson and Dan Brouthers

D. Set a new major league record, with 175 RBIs

E. Set a new major league record, with 191 RBIs

F. Set a new major league record, with 171 RBIs

G. Ended Babe Ruth's run of three consecutive seasons of leading the majors in RBIs when he got 155 in 1922

900

One more game of RBI records.

1. Jimmie Foxx

2. Lou Gehrig

3. Babe Ruth

4. Vern Stephens

5. Al Simmons

6. Joe Medwick

7. Hank Greenberg

A. Had the most RBIs in a season of any player between the years of 1932 and 2006—183

B. Became the active leader in career RBIs when Babe Ruth retired in 1935

C. Led the major leagues in RBIs in back-to-back seasons, but he was tied with a different teammate each time

D. Became the active leader in career RBIs when Mel Ott retired in 1947

E. The only player to lead the major leagues in RBIs in back-to-back seasons with at least 160 RBIs each year

F. Became the active leader in career RBIs when Lou Gehrig retired in 1939

G. Knocked Cap Anson off the top spot in career RBIs

899: 1-A, 2-F, 3-C, 4-B, 5-D, 6-G, 7-E • **900:** 1-E, 2-B, 3-G, 4-C, 5-F, 6-D, 7-A

Okay, *one* more. If you insist.

1. Yogi Berra   A. Became the active leader in career RBIs when Joe DiMaggio retired in 1951

2. Ernie Banks   B. The only player in the 1950s and 1960s to lead the major leagues in RBIs in back-to-back seasons

3. Johnny Mize   C. Became the active leader in career RBIs when Hank Aaron retired in 1976

4. George Foster   D. Became the active leader in career RBIs when Stan Musial retired in 1963

5. Cecil Fielder   E. Led the majors with the lowest RBI total (109) of all players from 1919 to 2006 (excluding the strike-shortened season of 1981)

6. Ken Harrelson   F. The only player in the 1970s and 1980s to lead the major leagues in RBIs in back-to-back seasons

7. Carl Yastrzemski   G. The only player between 1922 and 2006 to lead the major leagues in RBIs three consecutive seasons

902

Now hits.

1. Cal McVey   A. The first player to reach 200 hits in a season

2. Cap Anson   B. The first player to lead the major leagues in hits in back-to-back seasons

3. Dan Brouthers   C. Established a new hits record in 1896—240

4. Hugh Duffy   D. Established a new hits record in 1894—237

5. Ross Barnes   E. The first player to lead a professional league, the National Association, in hits in a season—66, in 1871

6. Jesse Burkett   F. The first player to lead the National League in hits in a season—138, in 1876

7. Tip O'Neill   G. The first player to reach 1,000 career hits

901: 1-D, 2-B, 3-A, 4-F, 5-G, 6-E, 7-C • **902:** 1-E, 2-G, 3-B, 4-D, 5-F, 6-C, 7-A

More hits.

1. Cap Anson

A. The last 19th-century player to lead the major leagues in hits in back-to-back seasons

2. Ty Cobb

B. Established a new hits record with 248

3. Ginger Beaumont

C. The first 20th-century player to lead the major leagues in hits in back-to-back seasons

4. Willie Keeler

D. The only non–Hall of Famer to be the active leader in career hits (2,705) between 1880 and 1976 (but for just one year)

5. Nap Lajoie

E. Became the active leader in career hits when Cap Anson retired

6. Jim O'Rourke

F. The first player to reach 2,000 career hits

7. Doc Cramer

G. The first 20th-century player to lead the major leagues in hits in a season—232 in 1901

904

Yes, the hit records just keep on happening.

1. Honus Wagner

A. Became the active leader in career hits with Honus Wagner's retirement in 1917

2. Ty Cobb

B. The first player to reach 3,000 career hits

3. George Burns

C. The only non–Hall of Fame player to lead the major leagues in hits in back-to-back seasons between 1904 and 1972

4. Nap Lajoie

D. The third player to reach 3,000 career hits (just a few months after number 2 joined the club)

5. Cap Anson

E. The only 19th- or 20th-century non–Hall of Fame player to lead the majors with more than 250 hits in a season

6. Joe Jackson

F. Second player to reach 3,000 career hits

7. Lefty O'Doul

G. The major league leader with the fewest hits in a season (not including the strike-shortened years of 1981 and 1994)—178

WHO, WHAT, WHEN, WHERE, AND WHY

1. Who is this man?

2. What's his job?

3. When was this photograph taken?

4. Where was he employed?

905:
1. Hall of Famer Jackie Robinson.

2. Brooklyn Dodger first baseman.

3. April 1947.

4. Ebbets Field in Brooklyn (featured directly behind him).

Another one.

1. George Sisler
2. Chuck Klein
3. Ty Cobb
4. Eddie Collins
5. Stan Musial
6. Sam Rice
7. Al Simmons

A. The only player from 1914 to 1948 to lead the major leagues in hits in back-to-back seasons

B. Became the active leader in career hits when Ty Cobb retired in 1927

C. Retired with 2,987 career hits, still to this day the player closest to 3,000 without reaching it

D. The first player to reach 4,000 career hits

E. The only player from 1934 to 1972 to lead the major leagues in hits in back-to-back seasons

F. Established a new hits record in 1920—257

G. Became the active leader in career hits when Rogers Hornsby retired in 1937

907

One last game of hit records.

1. Nellie Fox
2. Pete Rose
3. Tony Gwynn
4. Kirby Puckett
5. Steve Garvey
6. Robin Yount
7. Ichiro Suzuki

A. Became the active leader in career hits with Stan Musial's retirement in 1963—2,652

B. The only player from 1950 to 1988 to lead the major leagues in hits in back-to-back seasons

C. The last player to lead the major leagues in hits in back-to-back seasons

D. His 262 hits in a season broke the record that had stood for 84 years

E. Became the active leader in career hits with Pete Rose's retirement in 1986—2,599

F. Passed Bill Buckner in 1990 as the active leader in career hits

G. The only Hall of Famer to lead the major leagues in hits in back-to-back seasons between 1950 and closing day of the season in 2006

906: 1-F, 2-A, 3-D, 4-B, 5-E, 6-C, 7-G • **907:** 1-A, 2-B, 3-C, 4-G, 5-E, 6-F, 7-D

On to records for games played.

1. Jim O'Rourke
2. Sadie Houck
3. Bid McPhee
4. Andy Leonard
5. Cap Anson
6. Roger Connor
7. Jimmy Barrett

A. The first player to play in 162 games in a season

B. Holds the National Association record for career games played—286

C. Became the active leader in career games played when Cap Anson retired in 1897

D. The first player to reach 2,000 career games played

E. The first player to reach 1,000 career games played

F. Of all the players in this game, the first one to reach 100 games played in a season

G. The first player to reach 150 games played in a season

909

One more.

1. Honus Wagner
2. Ty Cobb
3. Brooks Robinson
4. Pete Rose
5. Cap Anson
6. Maury Wills
7. Hank Aaron

A. The first player to reach 3,000 games played

B. The first player to reach 2,500 games played

C. The first player to reach 3,250 games played

D. Set a new record with 163 games played in a season

E. The first player to reach 3,500 games played

F. The first player to reach 2,750 games played

G. The first player to reach 165 games played in a season

908: 1-E, 2-F, 3-C, 4-B, 5-D, 6-G, 7-A • **909:** 1-E, 2-A, 3-D, 4-E, 5-B, 6-G, 7-C

Let's see how you do with the even more obscure records for at bats.

1. Abner Dalrymple

A. The first player to reach 7,500 career at bats

2. Joe Start

B. The first player to reach 600 at bats in a season

3. George Wright

C. Led the NL in at bats in four of the league's first ten years

4. Arlie Latham

D. The first player to reach 5,000 career at bats

5. Tom Brown

E. The first player to reach 650 at bats in a season

6. Cap Anson

F. Passed George Wright in career at bats in 1880 to become the new major league leader

7. Jim O'Rourke

G. The only National Association player to collect more than 400 at bats in a season

911

1. Ty Cobb

A. Broke the previous record for at bats in a season the very next year with 672 (the old record was 671)

2. Jack Tobin

B. The only player between 1876 and 1975 to lead the major leagues in at bats for three consecutive seasons

3. Honus Wagner

C. The first player to reach 10,000 career at bats

4. Rabbit Maranville

D. Became the active leader in career at bats when Frankie Frisch retired in 1937

5. Goose Goslin

E. The first player to reach 11,000 career at bats

6. Cap Anson

F. Set a new career at bat record with 10,430

7. Doc Cramer

G. Set a new record for at bats in a season with 671

910: 1-C, 2-F, 3-G, 4-B, 5-E, 6-A, 7-D • **911:** 1-E, 2-G, 3-F, 4-A, 5-D, 6-C, 7-B

WHO, WHAT, WHEN, WHERE, AND WHY

1. Who is this player?

2. What extraordinary feat was he the last to accomplish?

3. When did he do it?

4. What position did he play?

912:
1. Hall of Famer Carl Yastrzemski.

2. Win the Triple Crown.

3. 1967.

4. Left field.

1. Hank Aaron   **A. The only player from 1943 to 2006 to lead the major leagues in at bats three consecutive seasons**

2. Dave Cash   **B. The first player to reach 13,000 career at bats**

3. Woody Jensen   **C. Set a new record for at bats in a season with 681**

4. Willie Wilson   **D. The first player to reach 700 at bats in a season**

5. Lloyd Waner   **E. The first player to reach 12,000 career at bats**

6. Juan Samuel   **F. Set a new record for at bats in a season with 696**

7. Pete Rose   **G. Second player to reach 700 at bats in a season**

914

NAME THAT YEAR

Seven clues. One year. See how few clues it takes you to guess the year.

1 **George Sisler wins the AL batting title** with a .407 average.

2 **Eight members of the Chicago White Sox** are found innocent of fraud for their alleged actions during the 1919 World Series.

3 **Cleveland wins its first pennant,** then defeats the Dodgers in the World Series, 5–2.

4 **Bill Wambsganss makes the only unassisted triple play** in World Series history.

5 **Frank "Home Run" Baker sits out** the entire season to care for his terminally ill wife.

6 **The Red Sox sell Babe Ruth** to the Yankees.

7 **Ray Chapman, the Indians' shortstop,** dies after being hit in the head by a pitch from Carl Mays of the Yankees.

PITCHING RECORDS

UNSURPASSED AND SURPASSED

Baseball Trivia

915

Let's begin with games pitched in the 19th century.

1. Jim Devlin

2. Will White

3. Pud Galvin

4. Al Spalding

5. Charles Radbourn

6. Bill Hutchison

7. Bobby Mathews

A. The first pitcher to reach 500 career games pitched

B. Established a new major league record in 1879 for games pitched in a season—76

C. Led the National League in games pitched in the inaugural season of 1876—68

D. The first pitcher to lead the major leagues in games pitched for three consecutive seasons

E. The first pitcher to reach 600 career games pitched

F. The first pitcher to lead the major leagues in games pitched in back-to-back seasons with at least 75 games pitched in both seasons

G. Holds the National Association record for career games pitched—282

916

More pitching records.

1. Tim Keefe

2. Cy Young

3. Pud Galvin

4. Joe McGinnity

5. Vic Willis

6. Walter Johnson

7. Ed Walsh

A. Became the active leader in career games pitched (600) when Pud Galvin retired in 1892

B. The first 20th-century pitcher to appear in at least 50 games in a season

C. The first pitcher to reach 700 career games pitched

D. Second pitcher to reach 800 career games pitched

E. The first pitcher to reach 800 career games pitched

F. The first 20th-century pitcher to lead the major leagues in games pitched in back-to-back seasons

G. The first 20th-century pitcher to lead the major leagues in games pitched (48, in 1901)

915: 1-C, 2-B, 3-E, 4-G, 5-F, 6-D, 7-A • 916: 1-A, 2-E, 3-C, 4-G, 5-B, 6-D, 7-F

WHO, WHAT, WHEN, WHERE, AND WHY

1. Who is the young man holding the trophy?

2. What had he just done?

3. When?

4. Where?

917:
1. Roger Clemens.
2. Win the All-Star Game MVP Award.
3. 1986.
4. Houston.

501

Still more.

1. Jack Powell

A. The first pitcher to reach 900 career games pitched

2. Firpo Marberry

B. Became the active leader in games pitched when Cy Young retired in 1911—578

3. Eddie Plank

C. Became the active leader in games pitched when Walter Johnson retired in 1927—665

4. Ace Adams

D. Became the active leader in games pitched when Bob Feller retired in 1956—554

5. Grover Alexander

E. The first pitcher in history to lead the major leagues in games pitched for three consecutive seasons

6. Cy Young

F. The only pitcher between 1927 and 2000 to lead the major leagues in games pitched for three consecutive seasons

7. Murry Dickson

G. Became the active leader in games pitched when Christy Mathewson retired in 1916—623

919

One last game of games pitched records, accomplishments, and progressions.

1. John Wyatt

A. The last pitcher to perform in 90 games in a season

2. Steve Kline

B. Second pitcher to reach 1,100 career games pitched

3. Salomon Torres

C. Set a new major league record for games pitched in a season—81

4. Mike Marshall

D. The first pitcher to reach 1,200 career games pitched

5. Jesse Orosco

E. The first pitcher to reach 1,000 career games pitched

6. John Franco

F. The last pitcher to lead the major leagues in games pitched for three consecutive seasons

7. Hoyt Wilhelm

G. With 106 games pitched one season, he's the only pitcher ever to break the 100-game mark

918: 1-B, 2-E, 3-G, 4-F, 5-C, 6-A, 7-D • **919:** 1-C, 2-F, 3-A, 4-G, 5-D, 6-B, 7-E

Now records and accomplishments for innings pitched.

1. Will White	**A. The first pitcher to lead the major leagues in innings pitched with less than 500 innings (482, in 1893)**
2. Pud Galvin	**B. Holds the National Association record for innings pitched in a career—2,351**
3. Al Spalding	**C. Led the National League in the inaugural season of 1876 with 622 innings pitched**
4. Jim Devlin	**D. Broke the record for innings pitched in a season in 1879 with 680, a mark that has never been broken**
5. Bill Hutchison	**E. The first pitcher to reach 5,000 career innings pitched (and later became the first to reach 6,000 innings)**
6. Bobby Mathews	**F. The first pitcher to reach 3,000 career innings pitched (and later became the first to reach 4,000 innings)**
7. Amos Rusie	**G. The last pitcher in history to top 600 innings in a season (622 in 1892)**

921

One last game of innings-pitched records and accomplishments.

1. Cy Young	**A. The only pitcher in history to lead the major leagues in innings pitched for five consecutive seasons**
2. Bill Hutchison	**B. The first pitcher to reach 7,000 career innings pitched**
3. Robin Roberts	**C. The last pitcher to lead the major leagues in innings pitched for three consecutive seasons**
4. Greg Maddux	**D. The last pitcher to hurl at least 400 innings in a season**
5. Ted Lyons	**E. The last pitcher to hurl at least 500 innings in back-to-back seasons**
6. Ed Walsh	**F. The first 20th-century pitcher to lead the major leagues in innings pitched with less than 300 innings—297.2**
7. Steve Carlton	**G. The last pitcher ever to break 300 innings in a season**

920: 1-D, 2-E, 3-B, 4-C, 5-G, 6-F, 7-A • **921:** 1-B, 2-E, 3-A, 4-C, 5-F, 6-D, 7-G

Get ready for games-won records and accomplishments.

1. Pud Galvin

A. His 53 wins in 1885 made him the last 50-game winner in major league history

2. Charles Radbourn

B. The last 40-game winner in major league history

3. John Clarkson

C. National Association record holder for career wins—205

4. Ed Walsh

D. The last pitcher to win at least 40 games in back-to-back seasons

5. Albert Spalding

E. Holds the major league record for wins in a season—59

6. Cy Young

F. The first 300-game winner in major league history

7. Bill Hutchison

G. The first 400-game winner in major league history

923

More games-won records.

1. Cy Young

A. The only 20th-century pitcher to lead the major leagues in wins for three straight years with at least 30 wins each year

2. Jack Chesbro

B. Became the active leader in career wins (312) with Cy Young's retirement in 1911

3. Bill Hutchison

C. Second pitcher to reach 400 career wins

4. Kid Nichols

D. The last 19th-century pitcher to lead the major leagues in wins for three straight years with at least 30 wins each year

5. Grover Alexander

E. Of the three pitchers who've led the major leagues in wins for three straight years with at least 30 wins each year, he's the only one not in the Hall of Fame

6. Christy Mathewson

F. Holds the 20th-century record for wins in a season—41

7. Walter Johnson

G. The first 20th-century pitcher to win 30 games in back-to-back seasons

922: 1-F, 2-E, 3-A, 4-B, 5-C, 6-G, 7-D • **923:** 1-G, 2-F, 3-E, 4-D, 5-A, 6-B, 7-C

Still more.

1. Dizzy Dean	**A. Won 31 games for the World Champion Indians in 1920**
2. Eddie Plank	**B. The first pitcher to reach 500 career wins**
3. Cy Young	**C. The only 29-game winner in the major leagues since Eddie Cicotte's famous 29-win year in 1919 in which White Sox owner Charlie Comiskey ordered Cicotte benched so he couldn't fulfill a 30-win bonus clause in his contract**
4. Jim Bagby	**D. The only NL pitcher since 1917 to win 30 games in a season**
5. Hal Newhouser	**E. Became the active leader in career wins (326) when Christy Mathewson retired in 1916**
6. Lefty Grove	**F. Became the active leader in career wins (257) upon Grover Alexander's retirement in 1930**
7. Burleigh Grimes	**G. The only active 300-game winner in the major leagues from 1931 to 1960 (and only for about two months)**

925

One last round.

1. Early Wynn	**A. The last 30-game winner in major league history**
2. Sandy Koufax	**B. The last pitcher to win at least 25 games in back-to-back seasons**
3. Jack Morris	**C. Became the active leader in career wins (286) when Warren Spahn retired in 1965**
4. Gaylord Perry	**D. Joined the 300-win club in 1982**
5. Robin Roberts	**E. Joined the 300-win club in 1983**
6. Denny McLain	**F. Became the active leader in career wins (235) when Bob Feller retired in 1956**
7. Steve Carlton	**G. Became the active leader in career wins (254) when Nolan Ryan retired in 1993**

924: 1-D, 2-E, 3-B, 4-A, 5-C, 6-G, 7-F • **925:** 1-F, 2-B, 3-G, 4-D, 5-C, 6-A, 7-E

WHO, WHAT, WHEN, WHERE, AND WHY

1. Who is this player?

2. What was his nickname, and how did he get it?

3. When did he suffer his injury? How?

4. Where does he rank on the career ERA list?

926:
1. Hall of Famer Mordecai Brown.

2. "Three Finger" Brown, because he was missing a finger on his pitching hand.

3. At the age of seven, on his family farm, Brown lost a finger to a corn grinder. Then, with his hand still in a cast, he fell while chasing a hog and broke two more fingers, which healed in a badly disfigured manner. This allowed him to grip a baseball in such a manner than his pitches dropped straight down.

4. Sixth all time at 2.06.

Now for the category pitchers want to think about least: Games lost.

1. Bobby Mathews **A.** Along with Jim McCormick, became the first pitcher to lose 40 games in a season (1879)

2. George Bradley **B.** Set a new major league record with 42 losses in 1880

3. Will White **C.** The first pitcher to reach 300 career losses

4. Pud Galvin **D.** Set the all-time major league record for losses in a season with 48 in 1883

5. Jim Devlin **E.** The last pitcher in history to lose 40 games in a season

6. John Coleman **F.** Lost the most games (35) in the National League's first season of 1876

7. Larry McKeon **G.** Holds the National Association record for losses in a career—112

928

More games-lost records.

1. Red Donahue **A.** The last pitcher to lose at least 35 games in a season

2. Tim Keefe **B.** Second pitcher to reach 300 career losses

3. Cy Young **C.** Became the active leader in career losses (177) when Eddie Plank retired in 1917

4. Jim Hughey **D.** Became the active leader in career losses (225) when Pud Galvin retired in 1892

5. Vic Willis **E.** Became the active leader in career losses (254) when Cy Young retired in 1911

6. Walter Johnson **F.** The last pitcher to lose 30 games in a season

7. Jack Powell **G.** Holds the 20th-century record for losses in a season—29

927: 1-G, 2-A, 3-B, 4-C, 5-F, 6-D, 7-E • **928:** 1-A, 2-D, 3-B, 4-F, 5-G, 6-C, 7-E

One last round of games-lost records.

1. Bill Steele

    A. The last 20-game loser in the major leagues

2. Red Ruffing

    B. Along with co-leaders Jack Powell and Earl Moore, his 19 games lost in 1911 were the fewest by the major league leader since 1872

3. Jack Fisher

    C. The last pitcher to lead the major leagues in losses in back-to-back seasons

4. Paul Derringer

    D. The only pitcher between 1878 and 1958 to lead the major leagues in games lost in back-to-back seasons

5. Ben Cantwell

    E. His 24 losses were the most by any pitcher in any season between 1963 and 2006

6. Roger Craig

    F. The only 25-game loser between 1934 and 2006

7. Mike Maroth

    G. His 27 losses were the most by any pitcher in any season between 1911 and 2006

930

See if you can match up these players with their records and accomplishments in the category of winning percentage.

1. Randy Johnson

    A. Posted the highest winning percentage (.893) of any 20-game winner in history (25–3)

2. Roy Face

    B. The only pitcher in history to lead the major leagues in winning percentage in back-to-back seasons with a mark of at least .800 or above in both seasons (28–5, .849; 31–4, .886)

3. Perry Werden

    C. The only player between 1873 and 2006 who has ever led the major leagues in career winning percentage

4. Albert Spalding

    D. The first of only four pitchers in history to lead the major leagues in winning percentage in back-to-back seasons

5. Ron Guidry

    E. The only lefthander to finish a season with a winning percentage of .900 or above (.900, 18–2)

6. Bill Hoffer

    F. Had a winning percentage of .923 (12–1) in his only season as a pitcher in the major leagues

7. Lefty Grove

    G. Had the best single-season winning percentage (.947) of any pitcher in history (18–1)

929: 1-B, 2-D, 3-E, 4-G, 5-F, 6-C, 7-A • 930: 1-E, 2-G, 3-F, 4-C, 5-A, 6-D, 7-B

931

Time for ERA records and accomplishments.

1. Al Spalding	**A. The only pitcher from 1901 to 1921 to be the major league leader in ERA with a mark over 2.00—2.48**
2. Walter Johnson	**B. National Association career ERA record holder—2.22**
3. Tim Keefe	**C. The only pitcher in baseball history (1871–2006) to be the major league leader in ERA with a mark above 3.00—3.18**
4. Red Faber	**D. Won the NL ERA title in the league's inaugural season of 1876 with an ERA of 1.23**
5. George Bradley	**E. The first pitcher in history to lead the major leagues in ERA in back-to-back seasons**
6. Ted Breitenstein	**F. The first of only two pitchers in history to be the major league leader in ERA for three consecutive seasons**
7. Lefty Grove	**G. The only 19th-century pitcher to finish a season with an ERA below 1.00—0.86**

932

More ERA records and accomplishments.

1. Walter Johnson	**A. Holds current pitching record for lowest career ERA (1.82)**
2. Ed Walsh	**B. Active leader in career ERA for the second most consecutive seasons—14**
3. Babe Ruth	**C. Active leader in career ERA (2.25) upon Walter Johnson's retirement in 1927**
4. Greg Maddux	**D. The last pitcher to lead the major leagues in ERA in back-to-back seasons with an ERA below 2.00 in both seasons**
5. Dutch Leonard	**E. Active leader in career ERA for the most consecutive seasons—16**
6. Tom Seaver	**F. Had the highest ERA (2.78) of any pitcher who was the major league leader between 1930 and 2006**
7. Saul Rogovin	**G. The only 20th-century pitcher who finished a season with an ERA below 1.00—0.96**

931: 1-B, 2-E, 3-G, 4-A, 5-D, 6-C, 7-F • **932:** 1-E, 2-A, 3-C, 4-D, 5-G, 6-B, 7-F

Complete-game records and accomplishments.

1. Charles Radbourn	**A.** The last pitcher with at least 60 complete games in a season (67, in 1892)
2. Will White	**B.** Set a new record for complete games in a season in 1879 with 75, a record that has never been broken
3. Amos Rusie	**C.** The first pitcher to lead the major leagues in complete games for three consecutive seasons (1880, 1881, 1882)
4. Jim Devlin	**D.** The last pitcher with at least 70 complete games in a season (73 in 1884)
5. Bill Hutchison	**E.** Tossed 66 complete games in the National League's first season of 1876
6. Jim McCormick	**F.** The last pitcher with at least 50 complete games in a season (50 in 1893)
7. Bobby Mathews	**G.** Holds the National Association record for complete games in a career—236

934

More complete-game records and feats.

1. Ed Walsh	**A.** The first pitcher to reach 500 career complete games
2. Bobby Mathews	**B.** The first 20th-century pitcher to lead the major leagues in complete games in back-to-back seasons
3. Walter Johnson	**C.** The first pitcher to be the major league leader in complete games with less than 30 in a season—29
4. Cy Young	**D.** The first pitcher to reach 700 career complete games
5. Grover Alexander	**E.** The last pitcher with at least 40 complete games in a season (42 in 1908)
6. Pud Galvin	**F.** The last pitcher with at least 35 complete games in back-to-back seasons
7. Irv Young	**G.** The first pitcher to reach 600 career complete games

WHO, WHAT, WHEN, WHERE, AND WHY

1. Who is this player?

2. What's significant about him in this uniform?

3. When did he receive his history-making decision?

4. Where was his offseason home, where representatives from every team except the Giants soon gathered, trying to sign him?

4. North Carolina.

3. December 2, 1974.

2. He was the first big star to be given his unconditional freedom by an arbitrator.

1. Hall of Famer Catfish Hunter.

935:

One last round.

1. Ted Lyons	A. Became the active leader in career complete games when Bob Feller retired in 1956
2. Robin Roberts	B. The only pitcher with at least 500 complete games who did not pitch in the 19th century
3. Warren Spahn	C. Holds the record for most consecutive seasons (11) as major leagues' active leader in career complete games
4. Walter Johnson	D. The last pitcher with at least 20 complete games in a season
5. Catfish Hunter	E. The only pitcher to lead the major leagues in complete games for five consecutive seasons
6. Rick Langford	F. The last pitcher with at least 25 complete games in a season
7. Fernando Valenzuela	G. The last pitcher with at least 30 complete games in a season

937

Now try these strikeout records and feats.

1. Tommy Bond	A. The first pitcher to reach 2,000 career strikeouts
2. Amos Rusie	B. The first pitcher to lead the major leagues in strikeouts for three consecutive seasons
3. Jim McCormick	C. The first pitcher to reach 500 career strikeouts
4. Hugh Daily	D. The first pitcher to reach 1,000 career strikeouts
5. Tim Keefe	E. Holds the National Association record for career strikeouts—167
6. Bobby Mathews	F. The first pitcher ever to reach 400 strikeouts in a season (483 in 1884)
7. Jim Devlin	G. Led the National League in strikeouts (122) in its inaugural year of 1876

936: 1-C, 2-E, 3-A, 4-B, 5-G, 6-F, 7-D • **937:** 1-C, 2-B, 3-D, 4-F, 5-A, 6-E, 7-G

More strikeout records.

1. Matt Kilroy

A. The first pitcher to lead the major leagues in strikeouts for five consecutive seasons

2. Cy Young

B. Became the active leader in career strikeouts when Tim Keefe retired in 1893

3. Rube Waddell

C. The first pitcher to reach 2,750 career strikeouts

4. John Clarkson

D. Became the active leader in career strikeouts when Cy Young retired in 1911

5. Dazzy Vance

E. Led the major leagues in strikeouts in all but one of the six years from 1923 to 1928

6. Walter Johnson

F. The first pitcher ever to reach 500 strikeouts in a season (513 in 1886)

7. Christy Mathewson

G. The first pitcher to reach 3,000 career strikeouts

939

Two more strikeout-record games to go.

1. Red Ruffing

A. The first pitcher to reach 3,500 career strikeouts

2. Dizzy Dean

B. The only pitcher between 1892 and 1965 to register at least 300 strikeouts in back-to-back seasons

3. Bob Feller

C. Became the active leader in career strikeouts when Lefty Grove retired in 1941

4. Herb Score

D. Led the major leagues in strikeouts in his first two seasons

5. Rube Waddell

E. Led the major leagues in strikeouts for four consecutive seasons, yet never registered 200 K's in any of the years

6. Early Wynn

F. Led the major leagues in strikeouts the last four years before WWII and the first three after the war (he missed the 1942, '43, '44, and '45 seasons due to military service)

7. Walter Johnson

G. Became the active leader in career strikeouts when Bob Feller retired in 1956

938: 1-F, 2-C, 3-A, 4-B, 5-E, 6-G, 7-D • **939:** 1-C, 2-E, 3-F, 4-D, 5-B, 6-G, 7-A

The last one.

1. Jim Bunning	**A.** The first pitcher to reach 4,500 career strikeouts
2. Nolan Ryan	**B.** The last pitcher (besides Randy Johnson) to lead the major leagues in strikeouts for three consecutive seasons
3. Frank Tanana	**C.** Became the active leader in career strikeouts when Nolan Ryan retired in 1993
4. Jack Morris	**D.** Became the active leader in career strikeouts when Sandy Koufax retired in 1966
5. Roger Clemens	**E.** Second pitcher to reach 4,500 career strikeouts
6. J. R. Richard	**F.** The only pitcher who led the major leagues in strikeouts in the six years between 1972 and 1977 besides Nolan Ryan
7. David Cone	**G.** The last pitcher (besides Randy Johnson) to lead the major leagues in strikeouts in back-to-back seasons with at least 300 strikeouts in both seasons

941

Look what the pitchers did to these batters.

1. Sam Wise	**A.** The first player to reach 500 career strikeouts
2. John Morrill	**B.** Holds the National Association record for strikeouts in a season—21
3. Danny Moeller	**C.** The only 19th-century player to strike out 100 times in a season (104 times in 1884)
4. Herman Dehlman	**D.** The first player to reach 1,000 career strikeouts
5. Gus Williams	**E.** The first player to lead the major leagues in strikeouts for three consecutive seasons
6. Babe Ruth	**F.** The first 20th-century player to strike out 100 times in a season
7. Tom Brown	**G.** Set a new record for strikeouts in a season (120) in 1914

940: 1-D, 2-A, 3-F, 4-C, 5-E, 6-G, 7-B • **941:** 1-C, 2-A, 3-F, 4-B, 5-G, 6-D, 7-E

942

Now it's time for shutout records and accomplishments.

1. Candy Cummings

2. Al Spalding

3. Cy Young

4. Pud Galvin

5. George Bradley

6. Grover Alexander

7. Tommy Bond

A. The only pitcher to lead the major leagues in shutouts for three consecutive seasons

B. Holds the National Association record (along with Al Spalding and George Zettlein) for most shutouts in one season—7

C. The last pitcher to lead the major leagues in shutouts in back-to-back seasons with at least ten shutouts in both seasons

D. The first pitcher to reach 60 career shutouts

E. The first pitcher to reach 20 career shutouts

F. Led the National League in shutouts (16) in the inaugural season of 1876, a record which will later be equaled but never broken

G. The first pitcher to reach 50 career shutouts

943

Two more.

1. Cy Young

2. Carl Hubbell

3. Walter Johnson

4. Eppa Rixey

5. Grover Alexander

6. Christy Mathewson

7. Red Ruffing

A. The first pitcher to reach 90 career shutouts

B. The only pitcher between 1917 and 1941 to post ten shutouts in one season

C. Second pitcher to reach 75 career shutouts

D. Became the active leader in career shutouts upon the retirement of Grover Alexander in 1930

E. Caught and passed Lefty Grove as the active leader in career shutouts with number 35 in 1940

F. The first pitcher to reach 75 career shutouts

G. Second pitcher to reach 90 career shutouts

942: 1-B, 2-E, 3-D, 4-G, 5-F, 6-C, 7-A • **943:** 1-F, 2-B, 3-A, 4-D, 5-G, 6-C, 7-E

Baseball Trivia

944

The last one.

1. Roger Clemens	**A. Pitched his 60th career shutout in 1991**
2. John Tudor	**B. The only pitcher between 1976 and 2006 to record at least ten shutouts in a season**
3. Bert Blyleven	**C. Pitched his 60th career shutout in 1984**
4. Jim Palmer	**D. Pitched his 60th career shutout in 1989**
5. Tom Seaver	**E. Holds the major league record for most consecutive years (13) being the active leader in career shutouts**
6. Nolan Ryan	**F. The last Hall of Famer to pitch ten shutouts in a season**
7. Eddie Plank	**G. Lefthander with the most career shutouts—69**

945

NAME THAT YEAR

Seven clues. One year. See how few clues it takes you to guess the year.

1 **Jake Ruppert** buys the New York Yankees.

2 **Honus Wagner** and Napoleon Lajoie join the 3,000-hit club.

3 **In a May 30 doubleheader,** St. Louis and Detroit combine for just 11 total hits, still the major league–record low.

4 **Babe Ruth makes his major league debut** for the Red Sox and pitches Boston to victory over Cleveland.

5 **The A's win** their fourth pennant in five years.

6 **A new major league,** the Federal League, makes its debut.

7 **The Miracle Braves,** in last place on July 4, win the NL pennant and then defeat the heavily favored A's in the World Series.

We've "saved" the best for last in this section: Save records.

1. Jack Manning   **A. Became the new career leader in saves with 26 in 1910 and held the top spot through 1925 with 49**

2. Joe McGinnity   **B. Became the new career leader in saves with 15 in 1894**

3. Firpo Marberry   **C. Holds the National Association record for saves in a season—8**

4. Al Spalding   **D. Became the new career leader in saves with 16 in 1899**

5. Mordecai Brown   **E. The first pitcher to reach 50 career saves**

6. Kid Nichols   **F. Became the new career leader in saves with 19 in 1907**

7. Tony Mullane   **G. Held the career record for saves from 1877 to 1893 with a total of 13**

947

Another.

1. Mordecai Brown   **A. The first pitcher to reach 25 saves in a season**

2. Ed Walsh   **B. The last pitcher to lead the major leagues in saves with less than ten in a season**

3. Joe Page   **C. The first pitcher to reach ten saves in a season (13 in 1911)**

4. Firpo Marberry   **D. Second pitcher to reach ten saves in a season—1912**

5. Bob Klinger   **E. The only Hall of Famer to lead the major leagues in saves between 1935 and 1976**

6. Chief Bender   **F. The first pitcher to reach 20 saves in a season**

7. Dizzy Dean   **G. Tied the all-time record for saves in a season with 13 in 1913**

946: 1-G, 2-F, 3-E, 4-C, 5-A, 6-D, 7-B • **947:** 1-C, 2-D, 3-A, 4-F, 5-B, 6-G, 7-E

And another.

1. Hoyt Wilhelm	**A.** The first pitcher to reach 100 career saves
2. Ted Abernathy	**B.** Second pitcher to reach 100 career saves
3. Firpo Marberry	**C.** The first pitcher to reach 35 saves in a season
4. Rollie Fingers	**D.** The first pitcher to reach 45 saves in a season
5. Dan Quisenberry	**E.** The first pitcher to reach 300 career saves
6. Wayne Granger	**F.** The first pitcher to reach 200 career saves
7. Johnny Murphy	**G.** The first pitcher to reach 30 saves in a season

949

The last one.

1. Bobby Thigpen	**A.** The only pitcher ever to record 50 saves in back-to-back seasons
2. Eric Gagne	**B.** The first pitcher to reach 400 career saves
3. Trevor Hoffman	**C.** Holds the all-time record for saves in a season—57
4. Dennis Eckersley	**D.** Second pitcher to reach 400 career saves
5. John Franco	**E.** The first pitcher to reach 350 career saves
6. Lee Smith	**F.** Third pitcher to reach 400 career saves
7. Jeff Reardon	**G.** Second pitcher to reach 50 saves in a season

948: 1-F, 2-G, 3-A, 4-E, 5-D, 6-C, 7-B • **949:** 1-C, 2-A, 3-F, 4-G, 5-D, 6-B, 7-E

WHO, WHAT, WHEN, WHERE, AND WHY

1. Who is this player?

2. What all-time major league record did he set?

3. When?

4. Why did he develop his submarine-style delivery?

950:
1. Dan Quisenberry.

2. Most saves in a season—45, which broke John Hiller's record of 38.

3. 1983.

4. Because of developing a sore arm in his senior year of college.

951

NAME THAT YEAR

Seven clues. One year. See how few clues it takes you to guess the year.

1 **Bill Veeck sells the Indians** and buys the Browns.

2 **Ralph Kiner wins his sixth** consecutive home run crown with 42 clouts.

3 **For the third time in six years,** the Dodgers lose the pennant on the last day of the season.

4 **Two Giants, Sal Maglie and Larry Jansen,** tie for the major league lead in wins, with 23.

5 **Willie Mays is chosen** as the NL Rookie of the Year.

6 **Bob Feller becomes the first 20th-century pitcher** to throw three career no-hitters.

7 **Ford Frick** becomes baseball's new commissioner.

951: 1951

BASEBALL GRAB BAG

952

Some numbers are virtually synonymous with certain players. Let's see how well you do at matching them up.

1. 130   **A. Pete Rose**

2. 714   **B. Lou Gehrig**

3. 31–6   **C. Joe DiMaggio**

4. .406   **D. Babe Ruth**

5. 56   **E. Ted Williams**

6. 4,256   **F. Rickey Henderson**

7. 2,130   **G. Denny McLain**

953

The 1993 season was the first in major league history in which all the double numbers, such as 22 and 33, were worn. Although most of these numbers were worn by more than one player that season, each of the numbers below was worn by one of the players listed. Match them up.

1. 00   **A. Jose Canseco, Texas**

2. 11   **B. Jack Armstrong, Florida**

3. 22   **C. Dick Schofield, Toronto**

4. 33   **D. Chili Davis, California**

5. 44   **E. Mitch Williams, Philadelphia**

6. 55   **F. Juan Guzman, Toronto**

7. 66   **G. Rene Gonzales, California**

8. 77   **H. Omar Olivares, St. Louis**

9. 88   **I. Don Slaught, Pittsburgh**

10. 99   **J. Rich Monteleone, New York Yankees**

952: 1-F, 2-D, 3-G, 4-E, 5-C, 6-A, 7-B • **953:** 1-H, 2-I, 3-C, 4-A, 5-D, 6-J, 7-F, 8-B, 9-G, 10-E

Good luck with this one. Each of the ten Hall of Famers below is listed with his famous uniform number. However, each player had a different number in his rookie season. See how many you can identify.

ROOKIE NUMBER	PLAYER AND FAMOUS NUMBER
1. 13	**A. Hank Aaron, 44**
2. 19	**B. George Brett, 5**
3. 43	**C. Roberto Clemente, 21**
4. 6	**D. Joe DiMaggio, 5**
5. 9	**E. Ryne Sandberg, 23**
6. 25	**F. Whitey Ford, 16**
7. 24	**G. Ralph Kiner, 4**
8. 5	**H. Mickey Mantle, 7**

955

NAME THAT YEAR

Seven clues. One year. See how few clues it takes you to guess the year.

1 **Bill Veeck unveils** the first exploding scoreboard.

2 **For the first time in history,** both leagues' batting champs hit under .330.

3 **Candlestick Park opens** on April 12 in San Francisco.

4 **Ted Williams slams** his 500th career homer on June 17.

5 **Charles O. Finley purchases** the Athletics.

6 **The Dodgers' Frank Howard is selected** as the National League Rookie of the Year.

7 **The Pirates defeat the Yankees** in the World Series, 4–3.

WHO, WHAT, WHEN, WHERE, AND WHY

1. What two players are at the center of this fight?

2. What prompted it?

3. When did it occur?

4. Where?

5. BONUS: Who is the player at the top of the photograph putting himself at risk against two bat-wielding Giants, and who is number 26?

956:

1. Hall of Famer Juan Marichal of the Giants and John Roseboro of the Dodgers.

2. Aggravating the normal tensions between the Giants and Dodgers, Marichal, while at bat, took exception when catcher Roseboro threw the ball back to his pitcher, barely missing Marichal's ear.

3. August 22, 1965.

4. Candlestick Park in San Francisco.

5. Hall of Famer Sandy Koufax is the player coming to Roseboro's aid, and number 26 is Tito Fuentes, who never used the bat he's shown holding.

Several players and a number of baseball notables have committed suicide. See if you know how they did it.

1. Marty Bergen, catcher, Beaneaters	A. Slit throat after an unsuccesful operation to save his pitching arm
2. Win Mercer, pitcher, Senators	B. While working as a cop, he shot himself on a street corner
3. Chick Stahl, outfielder-manager, Red Sox	C. Slit his wrists after killing his wife and two children with an ax
4. Eddie Hohnhorst, first baseman, Indians	D. Became a severely depressed drug addict, and ingested carbolic acid to escape the agony
5. Arthur Irwin, shortstop, Phillies	E. Inhaled gas after leaving a note about the evils of women and gambling
6. Pea Ridge Day, pitcher, Dodgers	F. Jumped off a ship into the Atlantic Ocean
7. Don Wilson, pitcher, Astros	G. Carbon monoxide poisoning

958

Sadly, seven more.

1. Otto Miller, catcher, Dodgers	A. Shot his wife and then himself
2. Jake Powell, outfielder, Senators	B. Shot himself in the eye
3. Dan Thomas, outfielder, Brewers	C. Jumped from a hospital window
4. Donnie Moore, pitcher, Angels	D. Carbon monoxide poisoning
5. Mike Reinbach, outfielder, Orioles	E. Drove his car over a cliff
6. Harry Pulliam, NL president	F. Shot himself inside a police station
7. Ron Luciano, umpire	G. Arrested for rape, hanged himself in jail

957: 1-C, 2-E, 3-D, 4-B, 5-F, 6-A, 7-G • **958:** 1-C, 2-F, 3-G, 4-A, 5-E, 6-B, 7-D

959

Try your luck with these unfortunate deaths of seven of baseball's Hall of Famers.

1. Addie Joss	A. Choked to death on a piece of meat while dining with his brother
2. Ed Delahanty	B. Drowned while trying to save his friend who couldn't swim, after their fishing boat capsized
3. Arky Vaughan	C. Was swept over Niagara Falls after either falling (or being pushed) off a railroad trestle after being kicked off a train for disorderly conduct
4. Mel Ott	D. Died from a sudden attack of tubercular meningitis
5. Jimmie Foxx	E. Died from a severe urinary tract disorder after an infection moved from his throat to his kidneys
6. Rube Waddell	F. Died in a Texas sanitarium from tuberculosis brought on by extended time spent standing in cold water helping flood victims
7. Ross Youngs	G. Died in an automobile crash

960

Lastly, try this set of untimely demises.

1. Jim Whitney, pitcher, Beaneaters	A. Died in a horse-riding accident just one month after his team won the World Series
2. Lyman Bostock, outfielder, Angels	B. Shot by two bank robbers during a payroll robbery at a bank
3. Ed Morris, pitcher, Red Sox	C. Stabbed to death at a Florida fish fry just before spring training
4. Bill Donovan, pitcher, Tigers	D. Accidentally killed by a shotgun blast to the head while riding in a car with the intended victim
5. Frank Navin, owner, Tigers	E. Killed in a train wreck in Forsyth, New York
6. Fred Knorr, owner, Tigers	F. Hit in the chest by a line drive and developed developed tuberculosis, which later killed him
7. Luke Easter, first base, Indians	G. Died in a bathtub accident in his home

959: 1-D, 2-C, 3-B, 4-G, 5-A, 6-F, 7-E • **960:** 1-F, 2-D, 3-C, 4-E, 5-A, 6-G, 7-B

961

Each of the players was the last active player for one of the listed teams of a bygone era. See if you can match player to team. By "last active player," I mean the last player of a now-defunct team to be an active major leaguer. For example, Reggie Jackson played with the Kansas City Athletics, a team that no longer existed after their transfer to Oakland in 1968. When Jackson retired, after the 1987 season, he was the last active player to have played for the Kansas City A's. Good luck.

1. Eddie Mathews	A. Seattle Pilots
2. Toby Harrah	B. New York Giants
3. Don Larsen	C. Boston Braves
4. Fred Stanley	D. Philadelphia Athletics
5. Vic Power	E. Milwaukee Braves
6. Reggie Jackson	F. 1971 Washington Senators
7. Willie Mays	G. 1960 Washington Senators
8. Bob Aspromonte	H. St. Louis Browns
9. Jim Kaat	I. Brooklyn Dodgers
10. Phil Niekro	J. Kansas City Athletics

962

Each of the books below was written by or about one of the following players in the right column.

1. *I Never Had It Made*	A. Joe Garagiola
2. *My Turn at Bat*	B. Tug McGraw
3. *Baseball Is a Funny Game*	C. Ted Williams
4. *It's Good to Be Alive*	D. Mickey Mantle
5. *Ball Four*	E. Jackie Robinson
6. *The Education of a Baseball Player*	F. Jim Bouton
7. *Screwball*	G. Roy Campanella

961: 1-C, 2-F, 3-H, 4-A, 5-D, 6-J, 7-B, 8-I, 9-G, 10-E • **962:** 1-E, 2-C, 3-A, 4-G, 5-F, 6-D, 7-B

963

See if you can match up these lesser-known major league baseball awards with the distinctions they honor.

1. Fishel Award

2. Ford C. Frick Award

3. J. G. Taylor Spink Award

4. Branch Rickey Award

5. Hank Aaron Award

6. Hutch Award

7. Lou Gehrig Award

A. Excellence in baseball writing

B. The best overall hitter in each league

C. Player who best exemplifies the character—on and off the field—of its namesake

D. Excellence in baseball broadcasting

E. Excellence in public relations

F. Player who best exemplifies the fighting spirit and competitive desire of its namesake

G. Excellence in community service

964

See if you can match these Triple Crown winners with their Triple Crown distinctions.

1. Lowest batting average by a Triple Crown winner—.316

2. Fewest homers by a 20th-century Triple Crown winner—9

3. Baseball's first Triple Crown winner

4. Baseball's last Triple Crown winner

5. Highest batting average by a Triple Crown winner—.440

6. Most home runs by a Triple Crown winner—52

7. Last National League Triple Crown winner

A. Hugh Duffy

B. Frank Robinson

C. Paul Hines

D. Joe Medwick

E. Mickey Mantle

F. Ty Cobb

G. Carl Yastrzemski

963: 1-E, 2-D, 3-A, 4-G, 5-B, 6-F, 7-C • **964:** 1-B, 2-F, 3-C, 4-G, 5-A, 6-E, 7-D

WHO, WHAT, WHEN, WHERE, AND WHY

1. Who is this player?

2. What was his famous trademark?

3. When did he have his best season, and at what age?

4. Where did he hit all of his home runs in 1943?

965:
1. Hall of Famer Mel Ott.

2. His high-leg kick while batting.

3. In 1929, at age 20 (.328, 42 HRS, 151 RBIs, 138 runs, 37 doubles).

4. He hit all 18 of his home runs at home, the Polo Grounds, and finished second in the NL.

Each of the players in the left column can lay claim to one of the feats in the right column.

1. Joe Jackson

2. Ray Schalk

3. Tommy Thevenow

4. Bob Nieman

5. Dave Philley

6. Mike Lum

7. Jim Tobin

A. Once had nine consecutive pinch-hits

B. Only pitcher to hit three homers in a game

C. Caught four no-hitters in his career

D. Only player to pinch-hit for Hank Aaron

E. Hit .408 in his rookie season

F. Most consecutive at bats without a homer—3,347

G. Only player ever to homer in his first two at bats

967

Match each man and his distinction.

1. Curt Flood

2. Clem Labine

3. Don Mattingly

4. Rennie Stennett

5. Ron Blomberg

6. George Lewis

7. Bobo Holloman

A. Only player ever to pinch-hit for Babe Ruth

B. First modern-era player to test baseball's reserve clause in court

C. First-ever designated hitter

D. Hit six grand slams in one season

E. A no-hitter in his first start, he never completed another game

F. Only 20th-century player with seven hits in a nine-inning game

G. Retired Stan Musial 49 consecutive times

966: 1-E, 2-C, 3-F, 4-G, 5-A, 6-D, 7-B • 967: 1-B, 2-G, 3-D, 4-F, 5-C, 6-A, 7-E

Each of the players listed below accomplished (to his great consternation!) one of the feats listed below.

1. Roger Peckinpaugh	**A. Compiled the lowest career batting average, .170**
2. Dock Ellis	**B. Lost 29 games in one season**
3. Vic Willis	**C. Lost 27 consecutive games**
4. Terry Felton	**D. Once allowed 29 hits in one game**
5. Ed Rommel	**E. Made eight errors in one World Series**
6. Bill Berger	**F. Lost his first 16 decisions**
7. Anthony Young	**G. Hit the first three batters he faced in his career**

969

Just for good luck, test your knowledge of some of baseball's most famous managers by matching them and their accomplishments.

1. Most years managing without winning a championship—26	**A. Frank Bancroft**
2. Most years managing in the National League—32	**B. John McGraw**
3. Most years managing in the major leagues—53	**C. Connie Mack**
4. Youngest manager to start a season at the helm—24	**D. Billy Martin**
5. Most consecutive years as a championship manager—5	**E. Gene Mauch**
6. Most clubs managed during a career—7	**F. Casey Stengel**
7. Most number of times managed the same club—5	**G. Lou Boudreau**

968: 1-E, 2-G, 3-B, 4-F, 5-D, 6-A, 7-C • **969:** 1-E, 2-B, 3-C, 4-G, 5-F, 6-A, 7-D

The whiff kings.

1. Bruce Campbell   **A. The only player between 1893 and 1975 to lead the major leagues in strikeouts for three consecutive seasons**

2. Hack Wilson   **B. The only player between 1915 and 1933 to strike out 100 times in a season**

3. Mike Schmidt   **C. The last player in history to lead the major leagues in strikeouts for three consecutive seasons before Adam Dunn in 2006**

4. Dave Nicholson   **D. The first player to reach 1,900 career strikeouts**

5. Adam Dunn   **E. The first player to reach 175 strikeouts in a season**

6. Willie Stargell   **F. Holds the record for strikeouts in a season—195**

7. Bobby Bonds   **G. Set a new major league record with 187 strikeouts in a season, and then broke it the next year with 189**

971

Only a handful of players belong to the 500-home run club. Each of the members listed below has the distinction of being the only 500-home run club member to claim one of the additional feats listed.

1. Highest lifetime batting average—.344   **A. Ted Williams**

2. Stole home ten times during his career   **B. Mark McGwire**

3. Had the most career hits—3,771   **C. Willie McCovey**

4. Struck out the most times—2,597   **D. Reggie Jackson**

5. Hit the most grand slams—18   **E. Babe Ruth**

6. Played the most consecutive games—717   **F. Ernie Banks**

7. Played the fewest years of all 500-home run club members—16   **G. Hank Aaron**

970: 1-B, 2-A, 3-C, 4-E, 5-F, 6-D, 7-G • **971:** 1-A, 2-E, 3-G, 4-D, 5-C, 6-F, 7-B

WHO, WHAT, WHEN, WHERE, AND WHY

1. Who is this?

2. What did he just do that has never been done before or since?

3. When did he do it?

4. Where was the game played?

5. BONUS: How did his feat come to an end?

972:

1. Harvey Haddix of the Pittsburgh Pirates.

2. Pitched 12 perfect innings (then lost the game in the 13th!).

3. May 26, 1959.

4. County Stadium in Milwaukee.

5. Third baseman Don Hoak made an error on a ground ball by Felix Mantilla to begin the 13th inning.

And now a palate cleanser. Match up these teams with their accomplishments.

1. San Diego Padres

A. The first team in history to hit back-to-back-to-back home runs in a game after the same feat had been done to them earlier in the same game (2000)

2. Kansas City Royals

B. The first team to feature a player with an artificial hip who, by the way, happened to hit a home run on the first pitch he saw on Opening Day (1993)

3. New York Yankees

C. The last team to feature a player who hit home runs in three consecutive innings (1995—only the fourth time it's been done in major league history)

4. Chicago White Sox

D. Had the oldest player in major league history to hit a grand slam (2004)

5. Colorado Rockies

E. The first team in history to hit three consecutive home runs at the start of a game (1987)

6. St. Louis Cardinals

F. The first team to feature two players who hit home runs from each side of the plate in the same game (2000)

7. Atlanta Braves

G. The only team in major league history to twice win a game by one run with a two-out walk-off grand slam (1970 and 1979)

974

Now match up these feats with members of the 3,000-strikeouts club.

1. Pitched the most shutouts—110

A. Bert Blyleven

2. Won the fewest games—251

B. Gaylord Perry

3. Walked the most batters—2,795

C. Nolan Ryan

4. Oldest in history (48) to pitch *regularly*

D. Don Sutton

5. Won the Cy Young Award in both NL and AL

E. Bob Gibson

6. Allowed a record 50 home runs in one season

F. Phil Niekro

7. In 22 seasons, was never once on the disabled list

G. Walter Johnson

973: 1-E, 2-A, 3-F, 4-B (Bo Jackson), 5-G, 6-C, 7-D • **974:** 1-G, 2-E, 3-C, 4-F, 5-B, 6-A, 7-D

975

Each of the facts applies to one of the 3,000-hit club members. See if you can connect them.

1. Ty Cobb	A. The only member of the club whose 3,000th career hit was a home run
2. Paul Molitor	B. The only club member to get his 3,000th hit off an eventual Hall of Famer
3. Dave Winfield	C. The only member of the club whose 3,000th hit was a triple
4. Cap Anson	D. Required the most games to get into the club—2,979
5. Rickey Henderson	E. The only club member with exactly 3,000 career hits
6. Wade Boggs	F. The oldest player to join the club—45
7. Roberto Clemente	G. The youngest player to join the club—34

976

More 3,000-hits club trivia for you.

1. Paul Molitor	A. Club member with the most career hits but no season with at least 200 hits
2. Eddie Collins	B. Club member with the most singles in one season—187
3. Carl Yastrzemski	C. Club member with the highest career batting average but no batting title
4. Pete Rose	D. Club member with the most career singles
5. Wade Boggs	E. Club member who had the highest single-season average
6. Stan Musial	F. Club member with the most career hits but no batting title
7. Napoleon Lajoie	G. Club member who finished a season the most hits ahead of the runner-up—44 (he had 228 hits to the runner-up's 184)

World Series nonwinners. None of these teams has ever won the World Series. What else do you know about them? (Note: Rangers questions include time in Washington; Nationals questions include time in Montreal; Brewers questions include time in both leagues.)

1. Tampa Bay Devil Rays   **A. The only NL team on this list that hasn't won a pennant or division title, either**

2. Seattle Mariners   **B. The only team in major league history to lose 100 games in a season despite having a winning record (41–40) at home**

3. Texas Rangers   **C. NL team with the most division titles—6**

4. Colorado Rockies   **D. Team with the most pennants—2**

5. San Diego Padres   **E. AL team with the most division titles—4**

6. Milwaukee Brewers   **F. Team whose only division title was tainted: they were simply ahead when the players' strike ended the season**

7. Washington Nationals   **G. Team's last division title was in 1982**

8. Houston Astros   **H. Failed to win the pennant even though it won 21 more games than any other team in baseball that season**

BASEBALL NAME-O-MANIA

See if you can fill out these fantasy teams' lineups with qualifying players at the appropriate positions. If a player played even one game at a position in his career, he qualifies for that position here, though I made every attempt to use players at the positions they normally played. Any player known by a nickname will be listed by that name, and not his given one. A copy of the out-of-print *Baseball Encyclopedia* or *Total Baseball* certainly would help when playing these games. Occasionally I have inserted a designated hitter, an owner, a pinch runner, etc., when their names were too good to pass up. At times, I've had to settle for part of a name. I filled in a few answers in the first round to get you started. Have fun! Answers begin on page 553.

The animal team—fur division.

Pitcher (Pirates, 1967–1976)
Bob Moose

Catcher (19th-century Hall of Famer, Giants)

First base (1,300 games at first for Pirates/Phillies)

Second base (Hall of Fame, White Sox)

Third base (1912–1921, Pirates/Cards/Phillies, though more as an outfielder)
Possum Whitted

Shortstop (Hall of Fame, Brooklyn Dodgers)
Rabbit Maranville

First outfielder (1984–1996, Brewers/Tigers)

Second outfielder (1925–1938, Athletics/White Sox)

Third outfielder (19th-century star with Louisville)

Manager (1949 Braves, managed 46 games after 20 years playing for them)
Johnny Cooney

979

The botanical team.

Pitcher (1981–1995, Royals/Giants)

Catcher (Helped beat the Black Sox in 1919)

First base (1908–1909, Braves)

Second base (The last player-manager in baseball)

Third base (1908–1923, Tigers/Senators, had 1,867 games at SS, but 43 at third)

Shortstop (1923–1933, Cardinals/Dodgers)

First outfielder (1878–1885, led NL in triples in 1879)

Second outfielder (1983 NL Rookie of the Year)

Third outfielder (1908–1916, Giants/Braves)

Designated hitter (One game at DH for 1995 Angels)

Manager (Hall of Fame, Browns/Cardinals)

980

The professions team.

Pitcher (Four-time 20-game winner for the Cubs)

Catcher (1971–1987, Brewers/Royals/Cardinals)

First base (1981–1991, mostly Dodgers)

Second base (1961–1964, Athletics)

Third base (1879–1892, mostly Cincinnati)

Shortstop (1911–1916, Pirates/Cardinals)

First outfielder (1915–1923, Senators/Cubs)

Second outfielder (1888–1894, mostly Louisville Colonels)

Third outfielder (1968–1986, Braves/Dodgers)

Designated hitter (1986, Royals, one game at DH)

Manager (Led 1979 Pirates to World Series title)

981

The presidential team.

Pitcher (1999–2004, Pirates/Cardinals/Twins)

Catcher (Hall of Fame, Expos/Mets)

First base (1996–2003, Cubs/Brewers)

Second base (1999–2006, mostly Angels)

Third base (1922–1934, Pirates/Cubs/Cardinals)

Shortstop (1977–1987, mostly Royals)

First outfielder (2001–2006, mostly Tigers)

Second outfielder (1904, Phillies)

Third outfielder (1986–1994, two-sport star)

Designated hitter (1991–1999, Indians/Red Sox)

Manager (Colorado Rockies)

Owner (Rangers)

Executive (League president)

982

The calendar team.

Pitcher (1901–1908, Red Sox)

Catcher (1983–1986, Reds/White Sox/Cubs)

First base (1949–1954, Indians)

Second base (1882–1887, pitcher, 28-game winner in '84, but with two games at second)

Third base (1943–1945, Cardinals, six games at third)

Shortstop (1884–1890, pitcher with 22 wins in 1890, but who had eight games at shortstop)

First outfielder (1966–1984; first free agent pick in baseball history by the KC A's)

Second outfielder (Later became a famous evangelist)

Third outfielder (1968–1977, mostly White Sox)

Manager (1985–2002, Rangers/Mets)

Owner (Cardinals)

983

The colors team.

Pitcher (1971 American League MVP)

Catcher (1974–1983, mostly Red Sox/ Cubs)

First base (Jewish Hall of Famer)

Second base (Hall of Fame, Cardinals)

Third base (1930–1946, A's/Tigers, 1,802 games)

Shortstop (1928–1931, Indians)

First outfielder (Had only one arm)

Second outfielder (19th-century 203-game winner as a pitcher, but with 23 games in OF)

Third outfielder (Yankee third sacker, but ten OF games; later became AL president)

Manager (Managed 1982 World Series champs)

984

The construction team.

Pitcher (Threw two no-hitters in 1952)

Catcher (1902–1905, Senators/ Tigers)

First base (1987–1988, Mariners, seven games)

Second base (1945, Phillies, one game at second)

Third base (1895, Brooklyn, one game at third)

Shortstop (1911–1912, Dodgers)

First outfielder (1985–1987, Pirates, nine games)

Second outfielder (Played 500-plus games with four different teams)

Third outfielder (1972–1980, Indians/Braves)

Manager (Union Association manager)

WHO, WHAT, WHEN, WHERE, AND WHY

1. Who are the two men?

2. What are they famous for?

3. When was their most notorious incident?

4. Which player precipitated this incident by bunting against orders?

5. BONUS: What did one call the other in a subsequent press interview?

5. Martin called Steinbrenner "a convicted felon."

4. Reggie Jackson.

3. July 1978.

2. Their constant battles and hirings/firings, leading to a major league-record five tenures for Martin with the team.

1. Manager Billy Martin and owner George Steinbrenner of the Yankees.

985:

986

The all-female team.

Pitcher (Best player ever, so say most experts)

Catcher (1926, Giants)

First base (1898–1911, Pirates/Phillies)

Second base (1909–1912, Indians/Dodgers)

Third base (1910–1919, Phillies/White Sox)

Shortstop (1906–1915, Cardinals/Rebels [FL])

First outfielder (1904–1919, 2,169 hits, Phillies/Reds)

Second outfielder (1915–1927, Browns/Red Sox)

Third outfielder (1890–1907, Pirates/Cardinals)

Manager (Hall of Fame, Athletics)

987

The clothing team.

Pitcher (1916–1933, Athletics/Braves)

Catcher (Yankees, Hall of Famer)

First base (1912–1917, Browns/White Sox)

Second base (1920–1925, mostly Pirates)

Third base (1920–1926, Browns/Red Sox, shortstop, but three games at third)

Shortstop (1916–1917, Dodgers)

First outfielder (1969–1974, mostly Expos)

Second outfielder (Cleveland named their team after him)

Third outfielder (1921–1927, Indians/Senators)

Manager (Cubs, 3,000-hit club, player-manager)

988

The poker team.

Pitcher (1966–1972, Reds/Angels)

Catcher (1878–1893, Hall of Fame, mostly with Cubs/Braves, played many positions)

First base (1893–1905, Dodgers/Red Sox)

Second base (1989–1997, Twins)

Third base (1947–1953, Giants)

Shortstop (1937–1938, Athletics)

First outfielder (1884–1890, Phillies/Pirates)

Second outfielder (1939, Dodgers, one career game)

Third outfielder (1969–1985, Yankees/Phillies/Indians)

Manager (Managed Marlins to World Series title in 2003)

989

The feathered-friends team.

Pitcher (1982–1991, Padres, Yankees)

Catcher (1937–1945, Red Sox, 518 games)

First base (Black Sox)

Second base (1906–1909, Pirates, 242 games)

Third base (1989–2003, White Sox/Mets)

Shortstop ("Gobbled" up grounders for nine games with the Red Sox in 1925)

First outfielder (Hall of Fame, Senators)

Second outfielder (Hall of Fame, Cardinals)

Third outfielder (1926–1927, Reds, 143 games)

Manager (1954–1966, Braves/Reds/Indians)

990

The anatomy team.

Pitcher (Hall of Fame, A's/ Brewers)

Catcher (1972–1983, Expos/Cubs/ Yankees)

First base (1947–1953, Indians/ Senators, 193 games pitched, but one game at first)

Second base (1980–1993, Mets/ Phillies)

Third base (1901–1908, Cardinals/ Dodgers)

Shortstop (1884–1902, Pirates/ Cardinals)

First outfielder (Hall of Fame, Tigers/Senators, 1923–1939)

Second outfielder (1976–1989, Mets/Giants)

Third outfielder (1952–1964, Red Sox/Orioles)

Manager (Hall of Fame, managed 26 years, Cubs/Giants/Dodgers)

991

The royalty team.

Pitcher (1925–1926, Phillies)

Catcher (1987–2003, Pirates/ Dodgers/Twins)

First base (1955–1963, Yanks/Mets, Miller Lite television commercials)

Second base (1896–1916, Hall of Fame, Cleveland)

Third base (1989–1999, Pirates/ Royals)

Shortstop (1908, Yankees)

First outfielder (1950s, Hall of Fame, Dodgers)

Second outfielder (1970–1986, Astros/Reds)

Third outfielder (1989–2006, Expos/Giants)

Designated hitter (1973, Rangers, four career games)

Manager (Hall of Fame, Orioles)

992

The family team.

Pitcher (1887, Cincinnati, pitched two games)

Catcher (1986–1998, eight teams, mostly Padres)

First base (1899–1904, Pirates/Dodgers/Tigers)

Second base (1888–1901, Cleveland/Cubs, 1,454 games)

Third base (1942–1950, Braves/Pirates)

Shortstop (1944–1962, Phillies)

First outfielder (Hall of Fame, Negro leagues)

Second outfielder (1981–1997, Dodgers/Braves, led NL in singles 1990, 1991, 1992, 1993)

Third outfielder (1963–1974, Astros/Braves, more SS than OF, led NL in singles in 1966)

Pinch runner (One appearance for 1937 Red Sox)

Manager (Black Sox)

993

The religious team.

Pitcher (1938–1954, Pirates/Dodgers)

Catcher (Caught 12 games for 1972 Padres)

First base (Seventy games at first for 1930 Phillies)

Second base (1924–1935, A's/Red Sox, 1,338 games)

Third base (1959–1973, Giants/Pirates)

Shortstop (1976–1991, Cardinals/Padres)

First outfielder (1952–1956, Indians/Orioles)

Second outfielder (1963–1979, Giants/Astros)

Third outfielder (1968–1970, White Sox/Tigers)

Designated hitter (1969–1976, mostly Oakland A's)

Manager (1907–1911, Red Sox/Indians)

WHO, WHAT, WHEN, WHERE, AND WHY

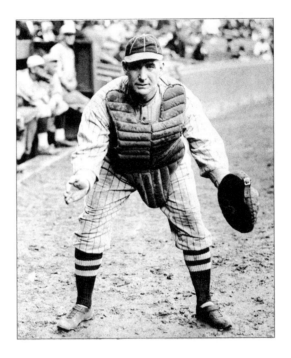

1. Who is this player?

2. What nonstatistics-related claim to fame does he have?

3. When did he do it?

4. What inspired him to do so?

4. He was tired of badly bruised legs from playing catcher.

3. 1907.

2. He introduced shin guards to the major leagues.

1. Hall of Famer Roger Bresnahan.

994:

995

The military team.

Pitcher (Won 50 games for the Senators in 1932–1933)

Catcher (1904–1910, Reds/Giants)

First base (1999–2006, Astros)

Second base (All 52 games of his career were at second base for the 1981 A's)

Third base (Six games for 1954 Phillies)

Shortstop (Two games for 1927 White Sox)

First outfielder (1884–1893, seven teams, mostly Giants, more noted as a pitcher)

Second outfielder (1887–1903, mostly Giants, possible future Hall of Famer)

Third outfielder (1965–1966, Mets)

Designated hitter (One game for 1980 Blue Jays)

Manager (Managed St. Louis to 27–14 record in 1890 American Association)

Executive (League president)

996

The weather team.

Pitcher (1982–1994, Orioles/A's/Royals)

Catcher (1944–1948, Cubs/Reds)

First base (1992–2006, Angels/Giants)

Second base (Seven games at second for 1925 Cubs)

Third base (One game at third for 1886 Athletics)

Shortstop (1884–1890, Phillies, mostly an outfielder, but 17 games at SS)

First outfielder (1884, Red Stockings/Nationals)

Second outfielder (Initiated the lawsuit over baseball's reserve clause)

Third outfielder (1936–1950, Indians/Giants)

Designated hitter (Three games at DH for 1989 Royals)

Manager (Ran the 1899 Giants for 66 games)

997

The money team.

Pitcher (Hall of Fame, 300-game winner with the early Braves)

Catcher (1906–1915, Yankees/Athletics)

First base (1958–1974, mostly Tigers)

Second base (Two games at second for 1887 Athletics)

Third base (Black Sox)

Shortstop (Hall of Fame, Cubs)

First outfielder (Home run record holder)

Second outfielder (Hall of Fame, Phillies)

Third outfielder (1960–1962, Cubs/Astros)

Designated hitter (1968–1983, Phillies/Brewers, though mostly a third baseman)

Manager (1884 Giants)

998

The geography team.

Pitcher (1977–1987, Giants/Phillies/Yankees)

Catcher (1943–1948, Braves/Reds)

First base (1901–1918, Tigers/Senators)

Second base (1996–2005, Devil Rays/Cardinals)

Third base (1982–1988, Reds/Orioles)

Shortstop (1947, Cubs, eight career games)

First outfielder (1984–1994, White Sox/Mets)

Second outfielder (1981–1982 Royals, two OF games in 11-game career)

Third outfielder (1968–1973, Cardinals/Reds)

Manager (Managed Phillies to their only World Series title)

999

1000

The topography team.

Pitcher (Hall of Fame, Mets/Reds/White Sox)

Catcher (1983–1993, Cubs/Cardinals/Phillies)

First base (Sixteen games at first for Pittsburgh in 1886)

Second base (1951–1956, Browns/Orioles/White Sox utility infielder with 99 games at second)

Third base (1924–1935, Pirates/Dodgers, 1,000-plus games at SS, but three at third base)

Shortstop (1983–1992, A's/White Sox/Angels, more second base, but 184 games at SS)

First outfielder (1970–1984, Angels/Yankees/Rangers)

Second outfielder (1952–1961, mostly White Sox)

Third outfielder (Five games in OF for 1884 Philadelphia Keystones of Union Association)

Manager (Piloted Phillies to last place in 1920)

The vehicle team.

Pitcher (1913–1927, Senators/Giants)

Catcher (1992–1995, Astros)

First base (1979–1982, Twins)

Second base (1944, Braves, one game at second)

Third base (1912–1913, Phillies/Reds)

Shortstop (1940–1942, Athletics)

First outfielder (1975–1985, Twins/Angels/Orioles)

Second outfielder (1897–1903, 738 games, Reds/Tigers/Cubs/Cardinals/Cleveland)

Third outfielder (One game, one at bat in career with 1918 Phillies, but I wanted his name!)

Designated hitter (1992–1997, KC/Oakland catcher, just one game at DH, but a great name!)

Manager (1884 KC team of Union Association)

1001

The baseball terminology team.

Pitcher (2004–2006, Blue Jays reliever)

Catcher (Star pitcher *and* catcher in the old Negro leagues)

First base (1990 and 1991 AL home run champ)

Second base (1997–2004, Yankees/Blue Jays)

Third base (Hall of Famer, 1908–1922, Athletics)

Shortstop (19th-century star, mostly with Buffalo Bisons)

First outfielder (1970–1984, Mets/Expos/Orioles)

Second outfielder (1958–1978, Dodgers/Expos)

Third outfielder (1938–1945, Cardinals/Phillies)

Manager (1960s to 1970s, Astros/Pirates)

1002

The food team.

Pitcher (1943 AL MVP)

Catcher (1917–1921, mostly Cardinals)

First base (Two games at first for 1941 Indians)

Second base (1962–1977, Phillies/Royals)

Third base (Hall of Fame, Pirates)

Shortstop (1884–1895, Baltimore/Brooklyn, outfielder, but 200 games at SS)

First outfielder (1942–1955, Cubs/Cardinals)

Second outfielder (Hall of Fame, Senators)

Third outfielder (1981–1995, journeyman OF with 1,410 games; played for Toronto in 1992 World Series)

Manager (Led 1978 Yankees to World Series)

WHO, WHAT, WHEN, WHERE, AND WHY

1. Who is this player?

2. When was the photograph taken?

3. Where?

4. What career change did he make this year?

5. BONUS: What major feat did he accomplish that season?

6. BETCHA-DIDN'T-KNOW BONUS: What team had he played for the previous year?

1003:
1. Hall of Famer Stan Musial.

2. 1946.

3. At Ebbets Field in Brooklyn.

4. It was the year he moved from the outfield to first base.

5. He became the first player in history to win an MVP Award at a second position. In 1943 he won the NL MVP Award as an outfielder.

6. For the U.S. Navy, playing exhibition games in Maryland and Pearl Harbor.

ANSWERS
(DREAM TEAMS BY THE NUMBERS and BASEBALL NAME-O-MANIA)

Dream Teams by the Numbers

804: C: Del Crandall; 1B: Jim Bottomley; 2B: Bobby Doerr; 3B: George Kell; SS: Ozzie Smith; number 1 OF: Chuck Klein; number 2 OF: Richie Ashburn; number 3 OF: Kenny Lofton; SP: Matt Young; MGR: Bill McKechnie

805: C: Mickey Cochrane; 1B: Ripper Collins; 2B: Charlie Gehringer; 3B: Red Rolfe; SS: Derek Jeter; number 1 OF: Heinie Manush; number 2 OF: Brett Butler; number 3 OF: Devon White; SP: Chief Hogsett; MGR: Tommy Lasorda

806: C: Mickey Cochrane; 1B: Jimmie Foxx; 2B: Frankie Frisch; 3B: Eric Chavez; SS: Alex Rodriguez; number 1 OF: Babe Ruth; number 2 OF: Joe Medwick; number 3 OF: Earl Averill; SP: David Wells; MGR: Bill Terry

807: C: Ernie Lombardi; 1B: Lou Gehrig; 2B: Billy Herman; 3B: Paul Molitor; SS: Miguel Tejada; number 1 OF: Mel Ott; number 2 OF: Duke Snider; number 3 OF: Ralph Kiner; SP: Charlie Root; MGR: Earl Weaver

808: C: Johnny Bench; 1B: Albert Pujols; 2B: Tony Lazzeri; 3B: Brooks Robinson; SS: Arky Vaughan; number 1 OF: Hank Aaron; number 2 OF: Joe DiMaggio; number 3 OF: Hank Greenberg; SP: Billy Pierce; MGR: Davey Johnson

809: C: Mickey Tettleton; 1B: Stan Musial; 2B: Joe Gordon; 3B: Scott Rolen; SS: Jimmy Rollins; number 1 OF: Mickey Mantle; number 2 OF: Joe Medwick; number 3 OF: Al Kaline; SP: Bob Lemon; MGR: Joe Torre

810: C: Ivan Rodriguez; 1B: Hal Trosky; 2B: Red Schoendienst; 3B: Eddie Mathews; SS: Harvey Kuenn; number 1 OF: Barry Bonds; number 2 OF: Mickey Mantle; number 3 OF: Joe Medwick; SP: George Earnshaw; MGR: Charlie Grimm

811: C: Bill Dickey; 1B: Willie Stargell; 2B: Joe Morgan; 3B: Bob Elliott; SS: Cal Ripken Jr.; number 1 OF: Chuck Klein; number 2 OF: Carl Yastrzemski; number 3 OF: Andre Dawson; SP: Bobo Newsom; MGR: Yogi Berra

812: C: Gabby Hartnett; 1B: John Olerud; 2B: Bobby Doerr; 3B: Minnie Minoso; SS: Matt Williams; number 1 OF: Ted Williams; number 2 OF: Joe DiMaggio; number 3 OF: Reggie Jackson; SP: Bob Feller; MGR: Joe Torre

814: C: Charles Johnson; 1B: Hal Trosky; 2B: Rogers Hornsby; 3B: Joe Sewell; SS: Arky Vaughan; number 1 OF: Roberto Clemente; number 2 OF: Joe Medwick; number 3 OF: Sammy Sosa; SP: Warren Spahn; MGR: Mike Hargrove

Baseball Name-O-Mania

978: P: Bob MOOSE; C: BUCK Ewing; 1B: KITTY Bransfield; 2B: Nellie FOX; 3B: POSSUM Whitted; SS: RABBIT Maranville; number 1 OF: Rob DEER; number 2 OF: MULE Haas; number 3

OF: Jimmy WOLF; MGR: Johnny COONey

979: P: BUD Black; C: IVEY Wingo; 1B: Fred STEM; 2B: Pete ROSE; 3B: Donie BUSH; SS: Jake FLOWERS; number 1 OF: BUTTERCUP Dickerson; number 2 OF: Darryl STRAWBERRY; number 3 OF: Fred SnodGRASS; DH: Kevin FLORA; MGR: BRANCH Rickey

980: P: Fred GOLDSMITH; C: Darrell PORTER; 1B: Mike MARSHALl; 2B: Charlie SHOEMAKER; 3B: Hick CARPENTER; SS: Art BUTLER; number 1 OF: Turner BARBER; number 2 OF: FARMER Weaver or Farmer WEAVER; number 3 OF: Dusty BAKER; DH: Mike BREWER; MGR: Chuck TANNER

981: P: Mike LINCOLN; C: Gary CARTER; 1B: TYLER Houston; 2B: Adam KENNEDY; 3B: Sparky ADAMS; SS: UL WASHINGTON; number 1 OF: Craig MONROE; number 2 OF: Deacon VAN BUREN; number 3 OF: Bo JACKSON; DH: Reggie JEFFERSON; MGR: CLINTON Hurdle; Owner: George W. BUSH; Executive: FORD Frick

982: P: George WINTER; C: Steve CHRISTMAS; 1B: Luke EASTER; 2B: Hugh DAILY; 3B: George FALLon; SS: Hank O'DAY; number 1 OF: Rick MONDAY; number 2 OF: Billy SUNDAY; number 3 OF: Carlos MAY; MGR: Bobby VALENTINE; Owner: AUGUST Busch

983: P: Vida BLUE; C: Tim BLACKwell; 1B: Hank GREENberg; 2B: RED Schoendienst; 3B: PINKy Higgins; SS: Jonah GOLDman; number 1 OF: Pete GRAY; number 2 OF: SILVER King; number 3 OF: Bobby BROWN; MGR: WHITEy Herzog

984: P: Virgil TRUCKS; C: Lew DRILL; 1B: BRICK Smith; 2B: Wally FLAGER; 3B: SCOOPS Carey; SS: Bert TOOLey; number 1 OF: TRENCH Davis; number 2 OF: RUSTY Staub; number 3 OF: Charlie SPIKES; MGR: Sam CRANE

986: P: Babe RUTH; C: Paul FLORENCE; 1B: KITTY Bransfield; 2B: DOLLY Stark, 3B: LENA Blackburne;

SS: Ed HOLLY; number 1 OF: SHERRY Magee; number 2 OF: BABY DOLL Jacobson; number 3 OF: PATSY Donovan; MGR: CONNIE Mack

987: P: SOCKS Seibold; C: Bill DICKEY; 1B: Bunny BRIEF; 2B: COTTON Tierney; 3B: DUD Lee; SS: Bunny FABRIQUE (fabric); number 1 OF: BOOTS Day; number 2 OF: Chief SOCKalexis; number 3 OF: Tex JEANES; MGR: CAP Anson

988: P: Mel QUEEN; C: KING Kelly; 1B: Candy LaCHANCE; 2B: CHIP Hale; 3B: LUCKY Lohrke; SS: ACE Parker; number 1 OF: Harry DECKer; number 2 OF: Lindsay DEAL; number 3 OF: Oscar GAMBLE; MGR: JACK McKeon

989: P: Andy HAWKins; C: Johnny PEACOCK; 1B: CHICK Gandil; 2B: Alan STORKe; 3B: ROBIN Ventura; SS: TURKEY Gross; number 1 OF: GOOSE Goslin; number 2 OF: DUCKy Medwick; number 3 OF: CUCKOO Christensen; MGR: BIRDIE Tebbetts

990: P: Rollie FINGERS; C: Barry FOOTe; 1B: Gene BEARDen; 2B: Wally BACKman; 3B: Dave BRAIN; SS: BONES Ely; number 1 OF: HEINIE Manush; number 2 OF: Joel YoungBLOOD; number 3 OF: GENE Stephens; MGR: Leo "the LIP" Durocher

991: P: Jack KNIGHT; C: Tom PRINCE; 1B: Marv THRONEberry; 2B: NAPOLEON Lajoie; 3B: Jeff KING; SS: QUEENie O'Rourke; number 1 OF: DUKE Snider; number 2 OF: CESAR Cedeno; number 3 OF: MARQUIS Grissom; DH: Don CASTLE; MGR: EARL Weaver

992 P: MOTHER Watson; C: Mark PARENT; 1B: POP Dillon; 2B: Cupid CHILDS; 3B: NANNY Fernandez; SS: GRANNY Hamner; number 1 OF: Cool PAPA Bell; number 2 OF: Brett BUTLER; number 3 OF: SONNY Jackson; PR: Bob DAUGHTERS; MGR: KID Gleason

993: P: PREACHER Roe; C: Joe GODdard; 1B: MONK Sherlock; 2B: Max BISHOP; 3B: Jose PAGAN; SS:

Garry TEMPLEton; number 1 OF: Dave POPE; number 2 OF: JESUS Alou; number 3 OF: Bob CHRISTIAN; DH: ANGEL Mangual; MGR: DEACON McGuire

995: P: GENERAL Crowder; C: ADMIRAL Schlei; 1B: LANCE Berkman; 2B: SHOOTy Babitt; 3B: Jim COMMAND; SS: Jim BATTLE; number 1 OF: CANNONBALL Crane; number 2 OF: George Van HALTren; number 3 OF: Danny NAPOLEON; DH: Joe CANNON; MGR: Count CAMPau; Executive: WARren Giles

996: P: STORM Davis; C: DEWey Williams; 1B: J. T. SNOW; 2B: GALE Staley; 3B: CYCLONE Miller; SS: Jim FOGarty; number 1 OF: ICICLE Reeder; number 2 OF: Curt FLOOD; number 3 OF: Roy WEATHERly; DH: Matt WINTERs; MGR: John DAY

997: P: Kid NICHOLS; C: IRA Thomas; 1B: Norm CASH; 2B: Tom POORMAN; 3B: BUCK Weaver; SS: Ernie BANKS; number 1 OF: Barry BONDS; number 2 OF: RICHie Ashburn; number 3 OF: Al HEIST; DH: Don MONEY; MGR: Jim PRICE

998: P: Al HOLLAND; C: Hugh POLAND; 1B: GERMANY Schaefer; 2B: Miguel CAIRO; 3B: Kelly PARIS; SS: Sal MADRID; number 1 OF: Daryl BOSTON; number 2 OF: Tim IRELAND; number 3 OF: Joe HAGUE; MGR: DALLAS Green

999: P: Tom SEAver; C: Steve LAKE; 1B: Frank MOUNTAIN; 2B: Fred MARSH; 3B: FOREST Glenn Wright; SS: Donnie HILL; number 1 OF: Mickey RIVERS; number 2 OF: JUNGLE Jim Rivera; number 3 OF: Elias PEAK; MGR: CLIFFord "Gavvy" Cravath

1000: P: Jack BENTLEY; C: Scooter TUCKER or SCOOTER Tucker; 1B: Jesus VEGA; 2B: Pat CAPRI; 3B: John DODGE; SS: CRASH Davis; number 1 OF: Dan FORD; number 2 OF: Dick HARLEY; number 3 OF: Ty PICKUP; DH: Henry MERCEDES; MGR: Harry WHEELer

1001: P: Brandon LEAGUE; C: DOUBLE Duty Radcliffe; 1B: Cecil FIELDER; 2B: HOMER Bush; 3B: HOME RUN Baker; SS: Davy FORCE; number 1 OF: Ken SINGLEton; number 2 OF: Ron FAIRly; number 3 OF: Coaker TRIPLEtt; MGR: Harry WALKer

1002 P: SPUD Chandler; C: PICKLES Dillhoefer; 1B: Vern FreiBURGER; 2B: COOKIE Rojas; 3B: PIE Traynor; SS: OYSTER Burns; number 1 OF: PEANUTS Lowrey; number 2 OF: Sam RICE; number 3 OF: CANDY Maldonado; MGR: Bob LEMON

PHOTO CREDITS